SHARK SQUADRON

SHARK SQUADRON

THE HISTORY OF
No 112 SQUADRON
R.F.C., R.A.F.
1917–1975

by
Robin A. Brown

CRÉCY BOOKS

First published in Great Britain in 1994 by
Crécy Books Ltd.

Copyright © 1994 by Robin A. Brown

ISBN 0 947554 33 5

Typesetting by Rom-Data Corporation Ltd., Falmouth, Cornwall

Printed and bound in Great Britain by
Hartnolls Limited, Bodmin, Cornwall

Contents

Illustrations

Preface

Certain squadrons in the RAF do achieve something that gives them a special reputation and respect. Sometimes it is a particular operation carried out by the unit which henceforth gives it a singular pride and honour. It is probably more often brought about by the good fortune of having dedicated leadership, being in the right place at the right time and establishing a reputation for bold and aggressive fighting qualities. In spite of the changing flow of flying personnel a good squadron generally inspires those following on to keep it that way or to make it even better.

Those of us privileged to serve with 112 of course considered our squadron to be something special, and it is true to say that 112 had more than its fair share of characters and outstanding leaders who engendered a spirit which permeated all ranks. With its constant turnover of pilots the stability of the squadron relies much upon its ground personnel who remain, to a large extent, with the unit throughout. There is no doubt that much of the spirit of 112 was fostered in this way.

The squadron's very birth in 1917 for a special rôle gave it a certain start and, sparse though the records are for this fascinating period of the squadron history during the first World War, this book contains the most meticulous account of day to day operations of a squadron engaged in front line action in two world wars. In particular their record of continuous service and action in WW2 are presented in great detail and will give the student of air warfare and the lay reader alike, a genuine history of fighter and fighter bomber operations during that time.

The Western Desert Air Force pioneered the rôle of close support for the land forces and 112 was in the forefront of this evolution along with its fellow squadrons of 239 Wing. They were in continuous and intense action throughout the desert campaigns from Egypt to Tunisia, the invasion of Sicily and the whole of the Italian campaign to the end of WW2.

The history of 112, although unique in some ways, is fairly typical of many fighter squadrons of that era and highlights some glaring faults and omissions in equipment and training which placed our fighter pilots at a very great disadvantage. Their equipment was outdated and outclassed. With the exception of the CR42 the Gladiator was no match for the Italian fighters and, of course, completely outclassed by the Me109 during the Greek campaign. Re-equipped with the Curtiss Tomahawk in 1941, 112 had a good aeroplane but it was still inferior to the 109 as a fighter, and the Kittyhawk was only slightly better. This machine only came into its own as a fighter-bomber with its good firepower and bomb carrying capacity.

It was not until 1943 that we achieved parity or a degree of superiority in North Africa with the advent of a limited number of Spitfire Mk 9's on the fighter squadrons. At least in World War 2 we had the time to develop and eventually to produce the right equipment with adequate performance. Nowadays, and in the future, time will not be on our side and we must hope that we have better, or the best, aircraft already in service.

Our pre-war fighter tactics and training were for the defensive rôle and the interception of bomber formations with our short range fighters flying in tight vic formation and squadron drill. The *Luftwaffe* offensive tactics, small fast moving flexible formations, were eventually adopted by the Allies but it took a long and expensive time for us to get the message.

The merits or otherwise of the Allied system of rotating pilots after 200 hours of operations compared with the *Luftwaffe* pilots who remained with their units through-out the war is open to debate. There is no doubt that, by their system, the Germans produced a large number of very experienced and highly successful fighter pilots.

It is perhaps ironic that having survived all that the enemy could inflict, 112 was eventually pulled from the skies and disbanded in 1957 in a form of self-destruct following the disasterous Duncan Sandys White Paper on Defence which virtually deleted fighter pilots from future Air Staff planning. Happily this was proved to be a policy without foundation and the fighter pilot in his multi-role aircraft remains irreplaceable.

There the story of 112 would end but for the final twist of fate which had the squadron re-formed as an Air Defence Missile unit in 1960, thus coming a full circle from its original foundation in 1917 as a Home Defence Squadron. Having been on the receiving end of so much ground to air flak' in its history, was this some bizarre reward?

Sqn Ldr Neville Duke, DSO, OBE, DFC, AFC.

Introduction

In wartime, with the over-riding requirements of security of information, few RAF squadrons have the opportunity to stand out from amongst the huge number of other units that are all engaged in fighting the enemy to the best of their ability. Now and then, by some quirk, or chance event, a squadron emerges from this fog of anonymity to catch the imagination of the public.

112 Squadron, RAF, by virtue of its famous sharksteeth markings was one, and, because of them, is remembered even today. As a schoolboy I remember seeing a newsreel and publicity photographs of those evil grinning mouths on Desert Air Force Tomahawks and Kittyhawks but little did I realise that barely fourteen years later I would be a Flight Commander on that very squadron.

An RAF squadron is a curious formation that is as unlike an army regiment as it is unlike a warship of the Royal Navy. In one the tendency is for personnel to remain together for years at a stretch while in the other the whole establishments moves around as a compact group until the vessel returns to port. In comparison an RAF squadron is an amorphous creature, continually altering as officers and men come and go and yet – if the unit is a good one – a thread of continuity persists so that, as in the case of 112 Squadron, the spirit of the squadron in 1946 would have been recogniseable to anyone who had been in it in 1940. This spirit is almost wholly dependent on the unit's morale, a virtue much encouraged by Field Marshal Montgomery who was well aware of its crucial importance in battle. Morale is sustained by many factors and one of the most significant is the quality of leadership. An ex-squadron pilot of the nineteen-forties recalls that the leadership of the officers and NCOs on 112 Squadron was of the highest standard throughout, and this is demonstrated on many occasions related in this history. The officers and SNCO pilots messed together, something that seems to have been unknown during the war on British airfields, and time and time again one reads of formations, made up of all ranks, being led by a sergeant or flight sergeant pilot. Like Nelson's happy band of brothers the men of 112 Squadron were of the highest quality.

When I joined 112 Squadron in June 1956 I asked the squadron commander, Sqn Ldr Frank Hegarty, whether I might write the history in the same way as I had compiled short accounts of No. 79 (FR) and 234 (F) Squadrons, my two previous flying units. Immediately I was led to a tall metal cabinet which, when opened, revealed, stacked from bottom to top, all the squadron diaries, combat reports, operations records and flight authorisation books that went back, almost without a break, to 1939. 'Get on with it!' I was told.

It wasn't until 1959 that I was able to produce a limited edition of 81 copies of the history, running to about 200,000 words, run off on a gestetner machine. These were distributed free (apart from the postage) to the many friends I had made during my researches. The people who have helped me, both then and since, range across a wide spectrum and I cannot do justice to each one individually, but the list would start with Nan Ricketts, onetime typist in the WRAF, who had been on 112 Home Defence Squadron in the Great War and who volunteered to type out the whole work in her spare time for no more reward than the pleasure of being able to contribute to the telling of the story. My list of acknowledgements continues with such well-known and respected aviation historians such as Chaz Bowyer, Leonard Bridgman, J M Bruce, Frank Cheesman, Chris Cole, Brian Cull, Ed Ferko, Reg Fowler, C Rupert Moore, J D R Rawlings, Bruce Robertson, Chris Shores, R C Sturtivant and Richard Ward. I have also received unstinted co-operation from the Air Historical Branch (MoD), the Commonwealth War Graves Commission, the Foreign Office, the Imperial War Museum, the RAF Museum, the Judge Advocate General's Department, the RAF Record Office (AR1b) and AR8(b) and the South African Air Force Association.

In a class of their own I have also gratefully to thank the ex-squadron members and their relatives or friends for their enthusiastic response to my appeals for information and wartime photographs. This list starts with two airmen from the Great War (as it was then called), A W James and J Tucker and pilots from the same period, J I Blackurn, C J Chabot, A C S Irwin, and A B Yuille. Mrs G E Lane, the mother of Matt Matthias, Mrs Georgina Barclay who was the fiancée of Michael White and Janet Wolley Dod, widow of Capt C F Wolley Dod, Mrs Margaret Castle, sister of Sgt Arthur Banks, GC, and Mrs Cynthia Williams of the Abergele Public Library. Aircrew and groundcrew from the 2nd World War such as Jack ('Ali') Barber, David B Brown, Johnnie Burcham, Clive R Caldwell, H W Carter, H F Churchill, Don Clarke, H P Cochrane, P D M Down, Neville Duke (who kindly pointed out to me some of my most obvious errors), Denis Featherstone, Air Marshal Sir E Gordon (Tap) Jones, H W Harrison, Bertie Horden, Peter Illingworth, J Kerslake, James Longmore, L W North, Peter Nuyten, T Ooosthuizen, Eddy Ross, R G Sayle, Bob Sinclair, J A Tingle, Gerry Westenra, E Norman Woodward and Jim Worsfold. Without their help much of the colour and comment that laces the stark military history would be missing.

This account is as frank and truthful as I can make it. I understand that it is becoming increasingly difficult to obtain accurate information about wartime losses from the archives of our ex-enemies in the 1939 – 1945 war and that there is also a tendency to deny that certain unpalatable events ever took place as if to moderate the reality of defeat. If this is so it is a regrettable development and one that does not serve the cause of historical truth. Readers of this account will find that it records not only victories in the air but also the aircraft destroyed and squadron pilots killed, wounded and made prisoner without any attempt at minimising the tragedy of warfare and the enduring legacy of personal misery and loss.

Robin A Brown
Woodcock Hall, 1994

Abbreviations

AA	Anti-aircraft artillery (see also *flak*)
ACH	Aircraft hand (an airman's trade)
AC	Aircraftsman (an airman's rank) this could be AC2 or AC1
a/c	Aircraft (also A/C)
AFC	Air Force Cross
AFV	Armoured Fighting Vehicle, usually a tank or armoured car
ALG	Advanced Landing Ground (see also LG)
ALO	Army Liaison Officer
AOC	Air Officer Commanding (an RAF Group)
ASR	Air-Sea Rescue (usually applied to a type of aircraft)
Bf	*Bayerische Flugzeugwerke* (Messerschmitt)
BPD	Base Personnel Depot
BR20	Fiat BR20 bomber
Ca	Caproni
C-in-C	Commander-in-Chief (of an Air Force such as the DAF)
CR42	Fiat CR42 fighter
DAF	Desert Air Force (the colloquial abbreviation of WDAF)
DFC	Distinguished Flying Cross
Div	Division (as in 51 Highland Div)
Do	Dornier
DR	Dispatch rider
DSO	Distinguished Service Order
e/a	enemy aircraft
E-boat	German or Italian torpedo boat
FGCP	Forward Ground Control Post
flak	*flugzeugabwehrakanone*: Hostile anti-aircraft fire
Flt	Flight, of a squadron
FW	Focke-Wulf
G50	Fiat G50 fighter
GP bomb	General purpose bomb
HDV	Heavy duty vehicle
He	Heinkel
HQ	Headquarters

Hs	Henschel
IO	Intelligence Officer
Jabo	*Jagdbomber*: Fighter bomber
JG	*Jagdgeschwader*: Fighter Group
Ju	Junkers
KG	*Kampfgeschwader*: Bomber Group
Lehrgeschwader	An elite unit formed to train *Luftwaffe* leaders
LG	*Lehrgeschwader*: an elite unit formed to train *Luftwaffe* leaders.
LG	Landing Ground, an abbreviation of ALG
LST	Landing Ship (Tank)
MC200	Macchi-Castoldi 200 fighter
MC202	Macchi-Castoldi 202 fighter
MBE	Member of the Order of the British Empire
Me	Messerschmitt
MG	Machine gun
MORU	Mobile Operations Room Unit
MT	Mechanical Transport, any sort of soft-skinned military vehicle
NCO	Non-Commissioned Officer, corporal, sergeant or flight sergeant
PoW	Prisoner of War
psp	Pressed steel planking, a type of airfield runway, quickly assembled
PzKw	*Panzerkampfwagen*: tank, usually followed by a type number – *PzKw IV*
RAAF	Royal Australian Air Force
RAF	Royal Air Force
RAOC	Royal Army Ordnance Corps
RCAF	Royal Canadian Air Force
RDC	Royal Defence Corps
Re2000	Reggiane 2000 fighter
RE2001	Reggiane 2001 fighter
RFC	Royal Flying Corps
RNAS	Royal Naval Air Service
Ro37	Rosatelli 37 *bis* reconnaissance biplane
R/T	Radio Telephony, voice transmission
RV	Rendez-vous or meeting place
SAAF	South African Air Force
SIB	Special Investigation Branch, RAF Police
Skg	*Schnellkampfgeschwader*: FW190 unit
SM	Savoia-Marchetti
Sqn	Squadron
StG	*Stukageschwader* later *Schlachtgeschwader*: Ju87 unit
Tac-R	Tactical (as opposed to Strategic) Reconnaissance
USAAF	United States Army Air Force
WDAF	Western Desert Air Force (see DAF)
WO	Warrant Officer, this could be WOI or WOII
W/T	Wireless Telegraphy or morse code transmission
ZG	*Zerstörergeschwader*: Light bomber unit

TERMINOLOGY

armed recce	a reconnaissance mission prepared to attack any targets encountered
bandits	enemy aircraft
dribblera	term used to describe damage done to a railway locomotive
flamer	an aircraft, or vehicle set on fire on the ground
mission or operation	a formation of aircraft sent to undertake some prescribed duty
recce	reconnaissance
'Rover'	Callsign for an FGCP
sortie	an individual aircraft's flight
strafe/straffing	an attack from the air with machine guns
50-plus (example)	some undetermined number over 50 but less than 60

UNIT ORGANISATION

RAF & Empire Air Forces	3 (later 2) Flights	= Squadron
	3 or 4 Squadrons	= Wing
	Any number of Wings	= Group
	Any number of Groups	= an Air Force
Luftwaffe	3 *Staffeln*	= *Gruppe*
	3 *Gruppen*	= *Geschwader*
	Any number of *Geschwadern*	= *Fliegerkorps*
Regia Aeronautica	2 *Squadriglie*	= *Gruppo*
	3 *Gruppe*	= *Stormo*
USAAF	3 Squadrons	= Group
	Any number of Groups	= Wing

British and Empire squadrons were autonomous units and were larger than *Luftwaffe staffeln* or *Regia Aeronautica squadriglie*.

COMPARATIVE RANKS

RAF, RCAF, RAAF	*SAAF, USAAF*	*Luftwaffe*	*Regia Aeronautica*
Group Captain (Gp Capt)	Colonel	*Oberst*	*Colonello*
Wing Commander (Wg Cdr)	Lieut-Colonel	*Oberstleutnant*	*Tenente-Colonello*
Squadron Leader (Sqn Ldr)	Major	*Major*	*Maggiore*

Flight Lieutenant (Flt Lt)	Captain	*Hauptmann (Hpt)*	*Capitano*
Flying Officer (Fg Off)	Lieutenant	*Oberleutnant (Oblt)*	*Tenente*
Pilot Officer (Plt Off)	2nd Lieutenant	*Leutnant (Lt)*	*2° Tenente*
		Oberfähnrich* *Unteroffizier (Uffz)**	
Warrant Officer (WO)	–	–	*Maresciallo*
Flight Sergeant (Flt Sgt)	–	*Oberfeldwebel*	*Sergente Maggiore*
Sergeant (Sgt) Corporal (Cpl)	–	*Feldwebel*	*Sergente*

*An *Oberfähnrich* was a cadet rank with no precise equivalent in the British or Empire Air Forces, but perhaps approximating to an RN Midshipman, while an *Unteroffizier* is an NCO pilot rank.

CATEGORIES OF DAMAGE TO RAF AIRCRAFT

In the narrative occasional reference is made to damage to aircraft as being Cat 1, Cat 2, Cat 3 or Cat 4. The significance of these categories is as follows:

Cat 1　= repairable on the squadron
Cat 2　= repairable on the airfield by a 2nd Line team
Cat 3　= repairable by a special working party from the nearest Maintenance Unit
Cat 4　= destroyed, only fit for scrap

CHAPTER ONE

Home Defence

On 25 May 1917 England was bombed in daylight by 23 Gotha G4 bombers on the first of eight daylight raids. Seventeen days later 14 aircraft of *Kagohl 3*, led by *Kapitän* Ernst Brandenburg attacked London. For Londoners this was a shattering experience. Seven tons of high explosive were dropped and 594 citizens were killed or injured. Sixty fighter planes were sent up but the tight formation of enemy bombers lost no aircraft. The lack of any early warning system meant that the out-dated RFC and RNAS fighter aircraft were still climbing to height when the Gothas were already on their way back to Ghent and their flying height was far beyond the reach of the AA guns.

The outcry that followed this raid resulted in the diversion of No 66 Sqn (Sopwith Pups) and 56 Sqn (SE5s) from the Western Front with orders to guard London against any further attacks. These two much-needed squadron were allowed to go against Trenchard's wishes and in the Third battle of Ypres the British 5th Army was left badly lacking in air support.

The Germans, with consummate grasp of strategy, now switched their attacks to the Western Front, upon which Trenchard hastily ordered 56 and 66 Sqns back to France. In the afternoon of 7 July 22 Gothas returned to London and were perfectly visible, circling the capital 3 miles high. Brandenburg reported 'only token resistance'. On the ground there were 252 casualties. This policy of switching from one target to another opened up a new dimension in strategic warfare but in England there was fury and consternation at the helplessness of the defences.

56 and 66 Sqns were again ordered back to England and there was an immediate review of the whole situation. Brig Gen E B Ashman of the Royal Artillery was selected to head a new defence organisation. Both he and Trenchard understood that the Gotha raids were designed to weaken the RFC on the Western Front but they also appreciated that the defence of Great Britain was an enormous task. The Gotha G4 had an endurance of up to 6 hours and a radius of action of about 230 miles, so the Germans could strike anywhere. The small number of Gothas and *Reizenflugzeuge* (R-types), rarely more than 43 at any one time, compelled the British to station over 800 aircraft in the UK of which about half were the most modern types available.

One of the three new Home Defence squadrons created as a result of these daylight raids was No 112, formed from 'B' Flight of 50 Sqn, then based at Bekesbourne, south-east of Canterbury, on 25 July 1917. 112 was initially established at Detling but moved to Throwley, five days later.

Throwley, a small grass airfield, lay between Charing and Faversham on the crest of the North Downs. It was one of a string of airfields that were positioned parallel to the Thames estuary, from Bekesbourne in the east to Biggin Hill in the west, located with the intention of intercepting the daylight raiders approaching London from the clutch of airfields at Ghent. Throwley had already been in use as a relief landing ground for No 50 Sqn, although in this rôle it had been little more than a prepared field with a store of fuel.

Initially, under the command of Major Gerald Allen, 112 was equipped with Sopwith Pups and three canvas (Bessoneau) hangars were erected. The Officers' Mess was located on the far side of the airfield, at Bells Forstal Farm. On 15 August 1917 Northern and Southern Wings were renamed the Home Defence Brigade (later 6 Brigade) and divided into three wings, Northern and Eastern (day operations) and Southern (night operations), the last two coming under the London Defence area. In October the organisation was changed again and 6 Brigade was split into five wings, Northern (46 Wing), North Midland (48 Wing), South Midland (47 Wing), Eastern (49 Wing) and Southern (50 Wing).

Meanwhile Brig Gen Ashmore had ringed London with improved anti-aircraft guns capable of reaching the Gothas' and R-Type Giants' ceiling. As a result of these improvements the bombers began to receive an unacceptable degree of punishment.

Major Allen was succeeded in his command of the squadron by Major Barry Moore but this officer never took up his post as, at his own request, he was sent to the Western Front. On 3 December the squadron was taken over by Major Claude Ridley, DSO, MC. This man was a character, even amongst the curious set of individuals in the RFC. When with 60 Sqn he went missing, flying a Morane Parasol. It was said at the time that he had landed in Belgium and had taken up residence with a farmer's wife. Tiring of her he then flew to Holland and later returned to his squadron. His DSO was awarded after being forced down and again escaping.

On 8 February, 1918, 112 Squadron, along with 50 Sqn, based at Bekesbourne, and 143 Sqn (Detling) were formed into 53 Wing, known as the Advanced Defence Group, with its headquarters at Stede Court, Harrietsham. The nucleus of personnel for 143 Sqn had been drawn from 112 Sqn. Early in the new year, 1918, 188 Night Training Sqn which had been formed at Retford, Nottinghamshire, moved to Throwley, equipped with Avro 504s to train pilots for the Wing. On 13 February the squadron was taken over by Major C J Q Brand, MC, who had seen service with 70 Sqn on the Western Front, also in the night fighting rôle. This sudden emphasis on night flying was due to the Germans' switch to night attacks in September 1917 as a result of their increasing losses by day.

The German High Command had begun with an extraordinary advantage which, had they realised it, could well have altered the course of the war. If they had continued with a concentrated and sustained series of bombing raids on London and other major cities they might well have paralysed British industry. Instead they neglected to press home their strategic advantage, probably because they did not realise the extent of their success. Numbers of bombers allotted to *Bombengeschwader 3*, the '*England Geschwader*' rarely exceeded about 43 and these were not used as often as they could have been.

'Irresolution, misjudgement, a fearful approach towards novel methods, and plain and simple shortsightedness led the Germans to rely on half measures . . . their strategic concept was valid but its execution was inept, yielding nothing more tangible than a few weeks of air superiority at the front'[1]

The British, though, had not been as efficient as they might have been in their response to the German air raids. The inter-service rivalry between the RFC and the RNAS meant that there was muddle, duplication and waste of effort. However it is probably true that it was the Gotha raids that eventually persuaded the RFC and RNAS to forget their differences and allow the formation of a combined air arm, the Royal Air Force on 1 April 1918.

Between September 1917 and the Armistice in November 1918 the Gothas and Giants raided England on 21 occasions, with numbers varying between one and 43 aircraft. On average one enemy aircraft was destroyed for each raid, together with 36 more which crashed in Belgium and three recorded as missing. We know very little about the activities of 112 HD Sqn during this period other than from lucky survivals such as the Flying Log Book that belonged to Lieutenant C H Wolley Dod which records his flights between June and October 1918.

The squadron had been re-equipped with Sopwith F1 Camels in March and it can be seen that his trips lasted between 2 hours 40 minutes flying in formation down to as short as 10 minutes on an Air Test. Curiously night flying was rare and flying was virtually all daytime training flights of one sort or another, although 'Night landings' and 'Searchlight practice' do figure occasionally. Unserviceability in the air seemed common with such remarks as 'cam rocker 'broken' 'engine dud, missing' followed by 'engine worse, missing all 'over', 'pressure pump unreliable' and 'pressure pump prop blown off'. Flying F2091 (his favourite machine) he records that on 27 June 1918 'Konked out, landing outside aerodrome, left axle bent, wheel off.'

No records appear to exist telling how often the squadron took off to intercept enemy aircraft although an Operation Order dated 10 September 1918 issued by the London Defence Area detailed the squadron to patrol a line from Throwley to Judds Hill to Warden Point on the receipt of an alert.

No doubt there were scores of fruitless sorties in search of the Gothas and they had no success until the night of 19/20 May 1918 when the Germans raided England for the last time and with the greatest number of aircraft. Forty three enemy machines, of which 38 were Gotha G5s (of *Bombengeschwader 3*), two were Reconnaissance and three were Giants (of *Reisenflugzeugabteilung 501*), crossed the coast and headed for London. The number of raiders was well over twice that ever sent out before. Thirteen enemy aircraft reached London and seven were brought down, three by AA fire, three by night fighters and one which force landed.

Of the three destroyed by the night fighters one was brought down by Major Brand flying a Camel fitted with twin Vickers and a Lewis gun mounted on the upper wing. He had taken off together with three other squadron pilots in complete darkness and without the aid of flares, climbing to meet the incoming stream of bombers. One Gotha G5 crossed the coast at Broad Salts, north of Sandwich, and flew westwards over Canterbury and then, at 23.16 hrs, turned north near Throwley. At about 23.23 hrs

---

[1] *'The Great Air War'*, Aaron Norman

Rochford

SOUTHEND

THAMES ESTUARY

All Hallows

GRAVESEND

Warden Point

Leyesdown

Eastchurch

CHATHAM

South Ash

Broomfield

Manston

FAVERSHAM

RAMSGATE

Detling

53

Judd's Hill

Broad Salts

MAIDSTONE

Frinstead

53

CANTERBURY

Throwley

53 Bekesbourne

SANDWICH

K E N T

CHARING

DEAL

Pluckley

ASHFORD

Dover

DOVER

Leigh Green

Lympne

FOLKESTONE

N

53 Airfields in 53 Wing

◯ Other Airfields

◀-- Gotha's flight-path, 19 May 1918

.... 112 (HD) Sqn patrol line

| 0 | 5 | 10 | 15 | 20 | miles |

| 0 | 5 | 10 | 15 | 20 | 25 | km |

SCALE

STRAITS OF DOVER

Map 1. South-East England, 1917-1919

RAB 1992

Major Brand saw this aircraft at 8700' over Faversham and, in the words of the London Gazette of June 1918, 'he at once attacked the enemy, firing two bursts of 20 rounds each' which put the Gotha's starboard engine out of action. The enemy machine turned sharply and began to descend 'Closing to a range of 25 yards he fired a further three bursts of 25 rounds each and, as a result, the enemy machine caught fire and fell in flames to the ground. Capt (*sic*) Brand showed great courage and skill in manoeuvering his machine during the encounter, and when the enemy aeroplane burst into flames he was so close that the flames enveloped his machine, scorching his face.'

The stricken Gotha crashed near the sea wall at Leyesdown on the Isle of Sheppey at 23.29 hrs where it was destroyed in the shallow water along with its crew[1]. The falling bomber had been seen from Throwley and when Major Brand returned he was 'chaired' into his office with such enthusiasm that his bearers banged his head on the door frame. He later had one of the Gotha propellors mounted with a clock set in its centre. For his victory that night Brand was awarded the DSO. Mrs N Ricketts, who, as a Miss Bowyer was a civilian clerk attached to 112 HD Sqn working in the CO's office in the Headquarters Flight, had a swagger stick made from the remains of a propellor and a letter rack covered in aluminium from one of the engine cowlings. The Wing claimed three Gothas in all that night.

Examination of the remains of the Gotha, which had fallen in shallow water, showed that its number was 979 and that it was camouflaged all over with a pattern of hexagons in the varied colours of black, indigo, very dark blue with a reddish tinge, dark purple and a slightly lighter blue.

A Mr Tucker and a Mr James who were airmen on 112 remembered seeing Major Brand's Camel the following morning. 'The underpart of the machine was ripped open the whole length of the fuselage, the varnish was burned off the propellor, the fur on his flying helmet and his moustache were badly singed' wrote Tucker.

With the advent of 188 Night Training Sqn Throwley airfield was expanded and a wooden hangar and additional Bessoneau hangars were erected. 188 NT Sqn lived under canvas on the opposite side of the airfield near Bells Forstal Farm and stock yard. Mrs Ricketts recalls that high up on the North Downs there was a water shortage and the airmen had to be taken into Faversham for a weekly bath. Later on a bore hole was sunk and a water tower built but all that came up was sludge.

The squadron was initially equipped with Sopwith Pups, of which only one extant photograph of a 112 example seems to remain, that of a machine called 'Madge'. This aircraft, with a beautifully polished engine cowling, was fitted with a 110 hp Gnôme Monosoupape engine with a segment removed from the lower quadrant of the cowling and slots cut out around the perimeter to assist engine cooling. The Pup was a formidable little fighter and, in Major James McCudden's words, 'could outmanoeuvre an Albatross no matter how good the pilot was'. However, against raiding Gothas, the Pup rarely managed to reach height soon enough to achieve an interception and they were soon to be replaced by the more powerful Sopwith F.1 Camel.

The Camel, in J M Bruce's words was 'the supreme dog-fighting aeroplane in the

---

[1] *Leutnant* Rudolf Bartikowski, aged 24, from Berlin, *Vizefeldwebel* Fritz Bloch, aged 29, from Niedenburg and *Vizefeldwebel* Heinrich Heiligers, aged 27, from Gerderhahn. They are buried in Cannock Chase Military Cemetery.

armoury of the Allies, only the Fokker Dr. 1 could match its manoeuvrability'[1] and its 'name probably symbolises 1914–18 aerial combat to more people that does that of any other aircraft'[2]. It was a snub-nosed little biplane with dihedral only on its lower wings. The nickname 'Camel' was the result of the curious hump just aft of the engine that enclosed the breeches of the twin Vickers-Maxim .303 machine guns. The Camels issued to 112 HD Sqn were powered both by Clerget and Le Rhône engines and some had clear vision panels opened in the upper wing centre section. From the few snapshots that still exist it appears to show that most of the Camels were the normal scouts and not the modified night-fighting version with the cockpit moved into position in line with the wing trailing edge. The Lewis gun on Brand's machine was mounted on the upper centre section so as not to blind him with the gun's muzzle flash when it was fired at night. Mr James also recalls seeing two Bentley Camels made by Boulton & Paul of Norwich with aluminium cylinders.

There were no official markings although aircraft carried some individual insignia. Lieutenant 'Earwig' Irwin's carried a pawnbroker's sign and the words 'The Odd One' and Captain 'Boozy' Baker's 'Tootsie' a diagonal stripe. Many machines seemed to carry girls' names, A B Yuille's was called 'Twinkle' and there was a 'Madge II', which presumably succeeded 'Madge' (the Sopwith Pup). The CO's aircraft, as was usual, flew strut streamers and the Flight commanders carried streamers attached to the rudder. Night fighting aircraft at that time were painted a drab olive green or black, with the serial numbers and roundels toned down. It seems likely, on 112, the whites of the roundels and rudder markings were overpainted in orange and the metal of the engine cowlings painted black once the squadron was confined to the night fighting role.

Night flying training was aimed at bringing the pilots up to a standard where they could land their aircraft safely at night without using underwing flares or relying on the flarepath. Airfield lighting was provided by gooseneck flares which were laid out aligned with the prevailing wind by the RDCs (Royal Defence Corps), elderly and veteran soldiers who were kept in uniform to perform odd jobs. One night the flares were laid out across wind so that every pilot either crashed or pancaked, except Major Brand who made a perfect landing. After that younger men were employed on flarepath duty.

There were no casualties due to enemy action although there was the usual crop of accidental deaths. On one occasion a Camel failed to get airborne and flew straight into 'B' Flight's Bessoneau hangar where a lot of airmen were gathered for pay parade causing many injuries. There are two graves in Throwley churchyard, one of Lieutenant E W F Hopgood who was killed on 14 October 1918 when he spun in from 4000' and another of 2/Lieutenant J T Mitchell who died on 24 January 1919. This aircraft also spun, falling into Hockley Wood about a quarter of a mile from the airfield, but no one saw where it crashed and the wreckage was not found until it was located from the air.

In 'Winged Victory', probably the finest book written about flying in the Great War, V M Yeates describes the difficulty of flying Camels. 'They were by far the most

[1] 'The Sopwith Camel', Part 1, '*Flight*', 22 April 1955, J M Bruce
[2] 'Sopwith F.1 Camel', Part 1, '*Aeromodeller*', January 1964, J M Bruce

difficult of service machines to handle. Many pilots killed themselves by crashing in a right hand spin when they were learning to fly them. A Camel hated an inexperienced hand, and flopped into a frantic spin at the least opportunity. They were unlike ordinary aeroplanes, being quite unstable, immoderately tail-heavy, so light on the controls that the slightest jerk or inaccuracy would hurl them all over the sky, difficult to land, deadly to crash: a list of vices to emasculate the stoutest courage, and the first flight in a Camel was always a terrible ordeal.'

On 9 July, 1918, Major Brand relinquished command to Major G W Murlis Green. Air Mechanic Tucker described Brand as 'a wonderful man, he had no time for drills or parades but work was what he wanted, a serviceable squadron at all times'. After the war, in February 1920, Brand, with Sir P van Ryneveld, in a Vickers Vimy, 'The Silver Queen', attempted to fly from London to Cape Town but crashed 530 miles south of Cairo. The engines were salvaged and installed in 'Silver Queen II' which they crashed near Bulewayo. Undaunted they completed the flight in a DH9.

Major Murlis Green DSO & bar, MC & 2 bars, *Karageorge* (a Serbian Order), another pilot from 70 Sqn was credited with 20 victories. He had fought on the Macedonian front, an 'ace' in the correct and accepted meaning of the term. He achieved nationwide publicity when 'The Daily Mirror' photographed him at 'Sutton Farm' in a billet which he had constructed entirely of petrol cans.

In February 1918 there was an influenza epidemic, not connected, it would seem, to the dreadful Spanish 'flu of September that year, but nevertheless the squadron lost 23 men in 10 days. In the summer of 1918 there was a Wing review at Throwley and aircraft flew in from far and wide – Bristol Fighters. FE2Bs. SE5s and Camels and there was a competition to find 'The Cock Squadron'. The events included formation flying, landing-on-the-mark and similar tests of squadron and individual skills, the winning squadron to receive a live cockerel. All stations were warned that the event required that piece of sky to be reserved for the day but halfway through a DH6 appeared, 'a most obvious first soloist flying very badly indeed . . . He not only filled the air with a beastly 90RAF clatter instead of our superior Le Rhône drone but kept on going and coming back again, in fact making a complete bloody nuisance of himself . . . One of the Camel boys leaped smartly into the air at which this DH6, instead of slinking away with its tail between its legs, proceeded to put up a complete mockery of a dog-fight . . . I have always, in my own mind, looked on this (Cock Sqn Competition) as the authentic ancestor of the RAF pageants . . .'[1] The review was taken by an Air Vice-Marshal who arrived in one of the astonishing little Bristol M1c monoplanes decorated with a large red spinner.

Up to June 1918 orders had been conveyed to pilots in the air by means of a complicated set of forty ground signals but experiments then started to try to send messages by W/T. About August of that year an attempt was also made to contact an aircraft by R/T but without any noticeable success at the first attempt. 'I remember' wrote Mr A W James, 'seeing one of the pilots (Capt Wolley Dod) speaking into a microphone to the pilot of a Camel telling him to turn left, right, climb, climb and turn, plus a few choice RFC words, for it seemed that the pilot of the Camel could not hear . . .'

[1] C J Chabot.

In that month many of 112's best pilots were called upon to form the nucleus of 151 Sqn at Hainault Farm, which was to be the first real night-fighter squadron. Once it was constituted it was transferred to France to counter the German bombers of *Bogohl 3* which were now being used to attack tactical military targets in support of their ground offensive.

Records exist which show that on 8 June 1918, 112 Sqn had 24 aircraft on establishment, of which 20 were serviceable. There were 20 pilots on strength and 60 other ranks. Like most RAF squadrons it was divided into 'A', 'B' and 'C' Flights and a Headquarters Flight. The squadron was fully mobile and was equipped with workshop lorries, a mobile blacksmiths' and welders' shop, transport lorries and tenders. Mr James remembers one man, a sailmaker for fabric repairs who also doubled as a french polisher, doper, artist and sign-writer. 'He was a very original artist'!

On 5 October, 1918, the squadron was taken over by Major C J Usborne, a French-Canadian ex-lumberjack and ex-Indianapolis racing car driver and ex-member of 40 Sqn. It was shortly after his arrival that the Armistice was announced. A few days before this there was a 'false' Armistice, generated by rumours. Officers and NCOs took a lorry into Faversham firing Verey lights and shouting 'The War's over!' while driving round the streets. Their celebrations were premature. On 11 November, the real day the war ended, Usborne was seen driving his car 'The Crimson Rambler' across the airfield with an enormous Union Flag attached to the radiator cap. Having no windscreen it was not long before the flag wrapped itself round his head and the car ended up in a ditch. The police had to be called from Faversham that day as everyone had rather too much to drink and were threatening to burn down the hangars. Verey lights were fired and shortly afterwards the WRAF airwomen, no doubt much against their will, were sent back to their billets.

One Sunday afternoon in the summer of 1918 an observer/pupil pilot of 188 NT Sqn, recently back from France, was walking across the airfield from the Officers' Mess towards the hangars. He saw a Camel coming for him very low and went down on one knee. In spite of this he was struck on the head by the propellor and instantly killed. The Camel, painted with a representation of the devil, immediately crashed and broke up with the pilot suffering severe head injuries. The inquest verdict was 'Accidental Death'.

In March 1919 the squadron was re-equipped with Sopwith Snipes but there was to be only a few months left to enjoy them as on 13 June 112 HD Sqn was disbanded. The Sopwith 7F.1 Snipe was a development of the Camel but had many improvements. The wings had two bays on either side and the fin and rudder were of modified design. The fuselage was tubby in comparison and the pilot sat higher up. It was as manoeuvreable as the Camel but not so sensitive on the controls and although its climb to height was better and it was faster, some Camel pilots did not like it as much.

Throwley airfield had been built on land belonging to Earl Sondes of Lees Court. At the time of the disbandment a large permanent hangar was in the course of construction, built to supersede the Bessoneau hangars, of which there were eventually five. In Dodds Willows, the wood alongside the airfield, a hutted camp was built where officers, airmen and airwomen were quartered.

THROWLEY AIRFIELD 1917~1919

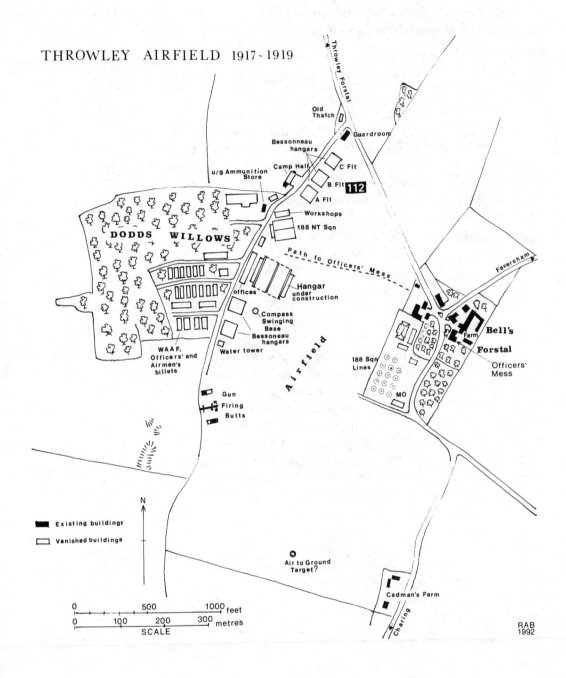

Throwley Forstal

Old Thatch

Guardroom

Bessonneau hangars

u/g Ammunition Store

Camp Hall

C Flt

B Flt **112**

A Flt

Workshops

188 NT Sqn

Path to Officers' Mess

Faversham

DODDS WILLOWS

offices

Hangar under construction

Compass Swinging Base

Bessoneau hangars

Water tower

Farm

Bell's Forstal

Officers' Mess

188 Sqn Lines

MO

WAAF, Officers' and Airmen's billets

Airfield

Gun Firing Butts

N

■ Existing buildings

☐ Vanished buildings

Air to Ground Target?

Cadman's Farm

Charing

| 0 | | 500 | | 1000 feet |
| 0 | 100 | 200 | 300 | metres |

SCALE

RAB 1992

A contemporary ditty, sung to the tune of 'A Little Bit of Heaven' perhaps sums up the proverbial misanthropic attitude taken by the airmen of their unhappy situation in life—

>   Have you ever heard the story how
>   Our aerodrome got its name?
>   If you listen you will understand
>   From whence this place first came.
>   No wonder the boys all want their tickets
>   To get away you see.
>   For here's the way a chap who knew
>   Once told the tale to me-
>
> *Chorus*   Just a little bit of rain and sleet
>   Fell from the sky one day
>   And settled on a mud heap
>   In a spot so far away.
>   And when the Brass Hats came to view
>   This scene of desolation,
>   They said 'Let's build an aerodrome
>   Five miles from town or station'.
>   Then they sprinkled it with wooden huts
>   And a Bessoneau hangar or two,
>   A row of squadron offices
>   That entirely spoiled the view
>   Then they dotted it with RDCs
>   Who should have been at home,
>   Put a few fed-up mechanics there
>   And called it Throwley 'drome.

CHAPTER TWO

Egypt, Greece and Crete

The aircraft carrier HMS *Argus* lying in Portsmouth harbour was the unlikely scene for the re-forming of 112 Squadron on 16 May 1939. Commanded by Sqn Ldr 'Slim' Somerville, the squadron set sail the next day for Alexandria, where they docked nine days later. On 26 May they arrived at RAF Helwan, one of the major permanent airfields in the Delta. The squadron was equipped with 16 Gloster Gladiator Is and IIs which had come from 72 Sqn at Church Fenton, plus eight in reserve. The Gladiator had emerged as a prototype in 1935 and was taken on in squadron service in February 1937. Four Browning .303 machine guns comprised the armament, two mounted in troughs in the sides of the fuselage synchronised and firing through the airscrew with 600 rounds each and one under each lower wing, mounted in fairings each with a 400 round belt.

At that time eight RAF squadrons were equipped with Gladiators, of which Nos 33, 80 and 112 were in Egypt. Although only 20 years had passed since 112 last flew, speeds had virtually doubled. The Gladiator could reach 226 mph at 5000′ and 236 mph at 20,000′. Climbing time to 20,000′ was about 9 minutes and its service ceiling was nearly 33,000′, its range was 428 miles and endurance just under 2 hours. Compared to the Sopwith Camel or Snipe these were considerable improvements. Based at Helwan the squadron adopted the usual three flight system, Flt Lt W C Williams commanding 'A' Flt, Flt Lt K H Savage 'B' Flt and Flt Lt C H Fry 'C' Flt. From photographs it would seem that the squadron aircraft retained their silver colour for some time, probably until the outbreak of war in Europe. There appears to have been no squadron markings at that time apart from the engine nacelles and wheel fairings being painted in flight colours. Ex-Flt Sgt Carter remembers that the code letters 'XO' were used around the time of the outbreak of war. The squadron's role was, naturally enough, the air defence of Cairo and the Delta. It seems certain that 112 also had several Gauntlets on strength, three serial numbers are known, and these were used for training while conserving Gladiator flying hours. The deepening crisis in Europe meant that the life-line to the Far East, the Suez Canal, was vulnerable, especially if Italy, one of the three Axis partners, was persuaded to join any war against France and Britain.

Britain and France entered the war on 3 September, 1939, but with only Germany as the enemy. Mussolini, for the time being, decided not to intervene. On 5 September, the first day that the 112 diary (F540) commences, the squadron was on 'standby' for a full 24 hours and the Operations Room was manned. There was no flying. The following day the squadron stood down from 19.00 hrs to 07.00 hrs, with only one Flight available, the remainder on a 4-hour recall. By 9 September the alert had subsided and the squadron resumed normal peacetime training. On 14 September the squadron was on Battle Flight and the F540 records that the aircraft reached 30,000' in 31 minutes. Peacetime training continued but nevertheless, about this time, the Gladiators were camouflaged in a locally devised colour scheme and the letters 'RT' were adopted as the unit code[1]. On 14 January 1940 Sgt C J W Tait, who had only been on the squadron eleven days, force-landed a Fairey Gordon (probably K2719) of the Drogue Towing Flt, which had been used to tow the air-to-air firing target, on an island in the Nile. It turned over onto its back but although Tait was unhurt, his passenger, LAC McLennan, a Fitter Mech, broke his wrist. We hear of LAC McLennan again later.

At the beginning of February the squadron was reorganised into two Flights, Flt Lt Charles Fry, an Australian, up to then 'C' Flt commander, became deputy 'A' Flt commander. This arrangement lasted until May when the three Flight system was re-adopted. On 11 March 1940 the squadron was engaged in an army co-operation exercise with the Hussars south-east of Heliopolis and four days later Sqn Ldr Somerville had to bale out when his aircraft caught fire in the air. He was admitted to the 2/10th General Hospital at Helmeih suffering from burns and, in his absence, the squadron was taken over by Sqn Ldr A R G ('Porpoise') Bax. At that time the programme for the squadron was reveille at 05.00 hrs, first working parade at 05.30, breakfast from 08.00 to 09.00 hrs with work continuing until 12.15 when all ranks were dismissed for the rest of the day.

From 7–17 May the squadron was involved in the Delta Defence Exercise. On 22 May 'C' Flt and a sub-section (3 aircraft) of 'A' Flt took part in a mass fly-past over Cairo of 81 aircraft from nine squadrons. It was said that the noise of this formation was out of all proportion to the number of machines taking part. Although this show of strength was designed to impress and reassure the local population one Egyptian was heard to remark 'There are more than three – it must be the Italians'. Meanwhile in Europe the Germans had just launched their *blitzkreig* on the Low Countries and France. By 22 May the evacuation of Dunkirk was in progress and hourly the intervention of Mussolini and the Italians was expected. On 29 May all leave was cancelled.

At this moment, as 112 stood on the brink of war, the squadron was organised as follows —

> Sqn Cdr: Sqn Ldr Somerville
> Adjutant: Fg Off Fraser
> Sqn Medical Officer: Fg Off McGregor
> Sqn Equipment Officer: Plt Off Gosschalk
> Sqn Intelligence Officers: Plt Off Lewis
> Plt Off Goar
> Sqn Armament Officer: Plt Off Lean
> Sqn Cypher Officer: Plt Off Page

[1] R C Sturtivant points out that 'RT' properly belonged to 114 Sqn.

'A' Flight	'B' Flight	'C' Flight
Flt Lt Williams	Flt Lt Savage	Flt Lt Fry
Fg Off H C Worcester	Fg Off Whittington	Fg Off Smith
Fg Off Price-Owen	Fg Off Hayward	(Fg Off Fraser [Adjt])
Plt Off Ross	Plt Off Evans	Plt Off Clarke
Plt Off Acworth	Plt Off Kirk	Plt Off Chapman
Plt Off Davison	Plt Off Sanderson	Plt Off Duff
Plt Off Smither	Plt Off Green	Plt Off de la Hoyde
Plt Off A Gray Worcester	Plt Off Hamlyn	Plt Off Bennett
Plt Off Harrison	Plt Off Wolsey	Plt Off Cochrane
Plt Off Wickham	Sgt Woodward	Plt Off Butcher
Plt Off Strahan	Sgt Tait	Sgt Donaldson
Plt Off Van der Heijden		

(Total strength: 35 officer & NCO pilots, 6 non-flying officers, 2 Warrant Officers, 7 Flt Sgts, 10 Sgts, 38 Cpls, 233 airmen)

This seemingly huge organisation compares oddly with a typical single-seater aircraft squadron of the present day, and the fact that they were commanded by an officer of only Squadron Leader rank suggests that perhaps things were somewhat simpler then.

On 31 May 1940 112 Sqn received orders that 'B' Flight, comprising 11 officers (including the squadron Cypher Officer, Plt Off Page), five NCOs, 62 airmen and 10 aircraft were to depart for Summit, an airfield south of Port Sudan on the Red Sea to act as a detached flight, subsequently known as 'K' Flt, prepared to act against the Italians in Eritrea. Two Valentias of 70 Sqn were to airlift the groundcrew and spares.

On 2 June 'B' Flight aircraft flew south stopping first as Aswan. After the war E Norman Woodward remembered this rather hair-raising trip. 'The fun started at Aswan, a small, narrow, sloping, rocky ground about 500 yards by 800 yards surrounded by steep cliffs with odd gaps here and there. We arrived in the middle of the day in the hottest month, temperature 100° plus in the proverbial no shade, and no wind. The CO landed his (sub-) flight in formation down the slope! Result – one burst tyre, one tail wheel missing and one bent wing respectively on the three aircraft. The remaining seven aircraft eventually landed individually in various other directions. The only servicing facilities were the four airmen in the Valentia. The bent wing tip (Plt Off Wolsey's L7612) was irreparable but we borrowed a tail wheel assembly and a main wheel. Having no trestles the aircraft had to be manhandled to fit them. To add to the fun Plt Off Evans had a prize pedigree dachshund 'Mitzi' which had just produced as wildly assorted a set of triplets as was imaginable. They were being conveyed in a Valentia and required virtually all the spare water available to keep them alive. Arriving at Wadi Halfa we had to refuel from 4 gallon petrol tins through chamois filters. Finally the taxi to Wadi Halfa broke down. The bar of the Wadi Halfa Hotel, which we finally reached at 9 p.m. was as near to paradise as I am likely to see!'

At Wadi Halfa they found an Italian SM75 of the *Ala Littoria*, the crew of which was doubtless very interested in the Gladiators' deployment. The next day, when the Italian

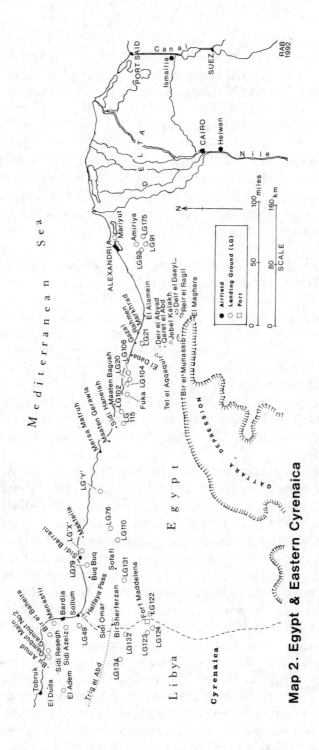

Map 2. Egypt & Eastern Cyrenaica

machine was ready to depart 'the pilot expressed his opinion of us by lining himself up with our row of Glads and running up all three engines at once. Wadi Halfa was very sandy!'

The next leg of the journey was to Atbara and this 'was made independently by (sub-)flights, two of which crossed each other about half way on courses about 90° apart. We arrived at Atbara about 1210hrs.' 'B' Flight eventually arrived at Summit on 3 June to form part of 254 Wing of the Advanced Striking Force.

The Italians declared war against France and Great Britain on 10 June 1940. That day four South African Air Force pilots were posted briefly to 'A' and 'C' Flights, the first of many who would join 112 Sqn throughout all the years of the war. It is worth recalling that the South African Air Force never required its pilots to serve outside the borders of the Union and that each one of these SAAF aircrew who joined the Desert Air Force and fought alongside aircrew of Great Britain and the other dominions was there of his own free will.

By nine minutes after midnight on 10 June all forward concentrations had been completed and the signal was received by 202 Group, which comprised a rather motley collection of aircraft under the command of Air Commodore Raymond Collishaw, (the leading RNAS 'ace' of the Great War with 60 victories to his credit) to dispatch reconnaissance aircraft into Libya. Facing the Royal Air Force were 200 modern Italian fighter aircraft with a superiority of about 2.5 to 1 and 200 modern bombers. 252 Wing (80 and 112 Sqns), in the meanwhile, remained in the Delta to defend Cairo. 203 Group in the Sudan, under the command of Air Commodore L H Slatter, consisted of three squadrons of Wellesley bombers (Nos 14, 47 and 223) and 'K' Flt – in all about 90 aircraft. Facing them were 200,000 Italian troops and 150 aircraft.

On 11 June nine Gladiators left Summit for Port Sudan where the officers were billeted in the Red Sea Hotel. Six aircraft were designated the Stand By Flight, ready for take off between 04.30 and 06.30 hrs and again between 16.30 and 18.30 hrs, dawn and dusk, the most likely times of an attack from the air. In addition one aircraft remained at readiness all through the day.

Those who were detached to Summit were slightly better off as it was 3500′ up, quite cool at night, and without the deadly humidity of Port Sudan. There 'the town festered in a humid shade temperature of 110° and sometimes more. In the cockpits of the aircraft patrolling down the Red Sea the temperatures were sometimes 130°; many in the town were suffering from prickly heat, the rash that blotches your face and arms with red scabs. The water in the pool at the front of the Red Sea Hotel was so warm that it was a slight relief in the evening to emerge from it into less warm air. In the hotel it was wise to fill your bath in the evening so that by the morning the standing water would have dropped a degree or two below the temperature of the flat, hot fluid that steamed out of the tap. One wondered how the crews of submarines in the Red Sea got along. . . .'[1] The airmen and the sergeant pilots, living in tents, regarded the Red Sea Hotel as something approaching paradise.

Five days later, on 16 June, it was decided to move 'B' Flt to Summit, leaving a sub-flight of 3 aircraft behind with a dawn and dusk watch of two aircraft at Erkowit, a short distance to the east. The same day the detachment had its first action. Plt Off G A

---

[1] 'Mediterranean Front' by Alan Moorehead.

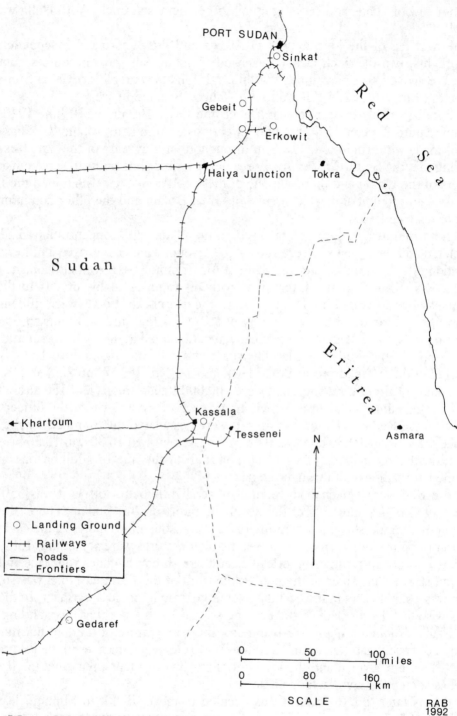

Map 3. Sudan & Eritrea

Capt Newton, 'C' Flight Commander (left) and Lieut Davies standing in front of a 110 h.p. Gnôme Monosoupape Sopwith Pup named Madge. Throwley Airfield, date unknown but probably between July 1917 and March 1918.
A. C. S. Irwin

112 Home Defence Squadron pilots outside the Officers' Mess at Bells Forstal Farm, Throwley, September/ October 1917. Those identified include Lieut Chandler (back row, 2nd from left), Lieut Cockerill, AFC (seated, 3rd from left), Major Allen (seated centre), Capt Newton (seated, 2nd from right), Lieut Davies (seated, far right).
A. C. S. Irwin

Lieut A. C. S. Irwin, 'C' Flight Commander, with his two dogs, Tinker and Tip, standing by his Sopwith F.1 Camel, serial number D6415. The fuselage serial number has been painted out and the roundels and rudder markings overpainted in night-fighting colours. The cowling has also been painted black. The aircraft flies a deputy Flight Commander's pennant from the rudder and beneath the lower wing is a night-landing flare.
A. C. S. Irwin

112 Sqn's Sopwith Camels in front of 'B' Flight's Bessoneau hangar. The nearest aircraft (D6473) carries an underwing flare and the cowling has been darkened. The further aircraft flaunts a large numeral 2 and an inscription that is illegible. The pilot seated in the cockpit is Lieut Gilbertson. *A. C. S. Irwin*

Capt Baker, 'B' Flight Commander, standing by his Camel Tootsie. The airman engaged in refuelling the machine was Air Mechanic Tucker. On the fin is a faint numeral 1 and there is a diagonal bar painted forward of the fuselage roundel. Despite the night fighting roundel and rudder markings, the cowling remains brilliantly polished. In the left of the photograph is an Avro 504 of 188 Night Training Sqn and the building seen in the distance on the right are Bells Forstal. *J. Tucker*

112 Sqn pilots in June 1918. Standing in rear row (left to right): -?- ; Capt Yuille, DFC: Lieut Blennerhasset MC: Lieut Scotcher; Lieut Barrager; Lieut Broome, DFC, AFC; Lieut Frampton. Seated: -?- ; Capt Baker; -?- ; Major Brand, DSO, MC, DFC; Capt Newton; Lieut Collier, DFC; Lieut Irwin. Front row: -?- ; -?- ; -?- ; Lieut Aitken; Lieut Wykes; -?- ; -?-. *A. C. S. Irwin*

Flt Lt Scotcher in Pixie III. Note the swastika and diamond shaped device. *A. B. Yuille*

The three Bessoneau hangars for 'A', 'B' and 'C' Flights of 112 Sqn at Throwley Airfield. The building in the distance was the airfield guardroom. *N. Ricketts*

Capt Quinton Brand, MC, outside the Officers' Mess at Bells Forstal Farm, Throwley. *Chaz Bowyer via Sqn Ldr D W Warne, RAF*

Three of 112 Sqn's night-fighting Camels. Nearest machine carries a swastika good-luck symbol on the fin. The centre aircraft is named Madge II. *A. B. Yuille*

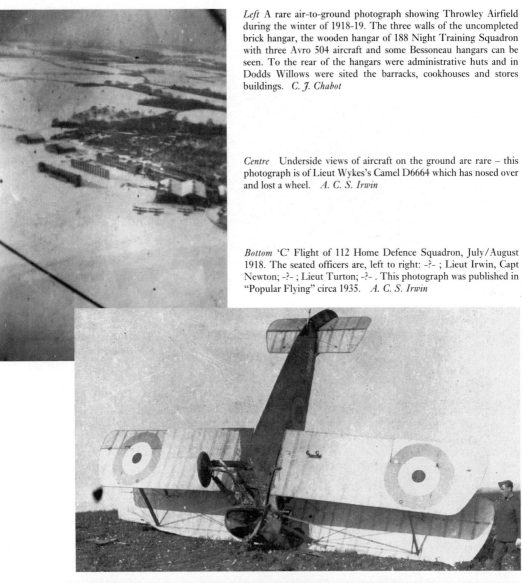

Left A rare air-to-ground photograph showing Throwley Airfield during the winter of 1918-19. The three walls of the uncompleted brick hangar, the wooden hangar of 188 Night Training Squadron with three Avro 504 aircraft and some Bessoneau hangars can be seen. To the rear of the hangars were administrative huts and in Dodds Willows were sited the barracks, cookhouses and stores buildings. *C. J. Chabot*

Centre Underside views of aircraft on the ground are rare – this photograph is of Lieut Wykes's Camel D6664 which has nosed over and lost a wheel. *A. C. S. Irwin*

Bottom 'C' Flight of 112 Home Defence Squadron, July/August 1918. The seated officers are, left to right: -?- ; Lieut Irwin, Capt Newton; -?- ; Lieut Turton; -?- . This photograph was published in "Popular Flying" circa 1935. *A. C. S. Irwin*

A Sopwith Snipe, E7337, at Throwley in 1918. On the left of the group standing by the wing trailing edge is Lieut Barrager. *C. F. Wolley Dod*

A line up of 112 Squadron Gladiators of the Delta Defence Force stationed at RAF Helwan in 1939. Engine nacelles and wheel discs were painted in flight colours. The second machine from the left is K8008. *Robin Brown*

112 Sqn's Gladiators in drab wartime camouflage. The nearest machine carries the early squadron identification letters "XO". *Clive Williams*

The second set of identification letters, "RT", carried on K6142, which is engaged in having its compass swung. The three officers are unidentified.   *Clive Williams*

Above The drab wartime colour shows up well in this photograph of K7963 which also has a modified fuselage roundel. Against the white desert sand these aircraft must have appeared to defy all the tenets of good camouflage!   *Clive Williams*

The large size of the Gladiator is shown well in this photograph, where the leading edge appear level with the standing man's face. Underwing roundel colours are also visible, and it will be seen that the fin flash had been painted out as well.   *Clive Williams*

A pilot boards a 112 Sqn Gladiator.
Robin Brown

Below A line-up of 112 Sqn Gladiators. The original photograph, from which this print was taken had the date 5.10.39 written on the back. The nearest aircraft has the serial number K7893 painted in small numerals on the cowling. The letter partially visible under the cockpit panel may be the "R" of the "RT" code.
Robin Brown

A line-up of 112 Sqn Gladiators. The nearest machine carries the serial number K7977 and, lacking the spinner, may be undergoing an engine test. The pilot, wearing a helmet and mask, stands at the wing tip. Four of the five aircraft have their engines running and the other machine appears about to start.
Clive Williams

An *Ala Littoria* SM75 taxying. This may be the occasion when 'B' Flight was at Wadi Halfa *en route* to Port Sudan on 3 June 1940.   *Clive Williams*

A group of 112 Sqn pilots at Sidi Haneish pose for a publicity photograph after the engagement of 20 November 1940 in which eight CR42s were claimed destroyed. Left to right: Flt Lt Abrahams, Plt Off Costello, -?- , Fg Off Bennett and Sgt Donaldson. The unknown pilot may have been Plt Off Acworth. *IWM (CM242)*

At Yannina (or possibly Paramythia), in Greece. Members of 'A' Flight. Left to right: Fg off MacDonald, Fg Off Bowker, Fg Off Brown, -?- , Fg Off Acworth and Flt Lt Abrahams. The coolness of the temperature is indicated by the heavyweight flying gear in comparison with the lightweight equipment worn in the desert.

Above Air-to-ground shots with hand held cameras are rare, but this one shows the snow-capped mountains of Greece between Yannina and Eleusis through the struts and wires of a Gladiator. *R. J. Abrahams*

Left At Paramythia. Sqn Ldr Schwab (centre, in dark glasses) with Fg Off Jerry MacDonald to the right ("X"). The Gladiator can be seen still bearing the codeletters "RT", the aircraft letter probably "Y". *R. J. Abrahams*

Below At Yannina (left to right): Probably Flt Lt Fraser, Fg Off Acworth and Plt Off Brunton. *Angela Acworth via Brian Cull*

"Sharksteeth"! A Tomahawk IIB carrying the newly adopted markings that were to be its singular identification throughout the rest of the war. The date of this official Air Ministry photograph is about September 1941, and the location is probably Sidi Haneish.   *IWM (CM1340)*

Jack Bartle seated in Tomahawk GA-K (AN413) which carries a boxing kangaroo motif and the name "Nan". Sidi Haneish, September 1941.   *Neville Duke*

Plt Off 'Butch' Jeffries standing by the nose of GA–V (AK578) at Sidi Haneish. Jeffries was killed in December 1941. *Neville Duke*

A group of sergeant pilots. This photograph dates from October/November 1941 at Sidi Haneish. Standing (left to right): Sgt Houston; Sgt Glasgow; Sgt Christie; Sgt Taylor. Front: Sgt Alves; –?– ; Sgt McQueen. Glasgow was killed in November, Houston in December and Alves made PoW in December. Not much is known about Taylor. *Neville Duke*

Above "The engine changing gang". Left to right: Sgt Butler; Jack Cookson; "Jock" McLennan; Sgt Harrison; Jim Worsfold. LG 102, Sidi Haneish, about October/November 1941. McLennan was the eponymous hero of McLennan's barge. *Jim Worsfold*

Right Sqn Ldr Tony Morello, CO of 112 Squadron from October 1941 to January 1942. *Neville Duke*

Below Plt Off Duke, Fg Off Westenra and Sgt Leu at LG122, Fort Maddelena. *Neville Duke*

Fg Off Ken Sands, Fort Maddelena, November 1941.
Neville Duke

Plt Off Neville Duke and Fg Off Peter ("Hunk")
Humphreys.   *Neville Duke*

The group of EPIP (Egyptian Pattern Indian Patent) tents that comprised the Pilots' Mess.   *Neville Duke*

Above The victim of a night landing accident occasioned by Plt Off Bowker, at LG122, November 1941. Here the sharksmouth seems to be registering misery and pain not determined aggression. *Neville Duke*

Right Plt Off Jeffries and Fg Off Sands. Note that pistols were carried on every sortie though (presumably) rarely used. Jeffries was killed in December 1941. *Neville Duke*

30th November, 1941. A photograph taken at LG122, Fort Maddelena at the height of the struggle for air supremacy over the Western Desert. Standing (left to right): Sgt Leu; Plt Off Duke; Fg Off Soden; Fg Off Humphreys; Sqn Ldr Morello; Flt Lt Ambrose; Plt Off Dickinson; Sgt Burney; Fg Off Westenra. Front row: Plt Off Sabourin; Plt Off Bowker; Fg Off Bartle; Sgt Carson. Neville Duke explains that his "pious expression" was due to his having just escaped death at the hands of *Obfw* Schultz earlier that day. *IWM (CM1820)*

The engine changing gang at work. GA-J, serial number AK475. The picture shows the extremely primitive conditions under which major servicing was done in the desert. Engines, at that time, rarely lasted more than 60-80 flying hours due to the effect of the sand. November or December 1941. *IWM (CM2039)*

Resting against an Allison engine are (left to right): Sgt Bert Butler; LAC Jack Cookson; 'Jock' McLennan and Jim Worsfold, all Fitters IIE. At El Adem in December 1941. *Jim Worsfold*

Wolsey and Sgt E N Woodward, taking off from Summit at 18.15 hrs had climbed to 2000' when they saw two Savoia-Marchetti SM81s about 300' above them flying north in the direction of Port Sudan. The Italian airmen did not spot the Gladiators until they had begun to open fire. The enemy returned fire from the upper and lower rear guns, breaking formation and jettisoning their bombs and then diving away until they were lost in the failing light.

The SM81 *'Pipistrello'* was a rather cumbersome looking three-engined aircraft with a fixed undercarriage which had seen its best days in the Spanish and Abyssinian wars a few years before. The machines intercepted on that day were probably from *29° Gruppo* based at Asseab.

On 18 June there was an abortive Italian air raid on Port Sudan. None of the bombs dropped caused any damage but the Gladiators were unable to make any interceptions because of the bombers' height, about 16,000'. On that day the squadron suffered the first of many accidental deaths when Sgt C J W Tait, attempting to slow roll his aircraft (K6136) over the Sergeants' Mess at too low an altitude, flew into the ground.

The aircraft now at Summit were K6134, K6135, K6136, K6143, K7479, K7977 and L7619. At Port Sudan were K6143, K7948, L7619. Shortly afterwards a new aircraft L7612 was delivered to replace St Tait's machine.

At Helwan the Battle Flight took off to intercept enemy aircraft and were caught in the searchlights and shot at by AA guns. When they returned to base the small problem of aircraft recognition was taken up with the Sector Controller.

The early warning system in the Sudan, as remembered by Sgt Woodward, seems to have been even less efficient. 'There were about ten (railway) stations between Haiya Junction, 40 miles south of Summit, and Port Sudan. The station master was responsible for reporting all aircraft, friendly or hostile and any hostile action. This worked out as follows. If the aircraft was high, that is 5000' plus, it was too far away to bother about and was ignored. If, however, a friendly aircraft happened along at 2000' and fired the colours of the day, this was interpreted as 'hostile action' and all and sundry on the ground vanished into the blue.

'On returning some time later, when it was assumed to be safe, contact was made with Port Sudan station by means of telegraph and a 'hostile aircraft flying very high' (that is higher than the local palm trees) was reported. Port Sudan station master passed this on to Civil Air Defence (whoever he was) who in turn informed Air HQ (if available). Permission for retaliatory action having been received, the procedure was reversed back to Sinkat, the airfield for Summit, about two miles away. The station master here was supposed to be able to speak English and had a telephone to 223 Sqn HQ to whom he reported the incident, using code letters for the place concerned.

'223 Sqn HQ was on the opposite end of the aerodrome so a runner had to be sent (or first found) to bear the good news to us. 55 seconds later the Glads were airborne. This, of course, merely led a vicious, if rather large, circle, as an hour or so after landing from a patrol, a further series of alarms trickled through. The Battle of Britain had nothing on us!'[1]

At Port Sudan on 29 June Plt Off J Hamlyn (L7619) took off at about 04.30 hrs to intercept enemy aircraft. Five miles south, when at 4500', he spotted an Italian trimotor

---

[1] E Gordon Woodward, correspondence

3000' above. He climbed and delivered a quarter attack, followed by a tail chase, by which time he had identified the machine as an SM81. The bomber dived down to 4500' but after Hamlyn had fired about 1000 rounds the enemy aircraft exploded and fell in flames into the Red Sea. Parts of the SM81 damaged the Gladiator's windscreen, airscrew and ring and bead sight and a large piece of piping lodged itself in the engine. Later in the day two of the crew were rescued from a coral reef just off the coast and one turned out to be the CO of the *Stormo*, the only one of 12 machines to reach the target.

The 'quarter attack' mentioned in this account was the classic manoeuvre taught to all fighter pilots for as long as their aircraft carried machine guns or cannons. It involved flying parallel, but somewhat higher than the target aircraft, and a set distance to one side. When the target was in a position slightly to the rear of the attacking aircraft the fighter would commence a diving S-turn judging it so that it would end up at an angle which would allow a full deflection shot that would rake the target.

In the meantime Plt Off P R W Wickham who had been attached to 33 Sqn based at Maaten Gerawla in the Western Desert had shot down two enemy aircraft, one, on the 29 June, a Meridionali Ro 37 *bis* army co-operation biplane[1] and the next day a CR32 fighter. It was decided around that time that pilots attached to other squadrons would have their claims credited to their parent squadron, so, within two days 112 had notched up 3 confirmed 'kills'. On 4 July Fg Off A Gray Worcester and Fg Off W B Price-Owen were sent to gain battle experience with 'A' Flt of 33 Sqn at Sidi Barrani. On an evening sortie that day, while escorting a Lysander, nine Fiat CR42s were seen taking off from Menastir Landing Ground (LG) west of Bardia. Fg Off Worcester, leading No 2 Section, shot down four of them while the other two members of his formation (33 Sqn pilots) shot down three more. Fg Off R H Smith and Fg Off R J Bennett, who had been with 33 only a day longer, each shot down one. Fg Off Price-Owen's aircraft was shot down but he came down safely by parachute and landed 15 miles inside the Egyptian border.

The Fiat CR42 *Falco* was then an extremely new fighter, the prototype having first flown early in 1939. Gianni Cattaneo[2] claims that the CR42 was perhaps the best biplane in service anywhere. 'Characterised by superlative manoeuvrability it combined all the qualities dear to the heart of the Italian pilots'. Several veterans of combat with the CR42 comment on the way the Italian pilots seemed to enjoy making an exhibition of their aerobatic prowess, something that frequently allowed RAF pilots calmly to dispose of them. The CR42 had a speed advantage over the Gladiator of about 13 mph and its twin 12.7mm machine guns, although producing a lower volume of fire, inflicted more damage than the .303s. Nevertheless *4° Stormo*, who had seen service in Spain, had so far not fared very well against the Gladiators.

At Port Sudan a 'suspicious aircraft' was reported which, when intercepted, turned out to be a Fleet Air Arm Walrus. On 10 July Plt Off R A Acworth and Plt Off E T Banks, also attached to 33 Sqn, found three Savoia-Marchetti SM79s bombing Sidi

[1] The Ro37*bis* was a two-seater and would have belonged to either the *64°, 67°* or *73° Gruppi Osservazione Aerea*.
[2] 'The Fiat CR42' in Profile Publications (No. 16)

Barrani. When they attacked the enemy machines they hurriedly jettisoned their bombs and fled out to sea.

The maximum speed of the SM79 of about 230 mph would have allowed it to escape from the Gladiators. The SM79 *Sparviero* had started life as a commercial airliner in 1934 but its high performance suggested to the military that, with the necessary additions of a nacelle for the bomb-aimer and positions for machine gunners, it might well serve as a bomber. It had its operational dêbut in Spain like so many Axis aircraft. The ones intercepted over Sidi Barrani were probably from *14° Stormo* based at El Adem.

On 17 July 1940 112 Squadron moved forward into the Western Desert to relieve 33 Sqn at Maaten Gerawla[1]. The following day Fg Off A Gray Worcester, who had already shown himself to have the makings of a brilliant fighter pilot, was killed, flying into a hillside while leading a formation down through cloud. Fg Off A M Ross became temporary flight commander until the arrival of Flt Lt L G ('Algy') Schwab, a Canadian. By 25 July the move of 'A' and 'C' Flights to Maaten Gerawla was completed and Fg Off P E C Strahan, on patrol near Bardia, saw eight CR42s and shot one down, although he himself was hit and landed a damaged aircraft. Once again, when Plt Off P R M Van der Heijden tried to slow roll his aircraft over Sidi Barrani, the aircraft crashed and he was injured. He did not return to the squadron.

In the Sudan 'B' Flight, which had moved temporarily to Khartoum, was sent closer to the Abyssinian border, to Gedaref, where it took part in operations against the Italians at Kassala. Enemy ground forces had advanced a few miles westwards and cut the railway line between Gedaref and Port Sudan. The raid, mounted by 254 Wing, included aircraft from all the squadrons in the Sudan. 'B' Flight's contribution was limited to attacking the railway station with machine gun fire. On 1 August three Gladiators were scrambled at 08.30 hrs, Plt Off P O V Green (K7974) immediately sighted a Caproni Ca133 500′ above him at 1500′ on his port beam. He managed to make an unobserved approach until dead astern. Green delivered about 12 attacks and fired off some 1700 rounds before the bomber crashed with white smoke pouring from its starboard engine. The engagement lasted about 50 minutes and the Gladiator was hit by one round, fired from a window gun.

The victory was later confirmed by the Sudan Defence Force who located the wrecked machine. It was later reported that, when attacked, the crew of the Caproni were playing cards. The Ca133 was a high wing three-engined bomber aircraft with a top speed of about 173 mph, developed from the Ca101 which had appeared in 1932. Although the Italian Air Force in Libya and East Africa had many hundreds of these machines they were soon found to be totally unfit for anything but transport work.

Despite this victory 'B' (or 'K') Flight, now back at Port Sudan, complained of the inefficiency of the early warning system and, following abortive scrambles to intercept friendly aircraft, to criticise 'the seeming inability of native spotters to identify their own aircraft'. 'K' Flight, now administered by 14 Sqn was shortly to form the nucleus of No 250 (Sudan) Sqn and thereby finally cut its links with 112.

In the Western Desert 'A' and 'C' Flights were positioned at 'Z' Landing Ground

---

[1] Place names follow the spelling given in the squadron's records, which may not always correspond to the versions given in other publications.

(Matruh West) and 'Y' LG – about 11 miles further west on 17 August. From here they were ordered to patrol over units of the Mediterranean fleet. They did not realise anything was amiss until they found themselves amongst the AA bursts from HMS *Warspite*, *Kent*, *Malaya*, *Ramillies* and eleven destroyers, and saw 25 SM79s dropping bombs. Flt Lt Schwab claimed one, Plt Off Wickham another. In all eight bombers were destroyed and there was no damage to the ships.

Throughout the North African campaign much of the Western Desert Air Force's operations were carried out from Landing Grounds (LGs). These invariably had natural surfaces and rarely were there any buildings. The lack of place names in the desert and their proliferation meant that they were usually identified by a number, although letters and the term 'Advanced Landing Ground' (ALG) were used in the early days of the first campaign. Because sites were so numerous they were used alike by Allied and Axis aircraft and there was never any point in demolishing an LG during a retreat since a site equally suitable could be found close at hand. In shape LGs were usually square with the perimeter or runway marked by empty fuel cans. Once abandoned they quickly reverted to their original state and today would be virtually impossible to find.

On 7 September the squadron moved to Sidi Haneish. Up to this time 202 Group had been carefully husbanding its resources. Although the enemy had presented some tempting targets Air Chief Marshal Arthur Longmore refused to allow his meagre forces to be frittered away. On 9 September recce reports indicated that Graziani was about to launch his long-awaited attack on Egypt. On the evening of 10 September the advance began. 'Cancel all orders. Scram. All posts retire eastwards, repeat eastwards on Matruh' were the instructions sent to 202 Group. On 15 September ten SM79s tried to raid Sidi Barrani. This time 112 were ready for them. Flt Lt C H Fry, Flt Lt R J Abrahams, Fg Off J F Fraser, Plt Off R H Clarke, Plt Off E T Banks and Plt Off R J Bennett were already on patrol at 16,000', thirty miles out to sea. No 1 sub-Flight (Fry, Abrahams and Fraser) took on the first formation of five aircraft and drove them off while No 2 sub-Flight closed on the second five and opened fire. Banks and Clarke both damaged one aircraft each. Two Hurricanes of 274 Sqn and two Blenheims got amongst the enemy formation as well and in the end all the SM79s except three were shot down. One Gladiator of 80 Sqn was lost and the pilot killed.

Graziani, with 200 tanks, four divisions and a fifth in reserve, had by now advanced and captured Sidi Barrani. There the advance halted. The Italians 'prejudiced by years of fighting against tribesmen patiently fortified each small outpost, with echelons of supply dumps stretching back to Makteila'[1]

The desert exerted a curious fascination to many who were obliged to work and fight in it. B J Hurren in his book 'Eastern Med' was sure that 'the desert is one of the most beautiful places in the world. It has an array of blending hues which is quite indescribable. There are matchless sunrises and sunsets. These owe their loveliness to the dust-filled air, each molecule of dust causing some refraction of the sun's rays. The next point of note is the great distances that the eye could roam freely. The desert offers nothing, nothing to distract you or remind you of the fret and toil of civilisation. Coupled with the loneliness is the quietitude. Voices in the scattered camps carry a

[1] 'The Desert Air Force' by Roderic Owen

tremendous distance. Ordinary speaking tones can be heard hundreds of yards away. . . . Most surprising (to the newcomer) of all desert features is the sudden change in temperatures from hot in the day to cold at night. In the sun in the central Libyan desert temperatures of up to 195° are known by day. At night under a star-dusted sky the temperature may be as low as 20° below freezing . . . a heating and cooling process which severely taxes strength and saps energy.'

The Italians had been advancing on the Delta in two columns, concentrated on the coastal road. But Graziani, short of tanks, transport and artillery, now waited for the next six weeks while roads and a pipeline were constructed. On 29 September Flt Lt H L I Brown, who had been with 112 since 4 September, was promoted to Sqn Ldr and took over command.

On 10 October the Italians bombed the airfield but merely succeeded in hitting the road between 112 and 80 Sqn and there were no casualties or damage. On 31 October there was a brisk fight to finish off the month. The Italians sent 15 SM79s escorted by 18 CR42s to try to bomb British forward positions. Flt Lt Abrahams, Fg Off Fraser, Fg Off Clarke, Plt Off B B E Duff, and 2/Lieut E R Smith (SAAF) took off to patrol the Mersa Matruh area at 13.00 hrs. Plt Off Duff gave chase to the bombers but failed to see the escorting fighters, six CR42s dived on him and shot him down but he managed to escape by parachute, suffering only slight burns. The fighters were engaged by Flt Lt Schwab, 2/Lieut Smith and Plt Off Acworth (who had just joined the patrol) and three CR42s were shot down. Acworth and Smith then collided and both had to bale out. Fg Off Fraser and Plt Off Clarke were ordered into the air and they engaged the bombers and Fraser managed to put one engine of an SM79 out of action. Clarke was posted missing at the end of this engagement, killed by return fire from an SM79. 112 and 33 Squadron between them accounted for at least eight enemy aircraft.

On 28 October, though, in a significant new extension of the war, Mussolini had launched an attack on Greece from Albania and Air Chief Marshal Longmore, AOC-in-C Middle East, found himself faced with a new campaign. The Greeks were faced with a dangerous dilemma. They felt that they were probably capable of holding the Italians for a while and requested help only from the RAF, fearing that support from the British army might precipitate German intervention in the Balkans. In consequence Longmore decided to transfer three Blenheim squadrons (Nos 30, 84 and 211) and one Gladiator squadron (No 80) to Greece.

On 18 November Flt Lt Schwab intercepted a lone SM79 and shot it down. Two days later the Gladiators showed that they were more than the equal to the CR42 as well. Flt Lt Abrahams, Fg Off Bennett, Plt Off Acworth, Plt Off A R Costello, Plt Off L L Bartley and Sgt G M Donaldson intercepted a formation of 18 CR42s and in the ensuing combat eight of them were shot down without loss. The scorers were Abrahams 1½, Bennett 1, Acworth 1½, Costello 1, Bartley 2 and Donaldson 1. This engagement resulted in the Air Force photographers visiting the squadron to take publicity pictures of the pilots concerned and they posed modestly by one of the Gladiators.

In Egypt the British offensive was about to begin and Air Commodore Collishaw began attacks in Libya. Marshal Graziani was still motionless, his mind fixed on building up his supplies, but General Wavell with shorter supply lines was ready first. Despite the committments in Greece there were 16 squadrons based in Egypt, including some Hurricanes. On 1 December 1940 112 started ferrying Gladiators to the Royal Hellenic Air Force and four pilots made their way to join 80 Squadron at Larissa.

Lt-Gen Richard O'Connor's counter-offensive started on the night 7/8 December and all available aircraft were committed to bombing and patrolling the skies over Libya. Makteila fell immediately and by 10 December Sidi Barrani had fallen. 38,000 Italian troops were captured including Army Corps General Sebastiano Gallina, who surrendered complete with his mistress. This high-ranking officer 'did not seem to mind the prospect of spending the rest of the war as a prisoner. He was most affable and distributed photographs of himself from a large stock that he carried round with him.'[1] At the fall of Bardia General Berganzoli, known as 'General Electric Whiskers', managed to escape but he was captured later after the bold thrust across unrecconoitered desert which resulted in the battle of Beda Fomm on 7 February 1941.

On 14 December the squadron moved westwards to ALG 79 at Sidi Barrani by which time all Italian troops had been pushed out of Egypt. On 31 December the squadron was relieved by 73 Sqn and flew back to Amiriya, south of Alexandria. 112 was not sorry to leave and was thankful to see the end of 'gruelling patrols . . . work carried on under impossible . . . conditions, machines on several occasions being brought home when visibility due to dust was practically nil . . .' Now the squadron could enjoy the luxury of hot showers and 'Wahid-Wahid-Etnein'[2] became non-operational. 112 was now earmarked for Greece and early in the new year more machines were ferried to Athens. On 18 January 1941 the advanced surface party left Amiriya to embark at Alexandria. On 23 January the aircraft began to fly to Eleusis, by way of Crete, the main part embarked at Port Said on the '*Ethiopia*'. They arrived at Suda Bay on 30 January, closely followed by the '*Desmoulea*' a tanker, decks awash, towed by HMS *Hasty*. The *Desmoulea* had been torpedoed by an E-boat not far behind the *Ethiopia* the previous day.

On 1 February 1941 the squadron, based temporarily at Eleusis, flew an 'offensive patrol' over Athens, doubtless to help reassure the populace. Nothing more happened until the squadron moved forward to Yannina, and by 10th, 'A' Flt could accompany 80 Sqn on a patrol over the Greek front line. The Greeks still retained the initiative in Albania but by mid-February it was plain that the Italians were building up their forces for a fresh offensive.

The squadron in Greece was now slimmer than it had been at the start of the war in the Western Desert —

> Sqn Cdr: Sqn Ldr H L I Brown
> Adjutant: Fg Off Manger
> Sqn Medical Officer: Plt Off Barclay
> Sqn Equipment Officer: Plt Off Gosschalk
> Sqn Intelligence Officer: Plt Off Fletcher
> Sqn Cypher Officer: Plt Off Faulk

[1] 'Flights of Memory', the autobiography of Air Vice Marshal Sir Leslie Brown, unpublished manuscript.
[2] The squadron's name for itself in Arabic, 'One-One-Two'.

'A' Flight	*'B' Flight (ex-'C' Flt)*
Flt Lt Schwab	Flt Lt Fry
Fg Off Costello	Flt Lt Abrahams
Fg Off Banks	Flt Lt Fraser
Fg Off Acworth	Fg Off Cochrane
Plt Off Bartley	Fg Off Bennett
Plt Off Brown	Fg Off Bartlett
Plt Off Harrison	Plt Off Groves
Plt Off R H MacDonald	Plt Off Smith
Plt Off D G H MacDonald	Plt Off Westenra
Sgt Donaldson	Plt Off Bowker

(15 officers, 177 NCOs and airmen)

80 Sqn now moved to Paramythia and 112 were billeted in Yannina. There was no water, no telephone, no light, no sanitation and most personnel were under canvas. The town was described as 'unusually dirty, even for this part (of Greece)' with garbage thrown everywhere. The saving grace was the remarkable scenery and the lake. This, however, was useless for anything as it was polluted with the town's refuse. Most of the time it rained.

On 20 February the weather cleared and the squadron was able to fly in support of the Greek army attacking Tepelene. Sqn Ldr Brown, Flt Lt Abrahams, Flt Lt Schwab, Fg Off H W Harrison, Fg Off Banks, Plt Off Bartley, Plt Off R H MacDonald, Plt Off J L Groves, Plt Off E H Brown and Sgt Donaldson went on an offensive patrol in which one Italian Fiat G50 was destroyed by Flt Lt Schwab. Later that day there was a second engagement. 15 Gladiators in five sections of three aircraft flying in vic formation, echeloned to starboard, were escorting two Wellingtons together with a Greek Junkers Ju52 which was taking food to the Greek troops in the Tepelene-Berat area. Eight enemy aircraft were spotted 'in no particular formation', all G50s or Macchi 200s. The enemy started by making head-on or stern quarter attacks and throughout the fight showed surprising persistence, although they were outnumbered. Their usual hit-and-run tactics were difficult to counter. Flt Lt Abrahams, Fg Off Banks and Plt Off Groves each damaged one G50 between them, the retracted undercarriage dropping down.

On 24 February, in order to improve their diet, the squadron bought eight hens and a chicken run was built. In an episode reminiscent of Anthony Armstrong's stories of RAF Prangmere in '*Punch*' the 'chickens achieved vertical take-off to neighbour's roof. Later force-landed with clipped wings.'

On 27 February Fg Off Acworth, flying a Hurricane with 80 Sqn, shot down a CR42 over Valona. However 112 was just getting its eye in as on the next day the squadron diary was able to report the greatest victory yet. Ten pilots joined in the Greek offensive over the area Sarande – Argyrokastron – Valona – Tepelene with the result that five G50s and five CR42s were shot down and two CR42s and one Fiat BR 20 damaged. The RAF formation, which consisted of 19 Gladiators and 10 Hurricanes flying at 14,000' saw enemy aircraft below them. In the resulting fight every pilot from 112 Sqn inflicted damage on the Italians. Flt Lt Fraser claimed two, a CR42 (the pilot's parachute not opening) and a G50 which flew into a mountainside, Flt Lt Fry one CR42 and one G50, Sgt Donaldson a G50 and another probable, Sqn Ldr Brown a G50 on which he made an unobserved stern attack. This enemy aircraft banked steeply to starboard allowing the Sqn Ldr Brown to turn easily inside it and deliver full deflection shots. It appeared that the enemy pilot was hit as the G50 turned on its back and fell in an inverted spin. Fg Off H P Cochrane claimed a CR42, Fg Off Banks one CR42 destroyed and one damaged and a Fiat BR20 damaged. Fg Off Groves claimed a CR42 destroyed and Fg Off Smith damaged another. Plt Off R H MacDonald engaged a BR20 and caused it to fall out of formation. Flt Lt Abrahams was shot down while attacking the starboard aircraft of a formation of G50s.

Flt Lt Abrahams reappeared on 1 March having landed safely by parachute, claiming a G50 destroyed. The squadron diary stated that day that this engagement brought the squadron's total to 43 confirmed victories. This differs from the figure arrived at on examination of the contemporary records which would appear to show 38 destroyed and 11 damaged, but it is possible that some of the damaged e/a were later confirmed as destroyed. Even by this date it is impossible to reconcile conflicting totals and the best that can be done is to accept the official figure.

The Fiat BR20 *Cicogna* had appeared in 1936 and was equipped with four 7.7mm machine guns, one in the nose, one firing aft beneath the fuselage and two retractable guns in the dorsal cockpit. BR20s were sold to several foreign air forces including Japan and they also served in the Spanish Civil War. Over Britain the BR20s of *Stormi 13°* and *43°* had proved something of a failure, 20 machines being lost between October 1940 and January 1941. In October 1940 *116° Gruppo* was in action over Albania and Greece and this unit was later joined by *18° Stormo (37° Gruppo)* and the *13° Stormo (11° Gruppo)*.

On 3 March 1941 Fg Off Acworth shot down his second Cant Z1007, another large trimotor bomber, of *50° Gruppo Autonomo BT* based at Brindisi. The *Alcione* was an ugly machine, as were most of the Italian bombers of that period. It was the largest aircraft in service with the *Regia Aeronautica*, built to replace the SM79, with a wingspan of 81'4", low wings and single fin and rudder. Of the three types in service, the 1007 *bis* was the most common.

On 4 March 17 Gladiators, of which 14 belonged to 112, were flying in sections of three, echeloned to starboard, off the Albanian coast south-west of Himare. Over half the squadron was thus involved. About ten G50s and five CR42s of *354°* and *355° Squadriglie*, were first observed flying slightly below and to port attempting to attack some Blenheims that were bombing the Italian navy which itself was bombarding Himare. The Gladiators went in and the enemy formation broke up. Flt Lt Fraser led 3 Section against some G50s which promptly disappeared into cloud. Sqn Ldr Brown saw aircraft engaged at various heights and also confirmed that the G50s took refuge in cloud. Fg Off Acworth was about to attack a G50 when he himself was attacked and this began a dog-fight that gradually became detached from the main *mêlée*, gradually descending to about 2000'. He managed to get some deflection shots at a range of 100' and the engine of his opponent started to smoke. He was then attacked and didn't see what became of his target. Fg Off Banks believed he shot down a G50 as he got in some good deflection shots and saw it spin and dive away and later observed a parachute.

The final score was that Flt Lt Fraser claimed one G50 and another was claimed by several pilots while five more were claimed but not confirmed.

On 7 March 'A' Flt flew to Paramythia, 80 Sqn having moved to Eleusis. 'B' Flt went on an offensive patrol that day accompanied by Wg Cdr Coote of 'W' (Western) Wing. On 8 March the squadron diarist remarked that 112 Sqn was now the only fighter unit left in western Greece, an ominous thought. The next day the long awaited Italian offensive began with 29 divisions on a 20 mile front from Tepelene to Corovode. In the initial attack ten divisions, supported by a large number of bombers and fighters, were thrown against the Greeks but no ground was gained. On 14 March the Greeks counter-attacked.

On 9 March 112 was airborne at 14.00 hrs to engage enemy aircraft over the Kelcyre – Tepelene area. The formation consisted of 15 aircraft in five vics of three echeloned to starboard, the usual arrangement. They sighted G50s, CR42s and BR20s of *22° Gruppo* and *37° Stormo* in tight vics of five aircraft each. Sqn Ldr Brown attacked two G50s diving from 14,000' and getting on their tails, giving one machine a long burst. The enemy displayed very poor evasive tactics and it was easy to keep behind them. One G50 fled while the other crashed into a hillside. Flt Lt Fry saw the BR20s jettisoning the bombs and the G50s scattering. The CR42s stayed high and were not seen again. Fry attacked a BR20, delivering a diving attack, and then turned on the G50s. One Italian aircraft dived away vertically and flew into the ground. Flt Lt Fraser led his section into a formation of BR20s and shot one down, the wreck falling near Garneo. The rest of his section engaged the escorts. Fg Off Banks attacked a BR20 but his long bursts had no visible effect. Later he chased a G50 down from 16,000' to 8000' but at that height his engine blew a sparking plug and he was obliged to return to Yannina. Fg Off Cochrane saw a Gladiator (N5823) falling in flames and a parachute opening. He broke off his attack and circled the parachute until he saw it fall into some trees by a river. He landed at the nearest Greek village and alerted the villagers who went to find the pilot. This turned out to be Plt Off R H MacDonald who was brought to safety although badly burned. In their reports both Sgt Donaldson and Fg Off Acworth remarked that they saw Italian pilots baling out of their aircraft and then fall to the ground without their parachutes opening. The final claimed score was seven victories.

Two days later there was another patrol which ended with five confirmed G50s and three probables. The squadron was escorting 211 Sqn Blenheims in the Buzi area with two new pilots, Plt Off N Bowker and Plt Off D F Westenra, fresh from Flying Training School, both claimed a victory each. Fg Off Cochrane, Plt Off Banks and Fg Off Acworth each got one with Banks remarking that the G50s must be armoured as they stood up to so much punishment. Flt Lt Fraser and Flt Lt Fry each claimed one unconfirmed kill. Fry reported that he attacked a G50 which spun slowly twice then flattened out and turned slowly onto its back with smoke coming from it. It went into cloud and he didn't see it again. He also attacked another G50 *bis* of *24° Gruppo* which went over onto its back and flew inverted into cloud. Sqn Ldr Brown emptied all his rounds into a G50 without effect. No doubt the all-metal construction of these monoplane fighters helped to hold them together.

Writing on the G50 Gianni Cattaneo[1] comments on the fact that 'the G50 pilots

---

[1] 'The Fiat G50' in Profile Publications (No 188)

learned that it was not advisable to try to dog-fight with the RAF biplane (Gladiator) but rather to exploit their superior speed.' He went on to remark that 'the ferocity of the air battles gave rise to quite discordant claims regarding 'kills' . . . on 28th February 1941 Italian claims totalled 12 while the RAF claimed 27 'kills' without loss mostly by the newly arrived Hurricane squadron (80 Sqn) and a Gladiator squadron (112) . . . Without distracting from the valour and aggressiveness of the pilots of both sides these examples illustrate the difficulty of gathering historically accurate data. . . .' As will be seen from the 112 combat report only one Gladiator was lost that day.

Robert MacDonald, badly burned, arrived back at Yannina on his way to Athens and hospital. Although full of spirit he died of his injuries a month later.

13 March 1941 was the fourth and final 'big show' by the squadron against 'Mussolini's bedraggled eagles' as the diarist described the Italian air force. Fourteen Gladiators led by Sqn Ldr Brown were airborne at 15.30 hrs north east of Tepelene when the squadron commander called 'Tally-Ho!'. At that moment they were at about 17,000', approaching Kelcyre, and below them was a formation of seven SM79s of *104° Gruppo BT* with a fighter escort. 112 decided to ignore the bombers which were heading for home and they followed three Hurricanes of 33 Sqn diving on the G50s (probably MC200s of *22° Gruppo*) and CR42s of *160° Gruppo*. Sqn Ldr Brown attacked the leader of a vic of G50s but it evaded him successfully. He got on the tail of another which turned and dived and eventually crashed. Flt Lt Fraser attacked three aircraft and shot them all down, not one of the Italian pilots getting out alive. First he attacked a CR42 which had not seen him and it burst into flames and fell near Buzi. He then attacked another CR42 which flick-rolled and dived away. He followed it down and got in two long bursts after which the enemy aircraft levelled off and lost speed, with the pilot slumped forward in the cockpit. The aircraft then dived vertically into the ground north of Corovode. Fraser then climbed back up to 8000' and got on the tail of another CR42 firing at it continuously until it burst into flames and was destroyed. Fraser commented in his combat report that the CR42 pilots always tried to flick-roll when attacked. The score that day was Fraser and Cochrane each three CR42s, Sqn Ldr Brown one G50, Groves two CR42s, Plt Off P C L Brunton one CR42 and Fg Off Brown one CR42 all for no loss. That day, however, Fg Off E T (Teddy) Banks, one of the few remaining original squadron members killed himself in a flying accident. When air-testing his guns over Yannina lake he misjudged his height in a steep dive and flew straight into the water, sinking immediately with his machine (N5913). His body was later recovered.

On 14 March there were only 12 serviceable aircraft ready for a patrol at 10.30 hrs. The Gladiators were joined by four of 80 Sqn's Hurricanes. This formation met about 40 G50s and MC200s of *22° Gruppo* escorting ten BR20s of *38° Stormo* and ten Cant Z1007s of *47° Stormo*. The Gladiators and Hurricanes made a head on attack and in the first few minutes Sqn Ldr Brown (N5916) had his tail shot away. His aircraft went into an uncontrollable spin and it was only with considerable difficulty that he managed to bale out and reach the ground safely. Flt Lt Fry attacked three formations of enemy bombers and shot down a BR20 which crashed near the front line near Kelcyre. In his combat report he noted that the Italian AA guns were firing at their own aircraft. Flt Lt Fraser's section was itself attacked from above and astern and the section broke up into a series of individual dog-fights. One G50 made a head-on attack from above but Fraser was able to skid his aircraft round and get in a short burst at which point the enemy aircraft rolled onto its back and the pilot baled out. Fg Off Bennett claimed a G50, Bowker saw one going down out of control and Cochrane saw an aircraft burning on the ground which he thought may have been the one he attacked. Smith damaged two and Sgt Donaldson saw two enemy aircraft dive away smoking. Brunton attacked one and appeared to knock bits off it so that it went into a spiral dive with smoke coming from it. The total claimed that day appears to have been three kills with three probables and two damaged – an overestimation in view of post-war research – two Italian aircraft only were destroyed and one damaged.

The next day, 15 March, the airfield was bombed. This was the last day of the fierce fighting which had begun with the Italian offensive of a week before and now the air effort began to slacken. For the loss of two Gladiators and one Hurricane (all pilots being safe) the RAF claimed 35 enemy aircraft destroyed and nine probably destroyed, of this total 112 claimed 23 kills and three probable. Nevertheless the bombing of Yannina was a sign of things to come. Fg Off Bennett, who happened to be flying low over the airfield found bombs bursting all around him. The blast of one nearly turned his aircraft onto its back but he managed to keep control and touch down between the craters, his mainplane full of bomb splinters. One Gladiator was set on fire but, despite the rain of bombs, two airmen, LAC Reed and LAC Walter emerged from their shelter, extinguished the fire and saved the aircraft. On 22 March there was another raid, the first indication being the sound of engines. The Gladiators were at standby and two were scrambled. Five Cant Z1007s with an escort of 15 G50s appeared but their total effort amounted to three small bombs dropped about two miles to the south-west.

Bomber escorts continued and on 25 March there was an offensive patrol over Kelcyre and the Mezgorani area, accompanied by Sqn Ldr R J C Nedwill, AFC, CO of No 211 Blenheim squadron which shared Yannina and Paramythia with 112. The next day four aircraft of 'A' Flt took off to intercept a raid on Paramythia. There were four enemy sections, the first which dived past the Gladiators to bomb and strafe. This attack was disrupted and Flt Lt Schwab possibly got a G50 near Perdika. He also shot at a Hurricane in error, not realising they were in the area. One Gladiator was destroyed on the ground and another badly damaged in the air. On 27 March all operational pilots moved to Paramythia and on 28th came the news that the squadron was to be re-equipped with Hurricanes. Flt Lt Fraser, Fg Off Cochrane and Fg Off Bennett left for Egypt to collect three of these long-awaited aircraft. The squadron, however, was to be disappointed. Although several post-war RAF histories state that 112 did receive Hurricanes[1], this did not happen and they were delivered to another squadron. The diary complained that they had now given up all hope of every having any other type of aircraft but Gladiators.

Towards the middle of February German 'infiltration' into Rumania had begun to look very much like the start of a drive through Bulgaria, with Salonika as the principal objective. On 1 March the German army entered Bulgaria and the situation in the

[1] Stemming first perhaps from Denis Richards' 'Royal Air Force 1939–1945' but repeated in the recent (1988) publication 'RAF Squadrons' by Wg Cdr C G Jefford, (Airlife Publishing).

Balkans suddenly began to look extremely serious; by 1 April the German invasion of Greece was imminent.

With the threat of a new front looming to the north 'E' (Eastern) Wing with its headquarters at Tsaritsani found itself with a more menacing enemy than the Italians in Albania.

On 3 April Wg Cdr 'Paddy' Coote and 13 of the squadron pilots escorted six Blenheims of 211 Sqn to bomb Berat. That day the squadron said farewell to Sqn Ldr Brown who handed over to Sqn Ldr (ex-Flt Lt) 'Algy' Schwab. On 5th the Germans declared war against Greece and Yugoslavia and launched their *blitzkreig*. Crossing into Macedonia by four routes they simultaneously attacked along the Stroumica valley in the south and from Dragoman to Nis in the north. At Yannina a German reconaissance machine appeared overhead.

On 6th Gladiators once again escorted Blenheims to Berat but on 10 April a Messerschmitt Bf 110 (perhaps from II/ZG26) appeared through a break in the clouds. Rumours were rife and the Germans seemed to be expected almost any day. The news was depressing and the pilots had no illusions about the relative merits of Gladiators against the *Luftwaffe*. The squadron diarist remarked glumly that 'If any Gladiators (are) left (their) next appearance no doubt (will be) in the British Museum.'

The Messerschmitt Bf110 seen over Yannina was probably a Bf110C-5, a reconnaissance version of the aircraft that had met its match during the Battle of Britain. Designed as a long-range escort fighter the prototype had appeared in 1935 and had been found to do 316 mph, which compared favourably with the top speed of the Hurricane. Pilots, however, found it a difficult machine to manoeuvre and sluggish compared to single-seat fighters. It was only during the Battle of Britain when Bf110 *Geschwadern* were mauled by the RAF's Spitfires and Hurricanes that the farcical situation arose whereby Bf109s were obliged to escort the escort fighters.

By 8 April the German invasion had penetrated into Thrace and Salonika had been captured. Twenty-seven German divisions had advanced westwards into Yugoslavia from Britolj supported by dive bombers of *Luftflotte 4*, aiming to join up with the Italians in Albania. The Greeks were thus about to be cut off and the retreat began. On 9th British troops holding the Florina gap were hotly attacked and, after stiff resistance, had been obliged to fall back. 112 Squadron continued to fly and 17 Gladiators assisted by covering the withdrawal of the Greek troops. The formation attacked eight SM79s and Sqn Ldr Schwab managed to surprise – for all its much vaunted good visibility – a lone G50 and shoot it down. Flt Lt Fraser noted that the enemy bombers had bright yellow engine nacelles and wide yellow fuselage bands. Fg Off Brunton failed to return from this mission but he turned up later riding on a mule – his airscrew had fallen off and he had landed near Koritsa.

By 13th the Germans had occupied Kastoria and were threatening the British army's positions on the Aliakmon line. The next day the loss of Kleisoura turned the defences, forcing the troops to fall back on Thermopylae. That day 112 took to the air in relays for eight hours continuous flying in order to cope with a possible raid on Yannina. Machines, in threes and fours, flew off in all directions hoping to intercept the enemy. While they were away the airfield was bombed from a great height by five SM79s which did very little damage. By the evening it was becoming increasingly obvious that twelve Gladiators could not hold western Greece by themselves. At dusk a Yugoslavian SM79 landed, escorted by six of 112's Gladiators, with a white flag waving from the cockpit. This machine was carrying King Peter of Yugoslavia, complete with the crown jewels and his Prime Minister, who was fleeing into exile. Later that night the royal entourage left for Menidi. More Yugoslavian aircraft, SM79s and Do.17Ks, arrived but at dawn on 15 April the airfield was attacked by nine G50s which came in from the east. An SM79 luckily attracted their attention and it was attacked repeatedly so that the Gladiators entirely escaped damage. A large proportion of tracers was used and, in the early light, it looked like a firework display. Bofors guns defending the airfield were firing and one G50 was turned over on its back by a near miss, but none were brought down. Six Gladiators which got airborne tried to attack the G50s but the enemy aircrafts' superior speed made it impossible for them to close and, in the end, it was the Gladiators that had to take evasive action. Plt Off Brunton got onto the tail of one G50 but his guns failed and he was wounded himself. He was in dire straits until a Bofors gun drove off his pursuer, undoubtedly saving his life. All the other local airfields were attacked that morning. John Herington ('The Air War against Germany & Italy') later wrote 'The squadron went out alone to meet anything which might come out of Albania, in other words the Italian air force . . . these Gladiators were not armour-plated, had no self-sealing tanks and were nearly 100 mph slower than the Italian machines . . .'

The collapse of Yugoslavian resistance and the British withdrawal to Thermopylae necessitated the evacuation on Yannina, a piece of news that the squadron heard with relief. As usual in dire times conflicting rumours filled the air – 'Larissa has fallen', 'Jerries on the road to Yannina' and so on. Gunfire had been audible for two days but no one seemed to know what was going on and it was only the BBC's news bulletins that told them how close the Germans were. 'E' and 'W' Wings were now disbanded and all squadrons were being pulled back towards Athens, coming under the direct control of HQ British Forces Greece.

All serviceable aircraft now flew to Agrinion and the ground party left by road. Only two Gladiators had to be left behind, and these were destroyed. One, which was about to be flown off by Fg Off Acworth tipped over onto its nose when taxying in the mud and the other, which was to have been flown by Fg Off Bennett developed engine trouble. Lorries made two trips to Arta and back, the second to salvage whatever stores were left. Flt Lt Manger, the adjutant, remained with the demolition party and finally left on the 16th, but their journey south was a slow one as they had to stop to destroy abandoned vehicles and pick up walking personnel. They did not reach Agrinion much before nightfall.

On 17 April, at first light, in rain and mist, the aircraft flew on to Hassani outside Athens. All the rest, which included a Greek officer acting as interpreter, Fg Off George Christides, left for Messalongion by train. There they managed to board a ship which sailed for Patras that afternoon. Here they tried to obtain transport but the local military governor refused to loan them any, even though he had forty lorries on hand. After a five hour wait they learned that a train would take them to Athens.

This train left at dawn on 18th but once started it then stopped again every forty five minutes for at least half an hour to allow packed refugee trains from Athens to pass. The airmen had never seen trains so crammed with people, with at least a hundred civilians on the roofs of each carriage. The Greeks now knew that the end was near but

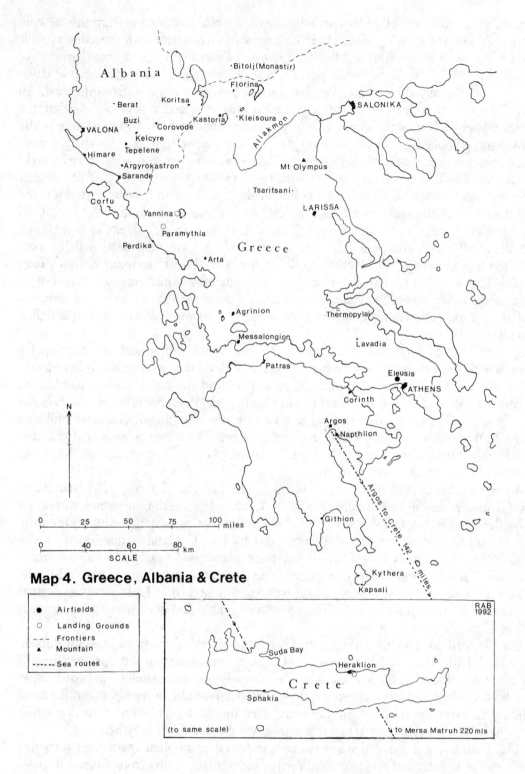

Map 4. Greece, Albania & Crete

their attitudes varied. After the war Wg Cdr H W Harrison wrote 'When we arrived originally in Greece in January we were quite often picked up and carried shoulder high down the streets of Athens as the locals were so pleased to see us. However during the few days we were in Athens (during the retreat) the population was very surly and the place was teeming with fifth columnists. We always walked about fully armed in case someone got a bit nasty . . .'

For the next four days all the airfields round Athens, except Hassani, were bombed but the Gladiators were kept on the ground. By late on 22nd all the stragglers had turned up, many having walked most of the way. That day the squadron was ordered to leave for Crete. The aircrew were under the impression that they would refuel in Crete and carry on to Egypt but 'there was a fair amount of confusion' (Wg Cdr Harrison) and it was eventually decided that the aircraft would remain at Heraklion and defend the island.

The ground party set off for Argos at nightfall and it was only their discipline that prevented the journey becoming a rout. Equipment was thrown into the sea and at Eleusis they met the main stream of the retreating army and from then on any attempt to keep together was useless. The vast cavalcade crept at snail's pace and any attempt to use headlights to negotiate the cliff road which was strewn with abandoned vehicles was met by a chorus of 'Put that f****** light out'. One estimate was that there were 300 overturned vehicles between Corinth and Argos, so perhaps the slow speed was a blessing in disguise. Just as they approached Corinth the column was joined by cavalry pack mules which further confounded the general confusion.

At Argos, after a trip of some 80 miles, the RAF were sorted out and moved to a nearby airfield. By now 11,000 Army and Air Force personnel were milling about and the Germans were believed not to be far behind. A ship in the harbour was dive-bombed and blew up with a terrific crash which was hardly noticed in the noise of the air raid.

About midday on 23 April 20 to 25 Dornier Do17 and Do215 bombers began coming over at height. The fighters based at Argos, about 13 Hurricanes, were thus all enticed into the air to chase them, at which Ju88s escorted by Bf109s dive bombed the airfield and the AA batteries. The only casualty appeared to be a Lysander of 208 Sqn which was shot down as it took off. This was not all as around two hours before sunset 25 Bf110s attacked the airfield again. While this was going on nearly a thousand airmen were crouching in the olive grove alongside the airfield but although the German machines dived time and time again they never thought to machine gun the trees. That night, dispersed on the hillsides, without blankets, the ground party found it too cold to sleep. It is estimated that about 17,000 RAF personnel were at Argos waiting to be evacuated. By this time all aircraft were being flown out and, although it may not have seemed so at the time, the evacuation was following some sort of plan. The roads were still jammed with vehicles and troops but during the morning of 24 April most of them managed to disperse and take cover, which was fortunate as Bf110s later ranged at will over the whole area searching for targets of opportunity and firing their guns to try to flush hidden troops out of their shelter. The squadron personnel had a narrow escape when a stick of bombs fell across their lines but there were no casualties.

That evening the main party was told to prepare to leave for Naphlion, about 5 miles distant. Here an invasion barge was brought alongside the quay and the airmen were transferred safely on board the '*Glen Earn*' which carried them to Suda Bay. Once on shore they found they had no tents or blankets so the airmen lay down under the trees and waited to see what would happen next. It was decided, by the toss of a coin, that 'A' Flight would continue to Egypt and 'B' Flight remain to cope with the coming invasion of Crete.

Flt Lt Magner, the squadron adjutant, was not to arrive in Crete until 29th. He, Fg Off Christides and a Fg Off Thompson had made their way from Argos and arrived at Githion, some 85 miles away. Here they found a Brigadier Hutson, a member of the Evacuation Committee and four other army officers who were not pleased to see them. It appeared that Githion had been chosen as the point where the secret evacuation of the Evacuation Committee would take place and Magner and Christides were an embarrassment, especially as more airmen kept turning up by the hour. Thomas Magner decided that, in view of this, it might be prudent to make his own evacuation plans. A Greek was hired for 150,000 drachma to take them to Crete in his boat and they embarked from Githion early in the morning of 25 April. The Greek then announced that the boat was unserviceable and declined to take them any further but luckily they managed to contact a Sunderland flying boat, T9084 of 228 Sqn, by flashing a pocket mirror. The pilot, a Flt Lt Lamond, agreed to take as many as he dared, 50 men, and return for the rest. In addition another sailing vessel was obtained and, as the Sunderland did not return, they set off in this to Kythera, about 40 miles to the south-east. After further adventures they managed to reach Kapsali on 28th where they were taken on board HMS *Aukland* and they finally arrived in Crete early the following day. A check by Flt Lt Magner revealed that not a single squadron member was missing.

112 Squadron was lucky in its evacuation from Greece as it had been one of the first to be withdrawn. Other squadrons continued operations for a week longer. Probably one reason for this was that while the antiquated aircraft that 112 possessed were considered a match for the *Regia Aeronautica* they were outclassed by the modern aircraft of the *Luftwaffe*.

'A' Flight embarked at midday on 29 April and departed for Egypt. Not surprisingly the squadron diary for May 1941 has not survived. Only 'B' Flight remained with a handful of groundcrew and half a dozen aircraft. There was a total of 14 Gladiators in Crete belonging to Nos. 33, 80 and 112 Squadrons, also 14 Blenheims of 30 Sqn and nine belonging to 203 Sqn and a few Hurricanes. Initially the fighters were used to provide air cover for the ships bringing the army to Suda Bay but later their task was to prevent German reconnaissance aircraft and finally to resist the invasion. The British garrison numbered about 28,500 and, by mid-May, when the Blenheims had been withdrawn, only about 24 aircraft remained, of which 12 were serviceable. Against them the Germans sent about 17,000 airborne and 7000 seaborne troops.

This apparent British manpower superiority on the ground was outweighed by the lack of air support, low morale and the crippling lack of equipment and supplies. For the invasion *Fliegerkorps VIII* and *Fliegerkorps XI* could throw about 650 bombers and fighters, 700 transport planes and 80 gliders. Crete lay well within the operational radius of the Dodecanese where the Germans were now feverishly constructing airstrips. The two British commanders, General B Freyberg and Group Captain G Beamish attempted to make the best of a bad job and the defence of the whole island was restricted to the defence of the airfields. Despite the odds, the attack came near to failure and it was only due to the inability of the troops on the ground successfully to stifle the preliminary parachute drop that allowed the battle to swing in favour of the Germans. It should also be remembered that it was the slaughter of the parachutists that precluded their use again during the remainder of the war – but particularly against Malta which lay across the Germans' lines of supply between Italy and North Africa.

Only four combat reports are preserved from 'B' Flight's stand in Crete, one dated 14 May 1941 when Plt Off Bowker attacked a Bf110 and shot it down into the sea and then damaged another and one dated the next day when Plt Off Westenra and a Fg Off Reeves attacked another Bf110 which also fell into the sea. On 29 May a Sgt Weir (not previously known to have been on 112) attacked and shot down an SM79 over Heraklion, a victory that was confirmed by the army, although the victim is more likely to have been a Ju52 than an SM79.

On 15th Flt Lt Fry, flying a Hurricane with four others, intercepted eight Bf110s of ZG26 at 6000′ near Heraklion. He attacked a Bf110 piloted by *Uffz* Witzke and it fell, but the rear gunner forced him to abandon his aircraft. Meanwhile Plt Off Neville Bowker, who had been taken ill, found himself in a German field hospital next to the pilot of the Bf110 that Fry had shot down, thus confirming his victory. Bowker's own victim on 14th was apparently *Oberleutnant* Sophus Baagoe, a pilot of ZG26, the '*Horst Wessel*' *Geschwader*, with 14 victories to his name and holder of the Knight's Cross.

What few successes the RAF had over Crete were hardly appreciated by the troops below. '. . . the spiteful and ignorant criticisms which were hurled at us were most annoying . . . to the army an aircraft on the ground was an aircraft fit to fly . . .' Early on the morning of 20 May, with the fighter opposition eliminated, the German airborne assault began. By the 27th the Germans had between 20,000 and 30,000 troops ashore and the defenders were hopelessly penned in. Astonishingly the fresh evacuation went well for the RAF and the main contingent was rescued from Sphakia on the nights of 28/29 and 29/30 May. Sunderlands achieved a remarkable success in this airlift and due to the ineffectiveness of the *Luftwaffe* at night none were lost. Plt Off Bowker escaped from the German field hospital on 27th by the simple expedient of walking out of it. He managed to rejoin a party of British troops and got on board HMS *Orion*. Although this cruiser was then badly damaged by dive bombers and suffered casualties, it reached Egypt safely and Bowker rejoined 112 Sqn on 16 June. By the end of 'B' Flt's campaign the squadron reckoned its score now stood at 76 e/a destroyed.

Particularly astonishing is the story of 'McLennan's barge'. On the 2 June, a day after the British forces on Crete had surrendered, three of the squadron airmen, AC1 McLennan, LAC Harrington and AC Malloy, together with Fg Off Bennett and Plt Off Len Bartley and men of various other units, found two abandoned German invasion barges on the rocks of the south coast of Crete. One was holed and the other had an unserviceable engine so the airmen transferred the good engine to the seaworthy barge. They managed to launch it and, having collected water and rations and fuel, set off for Egypt. In the early morning of the second day out they were intercepted by an Italian submarine which took off all the officers and ordered the barge to return to Crete. Those remaining decided to ignore this order and after four days, travelling at about 4 knots, they reached the Egyptian coast. After a while they recognised the sand dunes of Mersa Matruh and, seeing British troops, came ashore. The airman whose name was given to the landing craft was 539503 AC1 McLennan, G R, Fitter IIE. The squadron's losses in Crete appear to have been three officers and 21 airmen. The RAF's losses overall in Crete amounted to 38 aircraft but against this the *Luftwaffe* lost at least 220 aircraft destroyed and about another 150 damaged.

It seems natural that men away from their homes and loved ones always tend to produce songs and doggerel to bemoan their fate or while away the time. Flt Lt D H V Smith wrote this poem around March 1941:

1. In far off Egypt's desert land
   There lived a little band of men
   Assembled by the High Command
   To fight the vile Italian!

2. Their leader true, a Scottish type
   With mighty rump and smelly pipe
   Says 'What! What! What are you doin'?'
   And when he does there's trouble 'bruin'.

3. To Alex he led forth his crew
   Some by car and some by 'plane,
   For Middle East had promised true
   To give each man a Hurricane!

4. All were happy, many sang,
   Joe Fraser ever had some leave,
   And 'Stuffy' had a mighty 'bang'
   Complete contentment to achieve.

5. The Adjutant was happy, too,
   And went to Cabaret to woo,
   No more he cursed in ranting terms
   ('til he, poor chap, succumbed to worms)!

6. But all this joy was not to last,
   Fate spoke out, the die was cast!
   Our Hurricanes – they never flew!
   ****ed again, poor One-One-Two.

7. Some Officer of lofty rank,
   Either mad, or else he drank,
   Had found on some old rubbish heap
   Some Glads, Mark 2, all going cheap!

8. 'Just the very thing!' he cried,
   'To send across the other side!

On whom can we these old crates shelve?
Why, on the old One Hundredth Twelve!'

9. So saying, with a roguish grin
Approached with glee the horrid pile,
And from the wreckage forth he drew,
Some ancient 'planes for One-One-Two!

10 They hammered nails, they tied with string,
They scrounged a tailwheel, found a wing,
Screwed on bolts and filed a piston,
Counted the cylinders that she missed on,
Until the fateful day drew nigh
When all acclaimed with pride 'They fly!'

11. And so one's hopes have been in vain,
They've robbed us of the Hurricane.
We are the lambs without their fleece
And now we're flying Glads in Greece!'

Examples of the official wartime aircraft recognition material
supplied to No 112 Squadron in the desert.

CHAPTER THREE

Sharks in a Blue Meadow

At dawn on 14 June 1941 Operation 'Battleaxe' began. At that time there were ten squadrons in the desert comprising Hurricanes, Tomahawks, Blenheims and Mary-lands. For the first time SAAF squadrons fought alongside the RAF. Some aircraft had been removed from Egypt to help with operations against the Vichy French in Syria but reinforcements were arriving all the time. Facing the RAF in the Western Desert was I/JG27, 7/JG26 equipped with Bf109s, III/ZG26 equipped with Bf110s, two *Gruppen* of Ju87s and some Ju88s as well as about 70 Italian fighters and 25 bombers.

112 Squadron's 'A' Flight was spread between Lydda and Haifa in Palestine where it was refitting and flying 80 Squadron's Hurricanes. The squadron organisation at that time was —

> Sqn Cdr: Sqn Ldr Schwab
> Adjutant: Flt Lt Magner
> Sqn Intelligence Officer: Plt Off Fletcher
> Sqn Equipment Officer: Plt Off Gosschalk

'A' Flight	*'B' Flight*
Flt Lt Harrison	Flt Lt Fraser DFC
Fg Off Costello	Fg Off Cochrane
Fg Off Bartley	Fg Off Smith
Fg Off Brown	Fg Off Groves
Fg Off MacDonald	Fg Off Bartlett
Plt Off Brunton	Plt Off Westenra
Sgt Bates	Plt Off Bowker

On 5 June 1941 five officers and 216 men left for Fayid to start re-equipping. Flt Lt Fraser, only recently been awarded the DFC, was posted to the FTS at Ismailia[1] and 'B' Flt was taken over by Cochrane, who was promoted to Flt Lt. On 14th the first Curtiss P40C Tomahawk IIB arrived from 102 MU, but to the chagrin of the assembled pilots, it crashed on landing. Sqn Ldr Schwab, not trusting anyone else,

---

[1] Flt Lt Fraser survived the war but was killed in a car crash in Turkey

went to the MU to get the next Tomahawk himself on 25th. By the end of the day several pilots had flown in it and all were enthusiastic. Sqn Ldr Schwab, awarded the DFC and the Greek equivalent, now left the squadron and was replaced by Sqn Ldr D F Balden. On 8 July the second Tomahawk arrived but the next day, after a perfectly normal landing, the undercarriage collapsed. As the first Tomahawk was now due for servicing the squadron's serviceability was once again nil.

On 29th more Tomahawks arrived and the Gladiators were flown away. For all their antiquity the squadron was sorry to see them go as they had performed well against fearsome odds. At the end of the month it was learned that HM The King had approved the squadron's badge and motto, an Egyptian cat *sejant* (always referred to as the 'Helwan cat') with the motto 'Swift in Destruction'. Training on the new aircraft now began in earnest but, as always seems to be the case, one of the newest pilots, Sgt F K Johnstone, crashed and was killed while performing aerobatics over Mariyut. Meanwhile Bartley and Bennett, taken from McLennan's barge, were confirmed as prisoners of war in Italy. Flight Sergeant H W Carter the NCO i/c 'A' Flt who had been captured in Crete wrote after the war that one of the most heartening gestures was the flow of food parcels that were sent to the Prisoner of War camp by 112 Sqn up until Christmas 1941. After this the International Red Cross stopped the practice for some reason.

On 11 August a detachment from 'A' Flt went to Mariyut to relieve No 2 SAAF Sqn and take over the air defence of Alexandria. Flt Lt Cochrane and Flt Lt Fry (now a PoW in Greece) were both awarded DFCs, bringing the squadron's total to 5. On 31st Sgt Mills, another newcomer, was killed when he lost control and crashed. The squadron's casualty list now stood at six, one a pilot missing in combat while the other five were flying accidents.

On 8 September 1941 the squadron moved forward from Fayid to LG92 (south of Alexandria) and thence to LG102 (inland from Maaten Bagush at Sidi Haneish). On 14th they were airborne again and in action for the first time with the new aircraft. An R/T message was received that there was a 'bandit' over Mersa Matruh at 19,000'. The formation climbed to about 16,000' and spotted an SM79 below. Plt Off Bowker attacked (flying AN218) firing his wing guns only as his .5" machine gun had jammed. He reset the .5 and returned to the attack and at 150 yards he saw petrol streaming from the enemy aircraft. He pumped shots into the starboard engine and fuselage and the SM79 blew up.

This was the squadron's first victory flying the new aircraft and the diarist was able to record, no doubt remembering how the SM79 could usually get away from the Gladiators, 'Tomahawks overhauled enemy machine with ease and literally flew rings around it.' It was reported that the SM79 carried two horizontal white stripes on its tail.

The P40C Tomahawk IIB was an American aircraft manufactured by the Curtiss Airplane Division of the Curtiss-Wright Corporation of New York and was designed as a day interceptor fighter. Its power plant was an Allison CV-1760-D1 engine with maximum power of 1250 hp at 3000 rpm. Its dimensions were 37'3½" wing span, 33'8½" in length and 10'7" in height. It carried 123 gallons of aviation fuel including a 47 gallon reserve tank. At 15,000' its maximum speed was 367 mph with a service ceiling of 30,500' and a range of 625 miles. It could be an unforgiving aircraft to fly as pilots soon discovered and on 16 September Sgt McCormack, attached to the Mariyut detachment, had his engine cut on take off. He was about 150' to 200' above the ground and he made the mistake of attempting to turn to regain the airfield. He banked too steeply, spun and was killed.

On 25th ten aircraft were returning from Sidi Barrani having acted as top cover over a RN fighter squadron. They were bounced from out of the sun by two Bf109s. Plt Off Westenra who was part of the top cover, flying AK495, was suddenly attacked. He took evasive action and called an alarm on the R/T but no one heard him. Flt Lt Harrison, leading No 3 Section suspected something was wrong and he also gave the alarm, but again no one heard him. Nothing further happened for about 10 minutes when Westenra was again attacked and lost the tip of his starboard wing and aileron. By keeping his stick hard over and staying above 200 mph he managed to keep his aircraft on an even keel but near Sidi Barrani smoke started to come from the aircraft and his .5 ammunition began to explode. At this point he baled out.

This engagement cannot be traced in German records but *Oberleutnant* Homuth of I/JG27 claimed a Tomahawk the previous day when no RAF Tomahawks were lost so it seems as if JG27's diary is at fault. JG27 would soon have as one of its highest-scoring aces *Leutnant* Hans-Joachim Marseille who is supposed to have described the sky above the desert as that 'blue meadow of airman'[1].

About this time, September 1941, the 'sharksteeth' markings first appeared. As a design painted on aircraft there was nothing original about it as it had decorated warplanes since the First World War, but 112 Squadron was probably the most famous bearer of it. The Flying Tigers carried a similar design on their P40s in the Far East, copied, it is said from photographs of 112, and there are examples on AEAF Marauders and B25G Mitchells amongst many others. Photographs of the German *Haifisch Gruppe* of ZG76 must have been seen by many members of the RAF at various times. Furthermore Chris Wren, the resident cartoonist of 'The Aeroplane' magazine had recently portrayed the Tomahawk in the guise of a shark in his series called 'Oddentification'. Jerry (more correctly Gerry) Westenra relates that Fg Off Brunton painted the sharksteeth on his aircraft in order to distinguish it from the others at a distance. The result was dramatic since the Tomahawk with its great gaping air intake beneath the spinner seemed to have been designed for that very purpose. Westenra then suggested to the CO that all the aircraft should be painted the same way. Soon every machine carried the new markings, much to Peter Brunton's disgust. The sharksteeth design fired the popular imagination and still today people who would never recollect the number 112 remember the Shark Squadron, even though at times the captions under RAF publicity photographs referred to 112 by a variety of names such as 'The Killer Sharks' or 'The Tiger Sharks'. The colouring generally followed certain rules: black lips, white teeth, interior of the mouth red at the bottom and black above. Aft of the spinner was a pair of eyes, black rimmed, white with red iris and black pupil. When there was time the design was painted carefully and skilfully, but in the days of operational haste, when the aircraft came and went with alarming rapidity, the artistic efforts were not always of quite the same high standard. While it is facile to attribute too much to this flamboyant new marking it seems true to say that it soon became an object of pride to all squadron personnel. This type of pride breeds good

[1] quoted in 'The Desert Air Force', by Roderic Owen

ODDENTIFICATION—XIV

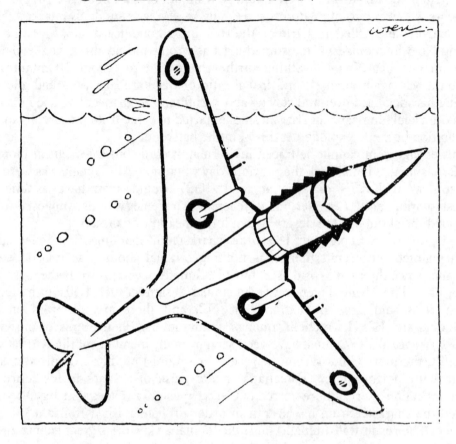

Except for the nose, which resembles a shark,
This fighter is nearly all wing.
We think of a bite that is worse than its bark
When Tomahawk's paises we sing.

'The Aeroplane' 27 June 1941

Chris Wren, illustrator on *The Aeroplane*, drew the Curtiss Tomahawk in the guise of a shark – perhaps suggesting the idea to the pilots of 112 Squadron.

morale and strong *esprit-de-corps* and the two together make for a more efficient fighting unit. 112 thus became for itself, and possibly for many other people, something special, lifting it above the level of its brother squadrons and making it, for those who have ever served on 112, 'the' RAF squadron.

Between September and November of that year the aircraft carried single letters foreward of the fuselage roundel but shortly afterwards the code-letters 'GA' were allocated, letters that remained on the squadron aircraft until the end of the war. On some machines the aircraft letter was repeated, quite small, on the 'knuckles' which were the fairings for the undercarriage bevel gears on the leading edge of the wings.

'Battleaxe' had ground to a halt towards the middle of June and there had been a stalemate since then. On 28 September the squadron took part in an escort to eighteen Marylands whose target was Bardia. The escort consisted of 44 fighters, representing four squadrons. The 8th Army came into being at this time and efforts were under way to mount a fresh offensive in November. The Middle East Air Force was now under Air Vice-Marshal Arthur Tedder, CB, certainly the greatest RAF commander of the Second World War. Reorganisation found 112 Squadron part of 262 Wing which consisted of six squadrons, a mixture of Tomahawks and Hurricanes and entirely mobile. Thus came into being the WDAF (Western Desert Air Force). Mobility and good communications was Tedder's recipe for effective air support and so Air Support Control units were instituted to sift requests from the army, decide on bomb lines and on ground-to-air signals. This system was not rigid and it was tried and tried again until a really effective form of supervision was evolved which was to carry the DAF, as it was always known, into the heart of Europe.

On 3 October 1941 the squadron sent eight Tomahawks to act as high cover for a Tactical Reconnaissance sortie by a 451 Sqn Hurricane west of Sidi Omar. Returning, they had the sun behind them, which allowed six Bf109s to bounce them. The first enemy pair consisting of *Oblt* Rödel and *Lt* Schacht of II/JG27 attacked and shot down Sgt I H Stirrat (AK502). Fg Off Groves managed to weave quickly and get a burst in on one of the enemy fighters which smashed the top of the fuselage behind the pilot's head. The comment afterwards was that a recce should not take place at that time of day which allowed the Messerschmitts to be scrambled and then follow the formation home and attack out of the sun. It is interesting to note that the Germans were, as always, operating as a tactical pair, a formation that had immense advantages over the rather unwieldy formations adopted by the DAF.

In the afternoon of 12 October 112 took over from No 2 and 3 SAAF who had been covering an army reconnaissance thrust near Bir Sherferzan. Close to Sofafi they ran into a formation of ten G50s with 15 Bf109Es and 109Fs. Individual dog-fights ensued spreading over a large area from Sherferzan to Buq-Buq. Fg Off Groves shot down one Bf109E and a G50 and Plt Off R J D Jeffries shot down a Bf109F. The reports mention the colouring of the enemy aircraft was a pale green and desert brown mottled effect with a silvery blue underside, also, for the second day running, the report stated that the spinners were not yellow. Presumably Intelligence were trying to identify a particular unit. 112's losses were two machines and their pilots who were reported missing. Plt Off F E Parker, an Australian (AN220) and Sgt R M Leu, also an Australian (AM396). Two machines were badly damaged, AM444 (Fg Off Groves) and AM481 (Sgt C F McWilliams, another Australian pilot), Plt Off Brunton was slightly injured. Parker and Leu were shot down by *Lt* Körner and *Hpt* Gerlitz of II/JG27. They were found that evening by the Coldstream Guards and returned to 112 a couple of days later. Yellow spinners seem to have been the identification colour for I/JG27 based at Gambut 3.

Preliminaries for Operation 'Crusader' involved 112's participation by intensified attacks on the *Deutsches Afrika Korps* (*DAK*)[1] and its lines of communication. The intention was to destroy the enemy's armour, relieve Tobruk and recapture Cyrenaica. Flt Lt Homer Cochrane was now promoted to squadron leader but a fortnight later he was posted to 204 Group. He was the last of the pre-war pilots to leave the squadron as Plt Off MacDonald and Flt Lt Harrison had both left that month. The squadron was taken over by Sqn Ldr F V Morello.

The appearance of the Bf109E, the 'Emil', swung the odds back again in favour of the enemy. Furthermore their units had adopted small formations, the *Rotte* or the *Schwarm* and allowed them to fly what they termed '*Freie Jagd*', a sort of individual unplanned mission to spread distress and dismay. The Germans also retained their pilots in the same unit so that their skill and expertise was there, handed down to newcomers. The RAF had the unfortunate practice of posting seasoned pilots back to base or to Training Units after a tour of duty, thus losing the advantages of their specialised knowledge, their places filled by untrained youngsters whose main hope was to stay alive long enough to learn what to do. In the German *Jagdstaffeln* the habit of *Freie Jagd* tended to produce a small number of very gifted high-scoring aces and it was understood that the junior pilots were expected to feed these heroes with the victims to add to their mounting score of kills. This system resulted in some jealousy as newcomers were not given the opportunity to open their score. The morale of the *Geschwader* was naturally boosted as the aces' scores mounted up but the death of men like Homuth or Marseille was, in consequence, a terrible blow to the unit, and indeed the whole German air force. No doubt there were advantages in the British system as the strain of months of daily combat against a determined enemy must have eventually taken its toll, both physically and mentally, and a posting to another theatre, a training unit or a mahogany bomber[2] could be seen as a necessary break.

To combat the Messerschmitt threat new tactics were devised. Instead of flying straight and level during offensive sweeps with a couple of aircraft weaving in the rear, the whole squadron now weaved. 'I should hate to tackle one of these formations' wrote Tedder, 'which look like a swarm of angry bees.' *Oberleutnant* Werner Schroer of JG27 described them rather differently: 'bunches of grapes' – presumably since they were so easy to pick off. At the beginning of November the squadron was still at Sidi Haneish but the Wing (now called No 2 Operational Wing) did not fly during the preliminary phase of 'Crusader'. On 12th and 14th the squadron moved to LG110, about 45 miles inland from the coast south of Sidi Barrani and the next day there was a Wing sweep, led by Wg Cdr Jeffrey, of the forward area, but no enemy aircraft were seen. The move west continued on 17th when the advance party left for LG122, near Fort Maddelena. 'Crusader' opened on 18 November 1941 with XXX Corps, which included most of

---

[1] To be precise the name *Afrika Korps* should refer only to the 15th and 21st Pz Divs, but today it is applied to all German land forces in the Western Desert.

[2] 'flying a mahogany bomber'; slang for a ground tour behind a desk

the armour, moving boldly round the enemy's open flank, aiming for Tobruk. It was planned that the decisive battle would be fought on the ridges around El Duda and Sidi Resegh. XIII Corps, with the infantry were to contain the main enemy positions and then join in the main battle outside Tobruk. Tedder could muster some 700 aircraft against the enemy's total of 283 in Cyrenaica, 186 in Tripolitania, and 776 spread out in Sicily, Sardinia, Greece, Crete and the Dodecanese. German airfields in Libya were closer to the front line than the DAF's but heavy rain meant that initially they could not intervene, while we were able to mount offensive sweeps over the battlefield. Sqn Ldr Morello led just such a sweep on the afternoon of 17 November to cause the maximum amount of damage to the grounded German fighters. 112 and 3RAAF Sqns escorted Blenheims and the Naval fighter squadron in an attack on Bir-el-Beheira LG, 12 miles south-east of Gambut. Again no enemy fighters were seen as they had withdrawn to Gazala. On 18 November bad weather bogged the squadron down and there was no flying, Axis aircraft being in a similar state. On the battlefield the army was closely engaged with the Italian Ariete Division and the 15th and 21st Panzer Divisions. The squadron made a sweep over the Gambut area, followed by another in the afternoon, determined to keep the enemy pinned to the ground. The squadron moved to LG 122.

On 20th the enemy made desperate efforts to support their ground troops but the squadron got amongst them in a decisive fashion. Ten Tomahawks of 112 and 12 of 3RAAF surprised about six Bf110s of III/ZG26 in pairs near Sidi Resegh, between El Adem and Acroma, the DAF aircraft having the height advantage of about 5000'. Sgt Carson (AN303) made two straightforward attacks on a Bf110 that took no evasive action and was shot down with smoke pouring from it. Plt Off Bowker (AN415) attacked another and its starboard engine blew up. As he broke away from that machine he encountered another which was already on fire from an attack by another Tomahawk. This aircraft eventually crashed with four Tomahawks chasing it. Plt Off Jeffries (AN413) attacked a Bf110 which began to stream glycol or petrol from both engines, causing it to lose speed and fly left wing low. The rear gunner managed to get some hits on AN413 which caused Jeffries to break off his attack. This machine, which he described as being painted in an all blue colour, was claimed as badly damaged. Fg Off J F Soden attacked two aircraft and blew the canopy off the second. The total claims for this combat were two Bf110s destroyed, one probably destroyed and two damaged. Since the RAAF squadron also claimed some destroyed it seemed likely at the time that the whole enemy formation had suffered badly.

On 21 November 11 aircraft, led by the CO, were patrolling the Gambut – Tobruk area when, on their way home, they caught two CR42s at about 500' near El Adem. Sgt Leu (AK509) forced one aircraft down to ground level where it crashed and the other was set on fire and destroyed by the combined efforts of Plt Off Jeffries (AK541), Plt Off N F Duke (AK402) and Sgt Carson (AK436). In the unemotional words of the combat report the Italian pilot was then strafed until he appeared to be dead. Duke concentrated on destroying the aircraft and considered killing the pilot an unsporting thing to do.

Neville Duke had joined the squadron on 12 November having served previously on 92 Squadron flying Spitfire Vs and he remarks[1] that having come from a squadron

---

[1] 'Fighters over the Desert' by Shores & Ring

flying very latest machines it was 'something of a change, and not for the better as far as performance and fire power were concerned.' Nevertheless he did have some good words to say about the Tomahawk which he found 'very robust and more sophisticated than British fighters, but, as a result, was heavier and consequently not so manoeuvrable or fast climbing.' Duke partly remedied this defect in the later Kittyhawks by sometimes having two of his wing guns taken out and carrying a reduced load of ammunition which gave him increased performance. He remarked that the Germans' use of tracer ammunition was often the first indication that you were being attacked and it also gave you a hint as to where the fire was going 'so that you could tighten or slacken your turn accordingly'. Subsequently, after leaving 112 in April 1942, he returned to command 'A' Flight of 92 Sqn and, later became CO of 145 Sqn. By the end of the war his personal score was 28 enemy aircraft destroyed, of which about six were credited to him on 112, and he had been awarded a DFC with two bars and a DSO.

Many 112 pilots had their 'own' aircraft, and some flew no other. Plt Off K R Sands always flew AM474 and AN330 had always been Sqn Ldr Cochrane's aircraft. Plt Of Bowker had two favourites, AK461 'A' and AN218. To have your own favourite aircraft allowed you to make certain personal modifications of the sort described by Neville Duke.

On 22 November Plt Off Bartle brought up a new aircraft, AK533, at the beginning of what was to be a great day for the squadron. At 11.40 hrs 13 aircraft led by Sqn Ldr Morello carried out a very successful strafe on an enemy road column on the Acroma road near El Adem. It was the first time the squadron was employed in attacking enemy ground troops in a rôle that would eventually become its speciality. The operation had been in response to an urgent call to attack a motorised convoy and, after one circuit, the CO ordered the squadron into line astern. With all guns blazing the road was raked with fire for about seven miles, with pieces of windscreen, fittings, wheels and tarpaulin flying off the enemy vehicles. Enemy personnel were seen to leap out, only to be machine-gunned on the ground. The whole convoy, which consisted of 3-ton trucks, was brought to a standstill, and the reckoning was that 15 to 20 vehicles had been damaged and about 50 to 100 casualties inflicted. The enemy opened up with small arms fire on later runs but the aircraft suffered no damage although Plt Off J P Sabourin (AN330) had baled out prior to the straffing run having been hit by flak from Sidi Omar. He landed safely amongst the Indian Division and returned a couple of days later becoming the first squadron member of the newly instituted 'Late Arrivals Club', whose badge was a small winged boot.

No less significant was the engagement that took place the same evening. Nine aircraft, led by Flt Lt Westenra, together with 12 of No 3RAAF Sqn, went on a Wing sweep commanded by Wg Cdr Jeffrey. At 16.15 hrs, south-east of El Adem, the formation was attacked by between 15–20 Bf109Fs and G50s. A combat ensued resulting in damage to both sides. A true picture of the combat cannot be given as it moved at high speed for the better part of an hour. For the first 15 minutes it was a free-for-all which gradually separated into individual dog-fights. Finally eleven Tomahawks formed a defensive circle with the Germans and Italians in a similar position, but slightly above. The circles flew round and round while every now and then an aircraft, seeing an advantage, would slip out and attack. While this was going on the enemy ground troops kept up a continuous fire of small arms and flak. In effect deadlock ensued, despite the enemy's superiority in every respect but there was nothing he could do to force the issue. Fg Off Duke destroyed a Bf109 after giving it a long burst at 100 yards. The hood and pieces of the fuselage falling off and the pilot, wearing a field-grey uniform, baled out.

Plt Off Bartle managed a sustained burst with all his guns on another Bf109F, killing the pilot. One G50 sporting black crosses was reportedly seen. Others observed a Bf109 burst into flames after a stern attack by an unidentified Tomahawk and a Tomahawk and Messerschmitt were seen to collide, the German machine spinning, its wheels down and pieces of wing falling off. With a score of two Bf109s destroyed 112's losses were Sgt Burney (AM390) who was shot down. Wg Cdr Fred Rosier, who happened to be with the squadron as he was trying to get to Tobruk in a Hurricane, landed beside Burney to try to pick him up. The Hurricane burst a tyre on take off and they had to abandon it. Enemy armoured cars were nearby so the two men had to hike 30 miles back to our lines where they were picked up none the worse for wear by the Indian Division. Meanwhile the fight had come to an end. The Germans, as night fell, flew off first as they were further from their base, leaving the Tomahawks, if not masters, at least in occupation of the skies. Their German opponents who had come from II and I/JG27 lost *Oberfähnrich* (Senior Cadet Officer) Waskott and *Feldwebel* (Sergeant) Hillert, both made PoWs. Waskott is believed to have been Duke's victim.

The Tomahawks were short of fuel and landed all over the place, Plt Off Bartle being the only one to reach LG122. Naturally some anxiety was felt but the next day all aircraft came back and, with the return of Sgt Burney, not one pilot was missing, although 3RAAF lost five. The significance of this combat was that the Tomahawks had held their own against an equal number of far superior aircraft. The Bf109s should have been able to do what they liked with the Tomahawk but the gallantry and skill of the RAF and RAAF pilots gained the day by default. It is not too far-fetched to suggest that from that day the *Luftwaffe* conceded air superiority to the Desert Air Force and never again did it challenge our fighters in a set piece aerial battle.

On the ground the battle was also being decided and for two days, 22nd and 23rd, a fierce slogging match was fought out until, in the end, our tanks were forced off the El Duda and Sidi Resegh ridges. That day, after the squadron had escorted Blenheims bombing enemy concentrations near El Adem, the situation, in the words of the tacticians, suddenly became fluid. Rommel's Panzers started to race towards the Egyptian frontier and the fate of the 8th Army and the DAF hung in the balance.

On 24th the squadron began the day by acting as top cover for some Marylands but the high speed of these bombers made it difficult for the Tomahawks to help them very much. A large concentration of enemy vehicles was seen on the Bir Sherferzan – Mediddi road about 30 miles west of the frontier, travelling east at great speed. Later that day the column turned south-east causing a flap at Fort Maddelena and at LGs 123, 124, 131, 132, and 134, which were evacuated. These aircraft took off too late to land at LG110 so they were obliged to cram in to LG122 where 112 Sqn was able to lay out a hurricane-lamp flare path. It was estimated that there were 175 aircraft on the landing ground and an anxious night was spent, with lorries lined up to evacuated the men if an attack should develop, pilots sleeping under the wings of their aircraft and the AA guns aligned to engage tanks. The German column missed the landing ground by about ten miles as it swept towards Egypt and thereby lost the opportunity of destroying most of the DAF's fighters.

Sqn Ldr Morello (AK538) led 12 aircraft to attack enemy AFVs and soft-skinned transport on 25 November. These they found badly dispersed and the Tomahawks, which flew at extremely low level, attacked about 150 vehicles, including 5–10 tanks and 20–30 armoured cars. Sgt W E Houston's aircraft (AN439) was damaged as was the CO's machine which had a hole through its wing. At least one tank and three or four other AFVs were left smoking and 20 other vehicles damaged. Plt Off Bowker was attempting to land to pick up the pilot of a shot down aircraft but before he could do so the pilot was made prisoner.

The same day there was a sweep over Sidi Resegh by 13 Tomahawks of 112 and 10 from 3RAAF Sqn, led by the Wing Commander. They arrived over the New Zealand troops just as they were being dive-bombed by a large number of enemy aircraft. This formation consisted of a top cover of 20–25 fighters, mostly G50s with some Bf109Es and Fs, while in the middle were 20 light bombers, mostly Bf110s and Ju88s, while at a lower level were were about 15 Ju87s with an escort of CR42s, a total of about 70 Axis aircraft. 3SAAF attacked the Bf110s and chased them out to sea, the Ju87s decided to make for home and the top cover came down to attack 112 Sqn. Even with the Stukas and 110s out of the way the squadron was still outnumbered nearly two to one. The G50s promptly went into a defensive circle and the Tomahawks had to pick off which ones they could. Fg Off P H Humphreys (AK405) attacked a CR42 which he shot down together with a Bf109F which was probably destroyed. Plt Off Bowker shot down a Bf110 into the sea and Flt Lt Westenra (AN303) left a CR42 spiralling down, although he did not see what became of it. The total at the end of the day, shared with 3RAAF, was ten destroyed, three probables and eight damaged. The combat took place over 'scenes of wild enthusiasm on the ground'. 112 lost Sgt F D Glasgow, a New Zealander, in AK461, who had only joined the squadron that month, shot down by *Oberfeldwebel* Albert Espenlaub of I/JG27. His body was never found.

The next few days were quieter, with very little enemy air activity. By 29th the enemy armour had turned back from its foray into Egypt and once again the centre of interest was around Tobruk where fighting was very heavy and losses were inflicted on 7th Armoured Division.

The month finished on another high note. At 08.30 on 30 November 12 Tomahawks of 112 with an equal number from 3RAAF Sqn intercepted a force of 35–40 enemy machines on their way to bomb our troops in Tobruk. The enemy were in several layers, 15 Ju87s at 6000', 20 G50s and MC200s from 7000'–8000' and five Bf109Fs as top cover. The Wing Commander detailed one section of 112 to watch the Messerschmitts and the remainder of the squadron, with 3RAAF, to concentrate on the middle and lower formations. The Stukas jettisoned their bombs and in the combat one MC200 and two G50s were destroyed and one Bf109F and one G50 damaged. Two of 112 Sqn's Tomahawks were lost, but both pilots were safe. One of the G50s was shot down by Sgt Leu (AK509) after a stern attack, Plt Off Bowker (AN338) claimed one MC200 destroyed, but he was then shot down by a G50 and was forced to crash-land on the outskirts of LG122, his machine being badly damaged. Plt Off Duke (AK402 'F') chased a G50 for a long way before finally shooting it down. He was then attacked from astern by two or three BF109s and a G50 or MC200. He turned and gave the Bf109 a short burst which appeared to damage it. He was followed home by another Bf109F and was hit in the port wing and main petrol tank. His machine went over onto its back at about 500′ and hit the ground on its belly just as he pulled it round. The aircraft took to the air again with a burst of power and crash landed. Duke leapt out and had only just cleared the aircraft and hidden himself in the scrub when it was straffed and set on fire. Later he was picked up by a Lysander and returned to base. His victor was *Oberfeldwebel* (Flt Sgt) Schultz of II/JG27 whose habit was to strafe downed aircraft for good measure.

So much has been written since the war on the Messerschmitt Bf109 in its various marks that to encapsulate this in a few lines will probably not do justice to one of the Second World War's most successful fighters. It has been said[1] that the high-powered low-wing monoplane aircraft was the progenitor for all international fighter aircraft of the 1930s and 1940s. It was conceived in the summer of 1934 and trials were undertaken in October the following year. The Bf (for *Bayerische Flugzeugweke*) was selected over its only rival, the He112V1. It was first used operationally in the Spanish civil war in 1938 and by the end of the world war in 1945 it had served on all fronts and with a number of foreign air forces and had gone through at least 14 different marks. The Bf109E was the standard *Luftwaffe* equipment in the Battle of Britain and was the first model that went into mass production. By contemporary standards it was an excellent fighter, it handled well and possessed excellent low speed control but it lacked the manoeuvrability and speed of the Spitfire although the Bf109E's climb rate and ceiling were superior and its handling above 20,000′ was better. In North Africa the Bf199E-4/N was the chief variant with a fuel injection system. The 109F had substantialy improved firepower and it was seen in North Africa as the 109F-2/Trop. Later the Bf109G-1/Trop, the '*Gustav*', carried a single engine mounted 20mm cannon and two 13mm machine guns in the wings. Throughout the war the Allies referred to these aircraft as Messerschmitt 109s, or Me 109s.

On 4 December 1941 ten squadron aircraft were airborne together with 12 of 250 Sqn, who shared LG122, when they ran into a large party of enemy aircraft over El Adem and Sidi Resegh. There were about 15 Ju87s flying in three groups of four or five at about 6000′. These were immediately attacked by the leading section. The second section attacked a mixed bag of about ten G50s and MC200s. These dived to about 6000′ and the Tomahawks were then bounced by about five Bf109Es and Fs. There followed a general dog-fight. Fg Off 'Hunk' Humphreys fired a lot of rounds at a Bf109E but was unable to see what effect this had. Neville Duke (AN337) attacked five Ju87s and managed to damage one so that it turned away and dived with smoke coming from it. Then he turned his attention to a MC200 which also dived away. Despite having his guns jammed and therefore unable to shoot, Duke chased the Macchi making dummy attacks until it flicked in a steep turn and spun, crashing about 2 miles from Tobruk landing ground. The score was two G50s destroyed by Flt Lt Gerry Westenra, one G50 and one Ju87 by Plt Off Bowker, one MC200 destroyed and one Ju87 probably destroyed by Plt Off Duke, one Bf109F probable by Sgt R H Christie and one Bf109F damaged by Fg Off Humphreys. Two Tomahawks were damaged.

---

[1] from 'Famous Fighters of the Second World War' by William Green

The following day the squadron achieved as great an aerial victory as the ones in Greece. At the end of the combat ten enemy aircraft had been destroyed by 112 Sqn and 12 by 250 Sqn. 250 Sqn was led by the Australian Flt Lt Clive ('Killer') Caldwell and the pilots of 112's formation that day were Flt Lt C F Ambrose (AK475), Fg Off Soden (AK377), Plt Off Duke (AN337'F'), Sgt Leu (AK354), Plt Off Bartle (AN372), Plt Off Bowker (AK509) and Plt Off Sabourin (AK457). The formation which was led by Flt Lt Ambrose, who had joined the squadron only a fortnight previously, took off at 11.20 hrs and sighted a formation of 30–40 Ju87s in vics of three, supported by 20–25 G50s and MC200s as close escorts. Twelve Bf109s were flying as high flank cover in two groups of six and there may have been about three MC202s. On sighting the Tomahawks some of the Stukas immediately jettisoned their bombs, but the majority, more daring, started their bombing dive. 250 Sqn started after the Stukas and 112 engaged the fighters. The G50s and MC200s stayed up as the Ju87s went down and in fact started to climb towards the Bf109s. There was a general *mêlée* and all the aircraft were mixed up. The Ju87s got involved with the retreating Italian fighters and, to add to the distractions, there was a hail of fire from the ground. Plt Off Bowker destroyed three Ju87s (two of which blew up in the air) and damaged a G50. He noted that when a Stuka was knocked out of the formation the remainder closed up and continued stolidly towards their target. Flt Lt Ambrose thought he had probably destroyed a MC200 and a G50. Fg Off Soden attacked a Ju87 and shot off its tail which fell off by degrees as the stricken aircraft dived. A Bf109F that he shot at lost its cowling and cockpit hood but was not seen to crash. Sgt Leu attacked a MC200 from out of the sun which spun in. He also attacked a Bf109F which 'seemed to falter in the air' and then dive, but he did not see it crash. Plt Off Sabourin shot down a Bf109E which fell in an uncontrollable spin with smoke come from it, and a G50 which also fell burning. He claimed a Ju87 which crashed near El Adem and also damaged a G50, a Bf109E and a Bf109F. Plt Of Bartle shot down one Ju87 and chased a G50 over El Adem where it was shot down by its own flak. Bartle claimed it as his victory as the enemy aircraft had been destroyed as a result of his action!

112's casualties were Plt Off Duke, who spun in from 10,000' down to 2000' and belly landed at Tobruk having been hit in the leg by an explosive shell. His radio had failed and his cockpit had sanded up so that he hadn't seen his attacker until cannon shells started hitting his aircraft. The squadron's score now stood at 108 aircraft destroyed for the loss of 44 pilots.

The Junkers Ju87, which was the host at this latest 'Stuka Party' as they were called by the DAF, had once appeared to be the battle winner when, in 1939 and 1940, it had paved the way for the advancing *Wehrmacht* in Poland, the Low Countries and France. 'Stuka' was an abbreviation for *Sturzkampfflugzeug* or dive bomber and it was its screaming near vertical descent that produced such a terrifying psychological effect on poorly trained troops and civilians. Over Dunkirk the supremacy of the Stuka was challenged for the first time by the RAF's fighters and they suffered heavy losses. In the desert the Ju87s of *Stukageschwader 3* had always to be heavily protected by escorting fighters as it was vulnerable and slow.

After this there was little activity until the 8 December 1941, the day after the Japanese attack of Pearl Harbour which brought America into the war. The trickle of Lease-Lend now became a flood. On the ground, in Libya, Rommel was withdrawing to Gazala. His retreat was far from being a rout although his position at Gazala were not very strong, so he retired again to Derna and thence at Jeddabia. It now became a race between the Germans and the British in Libya to see who could build up their supplies the soonest.

On 8th 112 and 3SAAF Sqns patrolled the forward area but were attacked by six Bf109s and Bf110s and Sgt J Alves machine (AK541) was damaged, but he got back safely. Later a force of Bf109s and Bf110s attacked the road south of the landing ground but were diverted from attacking the aircraft by a patrol of No 3SAAF Sqn. The Germans shot down a DH86a ambulance plane of No 1 RAAF Air Ambulance Unit which angered everyone[1].

The next day ten Tomahawks, along with 12 of the Australian squadron were jumped by six Bf109s of I/JG27 over the El Gobi – El Adem area. Sgt Carson's machine (AK533) was badly shot up and Fg Off Sabourin (AK509) was obliged to force land near XXX Corps with engine trouble. The German pilots shot down three of the Australians and Wg Cdr Jeffrey had to land at Tobruk. There were two Sgt Carsons on the squadron at this time, both Australian, both having arrived at about the same time, one with the initials K F and the other W E and as their service numbers were very close it doesn't take much imagination to work out that they were brothers. Of Sgt W E Carson little seems to have been recorded although he was on the Sqn as late as January 1942. Whether he was the pilot of AK533 that day is impossible now to discover. Sgt K F Carson remained on the squadron until June 1942.

There was now a general advance and the 112 Advance Party left for El Adem, arriving there on 12th. That day the squadron was particularly active to prevent any interference with the 4th Armoured Brigade's flanking movement. Later that same day 112 Sqn suffered a reverse. They arrived over Tmimi at about 16.00 hrs in time to see dog-fight already in progress. The formation, eight aircraft from 112 and eight from 3 RAAF Sqn, climbed to attack when it was seen that there were Bf109s and and M202s at all heights from 3000′ upwards. A general dog-fight followed in which four DAF squadrons were involved. Plt Off Bartle (AN372) claimed a Bf109 destroyed and a MC202 damaged. He fired a long burst at the 109 and saw smoke and oil pouring from the engine. The canopy of the MC202 broke away after his attack. He later chased another 109 and only gave up when his ammunition was exhausted. Sgt D N McQueen, an Australian flying AN303, claimed one 109F damaged, having hit it near the cockpit. When this aircraft was at 4000′ lower than he was it was on its back but he didn't see what happened to it. Later he was attacked himself and he had to dive into cloud to get rid of his pursuer. Plt Off E Dickinson (AM459), who had arrived on the squadron that month and who was to end up as 'A' Flt Commander only five months later, opened his score by attacking MC202s with Fg Off Humphreys. There was then a violent dog-fight in which he was attacked by two of the Macchis but he managed to turn inside them an scored hits on one which dived away. The final score was one Bf109F probably destroyed and damage inflicted on two MC202s and one Bf109F. 112's casualties included Plt Off Jeffries (AN413 'K'), Sgt Houston (AK457) and Sgt Alves (AK476). Houston, an Australian, was killed and his body was never found, Alves

---

[1] This incident is not mentioned in '*Jagdgeschwader 27*' by Hans Ring and Werner Girbig, so perhaps the Bf110s were the culprits

was made a PoW, released in July 1944, and Jeffries was also presumed killed, although his body was never found.

There are quite a number of squadron pilots who have no known graves, strange as this may seem when the desert over which they were flying was teeming with men and vehicles of all nationalities. No doubt, in such cases, the aircraft either fell into the sea or well away from the battle area and clear of tracks, disappearing into the sand, leaving only a few slight traces on the surface. Possibly passing tribesmen buried them where they fell and it is also possible that from time to time their bodies will still be found.

On 13 December the 8th Army continued their attack on Rommel's line at Gazala and the next day there was a small encounter, when five Tomahawks, led by Plt Off Duke saw eight Ju88s escorted by a similar number of fighters flying west. The Tomahawks were just about to attack when they were bounced by about six Bf109s. An inconclusive dog-fight followed. None of our aircraft were hit and except for possible damage to one Bf109 claimed by Sgt S C Johnson, there were no claims. The Messerschmitts were reported as being camouflaged in yellow with daubs of dark brown and green spots, giving them a leopard-like effect. This corresponds quite closely with one of the known camouflage schemes of I/JG27, based at Tmimi.

On 17 December Hunk Humphreys led five aircraft escorting Blenheims which were bombing enemy MT around Mechili and on the 18th there was an early morning patrol searching for enemy transport. A second patrol at midday had better luck and spotted dust rising about 20 miles south-east of Mechili. The enemy column was attacked along its length and about five trucks and a tank were left burning. A staff car was also shot at. There was scattered rifle fire and a bullet caused Plt Off Dickinson to land at Tobruk for repairs. By 17th, though, the battle of Gazala was over with the soft sand preventing the German armour from falling victim to the attempted encirclement by 7 Armd Div. On 19 December the aircraft flew forward to El Adem. The enemy had now disengaged and the Blenheims that the squadron escorted that day were 'let loose' as there was little chance of them dropping their bombs on friendly forces.

On a bomber escort mission the next day the squadron was attacked by fifteen Bf109s of I/JG27 near Marana. While 250 Sqn, who were acting as top cover, engaged the majority, five enemy aircraft got through and dived to attack the Blenheim IVFs of 45 Sqn and the Lorraine Sqn (Free French Air Force). One Blenheim of the Lorraine Sqn blew up and another started losing height with an engine on fire. The bombers jettisoned their bombs and started to split up, scattering into cloud, which was bad tactics as it made the task of the escorts more difficult. Plt Off Sands, an Australian, in AN372, managed to get in a long burst at a Bf109 and saw it wobble and lose speed. This machine had just attacked a Blenheim which had burst into flames on Sands's starboard quarter. At this moment Sqn Ldr Tony Morello (AN340 'B') was ahead of Sands and was overtaken by a flaming Bf109, possibly the one Sands had attacked. The CO was then hit in several places and his aileron control was shot away. He managed to pull out of the consequent dive at about 500' and make his way home. Sands was also having difficulties of his own as he had developed engine trouble. He did not return to base and was posted missing. Also missing was Sgt A H Ferguson.

On the second escort mission of the day Sgt H G Burney destroyed a Ju88. The Blenheims were covered by 112, 250, 2SAAF and 4SAAF Sqns. Leaving Gazala they were flying west when a single Ju88, its bombs racks full, passed them flying 500' above. Three aircraft of 112 immediately gave chase but, on losing it in cloud two returned to join the formation. Burney, in AN289, did not give up and caught the German aircraft west of Martuba. The Ju88, of II/KLG1, turned north and jettisoned its bombs, finally turning for home. Sgt Burney closed with it, firing all the way, following it down to 500′ until it blew up, falling close to Giovani.

The Junkers Ju88 was a twin-engined medium bomber which had turned out to be one of the most successful and adaptable aircraft the *Luftwaffe* possessed. It was used as a day and night fighter, bomber, torpedo bomber, dive bomber, reconnaissance aircraft, close-support aircraft and mine layer. The version shot down by Burney was a Ju88A-4/Trop, with underwing carriers that could carry various combinations of 550lb, 1100lb and 2200lb bombs. As the Ju88 had a maximum speed of 293 mph Burney would have had a longish haul to catch it.

On 22 December 1941 the squadron advance party was on the move once again, this time to Msus. That day six aircraft attacked Magrun airfield and took the defenders unprepared. The Tomahawks waited until there were no enemy aircraft airborne and then attacked out of the sun. It was a case of complete surprise. A number of Ju87s and a single Bf109F were just arriving or leaving and Neville Duke (AK354), after initially attacking and damaging a Stuka, attacked a Bf109 which was attempting to climb to intercept. South of Benghazi Duke then saw 15 Ju52s coming in from the sea and he then attacked the tail ender. Just as this machine seemed about to catch fire he himself was attacked by six Bf110s which were the escort. Being now short of ammunition he evaded and flew back to Mechili. Bartle and Westenra both attacked one of the Ju87s circling Magrun and, between them, shot it down. Sgt K F Carson, an Australian, attacked the Bf109 that Duke had already damaged and left it side-slipping uncontrollably towards the ground. He also attacked a Ju52 on the ground. The score was considered to be one Ju87 destroyed, one Bf109F, one Ju52 and one Ju87 probably destroyed, one Ju87 and one Ju52 damaged.

The Squadron Intelligence Officer wrote on 23 December 'Sands of the Desert returns'. Plt Off Sands, having last been seen in difficulty on 20th, had force landed about 20 miles north-north-west of Charubba. He left his aircraft and ran for cover because of low-flying Bf109s. Later he joined a friendly camel train of Senoussi tribesmen in a wadi near Si Saad, by the ruins of an old fort. He spent the night on a piece of rush matting covered by a threadbare blanket, sharing the night with Arabs, goats and fleas. His hosts had picked up German leaflets that showed Arabs being bayonetted and hanged by British soldiers. While being quite friendly the Senoussi were not particularly anti-German but they hated the Italians. The next afternoon the Arabs spotted two armoured cars but Sands had to watch them for a long time until he was satisfied they were British. They turned out to belong to the Kings Dragoon Guards. He gave the Senoussi £E2, all he had with him, and spent the following night sleeping in an armoured car. Eventually transport was found to return him to the squadron. He was posted shortly afterwards to become CO of 450 Sqn. Sgt Ferguson, also missing the same day as Sands, was never found.

On Christmas Eve Flt Lt Westenra led a strafe over El Agheila airfield. Apart from some enemy personnel, two Ju52s and one Bf109, the place was deserted. Sgt McQueen strafed a Ju52 with a pilot from 250 Sqn and McQueen had the pleasure of seeing it catch alight as he was firing. The other Ju52 was attacked by Sgt Burney but without any visible effect. They then shot at a large water tanker and brought it to a halt. On the road to Agedabia they attacked a truck and saw three or four men leap out. These they shot at, as well as the flimsy hut they had taken cover in; a Breda gun on a truck was also damaged. On Christmas Day the 8th Army entered Benghazi. 25 December was a normal working day without any of the usual trimmings. On the return journey from a sweep of the El Agheila area Lt Col Wilmot, DFC, led a carol-singing broadcast over the R/T, surely a disturbing sound.

Two days after Christmas five of 112 Sqn together with aircraft from 2SAAF, 4SAAF and 250 Sqns strafed enemy troops on the Agheila – Agedabia road. From this sortie Plt Off Bowker failed to return. He was last seen running in an easterly direction from his crashed aircraft. Later he was reported to be a PoW. He had 10 victories to his credit. On 29th the squadron received a belated Christmas present, seven Curtiss P40E Kittyhawk IAs. The CO and 13 pilots left for Kasfereit to collect some more. The Tomahawks, which were handed over to 250 Sqn, had been 112's aircraft for only four months, September to December 1941. Sixty-eight aircraft are recorded as having passed through the squadron, but this is a minimum estimate as several crashed before they were listed as flying operationally. Twenty Tomahawks had been lost in action but they had destroyed 36 enemy aircraft. Only two machines, AK457 and AK541 lasted the whole four months.

The Kittyhawk, although similar to the Tomahawk, incorporated several new improvements. The main visual difference between the P-40B Tomahawk and the P-40E Kittyhawk IA was the enlarged radiator air intake, a modified cockpit and the R/T aerial. The engine was shorter which raised the thrust line, allowing the length of the fuselage to be reduced by 6″ and the undercarriage shortened. The fuselage guns were removed and the wing guns increased to six, with 281 rounds per gun. There was provision for a ventral drop tank and for small bomb racks under the wings. The maximum speed was 354 mph. It was still not the answer to the Bf109, except possibly at low level, or the MC202, unless the Italian pilot was inexperienced, as this machine could out-turn the Kittyhawk. There were to be initial troubles with the engine bearings and jammed machine guns[1] due to the desert conditions but pilots still had to cope with the aircraft's tendency to ground loop.

Several days were spent in instruction on the new aircraft and the pilots were impressed by the improvements. Immediately, though, there was the usual crop of fatal accidents. On 4 January 1941 Sgt A T Crocker, who had only just joined the squadron, was killed on his first flight. The next day news came that Sgt Johnson had been killed flying through a dust storm near Halfaya Pass. Sqn Ldr Tony Morello was now posted, the new squadron commander being Sqn Ldr 'Killer' Caldwell, DFC & bar. Caldwell was already a well-known 250 Sqn pilot and John Herington[2] says of him that his '. . . phenomenal success was largely due to the cold determination with which he always pressed in close and his intelligent gunnery sense . . .' Roderick Owen[3] described him

---

[1] Though 112 didn't seem so badly served in this respect as the pilots of 260 Sqn, see 'Kittyhawk Pilot',
     by Wg Cdr James F Edwards
[2] 'The Air War Against Germany & Italy', John Herington
[3] Owen, *op cit*

more poetically as 'a lone wolf . . . one against the world . . . in the swashbuckling Elizabethan tradition.'

The squadron went into action with the Kittyhawks on 9 January. Led by Flt Lt Westenra eight aircraft along with eight of 250 Sqn's Tomahawks escorted Blenheims bombing north of El Agheila. Sgt Carson (AK672) was attacked by a Bf109F on the way back and was forced down but he returned to the squadron. WO Luscombe went out into the desert with a recovery party and towed the aircraft back the 25 miles from Msus. The *Kommodore* of *JG27 Oberstleutnant* Eduard Neumann, wrote after the war[1] that to the German pilots all versions of the P40 were 'Curtiss fighters' and their claims do not differentiate.

The squadron moved forward once again, this time to Antelat, about 60 miles south-south-east of Benghazi, the furthest west they had ever been positioned. The rear party arrived while a dog-fight was going on over the airfield. The 8th Army had now reached as far as it could go and supply lines were stretched to the uttermost. Someone in JG27 had written 'We come back! Happy Christmas!' on a door at Derna airfield before they departed, and now this boast looked like coming true. On 21st Rommel began an armoured thrust which the DAF could not counter as airfields were flooded. The squadron moved hurriedly out of Antelat and the rear party was shelled by the Germans as it left. Everyone reached Msus safely but the Advance Party was told to be ready to leave again at dawn. Nevertheless 112 provided cover to Blenheims going to Mersa Brega and Wadi Faregh. There was a dawn sweep on 23 January and enemy troops were seen in the Antelat – Agedabia – Hassiet area.

The next day 11 Kittyhawks went on a sweep of the Antelat – Saunnu area from Msus, returning to Mechili, about 85 miles to the north-east. There was a lot of difficulty getting the remaining aircraft away and they had to be lifted out of the mud and taxied with men under the wings and tailplanes to prevent the machines bogging down and tipping forward onto their noses. In the withdrawal transport also got stuck and the Mess vehicle, headquarters tentage and some of the pilots' kit was left behind.

The squadron led by Gerry Westenra escorted Blenheims going to Agedabia on a bombing mission on 25th. The bombing was reported as being 'poor', 112 apparently not having much respect for the Blenheims' efforts. On the return journey the Kittyhawks were attacked by five Bf109s of II/JG27 west of Msus, one of which was shot down by Sgt Leu. Flying AK637 he made a head-on attack and knocked a large chunk out of its starboard wing. The aircraft was seen to crash by another pilot. JG27's records do not mention any one of their pilots being killed that day. None of 112's Kittyhawks was damaged but one Blenheim was seen lagging, probably hit by flak.

That day some stragglers returned to the squadron, eight airmen who had been left behind in the retreat. They had been packing gear and servicing the remaining aircraft and MT vehicles when an officer of an RAF armoured car unit drove up and told them that an enemy column was nearby. This column, which was holding an escarpment on the Msus side of the Antelat road, had already lobbed some shells at the LG. Ammunition and aircraft were now being destroyed and that evening the armoured cars moved off towards the Benghazi road in a north-easterly direction. Around midnight they caught up with a mixed bunch of Artillery and RAOC. When they reached the

[1] Shores & Ring, *op cit*

main road they were straffed by a Bf109. They hid in a wadi and after about 10 minutes
the road was shelled. Uncertain what to do they decided to return to Antelat arriving
back during the afternoon. Two armoured cars went forward to investigate but they got
bogged down in the soft sand. Just as they had been dug out nine German tanks
appeared, firing as they came. The armoured cars, ten of them in all, old Rolls Royces
dating back to 1921 armed with one .303 machine gun each, bravely turned to engage
them and the trucks departed as fast as they could. They were chased for about 45
minutes and only four vehicles got away. Having refuelled they waited to see if anyone
else would turn up, but no one did. Late that afternoon they were spotted by two
Kittyhawks which indicated to them the direction to Msus, where they arrived that
evening. The airmen involved in this adventure were Cpls Luton and Hibbert, LACs
Robinson, Flower, Keighley, Barton, Cross and Thompson.

On 26 January there was an unsuccesful Tac-R of Trigh-el-Abd where they saw
nothing. At midday ten Kittyhawks led by Flt Lt Humphreys took off to strafe enemy
transport on the Antelat – Msus road. Sgt Burney found eight tanks with 25 supporting
vehicles refuelling about 20 miles north of Msus. He attacked and claimed hits on at
least ten vehicles and a number of men. Sgt R E Simonsen hit two VW *Kübelwagene* (a
derisory nickname meaning 'Bucket trucks') and a lorry and Sgt K F Carson, Sgt W E
Carson and Sgt R A Drew hit other vehicles. The next day there another strafe of
enemy vehicles in the Saunnu -- Antelat area. Flt Lt Westenra and Fg Off Brunton
claimed to have hit trucks along the Antelat – Msus road and Sgt Christie claimed to
have hit four vehicles and then attacked two tanks, one which fired back at him
although, as he remarked grimly, they didn't fire on his second run.

1078498 LAC Tingle, J A, writing after the war described life in the desert
around that time. 'As you well know 112 Squadron was always up with the army and
therefore our living conditions were what we made them, a dugout in the sand with
a bivouac over the top; for a bed a piece of sacking nailed to two lumps of wood with
two end pieces to keep it tight – of course not everyone had it so comfy, for some it
was just a blanket and head down in the sand. For food it was mostly Bully (beef)
done 1000 different ways but always well flavoured with sand. Speaking of food, I
remember once at LG49, Fort Capuzzo, the ration waggon brought in the rations
and with them some biscuits of a different kind, about 3″ square they were. When
we had to eat them we found only the hard shell, the inside had been eaten away by
maggots and, as no others were to be got, they had to do and if you had seen the
ways those biscuits were made eatable you would probably turn green. Then there
were the sand storms. One could see them coming, a large brown cloud far off in
the distance. That was the time to get out a ball of string, tie one end to a stick in
your dugout and take the other end to the cook house. The reason for this was that
sometimes these storms lasted 3 and 4 days and to be lost in a sand storm – only
those that have been lost in one know what it's like.' Sand got into everything,
engine air filters had to be changed after every flight, engines after 60 flying hours
and guns tended to jam when they were fired. Sgt Bert Butler, Jack Cookson, 'Jock'
McLennan, Sgt Harrison and Jim Worsfold, all Fitters IIE, were the engine-
changing team ('*par excellence*' says Jim Worsfold). It took one day to change an
Allison engine.

As a result of Rommel's diversionary thrust towards Mechili on the 28 January 1942,

112 started to move eastwards again, this time to Gazala. Flt Lt Westenra, Plt Off Duke, Plt Off Dickinson and Sgt A T Donkin made a sweep from Mechili to north of Msus, along the Sceleidima road for an hour. At Sceleidima Fort a concentration of six vehicles and a tank were selected for attention and all were raked in turn by each pilot in a run either way. There were at least 12 tanks and several hundred vehicles dispersed around the fort. The diarist referred to this as the last show of the fighter Wing's lone stand against Rommel. Having caught the British off balance he now made a sudden thrust northwards, and Benghazi fell.

That afternoon the ground gunners, HQ staff and No 2 Party left Mechili for Gazala, about 65 miles to the east, leaving the remainder to travel as a composite party by moonlight. The diarist, giving another momentary insight into the confusion wrote 'The mysterious withdrawal in the face of Rommel's alleged inferior forces begins to assume something uncomfortably resembling a disordered and inexplicable retreat.' A disordered retreat it was, so much so that XIII Corps was now left without air cover. The rest of the month was spent reorganising. The squadron was still, on paper, divided into two Flights, but all pilots flew together and the Operations Record gives no indication as to who was in which. There were six Australian pilots (shown thus: 'Aus') and one Canadian ('Can') —

Sqn Cdr: Sqn Ldr Caldwell (Aus)
'A' Flt Cdr: Flt Lt Westenra
'B' Flt Cdr: Flt Lt Humphreys

Squadron pilots:		
	Plt Off Brunton	Sgt Carson, K (Aus)
	Plt Off Bartle (Aus)	Sgt Carson, W (Aus)
	Plt Off Duke	Sgt McQueen (Aus)
	Plt Off Dickinson	Sgt Christie
	Sgt Holman	Sgt Taylor (Aus)
	Sgt Drew	Sgt Donkin
	Sgt Leu (Aus)	Sgt Hoare
	Sgt Burney	Sgt Simonsen

Non-operational:		
	Sgt Evans	Sgt Elwell
	Sgt Cordwell	Sgt Jackson
	Sgt Tackaberry (Can)	

(NCO pilots now outnumbered the commissioned officers by 17 to 7).

Based at Gazala the squadron began the month of February with some flying practice after which 'A' and 'B' Flts left for El Adem. On 3rd there was a strafe of the Derna road. Flt Lt Humphreys led the formation which flew along the coast to Derna and then turned out to sea, but doubled back to make a surprise attack on an enemy motorised column on the escarpment west of the town. Nine vehicles were attacked. Going south they attacked a similar convoy on the lower road, ten miles inland. At least ten vehicles and 20 men were probably hit. The only casualty was Fg Off (just promoted) Brunton who failed to return, no one saw what happened to him but in fact he was killed by ground fire. He had served just over a year on the squadron, the most senior pilot.

At El Adem on one occasion there was only one serviceable aircraft except that it had a hole through one wing. Nothing daunted 'Pru' Passfield (he had worked for the Prudential before the war) took off his shirt and doped it over the holes on the upper and lower wing surface to allow it to fly.

After a day of dust storms during which nothing could be done there was another strafe on the 5th, led by Sqn Ldr Caldwell. Eight aircraft took part from Gambut Main and headed out to sea, coming in again over the main road at Fare Point, between Derna and Tmimi. Here four aircraft criss-crossed the road, picking off the odd vehicle and thoroughly wrecking them one by one. Traffic was not heavy and there was some small arms fire in return. Sgt Carson was hit by a bullet but he brought his aircraft back safely. One truck heading towards Gazala was seen to be British-made, but the troops inside were German so it was attacked. El Adem and Gambut Main airfields were both bombed by aircraft that were supposed at the time to have come from Crete but were probably Ju88s of I/KLG I.

The constant harassment of the *Afrika Korps* from the air was beginning to slow down the enemy advance. By 10 February the enemy had captured most of the Cyrenaican 'bulge' as far as Gazala. Here the Germans halted and both sides hurriedly began to build up their supplies. A Ju88 attacked Gambut again on 6th and Cpl Searles was hit in the hand by a bomb splinter. Flt Lt Humphreys and Sgt Donkin scrambled in pursuit but failed to overtake it. The next day the same thing happened at Gambut, where 'A' Flt had moved. Sgts Simonsen and Carson, K, again scrambled but the enemy aircraft was dealt with by a Hurricane.

On 8 February 1942 there was an escort to 11 Blenheims which were targetted on Derna. Nos 3RAAF Sqn and Hurricanes from 73 Sqn were also there to act as top cover but four were obliged to return to base with engine trouble. Those left were intercepted by a surprise attack by three Bf109s, and one Kittyhawk was shot down and another so badly damaged that it barely made it back to Gambut. The 109s flew off before they could be dealt with but in the confusion five of the Australian Kittyhawks lost contact with the Blenheims and returned to base so that 112 were left by themselves except for one other. There was a rearguard fight and three pilots Sgt Elwell, Sgt Donkin and Sgt Hoare failed to return, all, as it happened, relatively new pilots. One Bf109F flew parallel with the formation as if acting as a decoy. Flt Lt Humphreys managed to get an attack in on him before other enemy aircraft started 'dive and away' tactics. The decoy was finished off near Bomba by Sgt Burney who also saw a Kittyhawk and another Bf109 crash into the sea about 20 yards apart east of the Gulf of Bomba. Elwell and Hoare were almost certainly shot down and one of them took a 109 with him – perhaps the two that Burney saw crashing as neither of their bodies has ever been found. The total that day was three all.

The records of all three *Gruppen* of JG27 appear to show that no pilot were lost that day but 112 were almost certainly engaged with I/JG27. Two of the Kittyhawks were claimed by *Lt* Marseille and with two others he claimed, which were from 73 Sqn, this brought Marseille's score to 40, the highest in Africa. On 9th there was another raid on Gambut and two aircraft were burned out by incendiaries and some were damaged.

There was an influx of eight new pilots between 8 and 10 February, all Polish, and the RAF publicity newshawks were on the scene to take photos of them being briefed by Sqn Ldr Caldwell. They weren't long on the squadron and, apart from one, Fg Off F Knoll who stayed until July, they only remained until the beginning of May, the shortest stay of all being Fg Off C Matusiak who was killed while circuit flying on the 12th. This didn't seem to be long enough to allow them to start scoring as it was well known that Polish pilots flew with a particular hatred of the Germans. *Lt* Stahlschmidt of I/JG27 who was captured by Polish troops about this time said he was knocked about and given a rough time.

On 11 February Sgt Leu led a patrol over El Adem. There was some confusion over the R/T which led indirectly to the death of Sgt Holman. The formation was nearing El Adem when Leu had to relinquish the lead to Burney as his R/T was not functioning very well. Somehow Holman must have got left behind because near Gazala they were attacked by six Bf109s and two MC202s using 'dive and away' tactics and although Holman evaded the first attack he was picked off at the second – a case of '*Den Letzten beissen die Hunde!*'[1]. He was not seen to bale out. Burney fired at a MC202 but this had got away by spiralling downwards and making off at ground level. The rest of the formation in the meanwhile had been vectored out to sea but, failing to receive any further instructions, they returned to Gambut.

On 14 February 1942 there was a fine squadron victory of the sort that had been lacking for some time which was inevitably referred to as the 'St Valentine's Day Massacre'. Ten Kittyhawks led by Plt Off Bartle (AK700) with Sgt Simonsen (AK682), Plt Off Duke (AK578), Sgt Leu (AK781), Plt Off Dickinson (AK804), Sgt R B Evans (AK637), Sgt Drew (AK653), Sgt Christie (AK761), Sgt W E C Cordwell, Sgt Burney (AK702) with eight aircraft of 3RAAF Sqn were scrambled to meet an approaching enemy formation. After flying north to Tobruk the Kittyhawks turned west over the perimeter defences and climbed steadily until, over Acroma, 3RAAF were at 8000' with 112 slightly ahead and above, just below the cloud base at the ideal height for the Kittyhawk. At that moment they spotted about a dozen MC200s and MC202s in a loose vic formation 2000' below. Plt Off Bartle warned the Australians who, however, were more interested in a formation of enemy bombers with a close escort flying lower than 2000'. 112 concentrated on the fighters who by now were climbing to meet the attack. However their courage failed them and they hurriedly and half-heartedly tried to form a defensive circle. The Kittyhawks dived into them and in the initial attack every aircraft of 112 must have scored hits. Sgt Burney, having dived through the Italian fighters found himself amongst the bombers, probably BR20s, and shot one down (he claimed a Breda 65, a curious recognition error). His victim attempted to evade but it hit the ground and Burney strafed it. By the time he regained height aircraft were milling around everywhere. Sgt Cordwell, in his first action, shot away about three-quarters of the wing of a Bf109F which spun in out of control. Sgt Drew claimed two MC200s, one of which he saw hit the ground. 'It was as easy as breakfast in bed' he said afterwards. Neville Duke attacked a MC200 which was seen to spin and crash by Sgt Evans. He also attacked another Macchi at ground level from dead astern and it too flew into the ground and burst into flames. This kill he shared with Sgt Reid of 3RAAF Sqn.

---

[1] 'The last one gets bitten by the dogs!' – a phrase current on JG27

The enemy's defensive tactic when evading was to drop down to ground level in rolls and vertical dives. Sgt Leu attacked a MC200 which blew up and another which flew into the ground. Sgt Simonsen certainly got a MC200 which he saw spin down and he probably damaged another. Plt Off Dickinson made a stern attack on another MC200 which was enveloped in a sheet of flame at 1000'. Sgt Christie claimed two MC200s destroyed and one damaged. His account told of how he dived and gave one Macchi a heavy burst so that the aircraft pulled up steeply and then spiralled and crashed, bursting into flames. He then dived on a second which stalled, pouring out black smoke and going into a dive. He had a go at a third and probably damaged it but without any visible effect. Sgt Evans also attacked a MC200 which was seen to lose about 2' off its starboard wing. It dived away so steeply that it seems doubtful whether the pilot could have pulled out. Plt Off Bartle gave another MC200 a long burst which sent it down out of control and damaged a Bf109 which he chased all the way to Tmimi. No3RAAF Sqn in the meantime had fallen upon the bombers but they spotted about six Bf109s lurking close by. They wheeled round in time and in the ensuing dog-fight four enemy machines were destroyed and another damaged. Then, at last, they were able to concentrate on the BR20s. By the time the battle finished the remnants of the Axis aircraft had fled. The total estimated strength of the enemy at the start of the engagement was 32 aircraft of which 20 were claimed as destroyed, two probably destroyed and ten damaged. What is astonishing is that neither of the Kittyhawk squadrons lost a single aircraft in what was described as a text-book example of a successful interception – both top and extra cover having been dealt with before the bombers were attacked. 112 Sqn's share of the total was 11½ destroyed, two probables and three damaged.

As no German losses were reported that day it would appear that the Bf109s claimed were probably misidentified MC202s. In the excitement and heat of combat it is hardly surprising that occasionally enemy aircraft are wrongly reported.

The Macchi 200 *Saetta* was a curiously ugly low-winged fighter with a radial engine with distinctive bulges round the cowling, which were the rocker arm fairings, and the cockpit set high amidships. It was armed with two .5″ machine guns. The prototype had flown towards the end of 1937 but official mismanagement meant that it was not delivered to front line squadrons until September 1940 and it was April 1941 before it appeared in North Africa. The MC200s of *8°, 13°* and *150° Gruppi* were used extensively as bomber escorts and it was probably these units that 112 met that day.

The MC202s were a different matter. They were used as high cover on these missions and, apart from the similar wing shape and rear fuselage, they were unlikely to be confused with the older MC200. The *Folgore* mounted a liquid-cooled in line engine which allowed it to have an altogether more streamlined engine. The prototype had first flown in August 1940 and immediately it was hailed as a successful design. The MC202 was undoubtedly the most effective fighter used by the *Regia Aeronautica* during the Second World War. The lack of really powerful armament that had characterised earlier Italian fighters was remedied by installing two .5″ machine guns in the cowling and two .3″ machine guns in the wings. The rather late arrival of the MC202s in Libya meant that it was not until January 1942 that they appeared in any numbers in the Cyrenaican skies.

The next day, 15th, there was a Wing sweep which was accompanied by Kittyhawks of 94 Sqn, led by Sqn Ldr E M 'Imshi' Mason over Martuba. *Oberfeldwebel* Otto Schultz of II/JG27 managed to take off. He immediately shot down four of 94 Sqn's aircraft, including the legendary Mason, and then attacked Sgt McQueen and badly damaged his aircraft and wounded him; he was lucky to have been able to limp home. Fot this action Schultz was awarded the Knight's Cross as it brought his personal total to 44.

That day the squadron moved to El Adem for a couple of days, but they had little rest as that night they were dive bombed. The cookhouse and a water truck were damaged. The next day they were bombed again and some Hurricanes were damaged. The front line was now stabilised between Gazala and Bir Hakeim and, although 'Crusader' had ended badly, the Allies were still further forward than when they had started their offensive and all the airfields in eastern Cyrenaica remained in our hands.

On 21 February Sqn Ldr Caldwell led 11 aircraft on a sweep near Gazala, meeting seven Bf109s. The squadron had now adopted the fluid pair formation in two sections, one of six and one of five. The CO shot down one Bf109 which fell in flames, an attack from some distance below which had astonished the Germans. The victim was *Lt* Stahlschmidt who had escaped from captivity. He managed to crash land his aircraft and return to his base at Martuba, plainly blessed with a charmed life. Sgt K Carson was able to give another 109 a steady burst at close range but without apparent result but later it was learned that an enemy aircraft had crashed between Tmimi and Gazala and this was credited to Carson. Two Polish pilots were shot down, one of them, Sgt Derma, was all right but the other, Fg Off Jander was taken to Tobruk with a broken leg. Sgt P T Elliott's machine was hit and he was wounded but he landed safely at El Adem. Two of these losses were claimed by Marseille and the other by Homuth.

Clive Caldwell, writing after the war, was full of praise for the Polish pilots and commented that 'they added their share to the squadron's battle honours as well as to life in the mess.' He went on to say how much he liked the desert and he 'thought there was more beauty there in colour and light effect' although the lack of things to do when off duty was irksome.

On 22nd the squadron moved to a new satellite airfield, Gambut No 2. There were a couple of days of patrolling without incident.

The squadron had left two aircraft behind when they moved. Cg Capt Cross had insisted on making his first flight in a Kittyhawk but this had resulted in two aircraft being damaged – Caldwell is not specific as to what happened other than saying that he was 'critical of the Group Captain's performance'. At Gambut the Gp Capt obtained a brand new Miles Magister for his personal use and the squadron Medical Officer, Fg Off C Joseph, persuaded Caldwell to give him a trip as he had never flown before. The Magister's engine stopped in flight and they had to make a forced landing in rough country below the escarpment completely writing off the Magister and knocking out the MO, who 'was later very critical of the whole performance. So was Gp Capt Cross.' Honours on that occasion appeared to be about even.

On 27th eleven aircraft, led by Plt Off Bartle, flew to Gambut Main to stand at 'readines'. They had hardly left their aircraft for the safety of the pilots' dug-out when the airfield was straffed by five Bf109s. Two Kittyhawks were left burning, one of them being Neville Duke's new machine, AK707 ('Y'). Two were badly shot up, two Cat 2 and another damaged. The remaining four machines scrambled later whereupon Sgt

Jackson (initials unknown), a relative newcomer, pulled too tight a turn, stalled and spun in.

March began with a patrol of six aircraft led by Plt Off Dickenson in the El Adem – Tobruk area. Near El Adem they saw a parachute descending but no sign of any aircraft crash. A search of the area by Dickinson found 20 aircraft scattered around, but they were all burned beyond recognition. That day the Desert Air Force was again reorganised, this time into Groups that each contained three Wings. 112 found itself part of 239 Wing along with 3RAAF, 250 and 450 Sqns, all equipped with Kittyhawks, as part of 211 Group.

Heavy rain curtailed flying activity for the first two weeks of March but the squadron began to receive Kittyhawks fitted with new bomb racks. On 8th Flt Lt Westenra led seven aircraft on a sweep from El Adem to Gazala. At this point Ops (codename 'Blackbird') vectored the formation on to some enemy aircraft five miles north-east. Westenra spotted some MC200s and with his No 2, Sgt Evans, dived to attack them. One went down and flew into the sea but as Jerry Westenra was about to attack again 15 Ju87s appeared out of cloud flying north-west as fast as they could go. Evans saw them and attacked one on the extreme port side firing three bursts. The Stuka crashed into the sea. Fg Off Knapik spotted two Bf109s but because his windscreen then became oiled up he was unable to join in. In face of the lack of opposition it now seems as though this formation was the remnants of one that had been mauled by 450 and 3RAAF Sqns only a short while before. The MC200s and Bf109s were probably part of the original escort and were trying to get home without any more trouble. The Italians had apparently mistaken the Kittyhawks for friendly fighters and had stayed in a tight formation until the moment of attack. There was inevitably some bad feeling generated between the two Axis partners after this *débacle*. That evening Sgt Leu was awarded the DFM.

The squadron moved to Gambut Main on the 9 March 1942 and were lured into the air by a decoy Ju88. Shortly afterwards Bf109s carrying bombs attacked the airfield, one of which disabled a 238 Sqn Hurricane. The Kittyhawks were unable to intercept. On returning Sgt Elliott, an Australian, in AK700 was seen to roll over, dive from about 8000′ and crash near the airfield. No reason was discovered for his death but the opinion at the time was that he was the victim of a sneak attack out of cloud.

On 10 March 1942 there was a significant development. Sqn Ldr Caldwell made the first practice bombing dive, carrying an unfused 250-lb bomb to see whether it could be dropped without carrying away the propellor. Since this might have led to the aircraft crashing the test was done over the sea with the Air-Sea Rescue organisation in attendance. The experiment was a success and that afternoon it was repeated with a live bomb. This was the beginning of a new form of offensive operation for the Kittyhawk since, although the aircraft was far from being outclassed as a fighter, its potential in the battlefield interdiction rôle was now being appreciated. The machine could carry quite a load of bombs and its ability to absorb punishment was already legendary. Thus the 'Kittybomber' was born. Jack Bartle and Peter Down then worked out the method whereby the bomb could be aimed. On the following day Gerry Westenra, Jack Bartle and Hunk Humphreys, the three most experienced squadron pilots, did some practice bombing and at dusk the CO went off to Martuba to see what effect it might have on the enemy, but the bomb fell wide of the target. Jack Bartle, after the war, explained the technique. Initially the aircraft was made to dive at about 45°, aiming at the target. On pulling out, between about 3000′–2000′, you counted to ten, fairly rapidly (about 5 seconds) and released the bomb. The bombs were fitted with a striker extended by 2′ which gave the maximum blast effect. He went on to say that after releasing the bomb it was unwise to climb, so they always turned and dived again, down to ground level and 'hedge-hopped' all the way home, straffing as they went. Generally one flight acted as top cover while the other bombed. The Kittyhawk became rather unmanagable when in the dive and could only be controlled by having both hands on the stick. 112 Sqn had now become the first fighter bomber squadron. On 12 March news came that Neville Duke had been awarded the DFC.

On 13th there was a confused action which resulted in a draw, one all, one Kittyhawk lost and one MC202 destroyed. Twelve aircraft, led by Pit Off Bartle were scrambled just after midday. At 12.15 Sgt Drew dropped out with engine trouble and landed at Bu Amud. Five minutes later some unidentified enemy aircraft were seen to appear out of cloud, right on the formation's tail. In the resulting turnabout the two flights became separated. Bartle with Sgt J W Rozanski, Sgt Burney, Fg Off Knoll and Sgt Cordwell flew north-west towards El Adem. A lone Hurricane was seen at this point which tried to join the formation but was unable to keep up. Over the coast, near some cloud, Bartle and Rozanski were attacked by two Bf109s. They successfully avoided them but were attacked again when they broke cloud. Sgt Rozanski (AK834) was shot down by *Obfw.* Schultz but Bartle got in one burst at an enemy aircraft. Rozanski managed to belly-land and get out before his aircraft burst into flames. Meanwhile the other half of Bartle's section, Burney, Knoll and Cordwell, were aware of enemy aircraft all around them, four Bf109s and five MC202s at sea level going west. They were attacked by a MC202 which overshot Sgt Burney who immediately latched onto its tail and shot it down so that it fell into the sea about 15 miles north of Tobruk. The four Kittyhawks then straggled back to base. The other flight, who had missed all this, had been vectored out to sea by 'Blackbird' where they saw six Bf109s hanging about as though waiting for some bombers to escort, but since no bombers were seen they returned to base.

On 14 March 1942 the squadron had its final operational sortie before going on 14 days leave. 'A' Flt left for Sidi Haneish that morning and in the afternoon the CO led 12 Kittyhawks from Gambut on a diversion sweep to try to intercept enemy fighters shadowing our bombers on their return from Martuba. Near Bir Hakeim two Kittyhawks were seen flying north-east with four MC202s and two Bf109s in pursuit. The CO turned the formation and in the first attack Sgt Simonsen (AK900 'A') and Sgt Evans (AK878) were both hit. Simonsen was killed but Evans baled out and was taken to hospital in Tobruk. Caldwell with his No 2, Sgt Z Urbanczyk, followed the Bf109 down and they both attacked it whereupon it was seen to crash very close to Simonsen's aircraft. Fg Off Knoll attacked the second 109 but without effect. The CO then climbed back up to attack the Macchis, one of which pulled up violently. A few seconds later a fawn coloured parachute was seen drifting down but the machine was not seen to crash. It is possible from post-war correlation of aircraft lost on this day that the Bf109s were in fact MC202s misidentified. The squadron's score now rested at 135½ enemy aircraft destroyed, 24 probably destroyed and 39 damaged. Neville Duke wrote that 'life expectancy was not high due to 109 troubles and particularly later, around Alamein time (when) ground straffing losses were high. Morale was generally very good but living conditions were bad, one was usually unwashed and dirty and always on the move, frequently in retreat! It was not uncommon to remain in the desert for 3 months or more without leave, but life was good!'

On 16th and 17th at Sidi Haneish the squadron sorted itself out and had a pay parade, after which all ranks left for Cairo and Alexandria on what must have seemed a long overdue leave. Of the 23 pilots casualties, killed or missing, since 1939, nine were killed within one month of arriving on the squadron, four were killed within two months, one was killed after three months, three after four months, one after five, one after six and the other four after 12 months. Of the total of 23, 14 were lost in action and the rest in flying accidents. Gerry Westerna, who had joined the squadron in Greece, was now awarded the DFC and posted out, Flt Lt Peter Down took over 'A' Flt. Plt Off Bartle was promoted straight to Flight Lieutenant and given 'B' Flt. Sgt McQueen, who had been injured, returned to the squadron.

On 14 April the official squadron badge was presented to the squadron by the AOC, Air Vice-Marshal 'Mary'[1] Coningham. After the parade the airmen were treated to a rather belated 'Christmas' dinner. Flt Lt Down, recalling these events after the war, remembers that he took the parade as he was the only officer with any pre-war experience of such formal occasions. He relates that one practice parade was held during a sandstorm 'Sometimes I couldn't see the Flights I was shouting at and had to guess their whereabouts.' Immediately afterwards the squadron struck camp and moved up to Gambut No 1 satellite and made ready for operations. Flt Lt Costello rejoined the squadron after 12 months as an instructor, but he only remained for a fortnight. Clive Caldwell left the squadron, returning to Australia to fight the Japanese, handing over to Peter Down, and Hunk Humphreys and Neville Duke were posted out. Three veteran NCO squadron pilots were granted commissions Sgt Leu, Sgt Burney and Sgt Carson became Pilot Officers. Flt Lt Bartle led the first operation on 22nd with 12 Kittyhawks over Hallium and Ezzieat. On 24th Plt Off Leu was sent with 12 aircraft to try to intercept Ju87s bombing Tobruk, but they arrived too late.

On 27th the squadron was visited by Major General HRH The Duke of Gloucester. Peter Down recalls his visit and remarks that the Duke's perceptive comment was 'It's a very sandy place you have here.' Plt Off Dickinson was promoted to Flt Lt and took over 'A' Flt.

For the first few days of May training in fighter bombing took place. Nevertheless, initially, the squadron was still employed in the fighter role and on 7 May 1942 aircraft of 112 and 3RAAF were detailed to act as top cover for a bombing mission. On the return trip they were attacked by two Bf109s, one of which was shot down by 3RAAF and the other by a recent arrival, Plt Off F F J Edwards, on his first operational sortie. I/JG27 who were in action that day reported no losses except for *Lt* Stahlschmidt who crash-landed after one of his guns blew up just as he was about to fire on a Kittyhawk. Perhaps, unbeknown to Stahlschmidt, his aircraft was shot down by Edwards.

Practice bombing continued for several days and on 16th they were used in their new rôle for the first time. Six aircraft carrying bombs with four acting as fighter escort, attacked some tents near Sidi Zaid (Tmimi). Heavy flak was the reply but everyone

---

[1] 'Mary' was derived from his real nickname 'Maori', he being a New Zealander,.

returned to base in high spirits. A dawn patrol the next day attacked Tmimi roadhouse. Six bombs were dropped within a small compass and one was seen to score a direct hit on the inn. All went well until the Kittybombers came down to deck level to strafe. Flak was intense and two aircraft, AK763 with Plt Off J R Fisher (who had joined the squadron on 3 May) and AK994 with Sgt J V Davey failed to return. Sgt Drew was flying with Fisher as his No 2 when Fisher was hit by flak and was seen to crash in flames. Drew bent his airscrew flying too low but managed to get within 12 miles of base before he had to crash land. Sgt Davey was last seen over the target and a report from a South African patrol informed the squadron that an aircraft had crashed behind enemy lines near Temrad. Plt Off Johnson (initials unknown) returned with a shell hole in one of his wings and two aircraft landed at El Adem short of fuel. The bodies of Fisher and Davey were never found. Their names are commemorated on the Alamein War Memorial, but their date of death is incorrectly given as the 17th.

Sqn Ldr Down had left the squadron three days earlier due to illness and his replacement, Sqn Ldr Billy Drake, DFC, appeared on 25th. David B Brown, a later squadron member had this to say about Billy Drake. '. . . once a member of 1 Squadron in France (he) had been shot at while attempting to bale out and had since developed a keen hatred for black crosses . . . A first class CO, apt to be somewhat tough on the ground but a superb and patient leader in the air. As for his ability as a fighter pilot – the sight of him removing the tail of a 109 with one short burst was enough to convince the writer. . . .'

Shortly after leaving 112, Clive Caldwell, now promoted to Wing Commander, made a broadcast on the BBC's Sunday Night Postscript entitled 'The Desert is a Funny Place'. 'I've been fourteen months in the desert' the Wing Commander began, 'and when I left it was almost like leaving a family – I was leaving so many chaps that I knew and was friendly with. Because of the conditions out there you get to know everybody and there's an extraordinary good feeling . . . that is one of the compensations out there. Most of the time you never get away from your aircraft, all day long you've people talking about aeroplanes, and tactics and serviceability and so on and at night time there's no other topic of conversation except flying . . . Everybody, of course, lives in tents. The day starts half an hour before dawn. The engines are warmed up and uncovered. Breakfast is somewhere around 7 o'clock or 7.30 for the airmen who line up with their plates and it's dished out to them – some sort of porridge, not too good because it's made with water that's well-chlorinated and usually brackish, and tea made with the same stuff, which, although you get used to it, is hardly drinkable. Lunch is the same sort of thing – a slice of bully beef with hard biscuit, and you can have margarine, and of course more 'chi' again – that's Arabic for tea. You all get a gallon of water a day, from the CO down to the lowest ACH, half of it goes to the cookhouse and the other half gallon is for washing, shaving and so on. You shave every second or third day, and then there's cleaning teeth and washing. So if you want a bath you've got to save up and that takes you a week probably. But then everyone smells the same so it doesn't matter. It cancels out. And even bully-beef – it's wonderful what you can do with bully-beef when you try. You can have bully-beef with sand, without sand (sometimes), fried, stewed, curried, hot or cold, quite a variation. And then there's the grand day when you get a load of eggs. You can have them hard-boiled or soft-boiled, fried or poached. You can do a lot with eggs.'

Wing Commander Caldwell went on to describe the wonderful effects of light and colour in the desert, but then returned to talking about operations. 'You want to know what flying is like. Well, I should say it's like nowhere else on earth. There are no landmarks in the desert and the heat makes such a haze that there's no horizon at all. You've got nothing to fly on. I've often been up at say 18,000′ with reasonably good visibility. I could see an aircraft six or seven miles away all right. But below me was just haze.'

He continued in this vein but ended his talk with some considerations about the enemy. 'It never pays to underrate the Hun. I regard the Germans as reasonably tough propositions. I was always a stickler for flight discipline. The boys wanted, if they were new, to go flying all over the sky alone until they had learned the dangers of what would happen. The Germans were good at thinking up traps, so I used to have a notice printed up in the place "Use your head, then the guns", just to remind them. For instance you might be flying along under the clouds and then perhaps there'd be an open patch, and an enemy plane or two under that open patch. Well, it always seemed to me that the question is, why should they be there? There's always certain to be something up above and if a couple of ours rush in to get those two on their own, the others would come down and get them. No, there's no such thing as a sitter in the air – at least there is, but you can't tell beforehand.' And with those words of wisdom Clive Caldwell signed off.

Flt Lt Dickinson led another raid on Tmimi airfield on 26 May 1942 with Billy Drake taking part. All six bombs fell on the target, one amongst some tents, one on some MT and the rest on the landing ground. Fg Off Knapik was obliged to land at Gazala, slightly injured. He did not return to the squadron.

On 26th Rommel opened what Major-General Fuller[1] calls the sixth Libyan campaign. From Gazala the British front line ran south to Bir Hakeim but General Ritchie had placed his troops in a series of what were called 'boxes', or fortified positions with all-round defences. Rommel's forces consisted of the 15th and 21st Panzer and 90th Light Divisions, the Ariete and the Trieste Armoured Divisions and six Italian infantry divisions with about 550 tanks and about 90 self-propelled guns. Ritchie faced Rommel with the XIII and XXX Corps and 631 tanks. The RAF was to act now in greater collaboration with the army as Tedder had embraced the doctrine that the largest proportion of his air force's strength was to be used in support of the land battle. Rommel's plan, named 'Operation Theseus', was to hold the British front with the Italian infantry and then swing his armour round to the south and aim to take El Adem and Sidi Resegh, then to turn west and attack the Gazala area from the rear and capture Tobruk.

The fort at Bir Hakeim, garrisoned by the Free French, became the centre of some of one of the fiercest battles, while at 'Knightsbridge', the Guards brigade 'box' at the crossroads on the Capuzzo road between Bir Hakeim and Acroma, confused and vicious fighting took place in what soon descriptively referred to as 'The Cauldron'.

Ten squadron aircraft attempted interceptions on 27 May but without result. At 10.45 hrs five aircraft led by Flt Lt Dickinson took off to bomb pin-point targets. The

[1] 'The Second World War' by Major-General J F C Fuller

squadron carried out 30 bombing sorties[1] that day, dropping 22 250-lb bombs and, at the end of the day, had claimed 47 MT vehicles hit and nine totally destroyed. Flt Lt Dickinson was reported missing. The Wing averaged 350 sorties per day over the next few days. Dickinson returned to the squadron on 28th and there was another day of continuous bombing, aircraft leaving in relays. By the end of the day Flt Lt Dickinson was again missing but this time he did not return, having lost his life.

On 30th there was another full day's bombing and this time Plt Off Burney (AK772, 'Y') did not return. His body was never found. On the last day of the month Plt Off S S Mitchell was lost after barely six days on the squadron. Plt Off Leu was promoted to Flt Lt and given command of 'B' Flt.

On the ground the confused fighting was slowing down and on 31st Rommel appeared to be weakening. This was not the case, however, he was simply pausing for breath. On 1 June 1942 he attacked 150th Brigade 'box' and despite the massive air support that was launched to help the defenders, it fell with the loss of 3000 prisoners. 112 were not apparently airborne until the evening when a fighter sweep ran into six Bf109s and four Ju88s. Plt Off Edwards damaged a Ju88 as did Flt Lt Leu. Plt Off R K Wilson failed to return but was later reported to be a PoW. Sandstorms prevented operations the next day.

On 4 June straffing and bombing missions were resumed and Sqn Ldr Drake reported that he had had the satisfaction of planting a bomb among some troops listening to 'a pep talk by one of their Colonels'. Plt Off E Atkinson was missing that day, another casualty whose grave is not yet known. General Ritchie launched a counter stroke on the Cauldron but this ran into trouble and Rommel, far from being forced to withdraw, now overran the 10th Indian Bde on the 5th, the day that, according to some authorities, was the turning point of the battle. Once again the fighter bombers were switched to meet the enemy's main thrust. Ten aircraft under the CO took off at 10.15 hrs to bomb and recce in the Bir Hakeim area. Near there they spotted four Bf109s and dived on them. The result was that 3 of the 4 were destroyed and the fourth a probable. That day the garrison of Bir Hakeim sent a message of thanks to the squadrons, *'Bravo! Merci for le RAF!'* To which the RAF replied cheerfully *'Merci pour le sport!'* The enemy formation may have been from II/JG27 who were escorting Bf109Es reconnaissance aircraft of 4(H)/12. On the German side only one recce aircraft was recorded as lost.

The whole of 239 Wing flew in support of the ground battle that day as well as giving cover to the bombers although the dust and confusion of the tank battle below gave them little opportunity to intervene effectively. Air to ground missions continued until the end of the month, the results being similar on most occasions – although the scores mounted: 46 enemy vehicles destroyed (6th), two 'flamers' and 25 damaged (9th), eight 'flamers' and 46 others damaged on the 10th, and so on. Sgt D J B White (AL211) was shot down on the 8th but he was reported safe and with the forward troops. On 11 June Sgt E Adye and Sgt D F Greaves were both missing later but Greaves was known to be safe the following day, and Adye seems to have been all right as RAF Records show him as having been discharged in April 1946.

On the night of the 10-11 June 1942 the defenders of Bir Hakeim withdrew but they

[1] A sortie was an individual flight as opposed to a mission or an operation

had served their purpose well. German plans to encircle the British forces had been badly delayed and a staff officer of the *Luftwaffe* Historical Section went so far as to say 'Those nine days were irrecoverable'[1]. Rommel now turned north again and resumed his attacks in the El Adem and Knightsbridge area. British tanks, however, made little progress against the German anti-tank guns and on 14th the Knightsbridge 'box' was abandoned. Tobruk, a town which had on a previous occasion been held successfully, was once more to be left garrisoned in the Germans' rear.

On 12 June the squadron carried out 37 bombing attacks, and one target was described as consisting of one thousand MT vehicles and lorried infantry. The flak was 'intense'. Flt Sgt Cassell (initials not recorded) was shot down near El Adem but was known to be safe. For the next few days the squadron was working from dawn to dusk. On 13th Plt Off Edwards in AK949 was missing from the 19.00 hr operation, Plt Off Carson (AL105) failed to return on the 14.30 operation on the 16th and Sgt R H Newton was missing for a while on the same day. All the squadrons were now working under tremendous pressure and the groundcrew did not have any rest between 4 in the morning until the failing light of evening made it impossible to continue.

On 17 June 1942, as operations reached a crescendo, the Wing bombed and straffed Gazala airfield which was crowded with enemy aircraft and 112 claimed nine machines severely damaged, including one Bf109 and two Fieseler Fi156 *Storches*. Flt Sgt Drew lost his life over Sidi Rezegh, probably Marseille's 101st victim. That day the 'flap' started and all the aircraft were flown to Sidi Azeiz. Now that Bir Hakeim had fallen Rommel had a clear route for his supplies and had reverted to his original plan of smashing through to El Adem and Acroma. The Gazala position was exposed and General Ritchie had no option but to pull out. By 14th the retreat was in full swing and it continued for three days and three nights. By 18th Rommel had taken Gambut, a day after the Wing had hurriedly departed, and on 21st Tobruk, against all hopes and expectations, fell to the Germans.

On 18th the squadron moved back again, from Sidi Azeiz to LG75, near Sidi Barrani and within a couple of days they were bombing Sidi Azeiz. On 21st Flt Lt Leu force-landed behind enemy lines. Plt Off Johnson attempted to land beside him and pick him up but the terrain and enemy fire thwarted him. Fg Off J M S Crichton, a Canadian, was also reported missing but he returned later by way of the army. On 21st Flt Lt Geoff Garton arrived to take over 'B' Flight after the loss of Flt Lt Leu. David Brown remembers him as a paternal figure with a 'regal moustache, given to reading passages from the "feelthy book" from Cairo to the assembled members of his flight, to help boost morale as he put it.' It seems unlikely that he was able to indulge the members of 'B' Flt with such entertainment at this particular time though.

On 26th the squadron claimed that it held the record for the number of sorties flown in the Western Desert. That day the main effort consisted of bombing and escorting Bostons. The majority of pilots did four sorties each that day. Sortie lengths varied between about 45 minutes to one hour. Just before the last mission returned there was a panic and several pilots had to forego their evening meals. In the engagement that followed Fg Off W M Whitamore shot down a Bf109F and Plt Off A B Cuddon was posted missing. That night the squadron moved to LG106 (El Daba) as the enemy

---

[1] '*The Royal Air Force, 1939-1945*' by Richards & Saunders

were approaching rather rapidly. Fg Off J A Milne injured himself in a crash and was posted.

Flt Lt J A Walker, DFC, who had replaced Flt Lt Dickinson as 'A' Flt Cdr, was shot down on the 10.30 operation the next day but returned safely and on 28 June the CO led the squadron on a strafe, bombing trucks and guns on the escarpment around LG102. 'B' Flt left for LG91 (Amiriya), 'A' Flt following on 29th. The month finished with some bomber escorts. Flt Lt Garton was awarded the DFC having flown a bomber out of one of the airfields in the retreat, never having flown a 'heavy' before. Plt Off Cuddon returned having spent some time in an army ambulance.

The retreat had begun. The swiftness of movement and the rapidity of the German decision making completely outclassed the British. Rommel was always up with the front line and always managed to be where the action was crucial. The British, although they had superiority in tank numbers, spread them too thinly and shifted them around too much so that control was lost. 'It was not that the British generals were less able than the Germans. It was that their education was out of date. It was built for trench warfare of 1914-1918 and not for the armoured warfare they were called upon to direct'[1]. The 8th Army escaped, on the whole, and in good order. Rommel made the mistake of not ordering his aircraft to attack the nose-to-tail columns that poured back towards Egypt and by starting his offensive before Malta – that thorn in his side – had been subdued. Instead of halting and bringing up supplies he forced forward into territory that was dominated by the DAF. On 27 June I/JG27 could only fly one mission as it was so short of fuel. General Auchinleck, a tenacious and exemplary leader, took over from General Ritchie.

In the record of 112 squadron's losses in aircrew and aircraft there are peaks and troughs that correspond to the active and quiet times in the desert campaigns. May and June 1942 saw the greatest loss of aircrew, (12), and, naturally enough the highest losses of aircraft. 39 in May and 47 in June. July was also about to be another busy month, although, with the front line becoming static, the large numbers of aircraft lost and damaged did not necessarily mean a large number of aircrew killed and missing.

In Russia the German offensive had taken Sevastopol and now Rommel stood ready to launch his final offensive and capture the Delta. It seemed as though two huge Nazi pincer movements were poised to meet in the oilfields of the Caucasus and Middle East. In London Churchill faced the test of a vote of confidence in the House of Commons but his speech, in which he admitted that the British Empire was in mortal peril, earned him an overwhelming vote of 475 to 25 to remain as prime minister.

July started for the squadron with more bomber escort missions. 200-300 enemy vehicles were attacked. The next day Sqn Ldr Drake claimed a 'probable' when he left a Bf109 going down at low altitude with glycol pouring from it. Sgt White was shot down again on 3rd while attacking 50 troop-carrying vehicles and MT but was reported safe. Escorts to bombers continued as the DAF pounded the German supply lines and troop concentrations. Fg Off Whitamore claimed a Ju87 destroyed and a Bf109F damaged and Sgt Ibbotson claimed another Stuka destroyed on the 4th. Sgt Agnew returned with his aircraft (AK852) badly damaged. Flt Lt Magner, the adjutant for two

---

[1] Fuller, *op cit*

years, left the squadron and was replaced by Plt Off E ('Taffy') Evans.

'Taffy', who was destined to stay with 112 until November 1944, was an ex-school teacher. 'Small, tough and (with) an accent that was pure music hall. Despite his continual groans at the alleged inefficiency of everyone but himself, he did a marvellous job under conditions that could hardly have been worse, with the squadron moving like a travelling circus . . .'[1] He was also described in glowing terms by Peter Illingworth, the squadron commander when 112 were in Italy. 'He really was an excellent chap, we all admired him intensely. The only virgin in the Western Desert. I wonder if he ever married his little girl in Wales . . .'

Sgt D Ibbotson was missing the next day, 7th, having been last seen over the Qattara escarpment but he returned. On 8th there was a successful bombing raid on LG21 with ten aircraft. The CO destroyed one Bf109F and Plt Off Johnson damaged one. On 10 July *Porucznik* (Fg Off) Feliks Knoll, the last remaining Polish pilot on the squadron, was missing over LG102 in AK892. He was killed. Sgt White in a Mk1a Kittyhawk (ET794) another pilot who seemed to bear a charmed life was rescued once again, this time from the sea.

The 8th Army was now at last in a defensive position of strength. For the first time in the desert war both ends of the British line rested in natural features which could not be turned by the flanking movements so beloved by Rommel. On the right the line lay up against the Mediterranean while on the left the 8th Army's flank rested on the Qattara Depression, a vast inland sea of soft sand that was impossible to cross in wheeled or tracked vehicles. Both sides were building up their supplies as quickly as they could but Rommel knew that his lines of communication were now so long that the 8th Army would be ready first. As the line was now holding the first enemy pressure and with the immediate danger past, the squadron was released for 24 hours and there was a rush for the flesh-pots of Alexandria.

On their return the squadron continued very much as before, with more attacks on the enemy's transport. Sqn Ldr Billy Drake was awarded a bar to his DFC – 'Billy', incidentally was his correct first name, not William as some authors suppose. On 18 July seven 500-lb bombs were dropped on 50 MT vehicles on the Markhrad track. The weight of the bombs was now twice that which 112 Sqn had begun with in March.

On 19th there was a big show over LG21. 239 Wing, 233 Wing and some Bostons were sent to attack 'fifty-plus' aircraft, Ju87s, Ju88s and Bf109s. Good bombing resulted in two aircraft left burning and four Ju88s strafed and damaged. These were accounted for by the CO, Plt Off A C Baker (an ex-Battle of Britain pilot), Plt Off Johnson and Sgt Young (initials not known).

Another airfield strafe took place on 20 July 1942 when nine aircraft, led by the CO, took part in a Wing bombing raid on Fuka Main together with 233 Wing and 3RAAF Sqn. About 100 enemy aircraft were seen, including Italian ones. These were effectively bombed with six 500-lb and three 250-lb bombs and then machine-gunned. Flt Lt Garton claimed a MC202, Plt Off Bruce a Ju88, Plt Off J S Barrow two Ju88s, Sgt Ibbotson one Ju88 and Fg Off Crichton another Ju88. Fg Off Whitamore severely damaged a Bf109. Sgt R DeBourke was missing at first having been seen flying towards a flak-defended area with two Bf109s as company, but he returned safely having

[1] David B Brown, correspondence

crashed in our lines. Wg Cdr Mayers OC 239 Wing also failed to return. This was a great loss as Mayers was an excellent Wing leader with eleven confirmed victories. Although taken prisoner that day it is believed he lost his life later when the Ju52 taking him to captivity was shot down.

The following day Flt Lt Garton led a raid on 100 MT vehicles and dug-in guns. Five fires were started amongst the MT. All aircraft returned safely and on 23rd there were 35 sorties over the battle zone and 500- lb and 250- lb bombs were dropped. Plt Off Barrow was shot down by flak, his aircraft, ET970, been seen to explode on impact with the ground. In the last show of the day eight of 112 Sqn's aircraft ran into a formation of twenty-plus enemy bombers and fighters. Fg Off Whitamore claimed to have damaged a Bf109E and Sgt Ibbotson claimed a probable. Flt Lt Walker was promoted to Sqn Ldr and posted to command 250 Sqn. On 23rd Flt Lt Garton and Sgt Young (AK866) both had to force-land but both returned.

On the ground General Auchinleck had begun a counter-offensive in which he hoped to push the Germans back towards the Egyptian frontier but it made very little progress and tanks were lost for no gain. On 24th there was a raid on LGs 20 and 104 with Baltimores and Bostons. The CO claimed a Bf109, Plt Off J E Loree, a Canadian, a Ju88 and Plt Off J G Wright, another Canadian, a Bf109F. The first two went down and burned on the ground and the third was confirmed by the Bostons. Plt Off Johnson was missing after being attacked by Bf109s by II/JG27 as he came out of his bombing dive but he was seen to crash-land 15 miles south-east of the target.

On 27 July there were 28 sorties. Two aircraft (ET865 and ET527) force-landed in our lines with oil trouble. Geoff Garton led an armed recce and the CO led an interdiction operation over the El Alamein area. Plt Off Cuddon who had force-landed ET527 thumbed a lift in a Lysander and was soon back with the squadron.

By the end of the month Auchinleck's rather sporadic offensive had petered out as the balance of strength was still not yet in our favour and our tanks were still outgunned by the Germans. Churchill was unimpressed by 'The Auk' who had declined to attack again until his reinforcements were acclimatised and so shortly afterwards there was a shake up in the Middle East command. General Sir Harold Alexander succeeded Auchinleck as C-in-C Middle East and Lieut-General Bernard Montgomery took over command of the 8th Army from Ritchie. Once again it was a question whether the British or the Germans[1] could build up their supplies faster.

The squadron went on leave from 3 to 10 August and did not return to operations until the 20th. There were flying practices from 12th to 19th and a new arrival, Sgt H V Schofield, was killed on 15th and was buried near the Cairo-Alexandria road. The first operational mission was on the 21 August when Wg Cdr David Haysom, later to become well-known as the originator of the Cab-Rank scheme with the callsign 'Rover David', led an armed recce in the central area of the Alamein front. Ten Bf109s appeared above and three attacked but to no effect. There was another Tac-R the next day but no bombs were dropped; later that day 50 vehicles were attacked.

Armed reconnaissance continued on 23 August and MT were bombed. The diary mentions that the Germans might use parachute troops in their next attack. Two hundred MT vehicles were found and attacked with four 500-lb and three 250-lb

---

[1] At this time the *Afrika Korps* was renamed *Panzerarmee Afrika*

bombs and a similar mission later found another large concentration of transport. Two days later the squadron moved from Amiriya to LG175, about eight miles to the south-east as conditions were better there with less dust. That day a concentration of 150 vehicles was bombed with four 500-lb and one 250-lb bombs which resulted in a fire and other damage.

On 28 August Capt Danny Saville, the new 'A' Flt Cdr, a South African, led a formation of eight aircraft to act as top cover to 250 Sqn on an armed recce of the Deir-el-Abyad area and south of the Qattara Depression. They were attacked by six Bf109s after the bombing run and Plt Off Loree (ET1017)[1] and Sgt Barlow (AK746), who had arrived that month, were shot down. One pilot was seen to bale out but this was probably Barlow who was later reported to be a PoW. One Bf109 attacked the formation on its return flight and Plt Off Wright claimed to have had a shot at it.

Capt E C Saville who had joined the squadron on 15 August on the departure of Flt Lt Walker was, in David Brown's pen picture, 'a cherubic-faced South African. Tousle-headed and inevitably dressed in the exiguous shorts which was the SAAF uniform when not flying. He was a first class fighter pilot and leader in the air, the good natured butt of countless jokes on the ground as his wit was not of the most brilliant and, when merry, he was for all the world like a very large and very sleepy baby.'

The CO led a mission of six aircraft on 30 August as top cover to No 3SAAF and 450 Sqns. Fifteen Bf109s and MC202s were seen and four Italian machines daringly attacked but without doing any harm. A second patrol confirmed earlier information that the Germans had concentrated 1500 to 2000 vehicles in a map reference square 8526-8725-8726. No doubt an omen of Rommel's coming offensive.

That night Rommel decided to wait no longer. His supply position was getting desperate. SIGINT's decoding of enemy signals allowed Royal Navy submarines and Malta based aircraft to notch up a significant number of sinkings and, with the German drive to Stalingrad taking priority, the Axis forces in the Mediterranean received less and less support. Rommel was nevertheless determined to strike first before Montgomery could launch his offensive. He opened with a three-pronged attack against the 8th Army. The northernmost attack was a feint, the central thrust was a holding operation but the real blow was designed to fall in the south, a right hook towards the Alam Halfa Ridge where the 10th Armoured Division stood. Had he succeeded he would have cut off the bulk of the 8th Army. In fact Montgomery had used the breathing space wisely. The morale of the troops had been boosted and the equipment they were now receiving was, at long last, as good as, if not better, than that of the Germans; also the skilfully sited anti-tank defences were instrumental in blunting the thrust of the panzer divisions. The fourth factor was the hammering Rommel's forces received from the air.

On the last day of August Capt Saville led four aircraft acting as medium cover to Bostons and Mitchells with the rest of the Wing flying as close and top cover. The bombing was reported to have been good and the 500 enemy vehicles were subjected to some nice pattern bombing.

September started with similar missions, one of which included escorts to USAAF B-25s. The Wing was scrambled from LG175 at 14.00 hrs and they encountered one

[1] This unusual serial number, and another, ET1024, are probably ex-USAAF.

Bf109 flying over Bir-el-Munassib; Capt Saville claimed it as a 'probable'. After that they waded into 50-plus Ju87s and 30 Bf109s heading due west over the Qaret-el-Abd area. The score was two Ju87s by the CO, one Ju87 by Capt Saville, one Ju87 by Plt Off H Phillips, a Canadian, and one damaged by Plt Off T Livingstone, with no loss to the squadron. In the final operation that day led Flt Lt Garton 112 acted as cover to Baltimores. Some enemy aircraft attacked and a Baltimore went down over the target area. General Bayerlein, Rommel's Chief of Staff, is said to have admitted that RAF air superiority was now complete and was perhaps decisive in the land battle.

On 2 September 1942 the squadron continued acting as cover to bombers whose targets were mainly pin-point positions in the Deir-el-Daayis area. On 3rd Baltimores attacked 400 enemy MT west of Reir-el-Ragil. Sgt Ibbotson (EV365) was attacked by four or five Bf109s while in a turn, but he managed to shoot one down and return with his aircraft Cat 1. Enemy aircraft were frequently seen but they seemed now far more hesitant to attack the formations.

The 4th was another day of escorts to the bombers, but on 5th the Wing was scrambled at 11.25 hrs and they were attacked by four Bf109s. Capt Saville damaged one but Sgt H E Thomas, a New Zealander, flying AK701 was last seen with a Messerschmitt on his tail and bullets streaming into his aircraft. Thomas is not known to have been killed and is not listed as missing, so it is possible he survived, perhaps wounded. That day Rommel started to withdrew under Montgomery's counter-attacks; the battle of Alam Halfa had been won.

On 12 September six aircraft were scrambled at 10.00 hrs together with 250 and 450 Sqns. They intercepted 25 Ju87s and 20 Bf109s over the El Alamein area. Sgt W E Pollock was credited with one Stuka confirmed and one damaged. Sgt Greaves claimed one probable and one damaged, Capt Saville got a Ju87 and a probably Bf109 and another Stuka damaged. Sgts D Hogg and W Money both claimed to have damaged a Ju87.

The total score was one destroyed, three probables and five damaged. 112's casualties were negligible. Sgt Money landed at LG100, short of fuel and Sgt Hogg (ET789) landed wheels down in the forward area having been damaged by a Messerschmitt. His aircraft was Cat 2.

On 13 September the CO led the Wing, 112 Sqn, 3RAAF, 450RAAF, and 250 Sqns, in a scramble over the front line. The El Alamein area was seen to be under attack by Bf109s and some of these were encountered shortly afterwards. The CO himself claimed one and Sgt Ibbotson claimed a probable. Sgt J H Morrison was shot down but landed safely wheels up, his machine being destroyed by fire.

Such combats were brief and straightforward but one during the late afternoon of 15 September was both involved and costly. Ten Kittyhawks of 450 Sqn acting as top cover to eight of 3RAAF were directed to a point ten miles south-west of El Alamein. There they sighted eight Bf109s above them and another seven up-sun, well positioned. Within a few minutes there was a general dog-fight in progress. More enemy fighters joined in but after 15 minutes of strenuous fighting 112 and 250 Sqns appeared on the scene. This time the advantage of height was with the reinforcements and the 109s were driven off. Four aircraft were burning on the ground and three parachutes were in the air and a Kittyhawk and a 109 were spinning down after colliding. The two Australian squadrons lost three pilots that day with another wounded but only claimed one. Sgt Young of 112 was shot down for the third time – on this occasion by 'white' (friendly) AA fire and was obliged to force-land his aircraft which immediately burst into flames. Nothing more was heard of him until the squadron learned that he was in the 64th General Hospital with severe burns. The Bf109s had consisted of 18 from I/JG27, 15 from II/JG27 and ten from III/JG27. Marseille claimed seven Kittyhawks shot down that day, *Lt* Liers claimed two, *Hpt* Homuth one, *Oblt* Börngen one, *Lt* Schroer two and a Spitfire and *Uffz* Stückler one, a total of 14 Kittyhawks and a Spitfire. In fact only six Kittyhawks appear to have been destroyed in this combat and this may underline the comment made[1] that this period saw a great number of rather dubious claims made by pilots of the Axis air forces. At the time there was no way of comparing unit records so it is possible that many claims on both sides were made in good faith.

In the same way that 112 had seen the distinctive spinners of JG27, JG27 had learned to recognise 112 as Hans Ring and Werner Girbig quote a comment about '*die . . . Curtiss der 112 Squadron mit den Haifisch-Schnauzen . . .*'[2]

On 16 September two MC202s appeared in front of the squadron formation having just done a diving attack on 3RAAF and 250 Sqns. Flt Lt Garton probably dealt with one, helped by Plt Off L H Curphey, an American, who had a shot at it. 'Bunny' Curphey had been on the squadron since early July and he and 'Big Joe' Crichton were inseparable buddies. Bunny, the smaller of the two was 'quick like a sparrow with a ready wit and a happy grin for one and all. Joe was built like a wrestler and used his muscles to good effect to coax a little more manoeuvrability out of the Kittyhawk. After ten minutes dog-fighting in the midday heat with both hands hauling back on the stick it became a question of stamina – and he had the answer. On the ground he was quiet-voiced, shy as a schoolboy'[3].

The next day Danny Saville received the award of the DFC and the squadron was involved in non-operational flying. Now the heat was off temporarily there was time to bring the new pilots up to scratch and stand-downs were more frequent. Missions were fewer that month than at almost any other time. Towards the end of September some American pilots from the 64th USAAF Sqn were attached to learn the ropes. On 29 September 1942 there was a brush with five Bf109s of III/JG27 and two MC202s but there was no decisive result. The last day of the month saw the squadron patrolling the front line. During this flight Sgt Morrison's aircraft (ET795) mysteriously caught fire in the air and he crash-landed near El Hanwariya. Except for cuts and bruises he was all right but he did not return to the squadron. He was luckier that day than *Hptm* Hans-Joachim Marseille of I/JG27 who baled out of his Bf109G at 10,000' when a fuel pipe fractured, but was hit by his tailplane and fell to his death without opening his parachute. Marseille, whose motto was taken from a quotation by Garcia Morato, '*Vista, Suerte, y al toro*'[4], was undoubtedly the highest-scoring pilot in the Western Desert. JG27 had lost three of its most successful *experten* that month.

The squadron was involved in two scrambles on 1 October, one at 14.25 hrs when

[1] Shores & Ring, *op cit*
[2] 'the Curtiss of 112 Squadron with the sharknose', Ring & Girbig, *op cit*
[3] David Brown, correspondence
[4] 'Good sighting, good luck and at the bull!', quoted in Owen, *op cit*

nothing was seen and one at 17.30 hrs when they were acting as top cover to 250 Sqn at about 6000' over El Maghara. They were vectored on to 14 Ju87s of III/St.G3 and 20 Bf109s of JG53. In the resulting dog-fight the CO (EV168) and Flt Lt Garton (EV136) shared a confirmed Ju87 and a probable Ju87 each, Plt Off Curphey (EV339) also got a confirmed Ju87. Other probables were claimed by Fg Off Livingstone and Flt Sgt R C C Smith; Sgt M H Lamont damaged a Stuka and Plt Off Wright damaged a Bf109. Sgt Money returned with bullet holes in his aircraft. The Messerschmitt pilots commented that, when attacked, the Stukas had split into two formations which made their task more difficult. 112's total score was two destroyed, four probables and two damaged.

The next day, the 2nd, there was a scramble at 08.55 hrs but this produced no result. On the 10.10 mission four aircraft took off on a training flight but at 17,000' Sgt G Rae, who had been on the squadron barely three days, crashed in flames and was killed. That afternoon, at 16.30 hrs, Fg Off Joe Crichton led six aircraft with 3RAAF Sqn as top cover over the front line. They were attacked by two groups of Bf109s. Sgt J M MacAuley (EV360) got in three bursts of fire on one enemy aircraft and saw the pilot bale out with black smoke streaming from the engine. Fg Off Crichton damaged another. These aircraft may have been MC202s and two machines from *4° Stormo* were lost that day. A later scramble led by Danny Saville chased four Bf109s which were bombing south of Deir-el-Dhib. Saville got two *Jabos* confirmed, both of which fell in flames. Plt Off Phillips and Fg Off Livingstone damaged another. On their return they received a dose of flak, probably from the 15th Panzers but this did not prevent Plt Off R G Sayle from shooting up a tent and receiving in return a bullet in his petrol tank. One of Danny Saville's victims was *Lt* Walter Burger of III/ZG1[1].

There were no ops until 6th when the squadron dropped nine 500-lb and two 250-lb bombs on a hundred enemy vehicles. There were similar sorties the next day and Plt Off G W Wiley force-landed his aircraft and broke a leg. Bombing, armed recces and bomber escorts continued until 20th without incident. On 20 October a formation from 112, acting as top cover to bombers raiding Fuka LG, were attacked by MC202s and Bf109s and followed all the way back to El Alamein. Sgt MacAuley claimed to have damaged a MC202 and Flt Sgt Smith, on a later mission, claimed a Bf109 which he attacked from below. His victim may have been *Uffz* Jürgens from the *Alert Schwarm* of II/JG27, all that was left of this *Jagdstaffel*, based at Fuka. Sgt Greaves was reported missing from this action having last been seen flying east in the area of LG21 (Qotafiyah III) west of El Daba. He was later reported to be a PoW.

Sgt Hogg (FR236) was also missing the next day after an escort mission with P-40Fs of 66 USAAF Sqn attacking LG20 (Qotafiyah I). He too was later reported to be a prisoner. Later 112 escorted 18 Mitchells raiding LGs 20 and 104 (Qotafiyah II). On 22nd Sqn Ldr Drake led a 'de-lousing' sweep with 66 USAAF and 145 Sqns again in the El Daba area. On the way home they saw four Bf109s which they attacked. Flt Lt Smith destroyed one, the CO a probable, a third damaged by Curphey and a fourth shared by Danny Saville and another (unrecorded) pilot.

That day Billy Drake got the whole squadron together and informed them that the battle of El Alamein would start at 22.00 hrs the following night. Montgomery now had three Corps, the Xth (Lieut-Gen Sir Herbert Lumsden), XIIIth (Lieut-Gen B C

---

[1] JG27, whose morale was now low, was withdrawn to Sicily for a month.

Horrocks) and XXXth (Lieut-Gen Sir Oliver Lees) comprising, in all, seven infantry divisions, three armoured divisions and seven armoured brigades, a total of about 150,000 men with 1100 tanks. In the air the DAF had 1500 first-line aircraft of which 1200 were in Egypt compared with the *Luftwaffe* and *Regia Aeronautica's* strength of 3000 machines in the whole of the Mediterranean, of which only 689 were in North Africa.

Rommel's army consisted of eight infantry and four armoured divisions, about 96,000 men and about 550 tanks. The Axis force was too small to hold 40 miles of front despite the extensive minefields and there was no convenient ridge, such as at Alam Halfa, which to pivot back on if necessary. What was more significant, though, was the fact that Rommel was back in Berlin and the *Afrika Korps* was commanded by General von Stumme who had made the mistake of spreading his forces, infantry and tanks, far too thinly instead of concentrating his armour in preparation for a counter-attack.

Montgomery's plan was one of deception. He managed to persuade the Germans that the main blow would fall in the south, intending to deliver it in the north. Dummy tanks and vehicles were laid out in the XXX Corps area while in the north camouflage was extensively used to conceal the mass of vehicles and armour. The time since the battle of Alam Halfa had been used by Montgomery to continue training, re-equipping and revitalising the 8th Army. With the new Sherman tanks and the huge forward supply dumps, confidence had returned to the Allied army. Rommel had also used the time wisely, building deep static defences that were to be held by the Italian infantry divisions stiffened by German paratroop units.

The painful lessons of Norway, France, Greece, Crete and Singapore had at last been learned and air superiority was, to all intents and purposes, complete. As a result enemy reconnaissance had failed to pick up the massive concentration of *matériel* and were apparently unaware of what was about to happen.

That day the squadron had flown 30 sorties, twelve at 07.05 hrs on a bombing raid on LG104 and six aircraft on a sweep of the central sector of the front. On the third and final mission twelve aircraft bombed LG104 again and all bombs were dropped. The standard load for the Kittyhawk III was one 500-lb bomb or two 250-lb bombs, supplemented occasionally by six 40-lb bombs on wing racks. Ageing Kittyhawk IAs, of which there were still some on 112, could only carry one 250-lb bomb. These were armed and released electrically, as were the 40-lb bombs, but in the MkIIIs the belly bomb was released by a handle on the cockpit floor.

David Brown, who had joined the squadron early in September, can look back on those days with equanimity and nostalgia. 'It was all very thrilling in retrospect' he concedes, 'but that wasn't quite the way we saw it then[1]'. He remembers that the new-comers were immediately made to feel at home, which was especially cheering after the months spent in transit camps and on temporary postings. 'For one thing, there was a touch of frontier spirit about the welcome, an open-hearted warmth expressed in a variety of accents from well-nigh all corners of the free world – including a surprising number from the USA – at having joined a "family" faced with a tough, rewarding job.' He was understandably shy about joining a new Mess where, in the curiously democratic community of the DAF, officers and NCO pilots all mixed

---

[1] from an article 'The Desert Sharks' '*The Air Enthusiast*', March 1978,

together. He remembered particularly the table just inside the entrance to the Mess where the aircrew piled their belts and .38 pistol holsters, the intense concentration of the poker school in the distant smoky corner of the tent, the magnificent 'desert lily'[1] just outside, the bar with the painting on the front of a 'Stuka party'. The conversation stayed at the social chit-chat level only briefly before returning to 'shop', talk of aircraft handling, tactics, the weak points of the Bf109s and Macchi 202s, the magnificent way the ground crews performed, and the army's appreciation of 112's efforts. 'When at last we weaved towards bed it was with the conviction that 112 was quite a bunch of characters'.

He then went on to describe the sight of the sharksteeth markings on the Kittyhawks 'That glaring mouth transformed the appearance of the stubby machine into an eager fighting aeroplane that made you itch to get your hands on her.' David Brown, a sergeant pilot in those days, had done his operational training on Hurricanes and Spitfires, and he had heard that the Kittyhawk was something of a handful to fly, undercarriages jamming half-way up, a tendency to spin, ground-loops when you landed and the haphazard arrangement of the flying instruments. 'The "upside-down" needle and ball indication of balanced flight, a solid stick instead of the split stick on Masters, Hurricanes and Spitfires, the increased use of electrics for vital services and the substitution of inches of mercury for psi (lb-per square inch) as the measure of supercharger boost' were all unfamiliar to him. A few days were spent by the newcomers 'back at school' learning to fly as a member of the team 'where there could be no passengers', practising battle formation flying, the use of minimum R/T, and learning how to be an effective No 2 by weaving properly and searching for possible enemy aircraft, not just staring at the sky. They were taught how to take off in close formation, how to patrol, dive-bomb, strafe ('sometimes camelthorn-close to the ground'), shadow-firing, dog-fighting 'with veterans who did utterly impossible things with their aeroplanes . . . sure in the knowledge that if they got on your tail it was up to you to buy drinks all round, tail chasing and finally landing in close formation, often with the CO watching.' David Brown remembers that flying discipline was very strict and any lapses were punished by the offender being made to trudge round the landing ground carrying his parachute. 'It was hard work but gradually by a combination of fair, sometimes harsh, criticism and the odd word of encouragement here and there, we found we were flying with growing confidence as members of the team . . .' After some time being nursed to a condition when his flight commander considered him ready for operational flying, David Brown wrote that 'one's first "show" tends to live in the memory as clearly as first solo; particularly those little points which no amount of practice could simulate; seeing you name on the operational "gaggle-board"; the hearty slap on the back and the thumbs-up signs from your ground crew as they helped you strap in; the sluggish feeling of the Kittyhawk on the "bombed-up" climb; a tendency to hunch into the far corner of the cockpit as the first puffs of anti-aircraft fire blossomed suddenly as we approached the target; the sheer incredibility of the steep angle of the first real bombing dive; the joyful horse-at-a-fence surge of the Kitty after bomb release; the thrill of the upwards-and-sideways zoom allowing the glimpse of a well-plastered target and, finally, the warm, lasting gut-reaction of delight in survival.'

[1] 'Desert lily', the thunderbox or latrine

He also remembers a time when, during a de-briefing session he happened to describe his opponents as 'the gentlemen with the white spinners' (I/JG27) at which Billy Drake, whose experience hanging from a parachute no doubt influenced his opinion, retorted 'They are not *gentlemen*, Brown, they are bloody Huns and it is our business to kill them.' Today, so many years after the war, it is something well worth recalling that the very real threat of German world domination, bringing in its wake the hideous creed and paraphanalia of National Socialism, required fanaticism in return – the unswerving determination to defend our liberty and defeat the enemy.

Once he was back at LG91, David Brown felt that at last he was qualified to join 'the little circle of pilots seated in camp chairs outside the Mess after the last trip of the day, enjoying a tankard of Stella and talking shop . . . we were becoming accepted as members of the family and soon, what with the increasing frequency and variety of operations – it became obvious that we would shortly bless every moment spent in training . . .'

At 21.40 hrs on the evening of 23 October when 1000 guns opened up on the six-mile front, the pilots drank a toast to the success of the 8th Army.

CHAPTER FOUR

Alamein to Tunis

At 22.00 hrs on 23 October 1942 the Allied infantry moved forward and by 05.30 hrs the next morning two lanes had been cleared by the engineers through the German minefields on XXX Corps' front. By 07.00 hrs the following day the first objective, the Miteiriya Ridge, had been taken and the 1st and 10th Armoured Divisions were advancing up to it.

Over the battlefield that day the squadron pilots could see very little except the artillery bombardment. 112 provided top cover on both the northern and southern sectors, and to bombers raiding near Gazal railway station. No enemy aircraft were seen.

The 25th was the crucial day of the battle as, with von Stumme killed, Rommel had hastily returned to take charge and was gathering his armour for the counter-attack. There were escorts to Baltimores and Mitchells attacking enemy forward positions but there were still no enemy aircraft and even the flak seemed less intense – the 88mm guns were probably busy in the anti-tank rôle. On 26th Billy Drake damaged one Bf109 which went down vertically with glycol pouring out. Glycol, so frequently noted in these attacks, was a fluid used as a coolant. Loss of this coolant would inevitably result in the engine seizing up. The black smoke that 112's pilots saw coming from the engines of Bf109s as they fell away was more likely to be evidence, not of fire, but of the fuel injection system being switched on to give additional boost. Plt Off Wright (FR279) and Fg Off K R Gardiner (FR263) were both missing on the return from the 09.00 hr operation. Gardiner was killed but Gary Wright returned with a bandage round his head and claiming a Bf109.

In the afternoon efforts on the ground were directed to preventing the Axis counter-attack from getting under way while the squadron was engaged in keeping enemy aircraft from interfering in the action by raids on LG20 and LG104, which were bombed with 500-lb bombs. Rommel had launched a series of violent counter-thrusts that day on XXX and X Corps which were all repulsed. Montgomery now regrouped his forces and ordered XIII Corps in the centre to remain on the defensive, X Corps on the northern flank was withdrawn and XXX Corps ordered to take its place and deepen the salient.

On 27 October the CO led 12 aircraft providing close cover for bombers going to Fuka. Three MC202s bounced the formation over the target and all three were shot down, one by Billy Drake, one by 'Bunny' Curphey and one by Plt Off D A Bruce.

Bruce followed his victim down to ground level and had the satisfaction of seeing it crash and explode. Sgt A Martin was missing from this operation but was subsequently reported safe. Later there was an escort to Sidi-el-Rahman and LG104, which was said to have been 'black with bomb craters'.

That day I/JG27, back from Sicily, resumed operations and JG/53 withdrew from Africa, never to return. Rommel, meanwhile, had been probing our defences for weak spots and, having found one, was forming up his Panzer divisions for an attack the next day. The DAF's bombing helped to disperse the armour again. Meanwhile 112 was attacking MT and tents in the Jebel Kalakh area and patrolling the central sector of the front. No enemy aircraft were seen on any of these operations. On 29th LG21 was again attacked by 12 aircraft and again no aerial opposition was encountered and only a little flak.

On 31 October there was a big scrap. After bombing a group of tents the Kittyhawks were vectored on to some Ju87s escorted by Bf109s of I/JG27 and II/JG77 and MC202s which were on their way to bomb 9 Australian Div that was under fierce pressure on the right of the Allied line. The enemy formation was intercepted and in the subsequent dog-fight the CO and Flt Lt Smith both claimed a Ju87 each, Plt Off Curphey, Plt Off Cuddon, Sgt Lamont and Sgt David B Brown all claimed probable Bf109s. Plt Off Phillips claimed a probable MC202. A second operation, led by Capt Saville at 11.40 hrs saw no enemy aircraft but that evening he had better luck. With 12 aircraft bombing and straffing between El Daba and Fuka, they met 20-plus Ju87s and some Bf109s. Fg Off Crichton claimed a Bf109F destroyed, Flt Sgt Newton one Ju87 probable, Flt Sgt W D Brown two Ju87s destroyed, Sgt Wild one Ju87 destroyed and one Bf109F damaged, Sgt Money one Bf109F destroyed and Sgt D S ('Butch') Watson, a pre-war RAF regular, one Bf109F damaged. Plt Off Bruce (FR281) was reported missing, but he turned up later having ditched.

David Brown described Flt Sgt W D ('Canada') Brown, as 'a real tough back-woodsman, always saying the wrong thing to the wrong person, getting tight and picking a fight with all and sundry, having his leg pulled unmercifully by all of us but ready to give the last shirt off his back to anyone who needed it. From the beginning he showed a fighting spirit in the air that made us lesser mortals quail. (Once) he bit off rather more than he could chew and got chased home by an unfriendly 109. His hair was literally parted by a cannon shell and he arrived back at the squadron with a rueful "What have I done now?" grin beneath a grisly-looking bandage, inordinately proud of the dried blood which caked his Mae West and parachute.'

On the ground Rommel had sent his armour north to try to relieve the 90th Light Division that was penned with its back to the sea by the 9th Australian Division. Heavy fighting continued in this area until the 1 November when XXX Corps was ready to attack on a 4000 yard front.

The Squadron officers and SNCO aircrew during October were as follows —

> Sqn Cdr: Sqn Ldr Drake
> 'A' Flt Cdr: Capt Saville
> 'B' Flt Cdr: Flt Lt Garton
> Sqn Adjutant: Fg Off Evans
> Sqn Intelligence Officer: Fg Off Carroll

Sqn Ground Defence Officer: Plt Off Rhodes
Sqn Engineering Officer: Plt Off Legg
Sqn Technical Officer: Fg Off Pepper
Sqn Medical Officer: Flt Lt Eberle

Fg Off Crichton	Sgt Greaves
Fg Off Livingstone	Sgt DeBourke
Fg Off Gardener	Sgt Hogg
Plt Off Phillips	Sgt Martin
Plt Off Wiley	Sgt Brown, D B,
Plt Off Cuddon	Sgt Snelgrove
Plt Off Ibbotson	Sgt Watson
Plt Off Bruce	Sgt Webb
Plt Off Curphey	Sgt Lamont
Plt Off Sayle	Sgt Clarke
Plt Off Wright	Sgt MacAuley
Flt Sgt Agnew	Sgt Wild
Flt Sgt Shaver	Sgt Money
Flt Sgt Howe	Sgt Shaw
Flt Sgt Smith	Sgt Marsden
Flt Sgt Brown, W D,	Sgt Lecours
Sgt Pollock	Sgt Newton

A total of 14 officer pilots, six non-aircrew officers and 23 NCO pilots. As before there is no clear indication as to whether there was a distinct two-flight system or, if so, which pilots were in which flight. The length of time a pilot remained in the same rank is striking in comparison with the RAF of the 1990s, but when wartime promotion came it was sometimes very rapid.

November 1942 started with six enemy aircraft claimed destroyed, three probable and two damaged. Geoff Garton led an armed recce of 12 aircraft at dawn on the 1st with P-40Fs Warhawks of the 66th USAAF Squadron of the 57th Fighter Group. American Fighter Groups were attached to DAF Wings around this time in order to gain much needed combat experience. After bombing some tents 30 Ju87s of I and III/St.G3 escorted by Bf109s of I and II/JG27 and I and III/JG77 was intercepted. In the fight that followed Flt Lt Garton (FR213) claimed one Ju87 destroyed with the pilot baling out, Sgt Watson (FR279) claimed another Stuka, Flt Sgt Smith (FR263) destroyed another in flames and damaged a second, Sgt Wild (FR789) destroyed one Ju87 and damaged another, Plt Off G F Allison, (FR215) an Australian who had been on the squadron since May, opened his score with a probable, as did Sgt T A Marsden (FR302) while Sgt DeBourke destroyed two Ju87s and damaged one. DeBourke was wounded in the shoulder but he managed to return to base and make a perfect landing. The only other casualty was WO J B 'Paddy' Agnew, recently promoted from Flt Sgt, who was obliged to force-land within our lines. It was reported that the Stukas, in their haste to be gone, jettisoned the bombs on their own troops.

David Brown describes the type of flying by saying that 'On fighter sweeps and armed recces the Squadron usually flew twelve aircraft in two sixes: Red and Blue

Sections, callsigns were "Babette" at first and "Ludo" later. Each section comprised three No 1s flying line abreast about 50 yards apart, with their No 2s weaving behind them. Red Section would lead with Blue flying above and to one side. Cross-over turns were used whereby the outer pairs would climb or descend depending upon whether they were on the inside or outside of the turn and cross to the other side of the formation. The standard of battle formation was generally excellent and it was an inspiring sight to see six aeroplanes flying this loose type of formation yet keeping a steady position at all times. If the formation was "jumped" (attacked) and if the "jumper" was not seen until the last minute the order "Scram left" or "Scram right" was given and then it was a matter of every man for himself with each pair pulling round in a steep turn, yet maintaining the fluid six formation. For dog-fighting the sections would split up into individual pairs, No 1s attacking and No 2s weaving and protecting. Naturally, in a prolonged engagement, pairs became split but this did not happen often and when it did it usually meant casualties. Fighter sweeps were usually flown at between 15,000' up to 18,000'. Once or twice, just after Alamein, Billy Drake led us up to about 22,000'. There the Kittyhawk was beginning to breathe a bit hard but the opposition, who at that time were accustomed to fly a little bit lower and look down for us, were duly surprised. For dive bombing we would usually aim to fly out about 10,000', 12 aircraft in the usual battle formation. When the target had been sighted the leader would usually approach so that the dive would be made out of the sun. In good time he would call "Echelon port" or "Echelon starboard", whereupon the left-hand pairs in each section would cross over, No 2s move out in echelon on their No1s and Blue Section would move down beside Red so that without delay there would be 12 aeroplanes in fairly close echelon, stepped up. At this stage there was no weaving and Black 2, or Green 2, at the tail of the echelon would feel a little vulnerable, but it didn't last for long. The leader, whenever possible, would aim to run up so that the target disappeared beneath his wing leading edge, between gun ports and the wing root. Then, as he estimated the target was approaching the trailing edge he would call "Going down!" and, as the target appeared he would call "Go!", wing over and then down as steeply as possible. The dive was usually about 60°, sometimes more, and all cordially agreed that the steeper it was the better we liked it. A shallow dive meant a worrying time for the last few members of the formation. The leader would dive to about 2000', gunsight centred on the target. Then he would pull out, count three, and pull the bomb release, then climb away fairly steeply at medium throttle to let the rest of the formation catch up. This would be done very quickly indeed, as can be imagined, with aeroplanes weaving and skidding all over the place to evade the black and white AA puffs which usually began to pop up at this stage. Skidding was quite effective in the Kittyhawk. As speed built up in the dive the aeroplane tended to yaw quite strongly to starboard. Instead of trimming, most of us would keep the ball (on the Turn & Slip indicator) centralised by brute force on the rudder then, during the pull-out, take our feet off the pedals. The resultant skid would have been horrifying in normal flying conditions but it was inordinately comforting when we thought of the Breda and 88mm gunners trying to follow a bunch or aeroplanes travelling in directions very different to those in which they were pointing. During this period the standard

Baling out slit trenches after the rains at Antelat in January, 1942. *Neville Duke*

The result of trying to land in a dust-storm on 27th January 1942 at Mechili. GA-X (probably AK583) seems virtually undamaged. The open panel on the fuselage suggests that someone had already been quick enough to remove the desert survival rations. *Sqn Ldr R. Testor via R. C. Jones*

Sqn Ldr Clive ("Killer") Caldwell, CO from January to April 1942, with Fg Off Peter ("Hunk") Humphreys. Antelat, January 1942. *Neville Duke*

GA-F, with the tarpaulin engine cover partly removed. Note the extended striker on the 250 lb bomb. This was to deliver an above-ground burst to maximise damage to materiel and injury to enemy personnel. Gambut, February 1942. Jack Barber believes this to have been Neville Duke's aircraft. *Jack Barber*

Sqn Ldr Clive Caldwell seen here driving an open Morris 15 cwt gharry with the intake of Polish pilots who joined 112 in February 1942 at Gambut Main. Amongst the group are Flt Lt Gazda, Fg Off Jander, Fg Off Matusiak, Fg Off Knoll, Plt Off Knapik, Sgt Rozanski and Sgt Urbanczyk. *IWM (CM2422)*

A group of six airmen well stocked with Stella beer. Freddy Markham on the left and "Pru" Passfield and Gerry Parson on the right. Gambut, February 1942. *Jack Barber*

A haircutting session, "Pru" Passfield and "Tiny" McGilroy at Gambut. *Jack Barber*

Plt Off Neville Duke wearing the ribbon of the DFC, awarded to him on 12th March 1942. *Neville Duke*

Dhobying, where every drop of water is precious. "Tiny" McGilroy and others at Gambut. *Jack Barber*

The presentation of the squadron badge. An occasion marked by a parade and inspection by AVM Arthur Coningham at Sidi Haneish on 14th April 1942. The AOC and Sqn Ldr Caldwell are seen here taking the parade with two Kittyhawks in the background – the variations in sharksmouth design is noticeable.   *IWM (CM2842)*

Two airmen stand by "their" Kittyhawk. In practice there was one Instrument Mech and one Airframe Mech (Rigger) to each aircraft and an Engine Mech between three. Note the aircraft letter "G" repeated on the undercarriage knuckle.   *R. Shama via P. Sampson & Chaz Bowyer*

Three of 112 Squadron's pilots. Left to right: Flt Lt Westenra, Fg Off Duke DFC, and Flt Lt Humphreys. A photograph taken just after all three had left the squadron in about April, 1942. Between them they had accounted for 11½ enemy aircraft destroyed, 3½ probables and 3 damaged. Note the unbuttoned top-tunic button, the "insignia" of a member of the Desert Air Force. *IWM (CM2504)*

Fg Off 'Babe' Whitamore in his Kittyhawk "Blonde Bombshell". *Jack Barber*

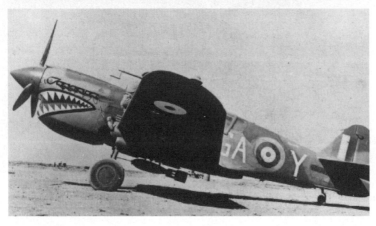

Kittyhawk Mk1A, GA-Y, AK772, named "London Pride" at Gambut Main. This aircraft served on 112 Squadron from March to 30th May 1942 when it was shot down with Plt Off Burney as pilot. *IWM (CM2895)*

Left Bombing up Kittyhawk GA-Y, AK772, with a 250 lb bomb, May 1942. The lengths of cord come from stoppers closing off the exhaust stubs and air intake on the upper engine panel. *IWM (CM2896)*

Below Sgt (Cook) Harry Trett stands by the wreck of a Ju87 "Stuka" at El Daba. What remains of the identification letters and numerals shows that this machine once belonged to the *Geschwaderstab* of *StG.3.* *Jack Barber*

A Kittyhawk taxying. GA-C, possibly ET919, an aircraft that was on the squadron from July to October 1942. A rare survivor for those days. Amiriya LG91 or 175.   *IWM (CM2897)*

Kittyhawk GA-C, ET789. This machine was forced down on 12th September, 1942, with Sgt Hogg as the pilot, in the El Daba area after combat with Ju87s and Bf109s over El Alamein. Later the aircraft was towed back to the LG175. Here the ground party inspect the aircraft, which was Cat 2, repairable on the airfield.   *IWM (EI7129)*

Kittyhawks opening up for take off. The fact that the hood of the nearest aircraft is open suggests that this photograph may have been taken after the event of 11th November 1942 when Crichton and Phillips were nearly trapped in their burning aircraft. The presence of an American supplied Jeep would also suggest late 1942 as the date of this picture. *IWM (NA7932)*

Wing Commander Billy Drake, DSO, DFC, and wearing the American Air Force Cross. A photograph taken after he had left 112 Sqn. *IWM (CM5117) via Chaz Bowyer*

The size of the bomb increases! "Pru" Passfield, Rigger, and a 500 lb slung under GA-D. *Jack Barber*

112's captured work-horse, the SM81, "liberated" at Castel Benito and made fit to fly. Seen here at Marble Arch LG sporting the GA insignia. *Matt Matthias via IWM (HU6952)*

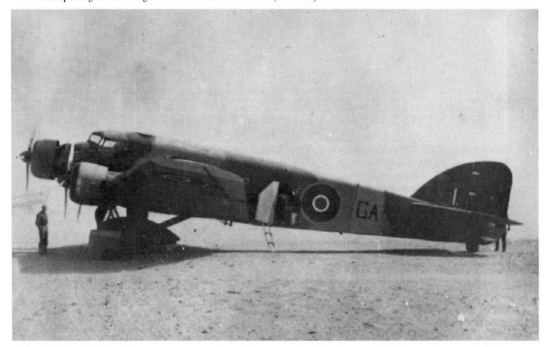

Left Reg Drown keeps cool in the gale from the airscrew.   *IWM (HU15597)*

Right An unknown pilot stands proudly by his aircraft, complete with map, parachute and Mae West. The man closely resembles Flt Lt Costello who had served in 112 Sqn in the Gladiator days and who returned for about 3 months in 1942, others believe it to be Sqn Ldr Garton who was CO from January to May 1943.

A group photograph probably taken at El Assa LG in February, 1943. Seated on the Kittyhawk's engine are (left to right): 'Canada' Brown; 'Molly' Lamont; Reg Wild; Bill Money; Ken Middlemist. Seated on the wing: Geoff Garton (CO); Flt Lt R. R. Smith; 'Goose' Guess; Herbie Snelgrove. Standing: -?- ; Gary Wright; 'Artie' Shaw; Bert Legg; Danny Saville; -?- ; MacAuley; R. C. ('Smithy') Smith; Ray Newton; Martin Barnes; Paddy Agnew; Dick DeBourke. Seated: David Brown.   *David Brown*

15th March 1943 at Neffatia, Tunisia. 112 Sqn officers and NCO aircrew after claiming their 200th aerial victory. At the rear (left to right): Plt Off Burcham; Fg Off Cherry; Flt Sgt W D Brown; Flt Sgt Lamont (top); Sgt Wild; Sgt McDermott. Centre row, standing: Flt Sgt Snelgrove; Sgt Hounsell; Sgt Blake; Flt Lt Hill*; Flt Sgt Money; Flt Sgt Shaw; Sgt Worbey; Flt Sgt Newton; Plt Off Barnes; WO Shaver (above); Flt Sgt D. B. Brown; Flt Lt Eberle (MO); Fg Off Wright. Rear front row: Plt Off Agnew; Fg Off Legg (Engr Off); Flt Lt Evans (Adjt); Fg Off Carroll; Fg Off Livingstone; Sgt Middlemist. Front row: Plt Off Guess (holding "Mickey"); Sqn Ldr Garton (CO); Fg Off Pepper (Tech Off); Fg Off Ross; Sgt MacAuley.
(*Flt Lt Hill was from 239 Wing). *IWM (HU6955)*

Flt Lt Matt Matthias took this in-flight snapshot of the reflector gunsight and fixed ring and bead sight on his Kittyhawk. *IWM (HU6953)*

Len Cherry, remembered as a snappy dresser even in the desert, with, on the wing (left to right), Johnny Burcham and his groundcrew, AC Markham, Fitter and AC Harrison, Rigger. *Bert Hordem*

Touching down. A short-tailed Kitty a few feet above the ground. The bomb rack is empty, mission accomplished. GA-D at this time carried an American serial number 245798. *IWM (HU15535)*

Bert Horden seated in his aircraft GA-Z (FR472), about May 1943, probably at Zuara LG. *Bert Horden*

Plt Off Johnny Burcham in his aircraft, also at Zuara and about May 1943. He is not strapped in and an airman is standing on the engine, so take off would not appear to be imminent. *Bert Horden*

At Zuara Sqn Ldr Garton briefs his two Flight Commanders, Capt Saville and Flt Lt Usher. The aircraft is Kittyhawk GA-L FR472. *IWM*

Herbie Snelgrove takes a bath. The extremely small desert wash–hand basin is here collapsed to allow a primitive form of bathing. A 20 litre Jerrican stands close by with a large "W" (for Water) for fear of mistaking it for petrol. *Bert Horden*

Left Gp Capt Jackie Darwen, DSO, DFC and bar. He is seen here in the cockpit of a Spitfire. *Chaz Bowyer*

Right Sqn Ldr George Norton, CO from May 1943, killed on his first operational mission with 112 Sqn on 13th July. *Bert Horden*

July 1943. Two short-tailed Kittyhawks touching down at Zuara LG. Colour photographs taken at about this time reveal that wheel discs and squadron and aircraft identification letters were painted in pale blue, not white. *Matt Matthias*

Sgt Alec Rowe in the cockpit of a Kittyhawk. At least four swastikas suggest four victories so it seems likely that this was not Rowe's aircraft. Bomb symbols would indicate the number of bombing missions the aircraft had accomplished. Note the useful addition of a rear-view mirror at the top of the windscreen. *Matt Matthias*

bomb-load for the Kitty III was one 500-pounder with relatively thin casing for maximum blast when attacking shipping and such like, or two 250-pounders with thicker casings and nose-rods for fragmentation against troop concentrations. Just before Alamein there were a few Kitty Is on strength and for those the load was one 250-pounder to compensate for their inferior performance. During the battle period we also carried six 40-pounders suspended from wing-racks and released by a button on the stick. That was the theory. Often they hung up, sometimes they waggled roguishly, never quite dropping free and sometimes they dropped off in the circuit during landing. They were not very popular.' In this amusing and eloquent description David Brown relates how the bombing technique had been refined from the initial method as recently as March that year. More close-cover was flown on 2 October but no enemy aircraft or flak was encountered. WO Agnew returned to claim one Ju87 destroyed, a second probable and two damaged. That day the 2nd New Zealander Division attacked west of El Alamein and a large number of cruiser tanks penetrated the final minefield, albeit at heavy cost. It soon became clear that Rommel was about to throw in the 15th and 21st Panzers Divisions whereupon X Corps ordered the 1st and 10th Armoured Divisions forward and a desperate battle commenced in the vicinity of Tel el Aqqaqir which the Germans lost that night.

On the 3rd 112 flew similar sorties as the previous day and again no enemy opposition was encountered. There was a new spirit in the air as the German front began to crumble. The squadron escorted bombers attacking just to the west of the bomb line. In the evening Geoff Garton led 12 aircraft straffing east of El Daba. Ten lorries, four gun emplacements and other vehicles were attacked. Top cover and escorts were provided for bombers on the 4th and again, after the bombers had finished, the Kittyhawks went down and straffed. They were attacked by Bf109s who did no harm, W D (known as 'Western Desert' or 'Canada') Brown damaged a Bf109G-2[1].

Rommel now knew he was beaten and he began to retreat, abandoning the greater part of his right wing, the Italian Ariete, Folgore and Pavia Divisions. By the 4th the advance was on. The Battle of El Alamein was one of the most decisive in British military history and absolutely vital for the Allied cause. Rommel's losses amounted to 59,000 men killed, wounded or captured of which 34,000 were German. 500 tanks and 400 guns were left behind on the battlefield. British losses were 13,500 killed, wounded or missing and 432 tanks destroyed or damaged.

On 5 November the squadron claimed four Bf109s destroyed and two damaged. The CO led 11 aircraft at 09.25 hrs to the west of Fuka at 18,000'. Six Messerschmitts were attacked at about 12,000' and Sqn Ldr Drake (FR293) claimed one destroyed and one damaged, Plt Off Curphey (FR195) one destroyed, Flt Lt Smith (FR217) one destroyed and one damaged and Fg Off Livingstone (FR266) and Flt Sgt L C Shaver (FR281) shared another 109 between them. At 13.30 hrs that day the squadron acted as top cover for 18 Mitchells bombing the Fuka – Matruh road. Ten Bf109s were

---

[1] This Bf109 *Gustav 'Black Six'* was flown that day by *Lt* Heinz Lüdemann of III/JG77 who was wounded. The aircraft was later found abandoned at El Daba and was used by Sqn Ldr Bobby Gibbes of 3RAAF Sqn. It still exists and is currently in flying condition based at Duxford in the Imperial War Museum collection, but is destined for the RAF Museum, Hendon, in 1995.

encountered and four attacked. One of the Kittyhawks was damaged but it returned safely. The squadron now began to move forward and 'A' Party left for LG102, south-west of Maaten Bagush.

'A' Party camped about five miles east of LG102 at dusk and 12 Italian and three German prisoners were guarded all night. Just before the evening meal was served two enemy aircraft dropped bombs close to the camp. No one was hurt and the prisoners, who had 'taken evasive action', returned to their positions near the cookhouse. The squadron aircraft arrived the next day and flew a bombing and straffing operation on Charing Cross and the Sidi Barrani road. Later intense rain fell and cloud came down to 500'. This rain, which lasted for 24 hours, allowed Rommel to disengage and thus robbed the 8th Army of the chance to capture his armoured and mechanised divisions.

On 7th Capt Saville led a recce of the Sidi Barrani and Sollum areas, but rain and low cloud caused the formation to lose contact near Fuka. A passing Ju88 was chased but it got away. Sgt R Webb failed to return, having been last seen near Fuka. In the same way that the manner of his passing is not known, his body has never been found.

Rommel, aided by the weather, was now conducting a text-book retreat, fighting as he went. Major-General Francis de Guingand, the 8th Army Chief of Staff, wrote[1] that the DAF was handled badly at this stage as, with complete air superiority and the disorganised state of the enemy, the Air Forces' contribution could have been far greater. The apparent reason for this failure to capitalise on the enemy's vulnerability was that very few squadrons were trained in ground straffing as the Kittyhawk Wings were, and the fighter and bomber squadrons 'were not allowed to come down low'. We also now know[2] that the DAF was itself suffering from supply problems together with an expectation that the *Luftwaffe* in North Africa was about to receive substantial reinforcements, a belief that resulted in all available aircraft being employed in providing air cover. A couple of missions on the 8th revealed very little enemy activity. Forward movement continued and the ground parties had reached LG115, having had great difficulty in the boggy ground on the top of the Sidi Haneish escarpment. Vehicles sank up to their axles and most of the day was spent digging them out. That day the Anglo-American armies landed on the French North African coast, and the *Afrika Korps* found itself fighting on two fronts.

The squadron aircraft left for LG76, about 25 miles inland from Sidi Barrani, on 9 November 1942. 'A' Party caught up with them eventually having been held up in a massive road convoy whose average speed was about 3 mph. Danny Saville led a formation of six aircraft acting as top cover to 3RAAF bombing and straffing Halfaya Pass. Three 'yellow nosed' Bf109s appeared but were chased away after a protracted and scattered dog-fight. Perhaps due to the rather hectic times this operation does not appear to have been recorded in the squadron operations diary. David Brown recalls it vividly since he came near to death. 'Three 109s appeared on the scene in the target area, attempting to jump 3 Squadron. We put an end to this nonsense but I cannot recall that any victories could be claimed. The opposition's standard of flying was higher than usual and the dog-fight became protracted and scattered.' David Brown then found himself 'dealing with two 109s, not because I was greedy but because I was

[1] 'Operation Victory', Major-General Sir Francis de Guingand (1947)
[2] Hinsley, Vol II, pp 452–453

dim enough to let myself be caught . . . One 109 indulged in head-on attacks, during which the German pilot and I let fly with everything available with little effect, while the second 109 waited his chance to slink in at six o'clock (astern) and deliver a crafty *coup de grâce* while the poor Kittyhawk struggled on its skyhooks. Fortunately this worthy's aim was poor and he only succeeded in putting a couple of holes in the Kittyhawk's tail – as well as a monumental breeze up its pilot! Finally the inevitable happened, the Kittyhawk went into a spin, certainly not this pilot's choice of evasive action as the altitude was just on 2000′ and spinning one of these "hot pursuit ships" was a novel experience indeed (not having practised it in the Kitty).' David Brown went on to describe some moments of stark terror and how, in this extreme situation he did what surely many a hardened and otherwise cynical person understandably does. He prayed. 'Sweet Jesus, if you love me, save me'. Then he described how everything in his mind went very calm and quiet and what came back to him, as though someone was speaking to him through his headset, were the instructions for dealing with a spin that he had been taught at Flying Training School on Miles Masters and North American Harvards. Throttle back, stick forward; centralise the rudder; when the spin stops, ease gently out of the dive. 'To say I was agreeably surprised to find that the Kitty recovered quickly is putting it mildly, nevertheless the close view of the ground during pull out was highly unpleasant. The wily Hun were evidently well-versed in the rumours of the Kitty's spinning habits, for while I was busy kicking the rudder, pulling the control column and praying, they both disappeared, although one that followed me had to pull so hard to avoid hitting the ground that streamers formed from his wing tips . . . Ground fire was inaccurate and the Kittyhawk (FR266 'H') bore its pilot homeward where he executed a very wide and very gentle circuit because just at that time anything more than a half-rate turn left him distinctly weak at the knees.'[1] Spinning the Kitty was discouraged as equipment such as aircraft batteries tended to come loose and fly around in the fuselage and belts of ammunition tangle up inside the wings.

The Germans fought a rearguard action at Sidi Barrani that day with only about 30 serviceable tanks – all that remained of the huge panzer force that had faced Montgomery at Alamein such a short while before. Two days later there was a long range sweep of the El Adem – Tobruk – Gambut area. During this operation Geoff Garton and Sgt Watson each destroyed a Ju52 at Gambut and Billy Drake damaged a Bf109F. Sgt Watson also shot up a Fieseler *Storch* on the ground and Sgt R A Wild damaged a 109F. Bobby Sayle recalled that 'Butch' Watson, his No 2, was capable of drinking a pint of rum without taking the bottle from his lips 'but he was usually u/s for a day or two afterwards!' Later that day there was an accident. David Brown describes the event. 'Taking off in pairs for a show, two of our aircraft, Joe Crichton and Tex Phillips the pilots, hit a third Kittyhawk which had previously crashed on the runway. The ensuing blaze, with tracers spitting wickedly in all directions from the heart of the flames, was a spine-chilling sight. The MO and an Army Liaison Officer, whose name escapes me (a Captain Nesborn) went into that mess, scrambled onto the wing of one aircraft, fought to release a jammed hood and eventually dragged the dazed pilot to safety. That was Joe Crichton. Then they went to the second Kittyhawk. Tex Phillips was unconscious and the hood jammed shut, defying all the frantic efforts of the Doc

---

[1] David Brown, correspondence and conversation.

and the ALO to open it. They stayed there, still trying, until an Australian airman arrived to help and at last they got the hood open and pulled Tex free. He was badly burned but eventually recovered. It was our practice, incidentally, to take off with cockpit hoods shut in the desert to avoid a miniature sandstorm in the cockpit. After that incident we kept them open' David Brown's pen-portrait of the MO, 'Doc' Eberle (pronounced Eberlé) – 'Tall, benign, and blessed with a God-given turn of wit when drunk, which happened all too rarely. He was the finest example of a Squadron MO that it was our privilege to know. Whenever we had to land at a tricky airstrip his ambulance was beside the runway with him inside it, smiling paternally as we passed. This was not just for the initial landing but on the return of every show, regardless of time, meals or anything else.'

That evening 'B' party turned up at LG75 only to hear that 'A' Party was already making ready to move forward again at dawn, this time to Gambut. On 12th the squadron flew as top cover for a strafe in the Gazala – Tobruk area and later they had a chance to beat up a German column on the Tobruk – Gazala road. For long-range strafes the Kittyhawks were now sometimes fitted with jettisonable 60 gallon belly tanks allowing an extra hour airborne. *Oblt* Werner Schroer[1], who served on JG27 and was the second highest-scoring pilot in the desert commented that whenever he flew low-level the British soldiers lay on their backs and shot at the Messerschmitts with their rifles, but that German soldiers would leap out of their trucks and run for cover when they were attacked by the DAF.

On 13 November Tobruk fell. Squadron aircraft flew up to Gambut Satellite No 1. The squadron was released from duty that afternoon and some of the pilots spent a profitless afternoon trying to erect a German tent, the CO being prominent with a sledge hammer. By 15th the squadron was occupying Gazala No 2 and there was a 'rhubarb' of the road west of Cyrene and MT were straffed, some catching fire. Billy Drake managed to shoot down a Heinkel 111.

'Rhubarbs', the name was chosen because of the laxative effect of these operations both on the aircrew taking part and the victims on the ground, were usually flown by sections of four aircraft, flying in echelon at deck level. The concentration of fire from six .5s per aeroplane proved very destructive while, according to PoW interrogation, the glaring sharks' mouths added to the general effect. The Kittyhawk could take an inordinate amount of punishment and was capable of flying minus 80% rudder and with holes as large as the proverbial head and shoulders in the wings and fuselage. On 16 November 'A' Party was off again, this time to Martuba No 4, arriving in pouring rain. There was more patrolling and a recce of the Benghazi area that day and eighteen Ju87s and six Bf109s were seen, but too far away to be attacked. Despite this one German baled out!

Geoff Garton was posted out that day as Sqn Ldr Flying at Wing HQ as a result of the deaths of Sqn Ldr Strawson and Flt Lt Terry while travelling to Martuba. Here 112 was detached from 239 Wing to join the USAAF 57th Fighter Group, comprising 64th, 65th and 66th Squadrons, to operate together as a tactical unit and give them the benefit of the DAF's experience. This secondment proved both successful and rewarding to both units. Martuba was too wet to be of much use but the squadron

---

[1] Shores & Ring, *op cit*

personnel amused themselves by investigating abandoned enemy dumps and scrounging a lot of useful gear. Later there was a straffing operation on the Benghazi – Magrun road and on the last mission Flt Lt Smith shared a Bf109 with Sqn Ldr Bobbie Gibbes of 3RAAF. Sgt Pollock had to return near Msus with engine trouble but he had not reached base by the end of the day. On 18 November Martuba was still too wet to be used and flying had to be done from Gazala. The CO commandeered a Ju87 which was made serviceable by the ground crew and the squadron 'liberated' a German field cooker mounted on a trailer with rubber tyres which was considered a worth-while acquisition.

The following day the CO led a sweep from Gazala to the Magrun – Benghazi road and between Sceleidima and Soluch they straffed 12 to 15 MT vehicles damaging most of them. The formation landed at Martuba. Later that day there was a scramble, aircraft taking off singly as quickly as they were refuelled. The CO was the first off and returned after 30 minutes claiming a Bf110 destroyed and one damaged. Plt Off Gary Wright encountered an Me210 and left it with one engine burning, claiming a probable. The Me210 was almost certainly from III/ZG1, the *'Wespen'* (Wasp) *Geschwader*, and the Messerschmitt claimed by the CO was probably from 7/ZG26. On 21st a Ju88 of 10/LG1 dropped bombs on Martuba Main, but AA fire drove it off and it was later shot down by 260 Sqn. Sgt Pollock returned to the squadron having force-landed on 17th, forty miles west of Msus. On 24th the squadron moved from Martuba No 4 to No 3. Sgt DeBourke rejoined the squadron, now recovered from his injury sustained at the beginning of the month. Nine squadron pilots went on leave to Cairo by transport 'plane (probably by DC3 Dakota which were now arriving in the desert) and Flt Lt 'Smithy' Smith flew the squadron Stuka to Martuba No 3. There were shipping searches on the 24 and 26 November but without any success. The Stuka was again airborne and it flew to Alexandria with Plt Off Bruce at the controls and Fg Off J H Pepper, the Sqn Technical Officer, and the Group ALO in the back – all plentifully supplied with green Verey cartridges in case they were attacked! The CO was awarded the DSO and Capt Saville a bar to his DFC. On 29th the advance ground party moved off again, along with a large convoy made up of the advance parties belonging to No 57 (Pursuit) Group, USAAF. The next day the squadron Stuka returned closely followed by four Hurricanes, who broke off when they saw the RAF roundels. The pilot and observer were asked why they hadn't fired the recognition Verey and they admitted they hadn't realised they were being chased!

Torrential rain prevented any flying for a while and conditions at Martuba were very unpleasant. The forward move to Belandah was delayed until the evening of 6 December 1942 when nineteen of the squadron aircraft arrived. There was an operational mission on the 7th when twelve aircraft raided the landing ground near Arco Philænorum[1], generally referred to as 'Marble Arch'. This was a huge pompous structure designed in the Fascist architectural style and erected by Mussolini before the war spanning the main coastal road between Tripoli and Benghazi. Most of the bombs landed near flak positions. Plt Off Ibbotson, one-time member of 112 but now serving with 601 Spitfire Sqn, was shot down and captured by Rommel's staff that day and was presented to the General. That night he managed to escape and returned to

---

[1] Named after two legendary Carthaginian brothers, the Philænae, buried there

base at El Hassiet. This was the second time Ibbotson had walked home.

The next day there was a 'de-lousing' sweep led by Capt Saville over Mersa Brega and to the south, which was described as 'profitless' at the time. The second operation of 10th was more eventful as the squadron, acting as top cover to No 66 USAAF Sqn, met 20–25 Bf109s and MC202s. Flt Lt Smith (FL880) shot down a Bf109G which crashed on land and an MC202 that fell into the sea. The squadron had been obliged to jettison their bombs in order to engage the enemy and there was a general dog-fight. Flt Sgt Shaver chased a 109F, giving it several bursts and finally seeing it crash behind enemy lines. He couldn't hang around to finish it off because of the flak. His victim may have been *Major* Müncheburg, *Kommodore* of I/JG77 as his account tallies. 'Smithy' Smith's aircraft was badly shot up.

There was another show the next day when the CO (FR293) led 11 aircraft covering a bombing raid by No 66 USAAF Sqn on enemy tents and MT, an attack which caused fires and one explosion. On the return trip the formation was attacked by four or six Bf109Es and Fs. Billy Drake claimed one which fell in enemy held territory and an MC202 which 'spun into the sea voluntarily'! He was chased by seven Messerschmitts and had to make a wheels up landing amongst the 11th Hussars, returning that afternoon in a Hurricane. At 15.10 hrs the squadron 'led by Flt Lt Smith, acting as top cover escorting two Hurricanes on a Tac-R. They again ran into enemy aircraft, about four to six . . . and had quite a gay party' – so runs the ops diary. Joe Crichton shot down a Bf109 into the sea, confirmed by Flt Lt Smith who also claimed a damaged one, Plt Off Bruce got a probable. Missing from this action was Plt Off 'Compo' Cuddon and Flt Sgt W D 'Canada' Brown but there was hope for them as rain and mist might have forced them to land elsewhere. Brown was later reported to be in hospital in Benghazi having landed at Magrun[1] with claims for a probable and one damaged. Cuddon was never found.

Despite foul weather which grounded the Wing, Belandah was visited by a lone Ju88 on 12th which, pursued by two Spitfires of 1 SAAF Sqn, strafed the airfield. All the Bofors guns opened up and the enemy machine fell in flames about five miles away.

On 13 December there was a call for maximum effort as the Germans were retreating from the El Agheila position. Eleven aircraft took off at 10.15 hrs to bomb pin-point targets. No enemy aircraft were seen. There were similar missions at 12.15 and 14.15 hours. At 16.00 hrs the CO led 12 aircraft on a bombing operation. They were warned that there were some Ju87s in the area, south of El Agheila, and they flew to investigate. Almost at once they saw ten-plus Bf109s to the north. There followed a general dog-fight in which four enemy aircraft were shot down. Sgt J G Lecours, a Canadian, in FR320 claimed one, Sgt DeBourke (FR213) another, Fg Off Curphey (FR195) a third and the CO (FR338) and Sgt 'Artie' Shaw, shared the fourth. Two others were damaged by Lecours and MacAuley. Sgt Lamont force-landed, short of petrol, at an emergency landing strip north of Agedabia. The squadron's total score now hung tantalisingly close to 200, at 198 destroyed, 51 probable and 72½ damaged. The diary complained that the *Luftwaffe* must have heard how close the squadron was to reaching 200 and were keeping well out of the way and there was even a plan to keep the CO's aircraft unserviceable so that someone else could reap the glory. Top cover

[1] This is probably the occasion related by David Brown above, p.78.

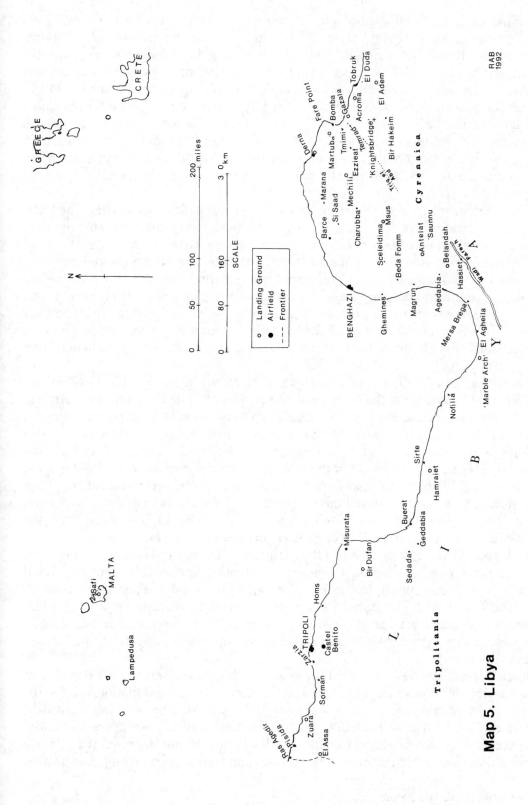

Map 5. Libya

SCALE

Landing Ground
Airfield
Frontier

RAB
1992

missions, recces and bombing occupied them for the next few days. By this time, David Brown remembers, the pilots of the 57th Fighter Group had, under 112's tuition, 'learned the ropes' but strict R/T discipline took a little longer to learn as the Americans tended initially to 'use their R/T as a kind of stream of consciousness medium'. The squadron Stuka flew to Alexandria to collect Christmas supplies. On 17 December a dawn recce of 12 aircraft led by Capt Saville was airborne for two and a half hours using belly tanks, and they brought back information that suggested the Germans were going to make a stand at Nofilia. Patrols continued but apart from seeing two Bf109s in the distance no contact was made with the enemy. Some pilots went on leave by transport aircraft and the squadron settled down to a relaxed Christmas.

The mention of transport aircraft being used to take squadron personnel to the Delta is a further indication that, at last, the DAF was using them in any number. Moorehead[1] has pointed out that 'Nine tenths of desert warfare is the battle of supply' and it now seems strange that for so many years the ground troops and air force personnel were supplied by road transport, particularly when the *Afrika Korps* had shown the advantages of using large aircraft such as the Ju52 for this purpose. It was only during the pursuit of Rommel's beaten army out of Cyrenaica, when air superiority was complete, that the RAF used air transport to proper effect. The long lines of supply vehicles, nose to tail on the endless desert roads, were soon to become a thing of the past.

There were no operations on Christmas Eve, all efforts being channeled towards the one objective of arranging the Christmas dinner. Capt Saville flew to Marble Arch to arrange for the transportation of the turkeys, pork and other delicacies. The airmen's dining hall was enlarged by the addition of another tent. There was some anxiety that evening as the transport aircraft, a Heinkel 111, known as 'Delta Lily' which was owned by 260 Sqn, arrived without the turkeys. Nevertheless Christmas 1942 was the best ever spent by the squadron in the desert. Food and drink were available in plenty and afterwards the airmen played the officers and NCOs at soccer and won by 3 goals to nil, due in part to the pilots being 'not very fit'. The aircrew also played the Americans at baseball and had slightly better success, losing by only two runs.

So the year ended quietly. In effect the campaign in the western desert was now over. The Germans were holding on to their last defensive line in Libya but the Allied advance was continuing relentlessly. The squadron moved again, this time to Hamraiet, about 20 miles inland from Sirte, and arrived there on 9 January 1943. Eleven aircraft covered a Tac-R sortie on 11th from Buerat, down a wadi to Geddabia. 'Big Joe' Crichton (FR216) was missing from this operation, shot down by flak and taken prisoner.

Similar operations were mounted the next day despite the severe dust storms that were blowing for most of the time. On 13th 12 aircraft escorted Baltimores to the Bir Zirdam and Geddabia areas. There was heavy flak for most of the way and marauding Bf109s and MC202s were around. One Messerschmitt was shot down, but, curiously, there seems no record of who was credited with it. Little 'Bunny' Curphey (FR195 'F') was shot down and baled out over enemy territory and was posted missing, but he died

[1] '*The End in Africa*', Alan Moorehead

and his body was never found. Two aircraft had to belly-land on their return, and two others, Fg Off Sayle (FR214 'A') and Sgt Watson (FR320 'J') were missing. 'Butch' Watson's aircraft fell victim to the fire of some well concealed enemy tanks and he made a wheels up landing at too great a speed. This, together with the fact that he was a large man, caused his harness straps to break and he gashed his head on the gunsight. He was taken prisoner almost immediately and was looked after quite well in the *Luftwaffe* mess. Subsequently however, he was treated rather roughly and even spent some time in Dachau concentration camp, being liberated in American troops in 1945. After the war Watson rejoined the RAF and served at Acklington and Waddington.

Bobby Sayle was also made a prisoner. Having crash-landed he was picked up by a Fieseler *Storch*. His pocket diary survives for the period he was on 112 and sketches the sometimes rather tedious days and nights on the squadron at that time. 'Went on "readiness" twice but did not meet with anything. Did a lot of practice "weaving" which is all important for a long life' is one such entry. In their spare time several of the pilots made model aircraft, Sayle a Kittyhawk, Dave Bruce an MC202 and Jock Livingstone a Spitfire and then an Me109. On 31 December he received news of his promotion to Fg Off, 'some class' he commented. His pay in his new rank was back-dated to 1 October. That evening he got 'pie-eyed'. It was the final entry. Bobby Sayle, a Canadian, is remembered for swearing in Chinese when he was in a festive mood and then pointing his .38 pistol into the darkness beyond the tent and letting fly with a couple of rounds 'to discourage unwelcome visitors'.

David Brown also recalls, perhaps wistfully, the companionship of the Pilots' Mess. The hum of the mobile generator in the starry darkness, the gritty recordings of 'Flamingo' or Mary Martin's 'Do it Again' played through the battered Mess radio, the closer knitting of friendships when losses were high, the share-out of comforts from the colonials' gift parcels, the pinning up of the 'Messpot' letters[1] and the woeful dirge as the victim bought his round of drinks, the startling versions of 'Little Angeline' floating loud and clear on the desert air . . .' Another correspondent recalls that the whole Mess listened to *Soldatensender Belgrad* closing down each night at 23.00 hrs when Lale Andersen sang 'Lili Marlene' to the *Afrika Korps*, DAF and the 8th Army alike —

Vor der Kaserne, vor dem Grossen Tor
Steht eine Lanterne, und steht sie noch davor,
Wenn sich die später Nebel drehn
Bei der Lanterne woll'n wir stehn
Wie einst Lilli Marlene,
Wie einst Lilli Marlen'

On the 14th there was one scramble but without any result. Later there was a bomber escort for six Mitchells and 12 Bostons to Geddabia. Sgt David ('Fat') Brown had his engine seize up in the circuit, right over Wing HQ. The assembled squadron commanders, hearing the aircraft's motor cut, wandered outside to see what would

---

[1] A 'Messpot' letter, like a 'Dear John' letter, was from a girlfriend back at home announcing the end of the friendship. On these occasions the girl's photograph, was pinned to the Mess notice board with a cross drawn through it.

happen, taking a personal interest in the proceedings since they thought at one stage the aircraft would dive through the roof of the HQ trailer. Sgt Brown put his aircraft down at about 150 knots and 'vanished into the limitless bundoo like a scalded cat'. Sqn Ldr Geoff Garton returned to the squadron from No 239 Wing and took over from Billy Drake. On the 17th there were 21 sorties mostly as top cover to other squadrons bombing. At Bir Dufan they saw stores being burned by the Germans and a tractor ploughing up the surface of the landing ground – two signs, it was supposed, of an impending retreat. A retreat from which, at long last, there would be no return.

This was proved correct a few days later when 'A' Party left for Sedada, *en route* for a landing ground near Bir Dufan. The aircraft followed the next day and operations began on 20th, flying as escort to 65 USAAF Sqn. There was a patrol over Castel Benito airfield, outside Tripoli, and the Breda guns were strafed. This attack, David Brown recalls, was accompanied by 'the inspiring if somewhat incongruous accompaniment of Italian grand opera' – due to interference on the R/T from medium wave radio. By the 25th the squadron had moved onto this former target and sorties continued with attacks on MT on the road between Tripoli and Mareth. A 3000-ton freighter and a tanker in Zuara docks were bombed and near-misses reported. The next day they tried again carrying 500-lb bombs and this time a direct hit was registered on the mole. Squadron personnel spent some time looking round the airfield which was littered with wrecked enemy aircraft. Sixty airmen and aircrew went into Tripoli 'to see the sights' but found all the shops shuttered and the civilians 'rather timid'. The squadron, having abandoned the idea of occupying some of the more permanent buildings on the airfield, set up camp in an orchard. 'Heaven knows what grows in the orchard' said one officer, 'but it's green, it's an orchard – it isn't desert any more.'[1]

It was at Castel B that 'Chiefy' Haynes came into his own. Ever since his arrival on the squadron, to the bewilderment of the groundcrew, he had carried a pair of roller skates in his kit bag. Now, at last, the reason for this curious behaviour became clear. At Castel Benito the hangars had the most beautiful quarry tile floors. Here, to the delight of the groundcrew, 'Chiefy' Haynes revealed himself as a professional roller skater.

Bombing of ships continued the following day between Pisida and Ben Gardan and near misses were claimed. The month ended with a raid on barges and schooners at Zarzia. That night the film 'Hellzapoppin' was shown to the airmen in the Castel Benito cinema, a rare luxury for men who had served so many years in the barren desert. By October 1942 the squadron had begun exchanging Kittyhawk MkIA aircraft for MkIIIs and now there were none of the older aircraft left. The Kittyhawk III, known as the P-40K Warhawk by the Americans, had a more powerful Allison engine which developed 1325 hp at take off. The first production models (the 'short-tailed Kitty') had the fuselage of the P-40E but with the increased power there was a tendency to swing on take off and a dorsal fairing was added to the fin to correct the fault. Later production models had a lengthened fuselage which served the same purpose. Mk III aircraft on the squadron carried the FR serial prefix letters. To carry the new 500-lb bombs aluminium wheels were used instead of steel ones and a smaller aircraft battery installed to reduce the all up weight.

Still at Castel B, the squadron had now returned to 239 Wing. On 3rd there was

[1] 'R.A.F. Middle East', anon.,

'great excitement' when Winston Churchill landed at the airfield. Stepping from his Liberator and wearing the uniform of an RAF Air Commodore, he was greeted by General Montgomery. While all this was going on, though, Flt Lt Legg, the squadron Engineering Officer, and his fitters continued to service the squadron's latest acquisition, an Italian SM81. The next day there was a parade for the Prime Minister. The whole of 239 Wing formed up outside the hangars and flying control tower and then, in dead silence, an armoured car appeared, then outriders and finally Churchill, accompanied by Montgomery, drove past in an open car. He was cheered to the echo by every man there.

On 5th there were more anti-shipping missions. Twelve aircraft led by Wg Cdr Burton also attacked MT at Ras Agedir. On the way back some enemy aircraft were encountered and one Bf109 was claimed as a probable and one damaged. FL730, flown by Sgt Lecours, failed to return and he was reported missing. The next day, after an attack on Ben Gardan along with 450 Sqn, 'A' Party was ordered to move forward, this time to Sorman, but that order was almost immediately amended to read El Assa, 55 miles further forward. The remainder of the squadron stayed at Castel Benito for a while longer and there was some bombing and straffing missions attacking enemy MT. On the 10th there was heavy rain and consequently no flying but the airfield guards were trebled as there was a report that saboteurs had been dropped by parachute. In the event nothing happened.

On 13 February the squadron's SM81 was serviceable. The crew and passengers consisted of Sqn Ldr Garton, pilot, Flt Lt Bert Legg, engineer and 2nd pilot, Flt Sgt Bacon, Cpl Duncan and LAC Kaye as crew. 'Taffy' Evans, the adjutant, was the only passenger. The CO was obliged to overshoot twice before he found out how to land it. David Brown recalls that the SM81 'was a very interesting aeroplane to fly: slab-sided as a removal van, with pneumatic brakes which were not very effective, leaving the aircraft very much to the mercy of a cross-wind during landing. It had a little auxiliary motor just behind the pilot's seat to drive the brakes' compressor and this was started with a piece of string as part of the pre-landing checks. It produced fumes and alarming heat in the cockpit. One charred sleeve of the writer's Irvin jacket was the result of leaving it in too close proximity. As for the aircraft's engine: controls worked back to front which made approaches interesting. None of us had multi-engine experience and the drill was to come in fairly high, close both outboard engines and use the centre engine only for the final approach. I cannot recall anyone else overshooting but, on looking back, it seems very likely that, had we tried to do so, we would probably have forgotten all about the other two engines and tried to persuade the poor old girl to stagger round on one.' The fuselage was suitably decorated with the squadron's 'GA' code letters. On 15th the squadron moved up to El Assa, close to the Tunisian border, with the CO bringing up the SM81.

The 16 February was a busy day, flying 36 sorties, all in the Medenine area on the Tripoli – Gabes road. The Axis armies, under the command of Field-Marshal Dietloff von Arnim in the north facing the 1st Army and Rommel in the south facing the 8th Army, were not in a very satisfactory state. Rommel was improving a fortified position, the Mareth Line, along the Wadi Zig Zaou with his left flank resting on the sea at Zarat and his right on the Matmata Hills. Rommel's lines of communication with von Arnim were, however, threatened by the advance of the US 1st and 34th Divisions. Knowing that Montgomery was not yet ready to attack, Rommel turned on the Americans on the 14 February and broke them at the Kasserine Pass. This surprising success was short lived and the Germans were forced to withdraw by the 23rd.

On the Mareth front things were quiet and the squadron football team was ferried back to Tripoli in the SM81 to take part in the semi-final of the Tripoli area RAF competition. Returning to El Assa the next day the SM81 landed in a dust storm and the huge aircraft unintentionally ended up in the domestic dispersal, near 211 Group HQ, luckily without anyone realising it.

On 23rd the squadron tried to attack an enemy landing ground but the target could not be located. Twenty-four sorties on the following day included 12 aircraft attacking the LG that was missed the previous day and then acting as top cover while 450 Sqn had a go. Similar raids on airfields continued until the last day of the month. On the second mission a dog-fight developed and one Bf109 was claimed as a probable. Sgt Marsden (FR130) failed to return and his body was never found. Tom Marsden, a north-country man is remembered as a quiet, efficient pilot with a dry turn of wit.

A Form 765A for the squadron in February gives the following statistics: the squadron establishment was 298 officers and men while the posted strength varied between 297 to 308. Of these about 14 were officer pilots, 12 NCO pilots, 5 non-flying officers and about 205 NCO and airmen ground crew. This latter figure included 36 RAF Regiment gunners whose duty was the defence of the airfield. The complement of aircraft ranged from 16 to 22. There was considerably more training flying done over this period and the records show that 13 hrs 5 min 'other flying' was logged. Operational flying on one afternoon expended 2560 rounds of ammunition, but this includes 1300 rounds written off in an aircraft that failed to return (FL730). Twenty-three hours and fifty minutes flying that day consumed 960 gallons of aviation fuel. Over the whole month 17,400 rounds of ammunition were fired, 45 500-lb bombs and 350 40-lb bombs dropped and 17,500 gallons of petrol were used.

On 2 March 1943 the squadron moved again, this time to Ben Gardan and much closer to the forthcoming land battle. Some hard work had to be put in to make the SM81 serviceable as it was due to take two pilots and the Fg Of Pepper, the squadron Technical Officer to Alexandria on leave. The next day the first operations for the month were flown with 12 Kittyhawks led by Flt Lt R R Smith, 'B' Flt Commander, from all accounts a man not remembered with any great affection by the pilots at that time. Along with 450, the aircraft set off on an armed recce of the route out of Gabes to Oudaref, Rommel's main supply route. Slight MT movement was observed and at one point 20-plus vehicles were seen driving towards El Hamma. One Bf109 was seen and flak in the Gabes area was reported as being heavy.

MT were again attacked the next day in the Bourdj Touag area and again Bf109s were seen, although they kept well away. In the afternoon 112 acted as top cover to 2RAAF and 450 Sqns. Heavy and light flak were again encountered while, in return, the Germans were at the receiving end of 45 40-lb bombs and 945 rounds of .5" ammunition.

On 6 March the squadron continued reconnoitering behind the Mareth Line to see what the Germans were doing. They were accompanied by 250 Sqn and Spitfire VCs of 601 (County of London) Squadron. There was not much to report due to low cloud on the hills. That day Rommel had struck against the 8th Army at Medenine but was sharply repulsed by anti-tank guns. His aim was to hold the Mareth line for as long as possible to prevent the two Allied armies from joining up. The following day the Kittyhawks were acting as top cover for 250 Sqn continuing the armed recces. 'A' Party left for Neffatia, even further forward, and the squadron followed, thus at last leaving Libya and entering Tunisia. From the Delta they had come over 1400 miles, the approximate distance between Berlin and Moscow.

In the morning of 10 March the Wing was visited by the AOC, Air Vice-Marshal Harry Broadhurst, DSO, age 38, the youngest Air Marshal in the RAF. Broadhurst's uncompromising message was that in the forthcoming battle those that would return would probably have to walk back, the rest would be dead, but regardless of this, the job had to be done. He was having the whole of the DAF trained to support the army by practising their low-flying, and to do this all the medium and light bombers were gathered into a newly formed tactical unit. The new organisation was still under the command of Air Marshal Coningham but it was now split into four sub-commands, of which the Desert Air Force (no longer officially the WDAF) was but one.

That afternoon the squadron finally achieved its 200th aerial victory, but there was little rejoicing as the price had been high, six pilots failed to return. Twelve aircraft had taken off, lead by Flt Lt Smith, at 15.45 hrs, to act as top cover for 250 and 260 Sqns who were straffing enemy positions north-west of Foum Tatahouin, in the Matmata Hills. As the two other squadrons dived to attack the top cover sighted 12 to 15 Ju87s and 20 to 30 Bf109s, a gaggle the size of which had not been seen now for many months. Combat ensued during which 'B' Flight Commander, Flt Lt R R Smith (FR325), Plt Off (ex-Sgt) R C Smith (FR131), Flt Sgt DeBourke (FR275), Fg Off Bruce (FR295), Sgt J H Oliver, a Canadian on his fourth operational sortie (FR361) and Fg Off Wiley (245798, an American serial number) failed to return. Two Bf109s and one Ju87 were claimed destroyed by Plt Off 'Goose' Guess[1] and Fg Off 'Jock' Livingstone, bring the squadron's estimated total to 202 confirmed.

At a stroke the squadron had lost several of its most experienced pilots so that pilots who were being nursed along as No 2s now found themselves promoted to leaders. David Brown, who was stuck at Marble Arch with the unserviceable SM81, counts himself lucky not to have been flying that day. He described Dick DeBourke as a quiet-spoken lad with a flowing moustache and skill with a guitar. He used to accompany 'Paddy' Agnew who, 'with an Irish glint in his eye, would sing the worst imaginable songs with a choirboy innocence. Their version of "When the moon comes over Madison Square" was a masterpiece of revolting rhymery that had been known to dispel the fiercest appetite if sung before dinner. Dick was an outstanding fighter pilot and was sorely missed. (Plt Off) "Smithy" went missing on the same show. He was older than most of us with a poker face that wouldn't have looked out of place above a machine-gun in Chicago of the Twenties. He looked tough, spoke little, had a wit as dry as tinder, but was really shy as a kid at his first school. When he did laugh, which was not often, his face creased up like an old fisherman's, as though he really enjoyed the chance to relax! George Wiley, a quiet-voiced Canadian, had joined the squadron as a Flight Sergeant and was commissioned soon afterwards. Shot down over Alamein he force-landed in a minefield and broke a leg. Some weeks later he rejoined the

---

[1] One of Guess's victims was probably *Lt* Heinz Lüdemann of *III/JG77*

squadron and began flying again. How he fooled the Medical Board we never knew – certainly his limp (when the Doc was out of sight) made us wince. Shot down again he was seen to start walking back but he was taken prisoner and ended up in *Stalag Luft III* and was one of the 50 shot while attempting to escape. . . .' Johnny Burcham, a new arrival, was detailed for this op but missed it as he was being interviewed by the squadron adjutant – he is sure he would have bought it that day if he had flown.

On 13th the CO led 12 aircraft on a sweep of the forward area, covered by 3RAAF Sqn. The SM81 reappeared from Marble Arch having spent the previous 10 days on the ground with Fg Off Pepper trying to get it to fly. This machine eventually proved too much trouble to keep serviceable and it was left behind at the next move forward.

In place of Flt Lt R R Smith a new 'B' Flt Commander was posted in, Laurie Usher. He found the squadron in a very low state of morale and he immediately made a tremendous impression by being totally 'round the bend'. It is said that he requested the CO's permission to marry the Black Widow spider that he swore shared his tent and then started canvassing everyone, apparently in deadly earnest, to have their teeth filed to a point like the sharksteeth on the aircraft cowlings. 'He conversed at length with lizards and whenever the occasion arose he joined forces with Reg Wild and Johnny Burcham to form a trio of amiable lunatics guaranteed to convince the remainder that they were sharing the Mess with the Crazy Gang'[1]

Baltimores were escorted on 16 March, and again on the 18th and 20th. Bombing was now in the forward area as Montgomery began the build up of his own assault on the Mareth Line. 'A' Party under Fg Off Carroll left for Medenine West LG and that night the 8th Army began its attack. There were two bombing missions on the morning of the 21st to cut the enemy's line of supply. The next day there was an armed recce and the second was a target in the El Hamma area. Enemy aircraft were seen, the bombs were jettisoned and in the ensuing scrap one Bf109 was claimed.

The Mareth Line, fortified before the war by the French, was an extremely strong position stretching only about 18 miles from the coast to the Matmata hills. Behind it lay the 15th Pz Div, the Trieste Div, the 90th Light Div, the Spezia Div, the Pistoia Div and the 164th Div. Along its front the Wadi Zig Zaou constituted a formidable tank obstacle, 50′ deep in places and about 80 yards wide. There was a route round the Matmata Hills by swinging far to the south by way of Ksar Rhilane, but nearing El Hamma there was a feature, the Tebaga Gap, known as 'Plum Pass', which was also fortified. To outflank the Mareth Line a left hook of about 150 miles was required but Montgomery decided to attempt this by holding the Mareth Line with XXX Corps and sending the 2nd New Zealand Division and the 8th Armoured Bde to fall on Plum Pass. The DAF was to act in close co-operation and dominate the battlefield at Mareth and Plum Pass. Broadhurst promised de Guingand, Montgomery's Chief of Staff, a 'Blitz' on the Germans such as had never been attempted before.

At 22.30hrs on the 20th a heavy artillery barrage was laid on the defences of the Mareth Line and the 50th Div stormed the Wadi Zig Zaou which was held by infantry of the Italian Sahara Group and the Pistoia Division. However, two days later, this attack was thrown back by a counter attack by the 15 Pz Div and 90th Light. Montgomery now decided to launch everything into the outflanking movement, but

[1] David Brown, correspondence

Plum Pass, a virtual bottleneck about 6000 yards wide, proved to be a very difficult position to storm. The DAF's 'Blitz', controlled by the new Forward Ground Control Posts (FGCP) for the first time, was an outstanding success and instead of the pilots having to walk back there were very few casualties. This, together with the artillery barrage, forced the Germans and Italians to retreat on the night of the 27th to Wadi Akarit. Rommel, now a sick man, had to hand over command of Army Group Tunis to von Arnim and fly back to Germany.

On 23 March Capt Saville led 12 aircraft on a top cover mission with 250 Sqn who were engaged in an armed recce, but little was seen. Similar missions were flown on the following day with similar results. After a weather recce on the 26th one operation was mounted to bomb and strafe north of the New Zealand troops, and bombs were seen to burst in the target area while straffing results included two MT 'flamers' and 18 MT damaged. On the 27th there was a bombing and straffing operation in the El Hamma area and the road to Gabes. Twenty-four 250-lb bombs were dropped on well dispersed MT. This was followed on the 28th by a similar mission. Prisoners captured later who had been in the El Hamma area expressed the opinion that it was the DAF's bombing and machine gunning that contributed largely to the 8th Army's success. German AA gunners admitted to being taken unawares by the weight of the air attack and that low-flying aircraft came in too low for the 88mm guns to be depressed to aim at them while the 20mm gunners were too busy taking cover to concentrate on producing accurate fire. Axis troops were forced to stay below ground level and were thus prevented from meeting the advancing infantry. A member of a Panzer unit had heard of a tank being destroyed by a tank-busting aircraft but others had more respect for bombs and cannons and he asserted that bombs did more damage by harming the tracks and bogies. One lorry driver said that his vehicle was attacked three times by different aircraft before it was finally destroyed by fire[1].

The 29 March was another busy day. The left hook through Plum Pass had turned the right flank of the Mareth Line defence complex and now the enemy were fleeing north. The squadron put up 47 sorties. At 07.15 hrs Capt Saville led 12 aircraft straffing and bombing MT on the Gabes – Sfax road. This formation landed at 08.35 hrs and at 10.30 the second operation was mounted bombing enemy transport north of Gabes. A target of 20-plus MT in a bottleneck was bombed with good results. At 13.05 hrs a third mission was airborne, bombing and straffing until 14.20. The day finished with a fourth operation lasting from 16.05 to 16.50 hrs which was against shipping. That day 90 250-lb bombs were dropped, 4000 rounds of ammunition fired and 54 hours of flying time recorded. The air activity reminded the old hands of the days before the Battle of El Alamein.

It has been said that the DAF's success in co-operation with the 8th Army did not receive the recognition it deserved at the time, nor was the lesson properly learned that close support was capable of demoralising and destroying the enemy's will to resist. At Monte Cassino in Italy and again at Caen in Normandy the mistake was repeated when tactical bombing and straffing was abandoned in favour of massed saturation bombing that merely created a wilderness of destruction. Official publications of this period,

---

[1] Air Ministry Intelligence Summary, 24 July 1943

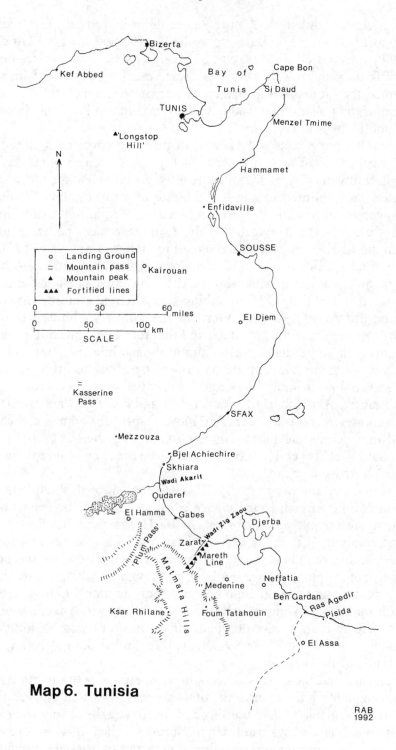

Map 6. Tunisia

RAB
1992

such as the Ministry of Information's 'Tunisia'[1], scarcely mentions the air effort at Plum Pass as being of any real significance. This may have been due to the Air Ministry's reluctance to admit that fighter bombers had such an important rôle to play in support of the army, fearful that the generals would now always expect a similar effort. In the upper reaches of the RAF command it would seem that the defeat of the enemy's air forces still ranked very high in the list of priorities when in fact this had now been achieved in the Mediterranean theatre. Luckily the importance of selective tactical air support was now being recognised so that it would come to fruition in Italy and, by June 1944, achieve its greatest success at Falaise in Normandy.

On 3 April 1943, as the army advanced northwards, the squadron was able to move to El Hamma. 'B' Party arrived there just as the airfield was being attacked by enemy aircraft, but intense AA fire drove the attackers off. The next day squadron personnel amused themselves by making fireworks from captured German cordite. The enemy obliged with a contribution themselves by shelling the airfield and on the 5th shells again fell in the area of Wing HQ and 450 Sqn's dispersals.

Johnny Burcham was detailed to act as Squadron Orderly Officer and he remembers being escorted from the Pilots' Mess to the Airmens' Mess by the Orderly Sergeant. Outside a sandstorm was raging and inside the erks sat with their plates of bully beef and mugs of tea. 'Orderly Officer; any complaints?' the Orderly Sergeant yelled in time honoured fashion, and Johnny, a 'sprog PO' as he describes himself, saw in their silence the patience of men who had endured much hardship year in and year out – in many cases airmen had been on the squadron since before the war as their tour of duty was three years. To them he must have appeared as the innocent newcomer. For all their hardship, though, the airmen were as much a set of characters as were the pilots. The two, for instance, who decked themselves out in looted Italian uniforms and then went over to the nearby PoW cage and were surprised when they were bundled inside by the RAF Police. Their release had to be negotiated by the CO; and the aircraftsman fitter who jealously guarded all that remained of the only 3/16ths drill bit on the squadron, sleeping with it to ensure its safety. Since Alamein, when it had been new, it had been worn down to a mere 1½'' in length.

Thirty nine hours and thirty five minutes flying was logged on three operations on the 6 April. To begin with 12 aircraft acted as top cover for 450 Sqn bombing MT in the Mezzouza area and heavy 88mm flak was encountered. This was followed by a bombing mission and finally a second top cover mission for 450 Sqn attacking MT on the road north of Skhiara. The Germans and Italians were now grimly holding on to their next defensive line at Wadi Akarit, desperate to prevent the link up between the 1st and 8th Armies.

Here a broken line of hills crosses the gap between the El Hamma salt marshes and the sea. General Messe was not, however, given time to prepare his defences nor mine the approaches even though the position was a strong one. During the night of 5 April the 2nd Gurkha Rifles on the extreme left advanced in total darkness and took the enemy by surprise and secured the Jebel Beida. At 4 in the morning there was a 15 minute barrage and a general attack. By mid-afternoon the enemy line had been broken and 9500 prisoners taken. That night the Axis troops fell back and British patrols made

[1] 'Tunisia', HMSO 1944

contact with advance units of the American 1st Armoured Div on the Gabes Road.

On the 7 April operations continued with 34 sorties, the first being a top cover mission to 260 Sqn; the second bombing MT on the Bjel Achiechire road where 250-lb bombs fell in the target area and there was one near miss on a group of three vehicles, one of which was destroyed in the subsequent strafe.

On the final mission, led by the Wg Cdr, vehicles were left in flames. Fg Off L C Cherry (FR412) and Sgt W Blake (FR137) both had to crash-land their aircraft but neither pilot was injured. Sgt J T Hounsell was missing until the following day having had to force land FR412 elsewhere.

Intensive air operations continued until the 8th, the usual sign that the land war was going according to plan. The Axis forces were now in full retreat to their next defensive position, a curved line across the north-eastern corner of Tunisia from Enfidaville to Kef Abbed, behind which the port of Bizerta and Tunis constituted the enemy's last hope of evacuation from Africa. Evacuation, however, had been forbidden by Hitler who had demanded that this final toehold should not be turned by the Allies into the the springboard for their assault on southern Europe.

112's air activity continued at high intensity with operations over Sfax. On the 9th six aircraft flew as top cover to 450 Sqn on an armed recce north of the town but they reported little activity and only slight flak. After this there were no operations for the next four days. Squadron personnel were given the chance to see themselves on film when 'Desert Victory' was shown at HQ 239 Wing. On the 13th 'A' Party under 2/Lt Winter, the IO, left for El Djem. This new airfield lay between Sfax and Sousse, but the squadron's stay there was brief as 'B' Party was instructed to continue north to Kairouan. This was the first occasion that the rear party, consisting of Sqn HQ, Maintenance and 'A' Flt ground crews, leapfrogged the advance party.

On 17 April 1943 there were fighter sweeps over the Cape Bon area during which vehicles were straffed. By the following night the whole squadron had gathered at Kairouan. Two aircraft were wrecked on landing, FR517 (Fg Off Ross) and FR338 (Flt Sgt 'Canada' Brown), neither pilot was injured. On the 19th there were more sweeps over Cape Bon and four Bf109s were seen but there was no action although 450 Sqn claimed a 109 and a Ju88. 'Canada' Brown again wrote off an aircraft (FL882). The following day Montgomery attacked Enfidaville, pushing out the 164th and 90th Light Infantry Divisions, but acting principally to occupy the enemy's attention while General Alexander could launch his attack in the centre with the 1st Army. That day saw 112 engaged in sweeping the Cape Bon area once more, perhaps hoping for a chance to get amongst the enemy transport aircraft, Ju52s or the lumbering Me323s, but with no success. One Ju88 was caught and although it was shot down no one pilot claimed it as the whole formation queued up to have a turn. In the end it crash-landed where it was straffed for good measure. The next day, though, during a fighter sweep over Cape Bon, the top section was bounced by four Bf109s of *II/JG27* who came out of cloud. The formation tried to break but Flt Sgt Lamont and two of the newer pilots, Sgt Hounsell and Sgt A E Prain were shot down by *Lt* Schneider and *Uffz* Stanglmaier. Their bodies were never found.

Breaches had by now been made all along the enemy's forward line and despite a counter-attack by the Hermann Göring Division, supported by Mark VI 'Tiger' tanks, the Allied advance continued. By 23rd 'Longstop Hill' (Jebel Ahmera) had been taken but the enemy's resistance was tough and the Allied advance costly. That day 112 Sqn flew twelve sorties, all fighter sweeps in search of enemy transport aircraft. Two days later, on 25th the squadron acted as top cover while 3RAAF bombed shipping off Cape Bon Point. The squadron shared a Bf110 with 3 Sqn and claimed 'eight-ninths' of the victim. The diarist wrote that the enemy aircraft 'sank . . . through sheer weight of lead'. The month finished with more anti-shipping sorties. Five Bf109s were seen and two of them made half-hearted attacks from 1000 yards but then broke away. The airmen were forbidden to go into the holy city of Kairouan for fear of catching diseases.

General Alexander's plan of attack on the ground was simply to apply pressure along the whole front line but to concentrate his main attack up the Medjerda Valley at the point closest to Tunis. This attack was timed to start on 6th May. 112 continued to roam the otherwise empty skies over Cape Bon and at Si Daud a jetty was bombed, and a warehouse which blew up with a large explosion. These missions continued for the first week of May without any interruption from the enemy air force. A Cant Z506B, a large trimotor seaplane, was straffed while taxiing in the Bay of Tunis by Flt Sgt F R Vance, who was a relative newcomer to the squadron. It sank.

On 8th May Bizerta was taken by the US 2nd Corps and the 7th Armoured Division entered Tunis. When the tanks reached the town centre they found German officers drinking coffee in the cafés, quite unaware of what was happening. That day the whole Hammamet line collapsed and the Allied armies, gathering speed, hurled themselves at the Germans, who turned tail and fled for the beaches desperately looking for boats. There were no boats, the Axis army disintegrated into a rabble.

On 9 May the squadron was sent to bomb the landing ground at Menzel Tmime and some trucks. The next day they escorted Bostons bombing Pantellaria, the tiny Italian-held island lying between Tunisia and Sicily. The final day of the North African campaign, 11th, was taken up with eleven sorties in the Cape Bon area and an attack on a flak position. Sgt R W Staveley (FL714) was hit and forced to pancake his aircraft near Hammamet, but he was unhurt and returned the same day. The surrender of the Axis forces in Tunisia was celebrated by Verey cartridges and small arms fire of every kind. 'It was a veritable victory night with a very striking resemblance to November 5th' wrote the squadron diarist.

Sqn Ldr Garton was posted out and on 17th the new squadron commander, Sqn Ldr G H Norton arrived from 450 Sqn. Victory celebrations continued and the airmen all received a quart of Tunisian wine. General von Arnim was captured by the Royal Sussex Regiment and Marshal Messe surrendered unconditionally. 252,415 enemy prisoners were taken, including 15 German and seven Italian generals. In all the battle for Tunis had cost the Axis 340,000 men and the *Afrika Korps* was no more. The Mediterranean was now open again to Allied shipping and the whole of what Churchill called 'the soft underbelly of Europe' was threatened with invasion. The Allied seaborne attack on North Africa had been the first great amphibious landing of the war and one in which many lessons were learned which would be of inestimable value when the Atlantic Wall was to be breached.

Between 18–22 May 1943 the squadron was involved in a move south to Zuara and the pilots' Mess was the old Railway Station Hotel. Eddie Ross was messing officer at that time and used to exchange the issue 'V' cigarettes for fresh meat in the guise of live sheep. The problem of slaughtering was overcome by employing a butcher in Tripoli who did the dirty work. This was most satisfactory and a welcome change from bully beef until one day when Eddie Ross went to look at his slaughterhouse he found the man preparing a goat – the pilots had never noticed the difference, and Eddie never told them!

Johnny Burcham remembers sharing a tent with Wally Rutherford, the large, quiet, placid Canadian, who appeared one day with a chameleon which he had adopted and which was called Gus. This poor creature was made to do its tricks by being placed on different coloured paper to see whether it would change its hue to match its background. In the end, perhaps out of irritation or perhaps because it became relatively tame, it reverted to a sort of unchanging pale yellow colour.

Burcham shared an aircraft with Len Cherry, a meticulous pilot who somehow always managed to stay neat and tidy throughout the rigours of the campaign. Cherry suddenly decided that he could make his aircraft go faster if he were to sandpaper all the camouflage paint off, which he proceeded to do, helped, out of a sense of duty, by Johnny but to the great amusement of the ground-crew who sensibly stayed in the shade. When this monumental task was completed Cherry was convinced he would be able to fly at least 3 to 4 mph faster. Unfortunately his theory was never thoroughly tested as the next day the aircraft was pranged by another pilot.

By the end of the month several of the aircrew 'old hands' had been posted out and new pilots posted in. It was a time for adding up squadron victories and losses and it was calculated that, by the end of the Tunisian campaign, 200 e/a had been shot down and confirmed and it was further claimed that, of all the DAF Kittyhawk squadrons, 112 was the highest scoring. There had also been a competition with 111 Sqn, the Sharks' senior by one digit, who were flying Spitfire Vs based at Mateur, south of Bizerta, as to which squadron would reach 200 first. Who won is not recorded. 112 had lost 122 aircraft as a direct or indirect result of enemy action.

Amongst the airmen the even 'older hands' remembered that when they embarked in HMS '*Argus*' in 1939, they had been told their tour in Egypt would be no longer than six months. When it was 'beer ration night' in the Mess Sgt Harrison, an ex-Brat[1], would lead the singing of 'The Hymn of 112' to the tune of '*Deutschland, Deutschland, über Alles*' —

> 'Goebbles, Goebbles! Binding bastard,
> Worked a flanker on 112!
> Sent them out to sunny Egypt,
> Only six short months to do!
> We will fix him, we will fix him!
> Send him out to One-One-Two!
> We will fix him, we will fix him,
> And we'll fix that (*cres*) binding bastard Hitler too!'

---

[1] A 'Brat' was an RAF Apprentice trained at RAF Halton

CHAPTER FIVE

From Sicily to Rome

The Desert Air Force and the North African Air Force were now amalgamated to form a single operational command, a Tactical Air Force, and although administered separately, they operated as one. Needless to say the squadron members continued to consider themselves as part of the Desert Air Force and continued to refer to themselves as such for the whole of the Italian campaign so as not to be confused with the johnny-come-latelies of the North African Air Force. On the aircraft and MT desert camouflage continued to be used until 112 re-equipped with Mustangs in mid-1944.

On 21 June 1943 the squadron flew to Sorman LG and the next day there was a parade for HM King George VI. Flt Lt Longmore, then on 450 Sqn, but later a Flight Commander on 112, wrote: 'The parade was a most inspiring sight. Over 100 Kittyhawks were lined up on both sides of the runway with 50 personnel lined up in front of each squadron. In addition there were Spitfires, Mosquitoes, Hurricanes and other aircraft. HM duly arrived sitting in the back of a car dressed in the uniform of a Field Marshal, accompanied by Montgomery and Broadhurst, with Sir Archibald Sinclair (Secretary for Air) and Air Marshal Tedder following in another car.'

Flying practice continued until the end of the month and 'toughening-up' route marches and PT were organised for the airmen. As a result of the new pilots posted in there was a spate of flying accidents – 245798 was wrecked on 20th, FL710 on 21st and FR448 on 29th, although what the causes were or who was involved is not recorded. At this time the Wing lost its Wg Cdr, Billy Burton, DSO, DFC, who was in a Lockheed Hudson that was shot down over the Bay of Biscay by a Ju88. Sqn Ldr O V Hanbury, DSO, DFC, who was going back to the UK to be married and Wg Cdr P T Cotton, DFC, all well-known DAF pilots, also lost their lives. Posted in to replace Wg Cdr Burton was Wg Cdr John ('Jackie') Darwen, DFC & bar.

Jackie Darwen was already something of a legend in the desert. He was a regular pilot from pre-war days and had served on 27 Sqn flying Westland Wapitis on the North-West Frontier of India and was, like so many pre-war RAF officers in India, a keen huntsman. On 8 March 1941 he and his young wife were dancing in the Café de Paris the night it was bombed and she was killed in his arms. The shock of this transformed Darwen into a man whose sole objective was to kill Germans with complete disregard for his own safety. It seemed, though, as if he bore a charmed life. On 9 October 1942, for instance, Darwen, then OC 244 Wing, flying a Hurricane on the 'Daba Prang', force-landed near LG104 after damaging his propellor tips flying too low. At that time Darwen had a scruffy mongrel dog, named Rommel, and the two of them, whenever there was an occasion, would go off hunting desert foxes in a Jeep. For some reason, never fully explained, Darwen would wear his hunting kit for this activity, complete with pink coat, breeches and riding boots. That day the Wing had been hurriedly scrambled and Darwen had had no time to change. Coming to rest in No Mans Land he was rescued by an armoured car belonging to the 11th Hussars and was taken back to their Mess where he was introduced to the Hussar's commanding officer. 'This is the first time I've seen an Air Force officer properly dressed!' was the cavalryman's comment[1].

On 6 and 8 July selected squadron pilots flew to Safi in Malta in order to see what the place was like, and on 9th 12 squadron aircraft flew there. The next day the invasion of Sicily began. At that time 112 Sqn consisted of 17 officer pilots, five non-flying officers, 17 NCO pilots, 229 groundcrew and 18 aircraft. Thus equipped the squadron prepared to begin its assault on the 'soft underbelly' of *Festung Europa*[2]. On 11th the squadron, flying from Safi, took part in its first operational mission in support of the landings on the southern coast of Sicily.

Whether the invasion of Sicily and the long slog up the length of Italy made sound strategic sense is arguable, but Stalin had been calling for a Second Front, and while this was not quite what the Soviet leader had in mind, it had the advantage of tackling one of the three Axis partners on his own home territory, pinning down German troops that might otherwise have been used to garrison the Atlantic Wall, obtaining airfields within range of Germany and helping the resistance forces in Yugoslavia. None of these objectives actually required the conquest of the whole of Italy – occupation of an area that included Naples and the Foggia clutch of airfields would have been sufficient – but, as will be seen in the following pages, once begun, there seemed no way of halting the slow, ferocious slogging campaign. British planners consistently urged the maintenance of pressure on the Germans in the Italy in order to grind down the *Wehrmacht* but General Marshal, the American commander, feared the creation of a Mediterranean vacuum which would drag in men and *matériel* required for the 1944 invasion of France. The invasion of Sicily began on 10 July 1943 with simultaneous landings by the 8th and 7th Armies, about 478,000 men, under Montgomery and Patton respectively, with Alexander in overall command. The Axis forces, the 6th Army, under the command of an Italian, General Guzzoni, numbered some 330,000 men.

Sqn Ldr Norton (FR440) led the squadron's first attack on Sicily with a formation of 12 aircraft which included Gp Capt Darwen of 239 Wing, bombing MT on a road near Carlentini. Direct hits were obtained. The diary records that the groundcrew who were still kicking their heels back at Zuara were getting restless at being left out of the action. On 12th another mission was flown from Safi, attacking gun positions in support of the forward troops in the Melilli area, inland from Syracuse.

The next day the squadron suffered two casualties. In a close support mission of 12

[1] Gp Capt J E Johnson, CBE, DSO, DFC, quoted in 'Freedom's Battle'; although he spells Darwen's name incorrectly.
[2] 'Fortress Europe', Hitler's phrase.

aircraft straffing MT on the road between Carlentini and Lentini where units of the Herman Göring Division were taking up defensive positions, the squadron commander in FR793 ('J') and Flt Sgt Vance (FR502, 'D') both failed to return. Fg Off R V Hearn was also missing for a while but he had force-landed at Pachino within the 8th Army bridgehead. The loss of Sqn Ldr Norton, the first CO to fall, was a severe blow to those who knew him. He had been a Flight commander on 450 Sqn and he was remembered by the 112 pilots for his famous story that began 'The sun came streaming through the window . . .'

Flt Lt A P Q Bluett, 'A' Flt commander who had been on the squadron since 22 May, led the mission on 14 July. Once again the target was MT but bombs were not dropped as our own forward troops were reported to be in the vicinity. Ray Hearn reported back having had his aircraft repaired by a Servicing Commando. The next day the squadron was taken over by Sqn Ldr Pete Illingworth from 260 Sqn. He began his tour of duty with the squadron that same day by leading a formation on a close-support mission between Gerbini and Raddusa. By that day the front had stabilised between Porto Empedocle in the west to just north of Augusta on the eastern side with seven Allied divisions already occupying about a quarter of the island. But now the resistance began to stiffen. The Italian coastal defenders had initially fled and the situation had been chaotic to the extent that the Italians had even managed to impede the Germans in bringing their forces to bear. Now, however, the German divisions began to fight obstinately. There were no squadron operations for the next three days and on 17th 'A' and 'C' parties left Malta in an LST for Sicily, arriving in Syracuse the following day. By the time they reached Pachino LG they found that the squadron aircraft had already arrived. The airstrip, which had been used by the *Luftwaffe* during the bombing of Malta, was sited in a vineyard where the natural surface had been levelled. The retreating Germans had ploughed it up but it had been easily repaired by the Royal Engineers. Back at Zuara Flt Lt Laurie Usher was posted away and 'B' Flight was taken over by Flt Lt W J M Longmore.

On 19 July 1943 the squadron began operations from Pachino by attacking a jetty and some fishing boats at Reposto. There were four direct hits. That day 'B' Flt at last received its orders to move and left Zuara for Tripoli.

The 20th was the busiest day of the month. Thirty-six operational sorties were flown, three missions at 07.55, 14.50 and 17.45 hrs. The first, led by Flt Lt Bluett, was an armed recce of three roads running from Catania round Mount Etna. Two 60′ barges, travelling in line astern, were attacked and one direct hit was scored on the leading vessel, from which came some accurate light flak. The second operation led by Wg Cdr R ('Raz') Berry of 239 Wing, flew a close-support mission to the army by bombing enemy troop concentrations at a cross roads. The final effort was bombing gun positions and all bombs were reported to have fallen within the target area. The army later sent a message to say that this attack had been very successful.

Bombing attacks continued for the next couple of days with operations against a warehouse, two stationary trains and MT between Troina and Randazzo. As a result of this latter attack three vehicles were left burning by the bombing and eight by the straffing, including a MkVI 'Tiger' tank. 'B' Party arrived at Syracuse from Tripoli after a long and chilly sea voyage. They docked in the middle of an air-raid and had some difficulty finding where they were supposed to go. After some confusion they left for Pachino at 15.30 hrs and arrived there about an hour later. Thus, for the first time since the debacle in Greece, the whole squadron was back on European soil.

At the front the Canadians, after heavy fighting, captured Leonforte, forcing the 15th Panzers back northwards. Lightning thrusts had taken the American 7th Army across the whole of western Sicily against weak opposition and Palermo had been taken on 22nd while at Trapani and Castellammare 20,000 Italians were forced to surrender. In the east the 8th Army was facing much stiffer opposition as the Germans withdrew behind a strong defensive line with Mount Etna as a splendid observation position.

There was an armed recce by the squadron on 24 July, led by the CO, bombing ten-plus MT. There were two direct hits on trucks. 'B' Party, now settling in, were apparently much impressed by the new 'Compo' rations as well as the abundance of grapes in every dispersal. Armed recce continued in support of Montgomery's plan to 'isolate' the battlefield. As far as 112 was concerned this meant straffing the roads round Mount Etna. This was referred to as 'going round the mountain' with the alternatives being whether they went round it clockwise or anticlockwise.

In the afternoon of that day the Fascist Grand Council in Rome finally summoned up enough courage to depose Mussolini and King Victor Emmanuel ordered his arrest. Some of the groundcrew went swimming in a nearby bay.

There were two operations on 26th, one of 12 aircraft in the morning and a second one in the afternoon, both armed recces. On the first a farmhouse and gun positions were attacked and on the second the railway station at Cartenanuova was bombed. There was one direct hit on four freight trucks and fires were started. The next day a bridge was attacked at Castiglione along with a factory and some MT. Four direct hits were claimed and the bridge was demolished, which was excellent bombing since bridges were notoriously difficult to hit squarely. Giordini marshalling yards were attacked later and a warehouse suffered. Twenty bursts of flak were seen over Catania but they caused no damage.

There were no operations then until 29 July when 12 aircraft attacked a railway terminus. Again buildings were hit and the next day Giordini marshalling yards were bombed. Sgt Staveley was forced to crash-land his aircraft but he returned to the squadron the same day. Now the whole Allied line was starting to swing, pivoting on the vital Primasole Bridge, slowly forcing the Germans into a tighter and tighter perimeter. Agira on the left of the 8th Army front was captured by the 1st Canadian Div and on 30th Cartenanuova fell to the 78th Div. the final day of the month was marked by 24 operational sorties. Twelve of these were on a road where they chanced upon some MT and enemy personnel which were straffed – 'Twenty-plus bodies' as the diarist recorded. The second mission attacked the road running out of Transavilla.

For the first time the squadron aircraft serial numbers can all be listed from squadron records along with their aircraft letters, something that up to now has only been rather fragmentarily recorded. Twenty-two aircraft ran the length of the alphabet from 'A' to 'K' (ignoring the letter 'I' which was never used, also 'G' and 'L') and then 'M' to 'Z' (ignoring the letters 'O', 'S', 'U' and 'Y'). Certain letters were plainly not used for fear of confusion – 'I' with 'J' and 'O' with 'Q' for instance, but there were sometimes squadron superstitions about certain aircraft letters which would not be used for long periods. 'S' was one such letter which was not used from October 1942 until January 1944 following a run of losses of aircraft carrying it.

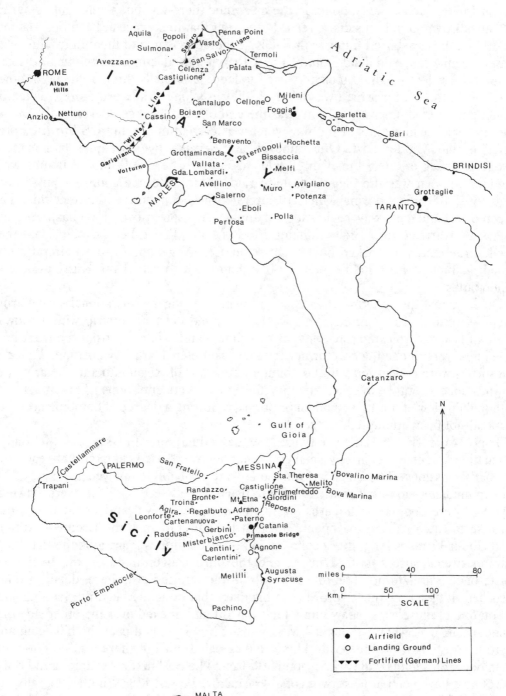

Map 7. Sicily & Southern Italy

RAB
1992

On 1 August 'A' Party, consisting of 'A' Flight's ground crew and armourers moved forward from Pachino to Agnone. In the meantime there was no operational flying. Flt Lt James Longmore, in his diary, records an event that took place at Pachino. At about 16.30 hrs, the sky started filling with B-24D Liberators, some of them in trouble, with feathered airscrews and dead motors. There then followed 'a most alarming air display' as these huge four-engined monsters tried to land. Eventually three of them got down onto the Pachino strip, which was barely 1200 yards long, while two more crashed on neighbouring landing grounds. This was the end of what has been described as one of the most spectacular raids of the war which was carried out by the US 9th Air Force based in the Middle East. One hundred and seventy five machines had made a low-level attack on the Rumanian oilfields at Ploesti where 260 tons of bombs were dropped in what was the biggest daylight raid so far. The operation had involved a flight of 2,400 miles during which 19 aircraft were shot down. The machines had become lost on their way back and had found themselves over Benghazi. Altering course they arrived over Sicily thinking it was Malta. The Liberator pilots said they needed fuel and when asked how much replied 2,400 gallons for each aircraft. The squadron fuel bowsers held a mere 700 gallons each to refuel the Kittyhawks' 157 gallon tanks.

On 2 August the squadron was back in business flying 24 operational sorties from Pachino, returning to Agnone. This was another old German airstrip with a runway made of lava and volcanic ash, lying, at that time, barely six miles from the front line. The tents were pitched near a former Italian coast defence artillery position. That day the sorties were concerned with bombing an area east of Regalbuto and the army put down smoke to guide the aircraft onto the enemy concentrations. This attack was within plain view of the 1st Canadian positions, requiring a degree of bombing accuracy that had not been attempted before.

There were six operations on 3rd, the day which saw the start of the Italian evacuation of Sicily. That day smaller formations were used, four aircraft each, on 'rhubarb' missions. The smaller formations were probably employed as enemy MT now immediately took cover whenever the usual armed recces, which were flown at 10,000', were spotted. 'Rhubarbs' were flown at deck level and counted on total surprise to catch MT in the open. The first four aircraft took the Bronte – Adrano road, about 12 miles long, the second, taking off five minutes later, took the Paterno – Adrano stretch, also about 12 miles, and the third concentrated on the road from Misterbianco to Paterno. The fourth group of four straffed elsewhere, details are not recorded. Flt Lt Longmore recorded in his diary that he 'got a beautiful flaming staff car on one of these trips. I saw him a long way off and ducked over the other side of a range of hills . . . when I thought I was opposite him I popped over the hill again and there he was, right on the bead. Three bodies baled out but there was no cover for them being on a long bridge with a good 50' drop. The car burst into flames and I think there must have been at least two 'good' Germans[1]. Fg Off Reg Wild, DFC, failed to return at 11.15. He was one of the most remarkable of all the Australian pilots, having arrived on the squadron as a sergeant in August the previous year. David Brown remembers his wide grin and nasal Aussie accent, his huge enjoyment of life and

[1] Germans were only considered 'Good' Germans when they were dead.

outstanding ability as a fighter pilot. As a Flight Sergeant he had led the Wing and his flying and marksmanship was second only to Billy Drake. The squadron waited to see if he would return.

That day Adrano was attacked, this town being the key to Centuripe which, in its turn was the key to Mount Etna, 19,758' high, which stood like some huge sentinel covering the three approach roads to Messina.

There were nine missions that day, the first eight being of four aircraft each, seven 'rhubarbs' and one recce and the final operation being of eleven aircraft over Mount Etna, then east to the coast, straffing every possible target. Flt Lt Longmore casts some light on this particular operation which was the brainchild of the Wing Leader, Gp Capt Darwen. Two squadrons flew in line astern, flying parallel in a northerly direction over Etna. At a given word of command every aircraft turned sharply right and, in two long extended lines abreast, swept down on the columns of vehicles moving along the roads which now lay across their line of flight. Straffing as they went the aircraft were out to sea almost before the flak gunners had realised what was going on – although plainly this didn't stop them inflicting some damage to the Kittyhawks.

Fg Off Rae ('Goose') Guess (FR429 'P') failed to return, Fg Off H J M Barnes baled out over the sea but later returned uninjured having been picked up by a Walrus and Flt Lt Bluett returned with almost the whole of his rudder shot away, an extraordinary example of the type of punishment the Kittyhawk could take and still fly. All that remained of the rudder amounted to about two square feet. On 5th the squadron moved camp up to the top of a nearby hill so as to avoid the mosquitoes that plagued them at the lower level.

Reg Wild returned on the following day, with his aircraft, having spent three days with the Americans on the northern side of Sicily. Three of his friends, including David Brown who recalls the occasion, were gathered in the Mess early that evening about to celebrate being recommended for commissions 'when the door opened and there was Reg, parachute and helmet under his arm, grinning as widely as ever and demanding beer. The party was something to be remembered.' David Brown also remarked that the British were usually in a minority as far as pilots were concerned, but all were very proud that 112 was a Royal Air Force squadron as opposed to 3RAAF Sqn and 'the motley bunch of hybrids known as 250, 450 and 260 Sqns, who made up the Wing. 112's tradition was immortalised by the letters R.A.F. emblazoned across the roof of the Mess tent to remind all colonials and lesser breeds . . .'

Flt Sgt I Treloar failed to return from operations on 7th which was an armed recce 'round the mountain' from Paterno – Adrano – Bronte – Randazzo – Castigliano, about 45 miles. There was some flak but few MT and only five vehicles were claimed. The second mission was a shipping recce and two small tugs were attacked, one was sunk and the other left listing. A Siebel ferry[1] was also hit. In the north of Sicily Patten was trying some combined operations, leap-frogging behind the German lines in a series of amphibious envelopments, causing General Hube to abandon the San Fratello position. Adrano finally fell on the 7th and Catania on the 8th.

Road straffing continued that day, resulting in a further four MT vehicles claimed as

---

[1] A Siebel ferry was a troop and freight landing craft with AA gun positions at each of the four corners and room for 150 men and two 88mm guns.

'flamers', eight MT and one *PzKw III* tank damaged on the first op and two vehicles destroyed and two damaged on the second. It was about this time that squadron pilots decided to do something about five Italian 14-pdr field-guns and about 2000 rounds of ammunition abandoned in a nearby coast defence battery. With no inconsiderable effort two of these 75mm guns were towed out of their gun pits and positioned outside the Pilots' Mess, facing seawards again. Fg Off Martin Barnes, because of his claim that he had had artillery training, was made OC 112 Field Battery and was ordered to train a crew. On 9 August 1943 there was an armed shipping recce of eight aircraft to the Gulf of Gioia, north-east of the Straits of Messina. A hospital ship was seen and one 50' barge, the latter being attacked. The second operation was somewhat further afield, round the 'toe' and 'heel' of Italy. No shipping was seen except a 60' barge which was attacked without effect. The squadron was visited by Wg Cdr Billy Drake who flew over from Malta in a Spitfire and the airmen went sightseeing in Catania.

One of the irritations of that particular period was 'Etna Emma', a German 210mm heavy howitzer which occasionally lobbed shells whenever there was transport on the roads bringing up supplies. If ever the Kittyhawks were sent to deal with it the gun was hauled quickly back out of sight into a cave. On 10th, as the German troops began their orderly withdrawal from Sicily, the squadron had a day off and personnel went bathing and sightseeing. The next day operations resumed with a strafe of the Fiumefreddo – St Theresa road. Five vehicles were damaged and one railway truck was left burning, one small barge was damaged and two machine gun posts silenced. That night, at 23.00 hrs the airfield was bombed and high explosives and incendiaries fell amongst the aircraft. This air raid was an attempt by the Germans to wipe out the DAF so that the evacuation of Sicily could go ahead unimpeded. The raid had actually begun earlier, around 21.30 hrs, just after the pilots had finished watching a Beaufighter get the better of a German aircraft that came down on the foreshore and burned itself out. The raid itself started with parachute flares dropping all around, so all personnel withdrew to dugouts and shelters, preferably where they could see the show. When they had picked out the airstrip a German aircraft dropped a green flare to attract the rest. The first bomb severed the telephone lines to the AA batteries and the incendiaries set fire to the grass and the peaty soil. 90% of the squadron were quite safe, being up on the hill and away from the landing ground but Gp Capt Darwen ordered everyone down from the heights to fight the fires, which luckily were not spreading. Many of the aircraft were found to be punctured by bomb splinters. While helping to extinguish a fire 539303 AC1 Croft was killed by a high explosive bomb which fell near him, close to the Ops Room and 1259301 LAC Wallis, a Medical Orderly was injured. The following morning 112 Sqn had twelve aircraft serviceable and by 10.00 hrs they were back at full strength. The Spitfire Wing based at Lentini fared worse and many of their aircraft were destroyed. AC Bob Sinclair, a Fitter IIE, had been due to stand guard that night but had been taken ill, apparently with jaundice and AC1 Croft had been detailed to take his place. Sinclair was evacuated to Tunis with Wally Wallis.

When their treatment was completed Sinclair and Wallis were obliged to find their own way back to 112 and there appeared to be no shuttle service that would take them. Eventually they hitched a ride in an American DC3 Dakota which, to their discomfort, they found to be loaded with hundreds of tins of petrol. After the aircraft had been airborne for a while one of the two engines packed up. Flying a heavily laden Dakota on one engine was not easy and the pilot got Sinclair and Wallis up front to help him hold the aircraft straight by keeping the rudder bar hard over, an extremely tiring task. Reaching Sicily it was discovered that there was a strong cross-wind on the runway where the Dakota was to land, and it took the American pilot seven attempts before he was able to get the Dakota safely down.

Through Wallis knowing a Gp Capt Medical Officer they were able to make their way back to 112 Sqn which, by that time, had moved to Bari, on the Italian mainland.

Wally Rutherford was now taking his pet chameleon Gus on operational sorties, perching the lizard on the aircraft's gyro gunsight where it seemed content until, at the bottom of the bombing dive, considerable G-force was required to pull out. At this moment Gus would always lose his grip and vanish into the recesses behind the instrument panel. At the end of each sortie Wally had to get out of the aircraft, take off his parachute and then clamber back in again to search for the missing Gus. After about five such sorties Gus got fed up with his life as a mascot and disappeared into the long grass, never to be seen again. Perhaps he found a mate and his progeny are living in Sicily to this day.

The German evacuation of Sicily was undertaken at night between the 11th and 17th but it is curious that the bulk of the 15th Panzer Grenadiers and the Hermann Göring Division were able to depart with most of their heavy equipment despite the Allies total command of the air. In part this was due to the very short sea crossing between Sicily and the mainland, the efficient German organisation and the extremely heavy concentration of flak guns on both sides of the Straits of Messina.

The squadron meanwhile continued operations on 11 August with one mission of 12 aircraft which straffed the Fiumefreddo – Messina road and railway line. At 14.00 hrs AC1 Croft was buried, together with six airmen from neighbouring units. It would appear axiomatic that it is the aircrew who suffer the casualties in wartime and it seems unusual for the groundcrew ever to come to any harm. Apart from some prisoners of war taken in Crete and some others in the retreat from Mechili, 112 appears to have lost only a very few airmen due to enemy action.

David Brown recalls a visit by an American newsreel cameraman, possibly from Paramount Pictures, who was determined to get some action shots of the Kittyhawks on a bombing raid. He tried to persuade the CO and the Engineering Officer to modify a 114 gallon ventral drop tank by inserting an optical flat at the front so that he could be carried under the belly of the aircraft on an operational mission. When the CO pointed out that whoever was carrying him would have no hesitation in jettisoning the ventral tank if the formation was bounced the news-hound replied 'Yeah, I know, but if it worked we'd have great pictures. If not I wouldn't be around to worry you!'

There was another shipping recce on the 13th, again to the Gulf of Gioia where an E-boat and a small barge were attacked. On the return flight a seaplane, afloat on the water, was seen and a Ju52 parked on a beach. Both were strafed. Ten-plus barges were seen in the Straits of Messina and a 3,000 ton ship that was just leaving the harbour. The Straits were a very unhealthy spot at that time and the vessels were not attacked. This type of mission continued for the next couple of days but on 15th a marshalling yard was bombed at a point near Bova Marina on the Italian mainland.

Over 300 freight waggons were seen and a large fire was started, all but one bomb falling within the target area.

At 22.00 hrs on 16 August 1943 Sicily was cleared of the enemy and the squadron finished off the campaign with thirty-six sorties from 06.30 to 16.10 hrs. Siebel ferries in the Messina Straits were attacked through intense flak from both shores, 88mm, 40mm and 20mm bursts being encountered which 'formed a curtain of fire from 4,000' to 8,000'', described by one pilot as '10/10ths flak'[1]. Later it was learned that the Germans had about 35 reinforced heavy batteries of 88mm guns quite apart from the flak guns of smaller calibre. By the evening, when two barges were attacked and destroyed in the Straits, the flak only came from the Italian shore. Major-General Fuller[2] is critical of the apparent immunity the Germans enjoyed during their withdrawal across the Straits of Messina 'in face of their enemy's absolute command of the air' but it would seem he was unaware of the reason for this apparent immunity.

That night there was a celebration in the Pilots' Mess. The two Italian field guns had not yet been fired. In the middle of the celebration the OC Field Battery came in to the Mess with a string and handed it to Gp Capt Darwen and asked him to pull it. 'Sure' he said, and gave it a tug. A shattering crash followed and two 17mm shells hurtled far out into the night across the bay. 'Who said you could fire the guns?' demanded Jackie Darwen, but when it was pointed out that it was he who had fired them he decided it was a jolly good idea and a second salvo was fired. It is said that when the Gp Capt was in the Mess they never played the gramophone record 'Oh, Johnny' as this was the tune Ken Johnson's orchestra was playing when his wife was killed.

David Brown recalls that Eddie Ross, something of a pyromaniac, was a keen member of the gun team. 'As might be expected . . . his face, as the guns boomed forth its challenge to the night and we listened for the splash of the shell far across the water, was a joy to behold . . .' The Royal Navy, however, were somewhat concerned by the unexplained explosions in the bay and when the source was located the 112 Field Battery was ordered to cease operations.

The next day, 17th, the Straits of Messina were again the target area. Siebel ferries and barges were bombed and one ferry sunk. Mobile heavy and light flak were seen on the Italian shore but the AA fire was growing less intense. Attacks on MT in Italy continued with underwing 40-lb bombs which were found to be useful at very low level if the pilot saw a target when it was too late to use his machine guns.

After this operations tailed off somewhat for a while although bombing and straffing missions over the mainland continued until the end of the month. Flt Sgt K F Middlemist (FR866 'T') returned from one low-level operation with his aircraft Cat 2 having hit a telephone pole. Ken Middlemist was a north-countryman with an exuberant personality and was also something of an artist. When he became the No 1 of a pair he was entitled to his own aircraft, which was always 'T'. On this, by the cockpit, he painstakingly painted, of all things, his old school crest. When one machine was damaged beyond repair he repeated this performance on the next 'T' that he was given and so on.

---

[1] A meteorological term usually used to describe the amount of cloud cover, 10/10ths would mean that the sky was totally obscured by cloud.

[2] Fuller, *op cit*

Squadron pilots had noted that on Catania airfield there were some Caproni Ca100 aircraft which had once belonged to the Catania Flying Club, 'Take the lot' said Gp Capt Darwen so 112 acquired three of these small two-seater backward-stagger biplanes of antique appearance, and a day was spent by the pilots and groundcrew assembling them. They were soon painted with RAF roundels and the squadron code letters, GA-1, GA-2 and GA-3. Thus was born the 'Shark Light Aeroplane Club'. These little machines, which resembled Tiger Moths, gave the squadron pilots some fun and enabled them to give the ground crew a taste of flying 'which, in their innocence, they were fantastically keen to sample'. The Ca100, in the Italian fashion, also had back to front throttle control which caused much derision from onlookers. 'The quickest circuit the writer[1] has ever seen was carried out by one pilot who suddenly sighted a small formation of marauding 190s . . .'

The enemy had evacuated some 100,000 troops, 47 tanks and 9,800 vehicles between 3–17 August and the three German divisions which escaped would prove still to be a capable fighting force in the months that followed. After Mussolini's overthrow Italy was governed by Marshal Badoglio who publicly pledged that Italy would continue on the side of the Axis but secretly began negotiations with the Allies. The Germans, fearful that Italy might defect, poured troops into the country and Italian troops were disarmed. Meanwhile the Allied High Command was riven with conflicting choices. The British, who had a long term interest in the Mediterranean, wished to enlarge the theatre of operations into the Balkans while the Americans were keener to syphon troops off to help with the build up for 'Overlord', the invasion of France but, at the same time, were hoping to transfer amphibious assault shipping to the Pacific. Conferences during the month finally decided that Europe was to be the primary theatre until Germany was defeated but that operations in Italy were merely to hold and occupy as many German divisions as possible while preparations went ahead for 'Overlord' which now had priority for men and supplies.

Operations by 112 resumed on 27 August with 11 aircraft escorting Mitchells bombing marshalling yards at Catanzaro. All the bombs fell in the target area and one large explosion was seen. After this there were no further ops for the rest of the month and only the Ca100s were airborne. In retrospect it can be seen that although the Germans in Sicily had been decisively beaten, perfection in the business of close co-operation between the troops on the ground and the aircraft had not yet been achieved. The DAF helped the ground troops only to a very small extent in the Sicilian campaign when it came to *direct* support. A single machine gun could still hold up an advance for half a day while a Kittyhawk could have dealt with it in minutes. This form of really effective air-to-ground co-operation was to evolve during the campaign on the Italian mainland.

Gp Capt Darwen was now experimenting with an unauthodox bombing technique against seagoing vessels which he called 'skip bombing'. This involved a level approach to the target at wave top height, broadside on to the ship, with the moment of bomb release planned to allow it to hit the water horizontally and then skip along the surface like a flat stone to strike the vessel amidships. After one or two unsuccessful attempts the idea was abandoned, much to the relief of the pilots who followed him on these

[1] David Brown, correspondence

attacks and under whom the leader's bomb was apt to explode!

On 3 September 1943 the army began its assault on the mainland. Two British divisions, led by the 51st Highland Div, crossed the Straits of Messina and moved inland against negligible resistance. It was hoped that this would draw the enemy forces down into the toe of Italy where they would be cut off when the main landing was made at Salerno six days later. This did not happen even though the Germans, who had detected the Allied build up, were unaware exactly where the next blow would fall. That day, the 3rd, the Italian signed a secret armistice.

The squadron was engaged in attacking German positions in a wooded gully from which came some light Breda fire. No enemy aircraft were seen. The phrase 'No E/A seen' had now been such a regular entry in the operations log that it would soon be dropped altogether. No hostile machines had been met in the air for three months now and the *Luftwaffe* in Italy was not a serious threat. The realisation that this was a fact soon resulted in the virtual disappearance of the old 'top cover' missions. Armed recces followed the next day along the road from Melito to Bovalino Marina, inland a bit and then back to the coast. Fifty-plus trucks were seen moving north-west but they were well dispersed and thus a poor target. Railway rolling stock was attacked at Bova Marina but no results were observed.

That day Gp Capt Darwen inspected the squadron MT which now all sported a ferocious shark motif on the doors. Jackie Darwen frequently flew with 112 and had, in effect, more or less adopted the squadron. His aircraft, FR868, had his initials 'JD' on the fuselage sides and this machine was always a problem with the armourers as they usually had to change the guns since he tended to melt the barrels with the long continuous bursts of fire he gave to any German who was unlucky enough to get in his sights. He invariably collected a bullet or two in return, his aircraft was rarely undamaged when he landed and frequently it had only about 5 gallons of fuel left in the tank as his solitary flights would take him all around Italy. Once, and not for the first time, the tips of his propellor blades were bent back having scraped the roof of an enemy truck.

On 5 September there was another recce of the Italian coast and inland roads. Despite thick cloud which obscured the ground 18 bombs were dropped. For the next few days similar, rather desultory missions were flown with few positive results. In fact there were very few enemy left in southern Italy for the air force or the army to deal with. The Germans, having divined what was going to happen next were rapidly moving north. On 9 September the Allied invasion at Salerno began under Lieut-General Mark Clark with the 36th US Div and the 46th and 56th British Divs. The beach-head was initially very precarious as hills looked down on it from three sides and the heights were dominated by the German 16th Panzers who, knowing they would be outnumbered initially, organised a mobile defence covered by minefields and wire hoping to contain the beach-head until reinforcements could arrive. The Allies were operating at about the maximum distance that close-support aircraft could operate from Sicily and consequently they could only stay for a short time over the battlefield.

That day the squadron was still roaming around looking for targets in the south and although the beach-head was desperate for air support, 112 were not employed. On the 10th they were packing up and over the next few days, the critical ones at Salerno, the ground party was moving by LCT from Syracuse to Taranto. That day the aircraft left for Grottaglie, just inland from Taranto, in the 'heel' of Italy. The Kittyhawks were accompanied by three DC3s in which 48 ground crew personnel and their necessary equipment were transported. Without the full squadron back-up the ground crews were obliged to work extremely hard for the first few days. Stores had to be manhandled and there was no MT to refuel the aircraft or carry the bombs and ammunition. Fuel had to be pumped into the Kittyhawks by hand using a pump borrowed from an MC202 squadron, and all supplies had to be flown in, also 112 was only separated from the enemy front line by a thin screen of the 1st Airborne Div.

It was not before the 15th that the squadron was in a position to come to the aid of the beach-head and the first sorties were flown to bomb and strafe road movement in the Salerno area, but this was abortive due to bad weather. Kesselring, the German commander in southern and central Italy, had now brought up elements of five Panzer and Panzer Grenadier Divisions to assist the 16th Pz Div in its attempts to push General Mark Clark's troops back into the sea before the 8th Army could reach the area. The 13 September had seen some of the fiercest fighting and the Germans had come close to cutting the British troops off from the Americans. By the 15th the Allies had managed to land much needed reinforcement, including the 7th Armd Div, and the beach-head was made safe. It has been pointed out[1] that if Rommel, who was then commanding the German troops in northern Italy, had seen fit to send two or three of his divisions south to help Kesselring, the Salerno landings would certainly have failed. As it was Rommel could see no point in defending southern Italy.

As soon as the weather cleared sufficiently 112's Kittyhawks were active in attacking MT in the Potenza – Muro – Eboli – Polla area. Vehicles and a tank were destroyed. Some 40mm flak and some accurate Breda fire were encountered and this probably accounted for the loss of Ken Middlemist, recently promoted to Warrant Officer, flying FR814 'T', when he tried a second run, usually an unwise thing to do, over some enemy positions near Pertosa. Operations continued on the 16th, the day the squadron's sea party reached Taranto but, due to lack of any transport they didn't reach Grottaglie until the evening. They were very welcome as they had brought the squadron's fuel bowsers. There was an armed recce of the Potenza area by five aircraft led by Gp Capt Darwen. The sixth, flown by Sgt Ken Cockram, pranged on take off. Darwen was not in the habit of waiting for the rest of the formation and, as he was invariably in a hurry to get at the Germans, he was away that day, literally in a cloud of dust. The second pair added to the dust cloud and the third pair, led by Sgt David Brown, was taking off 'on instruments'. Cockram swung slightly and hit a tree just after becoming airborne in FR839 'J'. David Brown believes that Allah was smiling on him that day as he 'rose up into the blessed sunshine with nothing worse than a severe attack of heart failure. We proceeded on the recce while I wondered what had happened to poor Cockram and my relief can be imagined when I landed to find him waiting to greet me'. He was evidently unhurt as he took part in a later operation that day. On the second mission, which was again an armed recce of the Potenza – Avellino – Vallata road three enemy vehicles were left burning and 12 were damaged. Visibility was excellent and the aircraft 'flew at zero feet'. Sgt S T Worbey (FL897 'A') failed to

---

[1] '*The West Point Atlas of American Wars*', Vol II, ed. Brig-Gen V J Eposito (Frederick A Praeger, New York & London, 1959)

return, but he arrived back that afternoon. The final operation was along the Avellino – Grottaminarda – Andretta road but nothing was seen and the aircraft returned with their bombs. On 17th the high rate of flying was sustained. The first mission caught fifty-plus vehicles on the Potenza road and these were bombed and straffed. Five were left on fire and 23 damaged, including one armoured car. More such attacks were carried out on the second operation which was on the road from Potenza to Guardia Lombardi. Twenty vehicles, two MkVI tanks and other transport, including a staff car, were attacked. The third and final mission was against Foggia airfield and its satellites at about 18.45 hrs. Two Ju88s were left burning and two more had near misses from bombs. Twenty Ju88s were seen at the satellite airfield and fifteen-plus single engined and one four engined aircraft on Foggia Main. Late afternoon operations from Grottaglie to the vicinity of Avellino and Vallata often meant that the aircraft returned after dark. Night flying was not the squadron's forte, particularly as the landing ground had only a single Chance Light to guide them home, and consequently the pilots found themselves having to learn the technique rapidly.

On the 18 September 1943 there were two operations, one which took off at 11.45 and the other at 16.55 hrs. The first, which lasted for an hour and twenty minutes, was an armed recce of the Potenza roads once more, and the second was in the same area. Ten vehicles were left burning and 23 damaged, including a tank. Some 88mm guns were seen lying just off a track between Guardia Lombardi and Bissaccia, but they did not open fire. Flt Sgt Staveley was hit at 500′ after a strafe and was seen to crash and was presumed dead.

The following day one of the longest-serving squadron pilots was killed, Warrant Officer W D ('Canada' or 'Western Desert') Brown, on the second operation between Potenza and Avigliano. There was intense flak along the road to Avigliano and at 15.20 hrs FR860, 'D', was seen to go down in a spin from 1500′ and burst into flames as it hit the ground.

The next day the squadron moved to Brindisi on the Adriatic coast where operations continued without a break. On the first mission, again an armed recce, the Paternapoli – Melfi – Benevento road was searched, but no movement was seen and the aircraft returned with their bombs. But on the second some MT were bombed from 1500′ without any results being observed. Similar operations took place on 21st. On the ground Kesselring was starting to withdraw as by 16 September elements of the 8th Army moving up from the south had made contact with a patrol of the 5th Army 40 miles south-east of Salerno. By the 18th the Germans were occupying the first of a series of well-prepared delaying positions in a countryside that was ideal for defence.

'B' Party under the adjutant, Flt Lt Evans, left Grottaglie on 22nd but made for Bari, leaving only a maintenance group to complete repairs on some of the aircraft that had been left behind. The squadron aircraft moved to Bari on the morning of 23 September and there was one operation along the Barletta – Foggia road, then to a railway yard and a wood. The search was on for tank transporters and the corner of the wood was supposedly an ammunition dump but there was no reaction when it was attacked. The next day 12 aircraft flew to Melfi and all the bombs fell in the target area but again no results were observed. After a day free of operations there was a 12 aircraft mission attacking transport along the road from Avellino to Grottaminarda and then from Valetta to Rochetta. Ten-plus MT were bombed and a near miss was seen. The subsequent strafe accounted for three flamers and twelve vehicles damaged

By the end of the month the front line across Italy ran from just south of Naples to just south of Termoli, but with a bulge to the south in the centre where the Apennines were easier to defend. Now Foggia and its clutch of satellites were in our hands. On 1 October Naples fell and Field-Marshal Kesselring withdrew to the line of the Volturno River. By this time also Sardinia had been evacuated by the Germans and Corsica by the 3rd. Although it was now assumed by the Allied Command that the Germans would soon withdraw north of Rome, Kesselring realised that the country favoured the defence and he assumed that, once the Allies had captured the group of Foggia airfields, they would halt and turn their attention to invading the Balkans. From this point on the whole campaign started to bog down, a 'slow, painful advance through difficult terrain against a determined and resourceful enemy'[1] as Kesselring began to build a series of fortified lines organised in depth and based on the various rivers. For 112 Sqn this was to mean a year and a half of dogged interdiction, close-support missions and very little else.

On 3 October the squadron started to move forward from Bari to Foggia and operations resumed on the 4th with a bombing raid in support of the army led by Wg Cdr 'Raz' Berry in his own aircraft (FR507, 'REB'). Two gun tractors and MT were strafed. Pilots established themselves in a flat in Foggia town and the NCOs and airmen were billetted on the airfield. It was difficult enough to find a habitable place for the pilots to live since Foggia was a city of the dead with hardly an undamaged building. Armed recces continued as far as Alfedina the next day, about 60 miles from base as the crow flies and the second mission was a close support operation bombing in the Termoli area where troops were reported to be hiding in a wood. News was received that WO Smith had received the MBE for his work on designing the Kittyhawks' 250-lb bomb racks.

6 October was 'quite the busiest day for some time' according to the diary. Thirty-five sorties were flown on three missions, armed recces, on roads near Termoli and Penna Point. Six-plus MT were observed amongst trees on one of these operations and all bombs were believed to have fallen in the target area. By this time many of the Allies' objectives had been achieved. Italy was out of the war and, indeed, was now a 'co-belligerent', a status that was not quite as prestigious as that of an Ally; the Foggia group of airfields had been captured; the port of Naples was rapidly being restored to working order after the German demolitions and, lastly, the Russian front and the Balkans were being depleted of troops as units were dispatched to Italy. Autumn was setting in and the rivers that lay across the lines of advance were filling with rainwater, streams became torrents and coastal swamps were flooded. The mountainous spine down the centre of Italy was ideal for the type of defensive operations that the Germans were so good at, the Allied troops were unskilled in mountain warfare and the lack of assault ships prevented any repeat of the Salerno landings in the rear of the German lines. However if the campaign had been halted at this point and the British and Americans had gone on the defensive there was always the possibility that a German counter-offensive would regain valuable ground. General Alexander wanted to keep

---

[1] from General H Maitland Wilson's report to the Combined Chiefs of Staff, 8 January–10 May 1944, p.1, quoted by Fuller.

the enemy rocking back 'on his heels' and there was also the lure of Rome, that plum just out of reach. Kesselring had ordered his troops to hold the Volturno until the 'Winter Line' had been constructed.

Torrential rain on the 7th made flying impossible although 260 Sqn managed to get airborne in the afternoon. On this mission Gp Capt Jackie Darwen was shot down, 'plucked from the sky' as Flt Lt Longmore put it, by a lucky hit from an 88mm shell when flying at 8000' as he started his bombing dive onto the target. His No 2, who had been told to 'follow him' whatever he did, went into the ground with him. Darwen would have been about 30 years old.

Flt Lt Hearn led an armed recce of 12 aircraft on 8 October on the roads near San Vito Chietino and Castiglione. Twenty-plus MT, badly dispersed, were attacked. There was a similar operation the next day during which a concentration of MT were attacked in a wood near Palata. Heavy ground shelling was seen five miles south of Termoli where Montgomery's 78th Div was holding the line. There is a mention in the report that 'Rover' was received loud and clear, and indication that Forward Ground Control Posts (FGCPs) and their associated 'Cab Rank' patrols were beginning to operate. Although it would be the end of November before the idea of the ground control of aircraft over the front line was perfected, the system, devised by Gp Capt David Haysom, DFC, an ex-79 Sqn Battle of Britain pilot, was quite simple. On the ground an Air Force officer, identified by his name 'Rover David', 'Rover Paddy' or suchlike, was installed in a jeep and equipped with a radio link to the aircrafts' frequencies. Working right up forward with the advancing troops he would select a point where he could see what was going on. If the advance was held up by any sort of resistance, whether it was a field gun, machine gun nest, or tank, he would call up the waiting Cab Rank, a flight of six ground attack aircraft that was patrolling in the vicinity. Using a gridded map he would indicate to the Cab Rank leader the precise position of the enemy resistance: 'Map reference L.8.3, a monastery, a big white building. I want you to put your bombs 200 yards south'. If there was no plainly visible reference the Cab Rank leader might be instructed to drop a bomb within a certain grid square and Rover would then transmit a correction and the remaining aircraft to bomb in relation to the original bomb burst. The Cab Rank would remain on station for about 20 minutes when they would be relieved by the next six aircraft. If, during their waiting time, the Cab Rank had not been vectored on to any target they were free to fly to a pre-planned secondary target and attack that. The Rover system was wasteful in fuel and it could only be attempted when the Allies had undisputed command of the air. Nevertheless it was an effective method of bringing extremely destructive weaponry down on the enemy within minutes – quicker often than bringing artillery fire to bear. It was the height of satisfaction to hear Rover's comments if the bombs fell where he wanted them, and they were also worth hearing when they were not where he wanted them, particularly if they were anywhere near him! *Luftflotte 4* on the Russian front had adopted a system in June 1941 where a *Panzerverbindungsoffizier* or Tank Liaison Officer was attached to German armoured columns keeping in wireless contact with close support aircraft. Rommel's *Panzerarmee Afrika* had *Fliegerverbindungsoffizieren* (*Flivos*) who were *Luftwaffe* liaison officers whose task was principally to keep *Fliegerführer Afrika* in touch with the position of the forward troops.

There were no operations on the 10th but the squadron commander, Flt Lt Longmore, Fg Off Pepper, Flt Lt Evans and the airmen under WO Doncaster attended a memorial service for the late Gp Capt Darwen, DFC. The next day there was another armed recce to Cantalupo but the aircraft returned without having seen anything as the ground was obscured by low cloud. Very heavy rain interfered with flying for several days and on 16th the diary records 'No operations and no enjoyment owing to bad weather'. This was to interfere with flying right through until the Spring and was the bane of the Allied air forces. Living conditions, as winter approached, became increasingly difficult, airfields were flooded or washed away and everyone was damp and depressed. In the centre of Italy the armies were pressing the Germans back and had established a salient across the Volturno. The enemy fell back slowly from one natural feature to the next and the effectiveness of their defence 'revealed a high order of leadership and skill'[1].

On 17 October an attack was planned on Boiano just behind the front line, but due to the 8/10ths cloud cover between 2000' and 10,000', Oritano was bombed by mistake. No results were observed. The destruction of villages, which had been such a feature of the Sicilian campaign, served little purpose – a lesson which was still not learned when it came to the battle of Cassino. Such bombings usually only killed Italians and did little harm to the Germans. In addition the blocked roads hindered the subsequent Allied advance and the troops then had to cope with large numbers of homeless civilians. A more productive mission was flown on 19th when the CO led an attack on the railway line north of Termoli. Some direct hits were seen. This is the first recorded railway interdiction mission, a type of operation which proved far more successful in sealing off the battlefield from reinforcements and reducing the enemy's transport system to impotence.

On 23rd the aircraft straffed a railway marshalling yard which contained 50–60 rolling stock and the next day a train was left motionless with the engine emitting clouds of steam. Four aircraft of a sub-flight espied a motor-cyclist and destroyed him. At the end of the month the squadron found itself obliged to vacate Foggia as the airfield was to be used by bombers and move to Mileni five miles to the north. A so-called 'iron ring' of bomber airfields had now been completed which would allow penetration into Austria, Germany and even Poland from the Mediterranean by aircraft of the 15th Strategic Air Force. News was received that the 2nd Cameronians had found the grave of WO Ken Middlemist near Pertosa.

In October 1943 the squadron officers and NCO pilots were as follows —

Sqn Cdr: Sqn Ldr Illingworth
Sqn Adjutant: Flt Lt Evans
'A' Flt Cdr: Flt Lt Bluett
'B' Flt Cdr: Flt Lt Longmore
Intelligence Officer: 2/Lieut Winter, SAAF
Sqn Medical Officer: Flt Lt McKenzie
Technical Officer: Flt Lt Pepper
Engineering Officer: Plt Off Weston

---

[1] Eposito, *op cit*

'A' Flight	'B' Flight
Flt Lt Hearn	Flt Lt McBryde (Aus)
Fg Off Horden	Fg Off Cherry
Fg Off Ahern (Aus)	Fg Off Wilkinson
Fg Off Burcham	Plt Off Gray (USA)
Fg Off Ross	WO Drown
Fg Off Matthias	Flt Sgt Nordstrand (NZ)
Fg Off Barnes	Flt Sgt Holmes (Aus)
WO Swinton (Aus)	Flt Sgt Worbey
Flt Sgt Hirons	Flt Sgt Stokes
Flt Sgt Snelgrove (Can)	Sgt Cockram
Flt Sgt Brown	Sgt Jellett
Sgt Peters (Aus)	Sgt Cocks
Sgt Rowe	

The squadron had 17 Kittyhawk III aircraft on strength during the month and, unusually, none had been replaced since the end of September – the extraordinary rates of attrition of the days when the squadron was in the desert were past.

November opened with 'the usual twelve sorties' but the formation split into sections of four to recce different roads. All aircraft returned by 16.10 hrs, one hour and forty minutes after take off. Some MT had been attacked and a gun on a *PzKw II* chassis thoroughly straffed.

On the second mission Fg Off 'Matt' Matthias led a mainly 'A' Flt formation bombing a road south of San Salvo, on the Adriatic coast. No movement was seen. On the 3rd Flt Lt Ray Hearn took a selection from both Flights to act as an old fashioned top cover to 260 Sqn bombing Celenza. 'Rover David' (Haysom) instructed them to bomb the north end of the town, but bombs fell at both ends. Montgomery, on the east side of Italy, had delayed his offensive until the 22 October when he had forced the Trigno River against severe opposition and had now pressed forward to the banks of the Sangro, along which lay Kesselring's Winter Line. The Germans had retired blowing up everything that lay in the 8th Army's path, bridges, roads and culverts and leaving a murderous legacy of mines and booby traps.

Bad weather again interfered with flying for several days but on 5th Flt Lt Longmore (FR492 'V') led a dozen aircraft, escorted by four Spitfires, to Aquila to attack some tanks and MT. North of Sulmona fifty-plus MT were seen moving south-east and these were straffed. On 9th a completely new theatre of operations was opened up to the squadron when they flew to Split in Yugoslavia. Here they attacked a single-funnelled ship of about 4000-tons lying against the southernmost jetty in the south harbour. There were three direct hits on the ship and eight on the jetty. Railway trucks were also hit and the aircraft left with a pall of smoke hanging over them. Torrential rain precluded any operations for a couple of days as the airfield was unfit for flying. On the 12th flying was resumed and the Operations Log for that day is reproduced here as an example of the type of entry —

12/Nov/43 Kittyhawk III

.. FR-492(V)	F/Lt W.J.M. LONGMORE Pilot	1130	1155	Kittyhawks flew to
.. FR-491(R)	F/Sgt WORBEY S.T.	..	1130	1320	Bracki channel and
.. FR-494(W)	F/Sgt SHAW A. (Can)	..	..	..	recced channel and
.. FR-839(J)	F/Sgt STOKES K.S.	..	..	..	ports on N. side of
.. FR-801(H)	F/Sgt PETERS B.H. (Can) ..	..	..	BRACKI ISLAND.
.. FR-439(K)	Sgt JELLETT J.L.	..	..	..	No activity was seen
.. FR-823(P)	F/Lt L. McBRYDE (Aus)	..	..	..	in channel and only
.. FR-806(Q)	F/Lt R.V. HEARN	..	..	..	small fishing boats
.. FR-824(A)	F/Sgt HORDEN H.A.	..	..	..	were seen off jetties
.. FR-496(N)	F/Sgt HIRONS G.L.	..	..	..	in SUPETAR and.
.. FR-803(F)	P/O J.O. GRAY (Can)	..	..	..	SUTIVAN. Noth-
.. FR-812(B)	W/O SWINTON N.E. (Aus)..	..	..	ing. seen in the s.

harbour of SPLIT.
Cloud 10/10 2000
to 10,000 feet over
sea, cleared off
BRACKI island.
No A/A. No E/A.

It would seem from this that Flt Lt Longmore was obliged to return to base after 25 minutes, presumably with some sort of unserviceability. Plt Off 'Tex' Gray is here shown to be a Canadian, presumably because, as an American citizen, he had joined the squadron in an unauthorised fashion, via the RCAF. David Brown remembers him 'Tex . . . a long, lean Texan with red hair and a friendly grin. He wandered into the Mess one afternoon at Grottaglie. Apparently he had got tired of the quiet life back at the Nile delta and hitched a lift up to the squadrons to get some action – just like that. It happened we were running a bit short of pilots and he knew Kittyhawks, so he stayed and became a valued member of the Squadron. This was a typical example, incidentally, of Wing HQ being helpful in arranging little matters like postings when the officer had already arrived and when operational conditions demanded it.'

After a day on road recces on the 13th, 112 were stood down for four days but when operations were resumed it was to act as top cover again, this time for 5SAAF who were bombing Barrea. The second operation encountered bad weather and all the aircraft returned with their bombs. Bad weather continued for over a week, although on 21st, the CO had led a dozen aircraft to attack a defended position south-east of Mozzadrognia. There was an intense box-barrage over Lanciano which burst about 3000' below. The month finished with two busy days in support of the 8th Army push across the Sangro. The first mission was of six aircraft which bombed a target immediately south-west of Fossagesia, directed by the FGCP. Bombing was from 8000' down to 1000', the pilots firing their machine guns as they dived. All bombs fell within the target area and the FGCP reported 'Excellent show!'. The second mission, at 09.20 hrs, again of six aircraft, bombed a target from 7000' down to 1000'. The third operation, led by the CO, attacked a road-rail bridge. Three gun emplacements in the target area were covered in bomb bursts and the bridge over the railway received a direct hit. Aircraft then went down to nought feet to strafe the road north-east from the target but they saw no movement. The fourth mission, at 12.35 hrs, was again controlled by the FGCP. Flt Lt McBryde and his No 2 bombed and the FGCP officer made the necessary correction, in this case a further 200 yards away from the bomb line, and then the remaining aircraft bombed. Four bombs fell in the target area. The final operation lasted from 15.00 hrs to 16.15 hrs and these aircraft attacked their secondary target which was near Lanciano.

The last day of the month was also busy. Another 24 sorties divided into four missions. The first six aircraft attacked a secondary target having patrolled for the stipulated 20 minutes without the FGCP giving them anything. Strikes were observed on a gun emplacement. The formation was warned that there was a Bf109 in the area but it was not seen. The second formation also attacked its secondary target while the third half dozen aircraft were called down to attend to a reference point a mile north of a monastery. The area was bombed successfully and all bombs fell within the target area. The formation saw what they described as 'a flaming ball' falling from about 12,000' about 30 miles north of Pescara, five miles out to sea – the fiery thanatogno-monic fall of some unknown aviator. The last formation for the day attacked its secondary target, the corner of a wood.

Mileni LG, which was built on a reclaimed swamp, was evacuated by the aircraft after overnight rain on 1 December 1943 to a neighbouring landing strip. From there, the next day, 22 operational sorties took off in the few hours of sunshine that there were. Two aircraft failed to return, but neither was seriously damaged. Flt Lt ('Happy') Ahern in FR132 'T' whose aircraft was hit in the glycol system, force-landed successfully behind our lines and Fg Off ('Tex') Gray in FR439 'K', who was hit in the port aileron on the second mission, force-landed at Canne LG. Both were casualties of the very accurate 88mm flak and intense 40mm Breda gun fire.

The pressure eased somewhat on the 3rd as the 8th Army was now across the Sangro River although German resistance did not weaken. The re-supply of ammuni-tion was a problem, tanks bogged down, casualty lists grew longer and because the shortage of reserves local victories could not be exploited. There was one operation by 11 aircraft against a particular corner of the village of San Martino, and some woods directly to the south-west of it, which was suspected of containing infantry and tanks. Nothing was seen and there was little flak.

Perhaps the ghost of Jackie Darwen, up in the pilots' heaven (as the USAAF aircrew song would have us believe) was comforted by the posthumous award of the DSO.

On the 5th flying was resumed after a day of bad weather with a second attack on the Yugoslavian port of Split. Here a 4000-ton ship was sighted together with two 2000-ton vessels in the west harbour. The larger ship was attacked from 7000' down to 1000' and strafed, but except for one bomb that landed on the quay and caused a fire, the other bombs must have missed. Bad weather prevented ops on the 6th and 7th, but the 8 December was a busy day. The CO, Sqn Ldr Illingworth, led two missions and Flt Lt Longmore one. These were big formations of 11 and 12 aircraft each and they went to bomb gun positions in the Casoli and Lanciano areas, on the high ground north of the Sangro valley. The second operation reported that their designated area had only just been attacked by Warhawks when they got there and the third formation reported that their target was hidden under haze from a previous raid.

'The busy period continued' (Sqn diary) on the 9 December when again three operations were flown with 11 aircraft. Every attack was on the same target, a pin-point west of Ortona. The both sections on the first mission bombed from north-west to south-east. Two veteran pilots, WO David Brown and WO Herbie Snelgrove left for No.2 BPD Tunis, operationally tour expired after fifteen months on the squadron. Of the eleven pilots who had been posted in at about the same time, September-October 1942, two had survived unscathed, two had been made PoWs and six had either been killed or been listed missing, believed dead. One other pilot had apparently joined the squadron (Flt Sgt D J Howe, a Canadian) but seems never to have flown on ops. and his date of departure remains unknown. In effect therefore pilots of the 1942–43 period could look forward to a 1 in 5 chance of surviving for a full tour, although this ratio actually decreases to 1 in 3 when considering the 1939–1945 war period as a whole.

On the 10th there were again three operations, one to the Ortona area, the second near Francavilla and the third along the Ortona – Chieti – Pescara road. Vehicles and machine gun positions were attacked and a tank hidden amongst trees was claimed as destroyed. After that bad weather curtailed flying for five days. On 11th Sqn Ldr Illingworth had lunch at 239 Wing with officers of the Soviet Red Army. On 15th, when the weather again cleared sufficiently, there was an abortive operation to Penna Point where cloud covered the whole battle area so the aircraft returned with their bombs. The next day was relatively quiet, with only 13 sorties, an attack on a gun position near Tollo where six direct hits were seen on buildings. After another day with no flying on the 17th, a Breda gun position near Ortona was silenced on the morning operation on the 18th. Gun positions continued to be attacked for the next few days in the face of heavy flak from all calibre weapons. Fg Off R M ('Hawkeye') Wilkinson in FR864 'M' was shot down over Ripa. He was seen to bale out of his flaming aircraft and it was hoped that he had survived. He had, and was made a PoW.

Similar attacks continued for a while near Ripa – a village so small that it appears on no maps of the area – and MT and Breda MG posts were straffed, despite the intense barrage. One aircraft returned Cat 2. The diary records that four South African pilots were posted in, making a total of six. The squadron diarist commented that in the Pilots' Mess Afrikaans was now spoken, English understood!

The last operation before Christmas took place the following day, 22 December. The aircraft attacked gun positions near Tollo and Miglianico. The Ops. Record records that the former target looked like nothing more than a collection of bomb craters and devastation. On the second mission pilots reported that possible smoke signals were seen coming from a point 500 yards east of Ortona, but this was not explained. From the 112 cookhouse though came the sound of pigs being slaughtered for the Christmas meal, and a fatigue party was employed plucking 30 turkeys. Christmas Day, 1943, was recorded as probably being the best in the history of the squadron. An excellent dinner was served to the airmen, as tradition demanded, by the officers at midday. This was followed by prolonged speech-making which extended the meal until 15.00 hrs by which time some of the weaker members had fallen asleep! The CO and the adjutant were seen leaving at about 16.00 hrs. The Christmas spirit evaporated only slowly as it wasn't until the 30th that the squadron continued with the war, and even then only with some training flights.

On the last day of the year 26 sorties were flown. Gun positions were attacked near Chieti and Miglianico. 2/Lt H J Hanreck one of the relatively new SAAF pilots, flying

FR839 'J', was hit on the first operation, just before starting his dive to bomb. He completed his attack and then flew towards the coast and ditched about 200 yards offshore. A rowing boat was seen to be making its way out to him and he returned to 112 in a few days.

About this time news was received of Len Bartley, a pilot on the squadron in 1940 and 1941 who had been taken off MacLennan's barge and made a prisoner of war. It was only now that the story of his adventures became known.

In Greece, when the retreat from Yannina began, Bartley lost his chance to fly a Gladiator to Eleusis through the toss of a coin and was obliged to hitch-hike his way to Athens with five of the ground crew. A Blenheim took him to Crete but once more, when the evacuation of that island began, he was again left without any means of escape until he was able to join McLennan's barge.

As has been previously related the barge was about 30 miles out when they were hailed by a submarine commander in perfect English. Believing this to be a Royal Naval vessel they answered cheerfully and received a burst of machine-gun fire in return. The Italian submarine commander probably then realised the British were unarmed and so merely took aboard what officers there were in the barge and submerged, leaving the remainder to their fate.

On board the submarine, the prisoners, who had not been able to wash for many days, were not only rather unwholesome but were also infested with fleas so the Italians took immediate steps to have them landed at Taranto, their first port of call. From there Len Bartley was taken to a PoW camp at Sulmona, some 75 miles east of Rome where he languished for the next twenty eight months.

In September 1943, when the Italians surrendered to the Allies, it seemed possible that all the prisoners would be released, but the Germans began moving in to take over control of the PoW camps. There were rumours that there would be a massacre of prisoners and the Italian guards attempted to defend them. In the confused fighting outside the wire Len made his escape, using a homemade wire-cutter.

Once free he, in his own words, 'kept running for 24 hours without stopping!' Although disguised by the old clothes he wore he inevitably aroused suspicion and was frequently interrogated by civilians as he made his way south but he managed to shake them off and only once did he find himself in any danger when a seemingly friendly farmer gave him a bed for the night in his barn. Later he discovered that the barn door had been bolted on the outside and he realised his host was probably getting in touch with the local military.

Determined not to be captured again, Bartley cut his way out and continued his journey south.

At a place called Alberona, on a tributary of the river Salsola, Bartley was able to meet the mayor of the town who spoke English and who controlled a band of partisans. This group set off hoping to reach Allied lines but their garrulously argumentative progress was so noisy that they alerted a German road block and in the shoot out that followed Bartley was wounded in both legs. Nevertheless he was able to avoid being captured and somehow made contact with 'Popsky's Private Army'[1], which was

[1] 'Popsky's Private Army' was a small scouting force attached to the 8th Army commanded by Lt-Col V Peniakoff, a Russo-Belgian officer who had at one time been associated with the North African Long Range Desert Group.

operating in the area behind enemy lines. With their help he reached Lucera, north of Foggia, and was soon liberated by the British advance.

Almost immediately, though, Bartley succumbed to malaria and his leg wounds and was hurried to hospital. He died in 1985 but is remembered as one of the few RAF pilots captured by a submarine.

1944 came in like a lion, with a gale that blew down a lot of tents. Operations were impossible and all that could be done was to issue everyone with a rum ration. The next day, though, the weather cleared sufficiently to allow a full day's flying. There were two attacks, both of 12 aircraft, on gun positions at Miglianico. The third operation was against 30 vehicles that had been reported. These were found, bombed and straffed and seven were claimed as destroyed – including one truck that the pilots thought might have been a *Wehrmacht* Ops Room.

Missions against enemy ground positions continued the next day but there was also a shipping mission over Korcula Carp. One schooner was sunk, one straffed and near misses were claimed on barges. Snow now fell and on 4th there was only one operation against MT and a reported fuel dump, although nothing was observed. Gales returned on the 5 January and the tents that had been flattened on New Year's Day were flattened again. However, by now the squadron had been issued with oilskins, gum boots and leather jerkins. Snow interrupted operations on the 6th but on the 7th the squadron was able to get airborne from Cellone LG which had a runway of Summerfield tracking, or psp. The first target was shipping in Markarska harbour on the Yugoslavian coast. Strikes were observed. One aircraft, believed to be an FW190 was seen at 9000′ over the target but it made off. The second attack was on gun positions near Manopello but no results were observed other than a house catching fire and a vehicle blowing up.

In better weather the squadron managed 23 sorties on the 8th. An 8000-ton vessel was the first target but this could not be found and the aircraft returned with their bombs. The second operation was against oil storage tanks on the other side of the Adriatic. During the bombing a bridge was destroyed. In view of the near misses on the oil tanks this was again the target the next day and the aircraft encountered intense Breda fire. One pilot, Lt N G Sharp (FR229 'Q') had to force land about six miles from Mileni, his aircraft being Cat 3.

Direct hits were scored on a barge that lay alongside a 2-masted vessel on the 10th, and the latter was lifted out of the water by three near misses. News came that Fg Off Nev Bowker, who had been seen sprinting away from his crashed aircraft on the 27 December 1941 near El Agheila, had been awarded the DFC. His score was 10 enemy aircraft destroyed and one damaged.

Anti-shipping strikes continued the next day. Seven bombs fell amongst the vessels in Markarska harbour but there were no direct hits. Two bombs were also dropped into some woods north of the bay where some Breda 20mm AA guns were firing. Velaluka harbour was straffed for good measure on the return flight and strikes were seen on a 60′ schooner which was left smoking. For the next couple of days the squadron did not fly, although the weather was excellent, but operations were resumed on the 14th with an attack on Sibenik harbour by 11 aircraft. There was a direct hit on a 50′ barge which sank, a near miss on a black camouflaged boat of 3000 tons and a direct hit on a vessel drawn up on a slipway. The bow of a sunken ship was seen in the south-west corner of the harbour. That evening the pilots entertained a party of RAF nursing sisters from No 25 Mobile Field Hospital at Foggia.

There was no flying on the 15th and squadron personnel went to Foggia for shower baths. The next day the first operation attacked a defended position near the Sangro River and the second mission was a similar attack near Vasto. The Germans had now withdrawn to their positions behind the Winter Line which lay along the Garigliano, Rapido and upper reaches of the Sangro rivers. The southernmost section, that which faced the Americans, also went by the name of the 'Gustav Line'. In essence the whole German front consisted of deep defensive positions covered by demolitions, extensive mine-fields, machine gun nests and mortar pits – some of which had been blasted out of solid rock and cunningly camouflaged. The enemy artillery had had time to register on every road, trail and even possible bivouac sites. Montgomery's attacks had managed to force the Sangro in its lower reaches, capturing Ortona, while the American 5th Army made limited gains, so that between 5 and 15 January the front line had been pushed up against the hill that was dominated by the abbey of Monte Cassino. Both the 8th and 5th Armies had, however, failed to reach their objectives and both were fought out. General Montgomery, in the meantime, had departed from Italy to take over the 21st Army Group and prepare for the invasion of Normandy[1].

On 17 January 1944 there was a successful operation against shipping in Pucisca harbour, on Bracki island. The town was hit and there was a near miss on a 300′ vessel. One large building was destroyed and other vessels strafed. These attacks on shipping were part of the interdiction effort designed to isolate the battlefield from any type of reinforcement. Troops and supplies that were being syphoned from Yugoslavia could plainly reach Italy more quickly by sea across the Adriatic than by taking the long road or rail route round by way of Fiume and Venice.

Ploca harbour was attacked the following day. The formation flew direct to the target at 10,000′ and bombed from 9000′ down to 1000′. There was a direct hit on a coastal vessel and a near miss on a two-masted craft, One coaster blew up after being straffed but the other vessels that were attacked showed no ill effects. The same target was attacked again later in the day and a 1000-ton ship against the wharf was hit and dense yellow smoke emerged from it. Gun pits and a Siebel ferry were also attacked. This type of harassment continued over the next few days and camouflaged Siebel ferries and what was believed to be a midget submarine were seen.

Belated recognition in the form a hand out of the Africa Star to all the squadron groundcrews came on 21 January which pleased everyone, although 112 was about the last to receive the medal. Attacks on the Yugoslavian ports went on unabated until the second operation on 22nd when there was an armed recce of the Avezzano – Popoli road and some MT were attacked. The Kittyhawk at this time was still a useful aircraft although straffing in the valleys was considered dangerous and the gradients of the mountain sides were somewhat steeper than the aircrafts' rate of climb. This, coupled with the increased efficiency of the light flak frequently made things uncomfortable for the pilots.

The distinct lack of Allied success against the Gustav Line had resulted in a plan to land troops to the rear. However the demands of 'Overlord' and the consequent

---

[1] Eposito, *op cit*

shortage of shipping meant that only a minimum force could be put ashore. The location chosen was the Anzio – Nettuno bay, about 30 miles from Rome. Once ashore, the six divisions, three American and three British under Major-General Lucas were to make for the Alban hills and cut the main road and rail links with the German 10th Army thereby forcing Kesselring to fall back from the whole Winter Line. These landings took place at 02.00 hrs on 22 January 1944. However 112, on the far side of Italy from these fresh events, had a quiet day on the 23rd and in the evening the squadron went to a concert starring Tommy Trinder, the comedian, in the Garrison Theatre at Foggia. Operations were resumed on 24th with armed recces against tanks in the Capestrano area. The target was 20-plus MT and ten *PzKw IVs*. The column was attacked and two direct hits scored on tanks and two near misses on another. The final score after the straffing run was three tanks destroyed, three straffed, four vehicles, including a staff car, destroyed and five damaged.

Sibenik harbour was the target for two missions on the 27th and a 1000-ton merchant ship and other vessels were attacked on both occasions but without scoring any hits although the straffing runs had some effect. A 100′ schooner was seen lying on its side on the mud of the Yugoslavian coast. On 28th the aircraft were attacking roads in the Popoli area and at Capestrano where six well camouflaged vehicles were straffed. There were also operations against Sibenik on the 28th, escorted for the first time by four P-47D Thunderbolts of the USAAF. Only near misses were again recorded although a bomb close to a 1500-ton vessel caused a column of black smoke.

On the 29 January the squadron moved forward from Mileni to Cutella LG, near Vasto on the beach. There were only six sorties from the new LG, a road recce from Avezzano to Sora. Three miles south-east of Sora ten-plus stationary MT were seen under trees. The aircraft strafed them at deck level scoring six destroyed and two damaged. Fifteen-plus single-decker buses were also attacked. One aircraft was hit in the belly tank which was jettisoned. This larger 114-gallon tank was an option that brought the total fuel load up to 272 gallons. Generally the space was occupied by a 500-lb bomb.

The squadron personnel found that Cutella was a pleasantly compact strip and the pilots were pleased to find that they had a Nissen hut as their Mess and the airmen had a large marquee. A sketch plan shows the type of layout adopted by the squadrons of 239 Wing. This layout is perhaps more typical of the time in the desert when everyone was under canvas, but it was an adaptable arrangement that had been used successfully in Sicily and Italy. In Italy there were frequent opportunities to use more 'civilised' accommodation and the tented sites were placed in relation to them under any natural cover that was handy. The minimum runway requirement with the Kittyhawks was 1000 yards, 1,200 yards if possible. A fully loaded aircraft needed most of this to get airborne with full bomb load of one 500-lb or two 250-lb or, later, with one 1000-lb bomb. The runway width had to be enough for pairs of aircraft taking off in close formation, about 150′. Airfield control was exercised by a Wing HQ unit sited close to the runway and using R/T. There were few problems, particularly since most LGs had only a single runway. Not much heed was taken of wind direction and squadrons, whenever possible, took off from the end nearest their dispersal sites and landed towards them. When the squadron was operating on its own the briefings were done in the Ops Tent, or truck, by the squadron Intelligence Officer or, if it was an army target, by the ALO. The 'readiness' Flight were usually called from the Pilots' Mess to report to squadron Ops for briefing which was usually short and simple. Road targets mostly originated from a Tac-R report and the location and the type of target would be specified. Known flak positions were pointed out, friendly aircraft in the neighbourhood mentioned and details of the weather in the target area. Usually within half an hour of being called to briefing the aircraft would be away.

Take offs were in pairs followed by a circuit of the LG by which time the rest of the formation would have joined up. They then spread out into their operational formation and course was set to the target area while in the climb. Sometimes the airstrip was so close to the bomb line to necessitate a 'rearward' circuit to gain a comfortable height of 6000' to 8000' to cross the lines. There was very little need for Flight Planning as it is understood today. The leader would map-read to the target providing weather conditions allowed it at the normal operating altitudes. MORU (Group Ops) listened out on the R/T to the pilots' chatter but it would chip in to warn them if any enemy aircraft were reported in the area or if there was a change of target. Likewise the leader of the formation would pass information to MORU if he saw anything interesting. For army targets particular attention had to be paid at briefings for the exact location of the forward troops. Sometimes, if the target was very close to our lines the ALO would make some arrangement for a smoke signal, either to indicate the target or the position of our men. Homing bearings were given over the R/T either from base or from MORU. Returning to base a formation of 12 aircraft would close into four line astern vics of three aircraft until airfield control gave permission to land.

The vics then went into echelon downwind forming line astern for landing spreading out to allow a runway's length between aircraft touching down. Post-flight debriefing, a term unknown in those days, took place in the Ops truck where the aircrew told their tales to the IO and ALO. This information was then passed by telephone to Wing and Group.

Differing conditions of warfare dictated variations in the formations used. At about this time, January 1944, the standard operational mission consisted of two sections of six aircraft, each section comprising three pairs. The No 2 of each pair weaved astern of his No 1 to cover him from attack from the rear. The lower, leading section was always Red Section, with Blue Section 500' above and to one side, always down sun. Each pair of aircraft was identified by a colour, as shown in this diagram —

	Red Section				*Blue Section*	
No 1	†	†	†			
No 2	†	†	†	†	†	† No 1
	(Green)	(Red)	(Yellow)	†	†	† No 2
				(White)	(Blue)	(Black)

Red and Blue leaders were, respectively Red 1 and Blue 1, with Blue 1 taking over the formation should Red 1 become inoperative for any reason. The formation callsign was always 'Ludo'. The sections bombed and straffed independently and the theory was that while one section was bombing the other acted as top cover, but now that the risk of interception was virtually nil, Blue usually followed hot on the heels of Red. When working with Rover sections of 6 operated on their own. 250-lb bombs now had

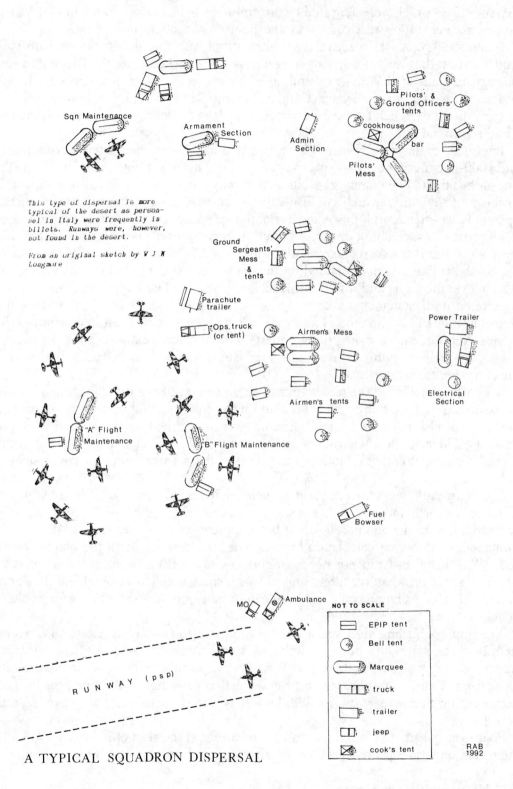

Sqn Maintenance

Armament Section

Admin Section

Pilots' & Ground Officers' tents

cookhouse

bar

Pilots' Mess

This type of dispersal is more typical of the desert as personnel in Italy were frequently in billets. Runways were, however, not found in the desert.

From an original sketch by W J M Longmore

Ground Sergeants' Mess & tents

Parachute trailer

Ops. truck (or tent)

Airmen's Mess

Power Trailer

"A" Flight Maintenance

B" Flight Maintenance

Airmen's tents

Electrical Section

Fuel Bowser

MO Ambulance

NOT TO SCALE

EPIP tent

Bell tent

Marquee

truck

trailer

jeep

cook's tent

RUNWAY (psp)

A TYPICAL SQUADRON DISPERSAL

RAB
1992

pressure fuses which were activated by the build-up of air as the bomb fell. Eight 40-lb anti-personnel bombs were carried under the wings on single-release racks.

When straffing it was every man for himself but with the No 2s sticking with their leader as best they might. A 'meaty' target might be attacked more than once provided there wasn't much flak coming up and the ammunition for the .5″ machine guns hadn't run out. When leaving the leader would call on the R/T, giving his position in relation to the target and his height and then waggle his wings to identify himself so that the rest could reform on him.

Interdiction attacks on roads, railway lines and bridges were carried out with 500-lb and 1000-lb cratering bombs using the conventional dive-bombing technique along the line of the target. The bombing results achieved by the Kittyhawk were not comparable to those of the Stuka which could dive at a far steeper angle with its hydraulically operated dive-brakes and thus place its bomb more accurately. Having no dive brakes, the Kittyhawk's speed built up considerably and when this happened the aircraft would twist and roll and any correction could result in a skid which in turn would often throw the bomb off line. Much depended on the leader choosing the right spot to place the section over the target and thus the correct angle of dive. The Kittyhawk pilots' reports were often understatements as they frequently reported 'near misses' on bridges and ships but they had no method of knowing how badly the bomb blast had damaged the target. Subsequent Tac-R photos often showed more damage than had been suspected. As in everything there was a large element of luck as well as skill in placing the bomb in the target area.

In straffing an airfield the target aircraft either caught fire or it didn't. If it did it was a 'confirmed destroyed' but if it didn't, and if the tracers could be seen to be striking home it was claimed as 'damaged'. Enemy aircraft attacked on the ground were not generally added to the squadron's score, it had to be an aerial victory to count in the official records, although doubtless many enemy aircraft were satisfactorily destroyed in this way.

The Kittyhawk, with one pilot and a single engine, could carry a 1000-lb bomb just as far as a light bomber. A light bomber, complete with a crew of 3 or 4 men, twin engined and carrying about 2000-lb of bombs, escorted by fighter aircraft, bombed in formation, so that a miscalculation by the leader could result in all the bombs falling wide. The Kittyhawk did not need a fighter escort and could carry out a selective bombing strike on whatever target looked worthwhile, was less vulnerable to flak and, having delivered its bomb could then come down and continue the attack with machine guns[1].

The unit establishment of aircraft was down to 18 in January, a reduction of seven from the previous month but, as numbers varied between 17 and 25 for no apparent reason this was probably nothing peculiar. What is peculiar is that FR236 changed its letter from 'T' to 'S' and became Flt Sgt J L Jellett's machine – the first time 'S' had been used for over a year, and FR388, Fg Off 'Matt' Matthias's aircraft, once 'Z', was now 'J'.

Poor flying weather reduced the number of sorties at the start of February 1944 and there was only one armed recce of six aircraft which went to the area of Popoli –

---

[1] All this information supplied by the late W J M Longmore

Vittarito – Avezzano. On 29 January on the Gustav Line the first of a series of battles began to try to take Monte Cassino. In the Anzio beach head the advance had come to a halt. Major-General Lucas lacked the necessary audacity to take advantage of his initial surprise and had hung about waiting to consolidate his positions. Kesselring, realising that his communications were not in danger from this cautious advance, contained the Allies and began to build up a strong counter-attacking force of seven divisions, with two more in reserve. On all the Italian fronts the ground battles now bogged down with scenes reminiscent of the Somme, Verdun and Passchendaele.

On the 3rd sorties were flown to Ancona harbour and some shipping was strafed. On the ground the squadron MT were finally repainted in standard Army green, the last memories of the desert were slowly disappearing. In squadron orders for that day a competition was announced to find a design, embodying the shark motif, to paint on the doors of vehicles. The winning entry depicted a ferocious diving shark surrounded by a black ring on which was written '112 SQDN DAF' – perhaps after all the desert was not completely forgotten. On the 4th ten aircraft flew to bomb a particular building near Casoli. At the same time Baltimores, escorted by P-47 Thunderbolts, were also attacking the town. There was a direct hit on the target, which had a tower, and two direct hits on buildings to the south of it. There was heavy and accurate flak from the target area and two aircraft came back Cat 1. The only other mission was a pair of aircraft doing a weather recce of the Chieti area.

In the late afternoon the gales returned in force and, as the diarist records, '. . . needless to say the Officers' Mess was the first tent down . . .' Bad weather continued for some time and there was an issue of rum. As always when there was no flying the squadron and flight commanders put their heads together to think of ways to occupy the men. On pay parade all ranks were ordered to wear respirators and the CO took great delight in hunting out pilots who were dodging by hiding in their tents. The weather cleared enough on the 8th for two operations, both were armed recces of the Sora – Avezzano road. Flt Lt Bluett led the first mission and about 100 vehicles were seen south of Sora and these were attacked. The claim was for five destroyed, three flamers (one a petrol tanker), three smokers and fifteen damaged. The second operation returned to the same area and a road and railway line were attacked. Four MT were claimed probably destroyed and one damaged. Gales returned that evening and the squadron had very little to do except try to keep their tents anchored to the ground. On 12 February Flt Sgt Douglas Holmes was missing on a non-operational flight (FR803 or FR823). He went up on an air-test and it is believed he got lost above cloud. A search was organised but without success and his body was never found.

The 14 February was a busy day. Twenty-three sorties were flown on two operations. The first, under Flt Lt James Longmore, was to have attacked a Siebel ferry at Omis, south of Split, but the formation could not find its way down through the thick cloud and ice began to form on the trim tabs so they returned. The second operation was also abortive. It was supposed to have attacked shipping off Uljan but once again bad weather forced them to return. Shipping attacks continued the next day at Rogoznica. There was not much shipping to see so the town was attacked. Two large explosions and dense black smoke resulted. Flt Lt Longmore mentions that these attacks on the Dalmatian coast were intended to disrupt supplies getting to the German garrisons on the many islands. There were also German gunboats and E-boats, heavily camouflaged, that lay in the creeks and harbours. Caiques and schooners were frequently used to transport fuel and here 'a short straffing session usually sufficed to discourage their further participation in the war'.

Other than these operations the squadron had the opportunity to inspect a North American P-51 Mustang. Mustangs, which had been designed and built principally at the request of the RAF who wanted a replacement for the Kittyhawk, had appeared over England in July 1942 and had seen its first operations over the Dieppe beaches in August that year. It had then been redesigned to take a Rolls Royce Merlin engine and it was this that turned an excellent aeroplane into a magnificent one. The squadron, however, was not to receive these new machines for some time so the best that could be done was to crawl all over them 'like seething ants' as the diarist puts it. One big question on everyone's mind was how the Mustang would look with the sharksteeth markings.

On that day the inhabitants of the Abbey of St Benedict on Monte Cassino were warned by means of leaflets to evacuate the building and the next day 229 bombers dropped 453 tons of bombs on the abbey and destroyed it. The ruin was now transformed into a German strong-point, 'an almost impenetrable maze of capsized masonry' in which the fanatical 1 Parachute Div took up residence. Fuller[1] describes the destruction of the Abbey as 'not so much a piece of vandalism as an act of sheer tactical stupidity'. On 18 February the Allied ground assault was launched under cover of five hours of artillery bombardment, but progress was so slow that on 19th General Alexander called off the attack. On 16th 112 Squadron should have taken part in this attack but weather aborted the operation. The aircraft flew out at 2000', climbing to 6000' along the Trigno River to Agnone. 9/10ths cloud persisted from 2000' to 8000' so plainly the mission was an impossible one. A similar abortive attempt was made the next day and from the 18th to the 21st there were no operations. Things were not going much better in the Anzio beach head where the German 14th Army had launched its attack on the 15 February at a time when the bad weather had hampered Allied air support. The initial assault had penetrated deep into the beach head along the Anzio – Albano road but General Mackensen failed to exploit this success and reinforced his troops only in driblets so that his push lost momentum. Lucas counter-attacked on the 19th and the German advance was halted.

On 22 February 112 resumed operations with 23 sorties. The first was against the Frosinone – Valmontone road, the main supply route from Rome to the Gothic Line. Two near misses were scored on a large 'covered' vehicle which was then straffed and left burning. Fifteen vehicles were observed at a point where the road ran alongside the railway line in a cutting and, although they were fairly well dispersed, they were attacked and hits were registered. In the straffing run one large vehicle with a trailer was destroyed, four probably destroyed and seven damaged. A Breda post manned by three soldiers was shot up. The second operation went to the Dalmatian coast to attack Siebel ferries and other shipping in Soline harbour on Dugi island. One three-masted caique was attacked with bombs and then straffed. These operations continued for two days with an operation to Marina, west of Split, where some barges were attacked,

[1] *Fuller, op cit*

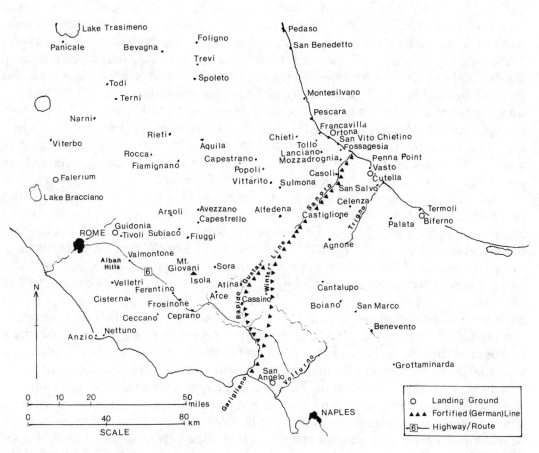

Map 8. Central Italy

RAB
1992

another to Zadara were a barge erupted with a large explosion and probably sank. A W/T station, described as 'new', was attacked and left covered with a pall of grey smoke. The next day barges off Uljan island was attacked. One barge received a direct hit which resulted in it breaking in half and turning over onto its beam ends. On the second mission six aircraft flew to Frosinone and up the main road towards Rome but cloud and lack of time forced the aircraft to climb and return to base before completing the operation. Bad weather everywhere restricted flying for the next couple of days.

The 24 February was a busy day with three operations. Six aircraft led by the CO went on an armed recce of the Capestrello – Sora – Isola – Monte Giovani – a point north of Arce and then secondary roads to Frosinone, another of General Vietighoff's 10th Army supply routes. The second mission led by Flt Lt Longmore was a recce of the Avezzano – Carsoli – Arsoli – Tivoli road. Some MT were seen and attacked. The final mission, led by Flt Lt Bluett attacked Tortorello railway station. The aircraft met some Spitfires and another squadron over Trigno and while 112 attacked the station the Spitfires recced the town for MT. The absence of many vehicles on these major supply routes to the front would suggest that the Germans were wisely moving all their supplies and reinforcements at night. Over Arce the next day cloud cover did not prevent quite accurate 88mm flak bursting around the aircraft.

The final operation of the month was flown by 11 aircraft attacking a military concentration near the Anzio beach head. The attack was pressed home through intense Breda fire and light flak. Four possible enemy aircraft were seen but they did not menace the Kittyhawks. Fg Off 'Tex' Gray in FL886 'K' was hit and obliged to force-land near La Villa, due, in Tex's own words, 'to increased wing loading imposed by a quantity of flak in my leg'. After he had come to rest the Kittyhawk began to 'hiss and crackle . . . in an unpleasant manner' and he made a hasty exit. Unbeknown to Tex his aircraft had finished up in a minefield and his dash for safety that took him all of 'ten seconds flat' was in contrast to his countrymen who took two hours to make their way back to the wrecked machine. To ask any of the squadron members at that time who 'the' character was on 112, their answer would invariably be 'Tex' Gray. In the air he was always rather a problem for his No 1 as he would take the first opportunity to 'get lost' so as to be able to carry on his own private war, looking for Huns at deck level. The mission often returned minus Tex but he would always show up later. At Mileni he had found a horse and he would go off on it to 'rope a steer' or 'call a hawg' for the Pilots' Mess cook. He was the last of a number of Americans who had included the Bostonian Dick DeBourke, 'Smithy' Smith from Detroit, Dicky Blake from Texas and Bill Pollock who had turned down tempting offers made by their own Air Force so as to stay with the squadron.

March started with wind and rain which kept the aircraft firmly on the ground but on the 2nd there were two operations against MT on the roads south-east of Rome. On both occasions vehicles were bombed and straffed resulting in seven destroyed and others left burning or damaged. Flak and Breda fire were intense and there was even some small arms fire while the aircraft were attacking. Lieut White (FR795 'B') landed with a burst tyre and the aircraft flipped over onto its back. On the 3rd there were again two operations, the first against roads leading north out of the Anzio beach head where MT at Valmontone were bombed, after this another convoy of about 20 vehicles was straffed resulting in claims of four burning trucks and many others damaged. The second operation, also against MT, resulted in a large six-wheeled vehicle being straffed, a staff car destroyed and three other vehicles probably destroyed.

To vary the monotony shipping was attacked on the first operation on the 4th, four 50' schooners being straffed. Returning to land the formation spotted a staff car which was destroyed and a locomotive which was left smoking. Tortorello railway station was attacked for the second time on the next mission and a good concentration of bombs was seen to fall on all the three lines in the station area. Ten waggons were strafed, then two vehicles and then back to the station to strafe another 30 trucks. Thus satisfied with their work the aircraft returned home. That evening 'Tex' Gray returned with a fresh stock of tall stories and 'speaking Italian with a perfect bridgehead accent' according to the diarist. Flt Lt Cherry left 112 on posting to 250 Sqn as a flight commander.

The 7th March saw the loss of Fg Off J H Burcham who had been on the squadron for over a year; experience bringing no immunity from the random nature of flak. The operation had been flown on roads to the east of Rome where MT were spotted concealed under trees on the side of a hill. One vehicle was hit and seen to disintegrate and there were two direct hits on the road and other MT were straffed. Johnny, in FR824 'A', was later reported to be a 'kriegy'[1] in *Stalag Luft III*. Lieut A K Taylor returned with his aircraft (FR283 'P') badly shot up and he had to make a forced landing on a nearby beach. He was unhurt but his aircraft was badly damaged. Johnny Burcham was remembered on the squadron as having come out from England as a young Flying Officer, quiet and well behaved but soon the magic of the desert and 112 Squadron altered him and he went gently round the bend, thoroughly enjoying the process. His conversation, David Brown recalls, took the form of short bursts like a machine gun, punctuated by wild chuckles. He cut down on his smoking by stubbing out half finished cigarettes on his tongue and eating the remainder. He and so many of the other characters on 112 were the stable nucleus of older hands that typified 'the squadron', there were others on the fringe who would mature in good time and gradually take their place and then there were the ones who simply came, stayed a while and went without apparently distinguishing themselves in the air or on the ground.

Bad weather allowed the squadron to have some rest for the next two days although personnel were busy securing the tents. Operations were resumed on 11 March 1944 but only eight sorties were flown as the squadron seems to have been getting short of aircraft. This mission was against MT in the Velletri area but was aborted due to bad weather. However they re-formed over the sea and came back over Avezzano where they saw four unidentified friendly aircraft bombing the Cisterna area.

Bad weather continued until the 13th when there was an armed recce of the roads east of Rome. Some MT were bombed by the lower section but their bombs undershot. The top section also bombed but again no results were observed. Flt Sgt Stan Worbey, also a squadron member of over a year's standing, was shot down by flak in FR812 'R' but was seen to bale out over enemy territory. Shortage of aircraft curtailed operations again on the 14th and six flew as top cover to 260 Sqn attacking shipping near Pedaso but the weather was poor and no bombs were dropped. A similar operation was mounted the next day when 260 Sqn bombed trucks and strafed near Valmontone and Ferentino.

---

[1] derived from *kriegsgefangene* or prisoner of war

Shipping in Ancona harbour were attacked on the 16th with 260 Sqn. After receiving a well-aimed burst of flak from Francavilla the formation shifted two miles further away from the coast. 260 bombed San Benedetto and 112 went further and attacked five or six two-masted caiques at the southern end of Ancona harbour. Roads were recced west of the town but not much was seen.

Nineteen sorties were flown on the 18 March, the increased number being due to aircraft transferred from 260 Sqn who were in the process of re-equipping with Mustang IIIs. The first operation was against a railway bridge which was approached by way of Aquila and Terni. The aircraft bombed from 8000' down to 2000' and there was one direct hit on the centre of the bridge. Another bomb hit the track but the remainder were not seen due to the dust and debris thrown up. Grouping was regarded as having been good and many craters were seen. The second formation that day bombed Castrocielo and Piedmonte just to the rear of the German lines at Monte Cassino and the latter village was reported as being totally ruined. Over Cassino lay a column of smoke.

The only operation on the 19th went to bomb a railway bridge north of Terni. There was a direct hit on the line and a very near miss on a house alongside the bridge. The weather was reported as 'glorious' with no cloud but haze up to 6000'. These attacks on the railways was part of 'Operation Strangle' which was designed to deprive the Germans of supplies prior to the start of the Allied summer offensive. Fuller[1] remarks that an average of 25 cuts were made daily on roads and railways and this was to rise by the end of May to 75 or more daily. 'There can be no doubt', Fuller writes, 'that this sustained attack on the enemy's transport system . . . did far more damage than had any of the '*colossal cracks*' (that is the massed heavy bombing of Monte Cassino – the italicised words are Montgomery's).'

A railway bridge over a river near Rieti was bombed on the following day. The aircraft dived through a break in the cloud and attacked the bridge which was a steel structure about 25 yards long. There was one direct hit on the side of the bridge which caused a 25° twist over to one side. One bomb fell directly onto the railway line near the devastated station and the bridge was left broken at its northern end. Some stationary MT were straffed for good measure, including a large bus with luggage on the roof, which was badly damaged. An aircraft was seen lying in the snow with footprints leading away from it.

On 21 March a total of 23 sorties were flown. The first was against a road bridge north of Rieti which received a direct hit and another bridge over a river was also hit but dust prevented accurate assessment of the damage. The second operation was over Yugoslavia where shipping at Korcula was attacked. Two camouflaged 70' landing barges were seen near Vis and the formation leader, Flt Lt Longmore, indicated the target with his bomb. The formation then attacked and there were some near misses and one barge was left listing. Two 20' boats were also straffed and one was sunk.

On 22nd the squadron commander, Sqn Ldr Pete Illingworth failed to return from the only operation. He was leading 12 aircraft against three E-boats that had been reported alongside a breakwater on the south side of Corvo Island. These were attacked and again there were some near misses and one boat started to burn amidships

---

[1] Fuller, *op cit*

and soon smoke was coming from all of them. Three 100′ schooners were also bombed but the bombs overshot. The aircraft then turned their attention to the town and a large white building which had a Breda gun post close by was attacked, together with a slipway and the boat-building yards. At this moment the CO was hit by flak and white vapour started coming from his aircraft (FR861 'M'). He called on the R/T that he had been hit and was making for the mainland. He flew off towards Trogir and sight of him was lost eventually against the background of hills. Aircraft recced the area but no smoke or fire was seen so it was hoped he had landed safely.

On the following day the squadron, temporarily under the command of Flt Lt Bluett DFC, flew 12 aircraft to attack Siebel ferries. One of them was seen camouflaged with green and brown netting although its outline was clearly visible. It was bombed from 1000′ and the first bomb fell dead amidships and the vessel split in two, ending up partly beached and partly under water. Two operations on the 24th were also against shipping. The first found a large 8000-ton ship which Control considered might be unfriendly, but a closer look from 500′ showed that it was a Swedish hospital ship, so the formation continued to Sibenik where a two-masted schooner was bombed and straffed although the near-misses seemed to have no effect. The second strike went north of Ancona to attack shipping but they got airborne too late to achieve anything and they returned before it became too dark.

A heavy storm and torrential rain prevented any flying for two days but on the 27th, despite the poor weather, two operations were flown. The first against a railway bridge which was hit in the second span which left a gap while other bombs also fell on the line and near misses damaged the piers and supports. Twenty-six 40-lb General Purpose bombs were dropped on about 15 railway trucks and a W/T station was straffed. Iesi and Loreto LGs were recced but no enemy aircraft were seen. Near Pesaro a Supermarine Walrus amphibian was seen on the water with a Spitfire covering it. The Walruses were used almost exclusively as air-sea-rescue aircraft. The second mission returned with a good score. Their target was a railway bridge near Aquila and although the terrain made bombing difficult there were two direct hits on the line north of the bridge although the bridge itself was not damaged. A level crossing was also attacked and 40-lb GP bombs were dropped on railway waggons. They flew to Aquila LG where a Fieseler *Storch* was seen landing. The aircraft had just touched down when the first burst of machine gun fire hit it. The second run turned it into a flamer and the pilot was killed as he ran from the wreckage. One MC202 was seen, hidden under camouflage netting, and strikes were seen to hit it. More railway trucks were then attacked with 40-lb bombs and one waggon blew up.

Bad weather again interfered with flying until 29 March which turned out to be the most active day of the month, with 32 sorties spread over three missions. The first, from 07.45 to 09.40 hrs, was an armed recce of Sibenik but nothing was seen and there was no report of anything being attacked. The second operation, 11.45 to 13.15 hrs, was against a bridge and there was one near miss which caused a wall to fall across the tracks. Some railway trucks were straffed and bombed and then two vehicles, one of which blew up slightly damaging one of the aircraft. Five smokers were claimed in a second attack on MT. The final operation, from 14.55 to 16.25 hrs, was also in the same area against camouflaged MT which well hidden in special blast bays under and around a hill. Finally a MC202 on Aquila LG was straffed and left smoking.

A railway bridge was attacked the next day and the target was reported well hit. A driver of a diesel locomotive that was on the bridge at the time must have had a *mauvaise quart d'heure*. The aircraft carried on to strafe railway trucks and MT. Three twin-engined aircraft were seen on Iesi aerodrome but they were not molested. The second mission was to attack a suspected HQ south of Rocca. Nine bombs fell amongst buildings and some hits may have scored on the target. The smoke signals that they had been briefed to expect from the troops on the ground were not seen. That day, 30 March 1944 George Wiley, prisoner of war in *Stalag Luft III*, was murdered by the *Gestapo* in a wood near Halbau, Lower Silesia, for his part in 'The Great Escape'[1]

The final day of the month was also a busy one. The first operation was against a railway bridge north of Pedaso. This was being repaired when '112 Destruction Company' appeared. Two spans of the six had already been crossed by a type of Bailey Bridge and there were two repair waggons on the bridge itself. There was a near miss of the 4th span and another half span was knocked out, three near-misses dislodged some masonry and some trucks were straffed. The second operation was targetted on a railway line but no direct hits were registered although a near miss may have undermined the embankment. A railway bridge was the target of the third operation which was bombed from 7500'. Two spans of the masonry bridge had been repaired with steel replacements. One near miss on the northern end lifted railway lines and sleepers from the rail bed and left them twisted at an angle. Parts of the masonry piers were chipped away by a near miss and the bridge was left unfit for traffic. A road bridge was then attacked and two-thirds of the roadway were blown out and there were other near misses.

April started with a no-flying day and the only news recorded was that Flt Lt Longmore was promoted to Sqn Ldr. The next day operations continued with two missions, both against railway communications. The Kittyhawks first attacked a stretch of railway line near a tunnel and a small 40' metal bridge. Seven trucks were also straffed. The ops diary recorded that the same target was then attacked by 24 Glenn Martin Baltimores, based at Biferno, 'without causing any noticeable damage'. However they escorted the Baltimores back across the bomb line. The second target was a railway bridge over a river north of Ancona. A couple of near misses twisted the railway line and caused a landslide and two other near misses caused masonry to fall from a pier. A recce after the attack showed that a span previously blown out by 112 was still missing.

On the 3rd the squadron flew with 1000-lb bombs for the first time. The first recipients of the new bomb were the Fascists at Macerata. The target was the town hall and the Fascist Party HQ. At Penna Point there was a 'Y' Service SIGINT[2] listening station in a disused lighthouse which, among other tasks such as intercepting and analysing enemy wireless traffic, received and transmitted information to Italian and Yugoslav partisans. It had been learned that some high-ranking German officers were to meet Fascist leaders in the Macerata town hall at 11 a.m. of the 3 April and, additionally, the security arrangements would be provided by extra German troops who

---

[1] Paul Brickill's 'The Great Escape' gives these details of Wiley's death
[2] see Hinsley's 'British Intelligence in the 2nd World War' on SIGINT work.

would be moved in to the nearby barracks. Broadhurst decided that the meeting would also be attended by the DAF.

The aircraft dived from 7500′ down to 1500′ with the new CO, Sqn Ldr Watts, leading. There were some near misses on the Fascist HQ, a building with a gabled roof, but all the bombs fell in the target area and the .5″ machine gun strikes were seen to be going through the front door and windows. The town hall was also hit by five bombs. 250 Sqn followed and their bombs also fell close to the targets. Marauders completed the job by bombing the barracks. The partisans later sent a congratulatory message saying that four direct hits had killed several important German officers and their Italian counterparts and many others had been injured. The second mission that day was targetted against an observation post at Tollo. Eight bombs fell close but no results were observed.

Sqn Ldr W K Watts, who had been posted to 112 on 29 March, came from No 3RAAF Sqn. Flt Lt Bluett, 'A' Flt cdr, left the squadron at the same time and his place was taken by Flt Lt L N Ahern.

A road and railway bridge were attacked on 4 April. The aircraft followed their now usual practice of flying out to sea and then turning in when abeam their target, thus avoiding crossing the front line with all its attendant dangers. Bombs fell on the railway bridge at Montesilvano in a good group and there were two direct hits on the rail track north of the bridge. It was considered that the structure must have been left unsafe for traffic. Accurate small arms fire came from the target area and Lieut Taylor was wounded in the leg. Although in some difficulty he was able to bring his aircraft back safely. The second operation was against a bridge carrying a road across a river. There was a group of near misses but the bridge was not hit. A Breda gun was straffed 100 yards south of the bridge.

That afternoon the squadron received news that Sqn Ldr Illingworth had returned safely. The next day he arrived back rather oddly attired but looking remarkably fit. He had managed to crash-land near Trogir and within a few minutes of coming to rest Yugoslavian partisans appeared and took charge of him, hiding him in a stone wall. After the Germans had given up searching for him he was taken on a series of lengthy night marches, lying up during daytime, across rough mountainous country to the partisans' HQ. There he was given the option of either joining them with the rank of colonel or being helped back to Italy across the Adriatic. His hiking experiences, if nothing else, prompted him to opt 'for an easier life on the squadron'.

Then began another series of night marches back to the coast where the partisans took him to the island of Vis where an Italian flying boat took him back to Bari. He arrived footsore and lousey but otherwise none the worse. He commented that during the day, when the partisans were lying up, he would share a large communal bed with the other members of the group, both male and female, but that the girls would have made more comfortable bedmates if they hadn't been slung about with hand grenades and rifles, which they wore all the time. His return resulted in 112 having three squadron leaders on strength.

In the Tunisian days the weight of bombs that were hung under the aircraft had required some modifications to be made. Principally this meant that aluminium wheels were fitted in place of steel ones, the artificial horizon was taken out and a smaller electric battery installed. Now that the clear skies of North Africa were replaced by the cloudy weather of Italy, the artificial horizon had to be put back in. Also it had been found that the aluminium wheels tended to crack after a while and so steel ones were put back on again. To compensate for all this extra weight, take-offs began with 20° of flap selected, full power on the brakes and a very nose-down attitude to gain flying speed with the minimum of delay.

On the 5th April the squadron flew on an armed recce with long range tanks fitted, staying airborne for two hours. They flew to Ancona but between there and Pesaro the visibility dropped and cloud finally forced them down to ground level so they returned. The 6 April was 'a most unpleasant day'. Twelve aircraft set off at 15.45 hrs with the CO, Sqn Ldr Watts, leading. This was again an armed recce of the Rieti – Terni – Todi areas, again carrying long range fuel tanks. The formation flew direct to Terni and there divided into two sections, each of six aircraft. Sqn Ldr Watts and his section found 30 stationary vehicles and these were attacked several times. Three were left burning, three smoking and many more damaged. The section then continued north-west and three miles north of Todi they ran into light but accurate 40mm flak. Sqn Ldr Watt's aircraft (FR822 'M') was hit in the glycol tank at about 3000' to 4000'. He turned south but had to bale out about five miles south-east of Todi. His last words over the R/T were 'Don't worry, I shall be back in a month, don't distress the wife.' He was seen to land safely in a coppice and wave to the escorting aircraft before running away from his parachute.

The other section had meanwhile found ten-plus railway trucks at Macerino which they bombed with 40-lb bombs. They then re-formed and flew north and found 15 large MT vehicles on a secondary road near Bevagna. They were parked close together, some with trailers, and the aircraft made five straffing runs and scored 10 vehicle flamers and four trailers burning. They must have been loaded with fuel and ammunition as smoke rose to 5000'. The section then re-formed once more and flew to Perugia (where they saw a burning aircraft) and on to strafe four more vehicles, leaving one burning and one smoking. Later another 20 MT were discovered, close together, with dumps of fuel and ammunition at intervals alongside the road. These were all attacked and a lot were left burning. In addition the section turned its attention to 60–80 petrol drums and at least half were set alight. The total score for the day, unpleasant though it had been for the squadron, was estimated at 21 enemy vehicles destroyed, 30-plus fuel drums destroyed and many MT damaged.

As fast as the ground-attack aircraft and light bombers cut the enemy's communications, they were repaired. Bad weather frequently interrupted flying for several days and the attacks themselves were not heavy enough nor accurate enough to cause much delay. The policy had to be two-fold, to pulverise the railway marshalling yards and repair facilities in the rear areas and to create a 'line of interdiction' past which no train or vehicle was allowed to go. The former was a long term policy and the latter short term. At this period results were good but not perfect and it was not until April 1945 that the doctrine was put into operation with complete success[1]

The 7 April was another memorable day. The first operation was straightforward, with an attack on shipping in Porto Civitanova. A dozen aircraft led by Flt Lt 'Happy' Ahern took off at 09.00 hrs and flew on course 330°, five miles out to sea, at 10,000',

[1] Richards & Saunders, *op cit*

and then turned west when abeam the target. This was a two-masted 500-ton auxiliary vessel in the south part of the harbour. Bombing from north to south the aircraft dived from 9500' down to 1500' through a break in the clouds. Flt Lt Matthias scored one direct hit on the stern. One very near miss and two near misses were also registered and the ship was left with its stern under water and a spreading patch of oil.

The second operations consisted again of 12 aircraft with Flt Lt Ahern leading (FT854 'B'), Fg Off Matthias (FR474 'Jinx'), Flt Sgt K C Warburton (FR857 'V'), Flt Sgt B H Peters (FR862 'E'), Flt Sgt W E Cocks (FR288 'Z'), Lieut M C White (FR507 'R'), W/O R W Drown (FR390 'F'), Lieut Hanreck (FR257 'H'), W/O N E Swinton, A New Zealander, (FR354 'W'), Fg Off Gray (FR309 'Q'), Flt Sgt Jellett (FR236 'S') and Flt Sgt A G Rowe (FL895 'A'). Take off was at 16.20 hrs with long-range tanks and 40-lb GP bombs, aiming for the Terni area. When approaching Rieti the formation sighted 12-plus FW190s on Rieti LG. Two of these were just taking off and three were already airborne. Flt Lt Ahern told the top six to stay up while he, along with his No 2, Flt Sgt Warburton, attacked one of the pair getting airborne. He saw strikes on this aircraft, which still had its wheels down, and Flt Sgt Peters, just behind, also fired at it. The FW190 blew up and fell just north of the LG. Flt Sgt Cocks, Peters' No 2, attacked a second one that was trying to get off the ground and it too crashed in flames on the edge of the airstrip. Cocks then attempted a stall turn but, misjudging it and being at too low a level, he went into a spin and crashed one mile south-east of the LG, aircraft and bombs exploding. Meanwhile 'Happy' Ahern made a couple of straffing runs on a pair of FW190s still on the ground and saw his rounds striking home. He then chased another enemy aircraft up a valley and saw bits flying off it as he fired. After this he made a head-on attack and again saw strikes. A second 190 was hit in the wings, ailerons and fuselage. Fg Off Matthias attacked the three that were already airborne and which were flying in formation, but made no claims. 'Jinx' his aircraft was badly holed. The top section of Kittyhawks now weighed in, led by WO Drown. He attacked one enemy aircraft and saw strikes on the fuselage and tail. Lieut Harry Hanreck chased another which hit a tree and knocked bits off its wing-tip and 'Tex' Gray attacked another. An FW was seen falling in flames but no one was sure who had attacked it. A voice was heard on the R/T saying 'I've been hit' and this was probably Flt Sgt Warburton, the only pilot who failed to return. As this complicated fight was taking place there was a hail of flak and Breda fire from the ground. The colouring of the Focke-Wulfs was dark green on top and light blue underneath, but this was a bad camouflage as they could be seen a long way off. The aircraft may have belonged to *Schnellkampfgeschwader (SKG) 10* who had had a bad time in North Africa and Sicily and whose pilots were, by this stage, pitifully inexperienced. On the return trip the squadron saw some Baltimores with a Spitfire escort and Flt Lt Ahern passed them a warning to keep a look out for the FWs.

On the 8 April 1944 there were only two operations, the first, of six aircraft, attacking a factory east of Popoli where three 500-lb bombs hit the building and a fourth overshot and hit the railway line, and the second, of eight aircraft, bombing a railway bridge which received two direct hits that took bites out of a third of the span.

The squadron had long been expecting to be re-equipped with Mustangs so when it was rumoured that new aircraft were about to arrive there was some excitement.

However this dissolved in disappointment when they turned out to be Kittyhawk Mk IVs. Four pilots went by Avro Anson to collect them from Bari and 12 more went the following day. On the 11th sixteen of the new aircraft arrived and the groundcrew set about them immediately to complete the necessary inspections. The armourers also got their hands on them to fit the new bomb racks which allowed a total of 2000-lb of bombs, one 1000-lb under the belly and two 500-lb under the wings. These new machines were Curtiss P-40Ns which had a modified cockpit canopy which gave a better rearward view, and Merlin-Packard V-1650-1 engines, later replaced by Allison V-1710-81s due to a shortage of Merlin spares.

112 flew with the new aircraft on 13 April 1944, but not with the full bomb load, and all 12 of them attacked a railway-over-river bridge. A post-attack recce reported that three very near misses had caused no apparent damage.

However the railway line had been hit north of the bridge by two bombs and on the south side by one. The pilots claimed they did not see much difference between the old Mk IIIs and the new Mk IVs. A railway bridge was again attacked the following day. The first one appeared to survive the rain of bombs although the line was cut. A man was seen firing a machine gun from the window of a house on the west side of the bridge. A recce of Aquila, Rieti and Foligno LGs revealed them to be empty of enemy aircraft. Eight Spitfires escorted this operation. Nine Spitfires provided cover for the second mission which also failed to hit the bridge but a near miss on the third span knocked off quite a lot of it.

'B' Flight commander, Flt Lt W J L (James) Longmore was posted out that day. He was the son of Air Chief Marshal Sir Arthur Longmore and he had joined the RAF in 1941 and had been posted to South Africa as an instructor. He was nearly killed there at the hands of an over-confident pupil pilot called Neville Heath who was later hanged for murder. On leaving 112 Sqn he was posted back to the UK where he was attached to a Wing of Canadian Spitfires.

The aircraft were loaded up with their full 2000-lb worth of bombs for the first time on the 15th. They again attacked a railway bridge and left it with a bite out of the second span and the line severed. The bridge that had been attacked the previous day was attacked again by the second mission and two direct hits were reported on the northern approaches, cratering the embankment masonry and severing the line. It was noticed that the previous day's damage had not been repaired. On the way home a ditched B-17 Flying Fortress was seen five miles off Ortona with two dinghies alongside and some fishing boats making their way out. That day Flt Lt Ahern was awarded the DFC and 35 of the airmen received their Africa Star with rosette.

More attacks on railway bridges followed on the 16th, again escorted by Spitfires. The first attack scored hits on the line and twisted it. FX366 'S' (WO Hirons) was hit by flak and the glycol tank, tyres, flaps and belly tank were punctured. He jettisoned his bombs and belly tank and returned to base. A bridge near Narni was attacked on the second operation and there was a direct hit on the south-east end, severing the line and leaving a crater. Seven single-engined enemy aircraft in blue-grey camouflage were seen on Rieti LG. The weather was now beautiful and the airmen began bathing from a nearby beach.

A twin bowstring type bridge near Rieti was bombed by the first mission the next day. Bombs fell on the track and also on the bridge which was claimed as damaged. Four unidentified enemy aircraft were seen approaching above a squadron of Kittyhawks escorted by Spitfires. The e/a did a turnabout and flew away. Later six grey-green camouflaged Bf109s were seen at 13,000'. They jettisoned some belly tanks but then vanished into the haze. The second operation was against MT reported at Knin in Yugoslavia. The aircraft made landfall at Sibenik and one aircraft recced Knin while the rest orbited. The recce aircraft saw a car park and a repair depot and attempted to mark it by skip-bombing. The bomb overshot and demolished two or three houses. The rest of the formation then bombed and all overshot with the result that an L-shaped cluster of houses north of the car park was considerably damaged. After that the aircraft straffed and claimed some MT.

Fuel dumps in Yugoslavia were the targets on 18 April 1944 which were reported located on a slope between two churches. The aircraft bombed and straffed and set fire to about 200 drums of oil and fuel. A strong wind quickly spread the flames. The second target was reputed to be an ammunition store but it turned out to be a church and a couple of near misses dislodged some tiles and partly demolished a wall. Two aircraft were instructed by 'Commander' to jettison their bombs and carry out an air-sea rescue search ten miles north-west of Vis. This was later cancelled so they orbited Vis and were promptly shot at by 20mm flak so 'Commander' told them to go home. On their return the squadron received a congratulatory message from the partisans who were evidently pleased with the results of the bombing.

Railway interdiction continued as the Allies slowly came to readiness for the next assault on the German positions. On the 22nd a new Flight Commander for 'B' Flt arrived, Capt Angus McLean of the SAAF. The following day there was a strafe of Perugia airfield. On the way they passed over Foligno LG and attacked aircraft there, a Ju88, A Caproni and a Fieseler *Storch* on the north-east side and a Do217 on the west side. All were left on fire. At Perugia two Ju88s and one Ju52 were also left 'burning brightly'. Then the top section straffed 20-plus twin and single engined aircraft dispersed in blast bays south of the runway in a large field. Strikes were seen but none of them caught fire. The hangars were also attended to and, not satisfied with this, the Kittyhawks continued south-west of Perugia where they found a large collection of railway trucks which were left damaged or burning. An overhead electric cable was severed and was seen to short-circuit. At Panicale some MT were straffed and two dumps of ammunition were left burning.

In the afternoon another ammunition dump near Lake Trasimeno was attacked. The revetments were described as sand-bagged and straw-covered. The aircraft made three runs over the target and five dumps blew up and ten others were left smoking. One large explosion at the southern end of the target area left a pall of black smoke over the area and debris was thrown up to 4000'. On the second pass, coming in over Lake Trasimeno, Lieut 'Fossie' Foster (FX516 'P') was hit by flak. His aircraft struck the ground, exploded and left a trail of burning wreckage for 50 yards through trees.

So it went on throughout the month of April. On 25th 'A' Party moved to a new LG at Sinello but the weather clamped down and conditions there were so bad that the squadron's move was cancelled and 'A' Party returned. By the end of the month wind and rain kept the aircraft on the ground and everyone stayed in their tents.

On 29th April the airfield was straffed by four USAAF P-47 Thunderbolts returning from an escort mission for Liberators and Fortresses bombing Wiener

Neustadt. Making landfall near Vasto the Americans, who were uncertain of their position, saw a Warhawk landing at Cutella. This machine carried a white spinner, unlike the normal red spinners of RAF machines, and the Americans assumed it was a Bf109. They came in, flying line abreast, and opened fire. Three aircraft belonging to 260 and 450 Sqns were damaged and WO Roland C Glew, DFM, of No 293 Air-Sea Rescue Sqn detachment, was killed. Glew, who piloted a Walrus, was married and the father of three children, but what made this costly mistake particularly upsetting was that Glew had recently rescued a number of American aircrew who had ditched in the Adriatic. Later, when the CO of the Thunderbolt Group, which was based at Foggia, flew in to offer his apologies, he was nearly lynched. All reference to the incident was hushed up and personnel were forbidden to write home about it and there is no mention of it in the squadron records.

The weather improved at the beginning of May and operations resumed but with much the same type of target – road and railway bridges and MT. On the 3rd the second operation was menaced by 20-plus Bf109s and FW190s which appeared at the 6 o'clock position (that is to the rear of the formation), circled and then pounced. The Kittyhawks turned to face the threat, at which the enemy aircraft split up to attack individual aircraft. The squadron formation seems then to have dispersed – perhaps it was that it was so long since they had been involved in aerial combat it was considered that discretion was the better part of valour – and they were instructed to rendez-vous over Aquila. Lieut Michael White (FX622 'W') failed to return and was reported missing.

Mrs Georgina Barley, from Johannesburg, wrote after the war that she had been part of a South African Entertainments Unit stationed near Foggia and had been Mike White's fiancée at the time. After he had been reported missing she began receiving letters from the squadron pilots because they felt that she would like news of the squadron, particularly because she had been the only girl who had never sent a 'Dear John' letter. White was not reported killed until after the war as no one saw him go down and his body was not found for a long time. Eventually the wreck of his aircraft was located near Rieti and a priest said that the pilot's body had been buried in the vault of a local church but because White had not been wearing his identity disc his name had not been known.

Attacks on railway bridges, stations and railway lines continued and on the 4th it was learned that Flt Lt Ahern was promoted to the acting rank of squadron leader and taking over as CO. On the 6th twelve aircraft attacked anti-aircraft guns near Perugia along with 250 Sqn as close cover and six Spitfires as top cover. Eleven 88mm guns were attacked in what seems to have been a unique operation up to that time. One direct hit was claimed on a gun pit at the western perimeter of the battery and another pit was seen to be on fire after the straffing. Good observation was difficult because of the vigorous and accurate fire from the 20mm light AA guns and small arms fire but somehow the Kittyhawks emerged unscathed from this hornets' nest.

Five new pilots arrived from No 239 Wing Training Flight, some of them being the first products of the recently instituted Air Training Corps – Sgt G G Clark, Sgt J R Greenaway, Sgt L W North, Sgt P L Rees and Sgt E Tickner – although an airman 1721704 AC1 Burgess, F G, also an ex-ATC cadet, had been on 112 since the 11 March 1944. The diarist commented that the new aircrew all seemed to be extremely young. Flt Lt Eddie Ross, no longer the Pilots' Mess catering officer, took over 'A' Flt. Operations resumed on the 9th after a spell of bad weather, with a road recce between Avezzano – Fiamignano – Aquila. Very little movement was seen and the two vehicles that were observed were quick enough to avoid being attacked by getting under cover. On the 10th, while bombing a bridge outside Spoleto, someone with sharp eyes noticed a dispatch rider leaving a red-tiled house and it was reported as a possible HQ.

General Alexander had, by now, built up sufficient forces to give him a numerical superiority over Vietinghoff. He had planned an overwhelming offensive which was designed to destroy the right wing of the German 10th Army and drive it back upon Mackensen's 14th Army which covered Anzio and the approaches to Rome. To achieve this the 8th Army now consisted of five Corps, three British, one Canadian and one Polish under Lieut-General Oliver Leese (a total of 13 divisions) and Lieutenant-General Mark Clark's 5th Army of three Corps (15 divisions) including Truscott's VI Corps in the Anzio beach head which had been reinforced and now comprised 7 divisions.

The 8th Army was to make the main attack against Cassino and advance up the Liri and Sacco valleys along Route 6 towards Valmontone. At the same time the Americans would attack from their bridgehead over the Garigliano and try to link up with Truscott. To confuse the Germans an elaborate deception plan was mounted to suggest that a large amphibious operation was to be launched against Civitavecchia. This had already had some effect as newspaper reports in early April had quoted German sources as saying that Allied landings were expected 'hourly' in the Gulf of Genoa and the Venice area and reinforcements had been hurriedly sent there.

In the meantime the squadron continued its ceaseless attacks on railways and roads. On 11 May the second battle of the Garigliano was opened with an artillery barrage of forty minutes extreme concentration on a front of 30 to 40 miles. Because of the air preparation and the summer weather the advance was successful and Kesselring saw that it was time to withdraw. The squadron's efforts were turned on field guns on the 13th and the first attack produced an explosion and a dense cloud of smoke that rose to 1000'. There were cab-rank patrols over Cassino but when they were told that FW190s were bombing and straffing Allied troops little could be done to intervene because of the thick haze. The following day Rover gave them a target after eight minutes on station, an enemy counter-attack forming up in a gully. This was bombed and Rover was pleased with the result.

Close support operations again on the 15th with attacks on field guns and mortar positions and the third target, a white building, was left burning. The area was left under what the diarist described as 'heavy artificial haze'.

17 May 1944 was celebrated by the squadron as its fifth anniversary overseas, not quite accurately as it happens, but near enough. Two operations were flown, both of 12 aircraft, the first against a suspected HQ building which was squarely hit and the second against a road bridge. When these necessary preliminaries were over a photographer was summoned and photos taken of the aircrew and groundcrew standing with an aircraft as a background. The Public Relations Officer from Advanced HQ of the Desert Air Force arrived to collect material for a brief write-up of the squadron's history. In the evening celebrations took place in the airmen's Mess that included a concert party and a large quantity of local wine. Congratulatory messages

were received from the AOC and all neighbouring squadrons.

During the previous months the squadron had also had an influx of 'trick cyclists' as psychoanalysts were disparagingly nick-named at that time. Pilots were subjected to endless questions about their attitude to flying and killing and no doubt many sheets of paper were filled up and sent away to be studied and pondered over. Much individual stress was absorbed by the simple expedient of getting drunk during the off-duty hours, a palliative which seems to have worked well since there were only a couple of instances of squadron pilots going LMF[1] at this time or earlier – a state of mind which, when it became obvious, ensured an instant posting back to base. The squadron, now that it was in a more settled environment and not perpetually gathering itself together and disappearing over the skyline, was also afflicted by any number of padres of various persuasions, who were politely accepted provided they didn't make too much of a nuisance of themselves. The principal criticism levelled against 'God botherers' and 'wingless wonders'[2] was the way they frequently attempted to ape the pilots' conversational slang as though to try to 'be one of the boys', an attitude that, even if it was understandable, was usually counter-productive.

On the 18th the town of Cassino was finally cleared of the enemy and the monastery – or what was left of it – fell to Polish troops. French Moroccan irregulars closed in on the road running north to Itri and Pico and thereby threatened the German line of retreat. The 'Adolf Hitler Line', an extension of the 'Gustav Line' held Kirkman's XIII Corps for five days, but it was breached on the 23rd. That day VI Corps in the Anzio beach head thrust north towards Valmontone and on the 25th Keyes' II Corps linked up with the beach head troops near Borgo Grappa. Although the Vietinghoff's 10th Army was now in great danger the Germans withdrew skillfully but Mark Clark shifted his advance in the direction of Rome and it fell on the 4 June. Although this great success was greeted with relief throughout the Western World its significance paled when, two days later, the invasion of Normandy began.

The squadron, throughout all these events, continued their nibbling away at the enemy transport system. Shipping was attacked on the 19 May, roads on 21st. Meanwhile there was a move afoot. 112 had been at Cutella since January, almost four months, the longest they had stayed anywhere since the beginning of hostilities. 'A' Party under WO Hooper left for San Angelo on the western side of Italy just north of the Volturno River, the scene of heavy fighting in October of the previous year. Armed road recces behind the Germans lines continued in the meantime. After a strafe along the Sora – Atina – Arce road Sgt D W Grubb (FX544 'K'), who had been on the squadron barely one month, reported that he had been hit in the glycol tank. He was escorted homewards but three miles south of Avezzano he had to put his aircraft down. He was seen to start to open the cockpit door to get out so it was presumed he was unhurt and probably a PoW.

That afternoon 112 flew to San Angelo but, although it was a squadron rule always to start operations again immediately after a move it was late by that time and nothing further was done until the next day. Two missions, both Cab Rank patrols were flown

---

[1] Lacking Moral Fibre, a term denoting cowardice or infirmity of purpose.
[2] 'God botherers' – padres of whatever denomination; 'Wingless wonders' – RAF officers without aircrew brevets

on the 23rd supporting the army's assault on the Gustav and Adolf Hitler lines. Gun pits were hit on the first operation and on the second Rover David vectored them on to a target of guns pulling out onto a road. A layer of cloud over the target from 800' to 1000' made it impossible for the aircraft to see the target so they attacked a house from which the flashes of guns were seen to be coming.

Intensive operations continued the next day, also Cab Rank patrols with much emphasis on attacking gun positions. Rover David then asked them to recce south of the pin-point but no movement was seen. The second Cab Rank was directed to search for bridges between the Liri River and the highway and they found one Bailey-type bridge which received one direct hit and a couple of near misses which caused it to sag into the water. The pilots noticed tracks converging on the bridge which suggested that queues had been forming up to cross it. The final two missions ended up attacking MT.

The rear party arrived at San Angelo that day and everyone was pleased with their new location as it was picturesque and the airmen were happy to find that a cricket and soccer pitch had been laid out for them.

On the 25 May, as the beach head linked up with Mark Clark's northward thrust, 112 were busy. Four missions were dispatched, the first two being of six aircraft and the second two of 12 aircraft each. A road recce resulted in a strafe of 20-plus MT and two tanks and ten vehicles were claimed as flamers. The second road recce was not quite so lucky and only claimed one flamer. The third operation was in search of a petrol dump described as being in or near two large haystacks by a farmhouse. Many such haystacks were seen and the formation split up to attack the most likely ones. One wonders at the bewilderment of the Italian farmers at the destruction of their cattle fodder. Afterwards dispatch riders and staff cars were attacked and a troop carrier with 'about fifteen bodies[1]' was thoroughly straffed and it was considered that 'many bodies (were) killed'. Blue Section attacked a tank and left it smoking. The final operation had a field day with enemy MT. Red Section found 30-plus vehicles and claimed two flamers and other well straffed, also a motor-cycle and sidecar; Blue Section claimed three smokers including an HDV.

The next day, with the German line pulling back fast, there were, naturally enough, road recces. The first which was along the Ceccano – Ferentino – Valmontone road found two stationary vehicles which were bombed. A wheel and an axle were blown off one truck and the engine was blown into the cab of the second one. The second mission is transcribed here as it appears in the Ops Record Book in its entirety —

'Target – armed recce. Direct to Ceprano – North of Highway 6 – A/D[2] Frosinone – North of Alatri – Ferentino – Fiuggi, single D/R[3] and M.T. seen. 3 M.T. pulled into side of road facing south-east, bombed south-west to north-east 7,000' to 1,500'. 2 direct hits, 1 near miss, 1 near miss road, road cratered for fifty feet. 1 set of bombs demolished house on north side of road and took bite out of road. G.3555[4] aircraft went down on M.T. already burnt out, G.4141 1 troop carrier with five plus bodies

---

[1] 'bodies', sometimes colloquially shortened to 'bods', here has the meaning of (living) personnel.
[2] A/D probably means 'altered direction';
[3] D/R = dispatch rider;
[4] G. 3555 etc = map reference points;

strafed, one flamer and five plus bodies claimed. G.4646 1 large camouflaged M.T. under trees well strafed, no claims. 1 D/R moving west at G.4147 damaged. G.3648 staff car, half upper portion of car blown off. G.3936 troop carrier 4 plus bodies well strafed, ran off road into bank, damaged. Claims, 1 flamer, 3 damaged, G.4530 medium accurate 20mm and 40mm[1]. G.4331 light accurate 40mm.'

It will be seen from this report that there is no mention of the number of aircraft taking part, or the times of take-off and landing – details that have to be cross-referred from the Flight Authorisation Book. The third operation that day had little to report other than 'at G.3155 aircraft went through a cloud of tinfoil' – presumably 1cm-band paper-backed metallic strips, codenamed 'Window', which were dropped by both air forces to confuse early-warning radar.

On the 27 May armed recces continued. Two aircraft dropped their bombs on one vehicle and had the satisfaction of seeing it disintegrate. On their way home they saw eight-plus MT but they could do nothing other than calling up other squadrons to attack them. Gun pits occupied the second mission, followed by a road recce. The third mission managed to catch a large lorry carrying drums of petrol which was set alight causing the fuel to explode for the next five minutes. This unremitting chipping away at the enemy's transport, expensive though it must have been in aircraft fuel, must also have caused individual German officers and soldiers great worry as the evidence of the success of this interdiction programme was heaped at the sides of every road and visible at every broken bridge. One can only imagine the terror that an MT driver or dispatch rider felt as these low-flying Kittyhawks appeared dead ahead of them along the road, machine guns 'spitting lead'. Back at San Angelo the summer weather allowed the airmen to bathe in the Volturno while another party went on a day's pass to Naples.

Armed recces of 28 May silenced 20mm (probably anti-tank) gun positions and the second mission, in the middle of a straffing run on some MT and tanks, had to leave hurriedly when Thunderbolts started to dive bomb the same target. Tanks in a wood were the primary target on the first operation the next day, followed by the usual road strafe. On the second operation Sgt C J Parkinson, an arrival on the squadron only five days before, was hit by flak when only 20' above the ground and the aircraft 'S' (most probably FX710) crashed-landed heavily, breaking its back. Half a minute later it was enveloped in smoke and flames and Parkinson was considered dead. It was only his second operation. The leader's aircraft was damaged when a vehicle disintegrated and he had to be escorted back to base. On the third operation Flt Lt Matthias's aircraft (FX777 'C') was hit in the glycol tank and he crash-landed it near Nettuno where he was picked up by an American unit.

Bad luck continued the next day when Sgt Rees, one of the five ATC cadets who had trained as pilots, failed to return from the second operation. Rees (FX670 'W') ran into intense and accurate MG fire and 20mm flak during a strafe of MT. He was heard to say 'I have been hit, cannot see anything, going down'. He was not heard from again and no wreckage could be found. He remains missing on RAF files. The month ended with another pilot missing, Sgt G F Davis (FX740 '?'), on his third operational sortie. He was taking part in an armed recce and was simply not seen again and was posted missing, but it transpired later that he had been killed. The squadron commander

---

[1] 20mm and 40mm flak guns

noted that thirteen aircraft had been lost or damaged and four of the new NCO pilots had fallen victim to flak during low-level straffing runs. Sqn Ldr Ahern considered that lack of experience was to blame although the fact that these men were very young was considered a contributory factor.

In May the squadron had had 30 aircraft on strength and not all the serial numbers were recorded (for an 'S' and a 'Z'). Some aircraft changed their letters and were transferred from one Flight to the other. The query symbol on Sgt Davis' machine was Flt Lt Eddie Ross, 'A' Flt commander's idea. He had given his aircraft the '?' device instead of a letter, and this remained the habit from then on. This was not unique in the DAF as 87 Sqn flying Spitfire VIIIs from Catania and 601 Sqn, also flying Spitfire VIIIs from Venafro are known to have had the query symbol. 112 may be considered unique, though, in readopting it when flying Hawker Hunters. At this time only four of the squadron officers, Flt Lt 'Taffy' Evans, the Adjutant, Fg Off Bob Page, the Engineering Officer, Flt Lt R H McKenzie, the MO and Matt Matthias were Royal Air Force. The squadron commander and eight others were SAAF and one was RCAF. On the other hand, of all the NCO pilots, only one was not RAF.

On 1 June 1944 armed recces continued but few claims were made. On the second operation the next day Sgt J R Carr, another recent arrival, flying FX687 'K', suddenly rolled over onto his back and fell in a slow spin ultimately crashing and bursting into flames. No parachute was seen, R/T silence was not broken and there had been no flak so his death remains a mystery. 2/Lt Don Clark was lost the following day flying FX792 'X'. On the second operation he called up 'I've been hit, am baling out'. The aircraft rolled over and a parachute was seen to open, he landed safely and waved before running into some trees. It was hilly country two miles north of Ienne so it was hoped that he would be all right. After the war Don Clark described what had happened: 'I was hit in the engine at the beginning of my bombing dive . . . immediately pulled up, reported I had been hit and was baling out. Then dropped my bombs on the road and (I) reckon I got a direct hit. Took off my flying helmet and opened canopy and started turning aircraft over and winding tail trim forward. Turned aircraft half way over and found I couldn't get it around any further, so released the stick and shot halfway out of the cockpit. I then climbed out the rest of the way and started somersaulting . . . After about 10 seconds I pulled the ripcord and my 'chute opened. After taking stock I found one flying boot and my revolver missing. I saw my aircraft crash and burst into flames in the hill nearby. I landed in a very rocky piece of ground, but without injury. Then released my 'chute, ran about 10 yards, stopped, waved to my No 1 indicating I was O.K. By this time some Italians had gathered, seemed very pleased to see me and carried on a conversation which was all one sided . . .' Clarke had lost his escape kit and his Italian phrase book, which didn't help much but he distributed his parachute and cigarettes amongst the locals and set off in an easterly direction for the high ground. 'After sliding down Mount Aurore and washing my feet, I met an Italian in uniform who gave me half a loaf of bread and some very bitter cheese which I didn't eat. Having been told that the Fascists were in Vellepetri, I set off for Trevi where I intended sleeping, but on seeing eight-plus Huns' MT in the village did a smart about turn to the hills. I reached an abandoned hut in the hills at 10 pm and found it bloody cold sleeping in a pair of (flying) overalls on the floor. Next morning I set out to cross the Trevi road but heard MT coming and dived under the bridge while two half-tracks went over the top. Then I went on my way, crossing a river up to my waist – damn cold too – and then up the mountains again, using now my second glove as a shoe, the first having worn out. Near Monabianca I met up with some Italian cave-dwellers, who persuaded me to stay the night with them. At about 4pm, as I was sleeping, a boy woke me telling me '*Tedesci*'(= Germans) were coming. I went into the bush and seven more came down the valley, going north in a hurry. After they'd passed I continued with my sleep. I was called out twice before sunset because of Jerries going through. The Eyetyes (= Italians) fed me there on brown bread, goat's milk and raw eggs. Next morning two Italians offered to guide me to our lines as they thought Jerry had left these parts. On the way I captured a Jerry HQ of some nature, complete with Orderly Room, beds, tables, chairs, blankets, bicycles and ammunition, all left in confusion. At this camp I lifted an Italian cavalry sword, previously lifted by Jerry. I also got myself a right boot. The guides helped themselves to the kit and bicycles left behind. I then set off down the road towards Guarcino carrying a white flag and a bayonet, inspecting MT, tanks, guns – a couple of 88mm – that had been bombed and straffed. Some had been burned out, others just blown off the road, and other completely riddled. Several German graves were by the roadside too. I passed quite a number of Indians (6 Div) who took no notice of me, but later got captured by a doctor and eight others pointing their guns at me. After making myself known they gave me a cup of tea, something to eat, a cigarette and transport back to Div HQ'[1].

The run of bad luck which suddenly seemed to be dogging the squadron was not over as on 5 June two more pilots were lost. Sgt Tickner (FT948 'J') was heard to call that he had been hit and his aircraft was seen to be losing oil and glycol but after that he was not seen again. Lieut H F Churchill, who had been on the squadron five months, flying FX800 'R' disappeared entirely. Both aircraft were probably hit by flak in the Castel del Tora area. Later it was learned that Tickner had been killed and Churchill was a PoW.

---

[1] This account comes partly from a letter to the author and partly from '*Desert Air Force*' by Chaz Bowyer & Chris Shores

CHAPTER SIX

Rome to Capitulation

Rome fell on the 4 June but the capture of the first Axis capital went almost unnoticed in the free world's press as on the 6th the Allies landed in Normandy at the opening of 'Overlord'. Kesselring's dilemma was that the next line of defence, the 'Gothic Line', which ran from Pisa in the west to Rimini on the Adriatic, was not yet complete. North of this the Appennines, so useful in defence, fade away into the valley of the Po river. It was therefore necessary for the Germans to delay the Allied advance for as long as possible, even in the teeth of total Allied air superiority. The advance of the 5th and 8th Armies continued north of Rome and by 7 June Civitavecchia had fallen and the complex of airfields around Viterbo was captured two days later. To the Allied High Command all seemed to be going remarkably well.

There were no operations on the 7th and the squadron was delighted by the return of 2/Lieut Don Clark, who had last been seen standing by his parachute on the 3rd. He did remark that he had had the greatest difficulty in walking with only one flying boot!

Bert Horden contributed an article to an aviation magazine[1] after the war in which he describes what it was like flying the Kittyhawk in those months when the principal operation was dive bombing. He makes the point that it was difficult to see one's own bomb burst 'but we saw the ones ahead of us and reported individual successes or otherwise on our return . . .' The constant dive bombing from high to low altitude 'was all very exciting but hard on the ear drums. In fact, as predicted by the squadron MO, we have all suffered from damaged or sensitive ears ever since . . .' He continues 'We had a saying in those days that you could tell a Kittyhawk pilot by the way he wore his wrist watch and by the twitch in his left leg. Comment about the pilot's watch stemmed from the fact that in order to avoid damaging it, a Kittyhawk pilot wore it on the inside of his wrist to avoid it being crushed between the throttle and the fuselage. The twitch in our leg came from the great pressure on the left rudder pedal needed during the dive-bombing manoeuvre.'

Flying resumed the following day with more attacks on railway lines. Some pilots flew twice. A staff car received a direct hit on the 9th and tank transporters were straffed. Flt Lt Reg Wild, who had joined the squadron as a sergeant in August 1942 when the 8th Army had its backs to the wall at E1 Alamein, rejoined 112 and thus brought an Aussie accent back into the Pilots' Mess tent. He was soon leading a section

[1] 'Fly Past Magazine', June 1989, p.37

once more. The story of an exploit when he was on 3RAAF Sqn deserves to be repeated. On the 14 May he found a large convoy of enemy vehicles near Subiaco and with one bomb cratered the road ahead of them and with his second cratered the road at their tail end, thus trapping them. He then passed the word to base and all available aircraft in the Wing were diverted there and between them they created absolute havoc, destroying 90 trucks and damaging 30. On 10 June the squadron began a move forward again, this time to Guidonia, not far from Rome. Operations that day were in search of a convoy reportedly of 200 vehicles but although three missions were sent off, this plum target could not be found. They had better luck on 11th when they successfully straffed 40-plus MT. There was only one operation on the 12th when 12 aircraft under Capt McLean flew to attack a factory near Rieti. Five sets of bombs had already fallen on the northern end of the building when the leader saw, marked very distinctly, the letters 'P O W' painted on the southern end. The rest of the formation were told not to bomb by 'Commander' (Gp Ops).

News was received that Plt Off (ex-Flt Sgt) Stan Worbey who had been missing since 13 March and presumed to be a PoW, had returned safely after 82 days behind enemy lines. After being captured he was being taken north by road when the convoy was attacked by 112 Sqn and his description of what it was like being straffed by his own comrades, the sight of the Sharks swooping down on the convoy and the destruction caused by them was very dramatic. Later he escaped and managed to find an Italian farmer and live with the family working as a farm hand, just waiting for the front line to reach him.

On the 13th at 05.30 hrs the squadron aircraft flew to Guidonia and at 09.05 hrs the first operation was mounted from the new LG. On the second operation Sherman tanks were seen moving into Narni, just south of Terni. The squadron made itself comfortable in its new home which was described as 'rather pleasant'. A liberty vehicle went into Rome and the duty of guarding the aircraft at night was taken over by a unit of the RAF Regiment, to the great satisfaction of the overworked Fitters, Riggers and Armourers.

On 15 June the squadron went back to armed recces and Cab Rank patrols but in the latter instance the secondary target was attacked, which was gun pits. The CO flew to Corsica for a few days leave and the squadron was taken over by Capt McLean in his absence. Attacks on German road transport continued as Kesselring began to settle down behind the 'Gothic Line' which was being transformed into the usual strong defensive position. The front now ran from Ombrone on the west coast to Civitanova on the Adriatic. Hitler had reinforced Kesselring with eight more divisions, sending troops from Denmark, Holland, the Balkans, Germany and even Russia. The Hermann Göring Panzer Division which had been earmarked to go to France was also retained.

The swiftness of the advance once again resulted in rifts in the Allied High Command regarding future strategy. Alexander was confident that the forces in Italy could break through the Gothic Line and advance into the Po valley during August. From there his forces could fan out either into southern France or into Austria and Yugoslavia. This plan found little favour with the Americans who wanted a seaborne invasion of the Côte d'Azur as soon as possible, an option that was strongly supported by the French. Stalin was not anxious to see the Allies moving into the Balkans which he considered should come under his influence after the war ended. Churchill eventually yielded to Roosevelt's insistence and troops were withdrawn from Alexander's command in preparation for 'Operation Anvil' which would protect the southern flank of the Normandy invasion force and supply the Allies with another much needed major supply port – Marseilles.

On 17 June the squadron was released from duty and stood down for 48 hours. Practically the whole squadron decamped for Rome, Tex Gray was prominent wearing a top hat and brandishing an umbrella in his rôle as 'Petrov the Russian'. The weather on the 19th and 20th was mercifully too bad for any flying which no doubt helped the pilots recover from the ill-effects of the Eternal City. The best news, however, was that 112 was at last about to re-equip with Mustangs.

Before this happened there were operations still to be flown with the Kittyhawks. Armed recces got airborne on 21 June. On the second operation Sgt A A Dowling (FX719 'H') found that he could not switch on his auxiliary fuel tanks and had to force land. Later that day six aircraft found an enemy vehicle at a cross roads which they had been targetted to bomb. Two direct hits fell on the west side, one direct hit on the south-east side and one near miss on the north-west side. The vehicle was blown into the centre of the roundabout where it was destroyed. The aircraft then straffed a VW *Kubelwagen* which went off the road and turned over. The occupants were considered to have been killed.

That day 'A' Party left for Falerium LG, near Lake Bracciano and Capt McLean and five pilots went to Blida to collect the new aircraft. On the 22nd 24 sorties were flown on two operations. The first attacked a cross roads and the second against an alleged concentration of 100 vehicles which was not located. These were the final operations in the Kittyhawks as that day saw the delivery of the first Mustang MkIIIs. Kittyhawks had first arrived on the squadron in January 1942 and they, above all other types, seem to have been the aircraft that 112 Shark Squadron are remembered by. Approximately 415 Kittyhawks from Mk Ia to MkIV had passed through 112 Sqn's hands of which 126 were destroyed by enemy action, crashed, went missing, force-landed or were abandoned in retreat. Allowing for the 23 aircraft that were on the squadron at the time the Mustangs arrived this leaves about 266 machines that left the squadron for various other reasons – replaced, damaged beyond repair or flown away for major servicing, an expenditure rate of about 1 aircraft every 2.3 days, something that could not have been done without the huge American production line churning out warplanes at a stupendous rate.

On 23 June the CO flew the first Mustang P-51-C while the pilots swotted up on Pilots' Notes and practised cockpit drills. The aircraft then flew to Falerium and training began. Sgt R D Davies, a new arrival, slightly bent one aircraft which had to be taken away for repairs, a 'black' which was swiftly followed by this NCO's posting to 450 Sqn which still flew Kittyhawks. The next day Sgt J M Dick also had an accident and was slightly injured, in consequence he too left the squadron almost immediately.

The squadron organisation at the end of June was as follows —

> Sqn Cdr: Sqn Ldr Ahern, DFC
> Sqn Adjutant: Flt Lt Page
> 'A' Flt Commander: Flt Lt Wild

'B' Flt Commander: Capt McLean
Intelligence Officer: Fg Off Hooper
Sqn Medical Officer: Flt Lt Crews
Engineering Officer: Fg Off Page
Equipment Officer: Plt Off Huntley

(division into Flights not known)

Lieut Hanreck	Sgt Dowling
Lieut Dottridge	Sgt Goodwin
Lieut Sharp	Sgt Daniel
Lieut Nuyten	Sgt Crowther
Lieut Liebenberg	Sgt Mann
Lieut Jones	Sgt Blair
Lieut McFie	Sgt Musther
Lieut Lund	Sgt Greenaway
2/Lt Illidge	Sgt Clark
2/Lt Clark	Sgt North
Sgt Dick	Sgt Brierly

The North American P-51-C, Mustang Mk III, which the squadron received at the end of June 1944 was not only an inherently versatile aircraft, but also one of the truly great fighter planes of the war. Powered with a Packard Merlin engine of 1520 bhp it was built at Inglewood, California and Dallas Texas, and designed to carry 150 gallons of internal fuel. The MkIII, with two 76 gallon wing tanks and a 124 gallon belly tank flew its first deep penetration mission on 13 December 1943 when it escorted B-17s based in England to Kiel and back, a trip of 490 miles, throwing the German air defences into disarray. These first aircraft were supplied with the sideways-hinging canopy which restricted the rearward view until the British designed Malcolm hood was fitted to some Mustang IIIs (not to 112 Sqn's). Later an entirely new bubble canopy was designed for the P-51D-25-NA (Mustang IV) along with a new fairing to the fin. The aircraft's dimensions were: wing span 37' 0¼", length 32' 2½", height 13' 8". It could carry 2000-lb bomb load, had internal tankage space for 280 gallons with a maximum speed of 439 mph at 26,000' and a sea-level rate of climb of 3,900'/min. The armament was four .5" machine guns mounted in the outer wing clear of the airscrew arc. The P-51Ds had six .5" machine guns with 270 or 400 rounds per gun. 112 Sqn now found itself equipped with an aircraft that was the best all-round piston-engined fighter used by any air force in the war.

Operations using the new aircraft did not start until 5 July 1944. The days prior to this had been occupied in Air Tests and looking for snags. Snags that revealed themselves included canopies flying off and bombs failing to release. The CO went looking for, and found, the grave of Sgt Parkinson who had been lost on 29 May. One of the airmen, a Cpl Chapman, died at No 30 MFH on 1 August and was buried in the British Military cemetery outside Rome.

Sqn Ldr Watts who had force-landed behind enemy lines on 6 April was reported to be a PoW. The first Mustang operations consisted of an armed recce led by the CO when bombs were dropped on a Siebel ferry and some schooners, but all the bombs undershot. Twelve aircraft were sent on the second operation but the final two missions, each of six aircraft, took off together and went to attack field guns. Ravenna LG was bombed, cratering the runway. The last of the Kittyhawks were flown away and 'A' Party packed up for the next move forward. The Mustangs looked pretty good with the sharksteeth markings. Perhaps, in the absence of the large air intake under the spinner, the effect was not quite as fierce as on the Kittyhawks, but it still looked menacing.

On the 7th there was only one operation of six aircraft on a close-support mission, but the aircraft could not make R/T contact with the troops on the ground who were to guide them to the target and they went to attack their secondary. 'A' Party left for Crete LG[1] just west of Lake Trasimeno.

The squadron continued to operate from Falerium the following day with attacks on railways and roads but, with 'B' Party packed up and ready to move there were no missions on the 9th and, at 18.00 hrs the aircraft flew to their new home. Here they found themselves quite close to the front line and it was the first time since the desert days that the groundcrew could watch the aircraft take off, bomb the enemy and return. In this case the target was some mortars near a castle which the army were able to signal correctly. Five 500-lb bombs failed to release and these were jettisoned on the return flight. Because of the nearness of the front line care was taken to disperse the parked aircraft and camouflage them and dig slit trenches. News was received that the grave of Sgt Carr, who had been killed in rather mysterious circumstances on 2 June, had been found in Subiaco cemetery.

Guns and roads were attacked on the 12th and the squadron was visited by some of the DAF armament staff to investigate the problem of the bombs not releasing. The next day things were a bit busier, with a series of six-aircraft missions against field guns. Sometimes the gun pits were seen but more often the aircraft merely dropped their bombs in the designated target area and hoped they would hit something hostile.

The grave of Lieut Foster was found that day in Panicale cemetery, he had been missing since 23 April when he had been hit attacking a bomb dump south of Lake Trasimeno.

The problem with the bomb release mechanism had not yet been solved as was discovered on 14 July. This led to Fg Off R H Newton, flying FB287 'Jinx', spending a couple of nerve-wracking hours in the air trying to get rid of it. Ray Newton, a New Zealander, was a recent arrival, but a veteran of the desert days as his first tour on 112 had been in 1942. The bomb was armed which made it impossible for him to land so for almost an hour he tried to shake the bomb free. In the end 'Commander' ordered him to point the aircraft out to sea and bale out. This he did but the faithful Mustang refused to leave him and circled playfully as he descended by parachute before plunging into the sea and exploding. Peter Nuyten, whose aircraft this had been, was not pleased when he returned from a few days leave to discover 'Jinx' had been lost.

In consequence, more technical types arrived the next day to investigate the problem. The weather was excellent and the squadron flew six operations, each of either five or

---

[1] Squadron records spell the name this way; Jefford, *op cit*, refers to it as Creti, which would appear to be correct, 5km east of Foiano della Chiana.

six aircraft. All the targets were guns and on the third mission, east of Arezzo, the intention was to drop leaflets, but the leader's aircraft, which carried them, had a jammed shutter so they could not be released. As the front line settled down there were more Cab Rank patrols and a cross roads, some mortars and self-propelled guns were attacked. In this latter mission they bombed the pin-point correctly only to see that the guns were about 100 yards away. The sixth mission had its target passed by Rover David, a convoy of 50-plus vehicles possibly including tanks. The convoy was found, pulled off the road, two miles south of Cagli, and was attacked. One direct hit amongst a group of six vehicles destroyed three tanks, a claim that was confirmed by 260 Sqn who attacked the same target later. Sqn Ldr 'Auntie' Ahern, who had flown his last mission that day, became tour expired on completion of 230 operational flying hours.

Twenty-two sorties were flown the next day with a Cab Rank patrol which was led to its target of guns and mortars by Spitfires. On the 18 July, going deeper behind enemy lines, they attacked a railway bridge but, on getting there, they found it was already cut. Being unable to contact 'Commander' for fresh instructions they bombed it again, further weakening the structure. The fourth operation was carried out against some well camouflaged guns west of Siena, 50 yards north of a cemetery. That day Sqn Ldr Ahern and the adjutant flew to Arezzo in a Taylorcraft Auster IV. These little high-wing monoplanes were used for communications duties and artillery air observation posts and this one probably belonged to 654 Sqn. On the 19th the squadron was released from operational duties and given the day off. Some went swimming in Lake Trasimeno and others went sight-seeing but torrential rain brought everyone back in the evening. The new CO was Sqn Ldr A P Q Bluett who had left the squadron in March and now returned for a second tour. Livorno and Ancona fell that day to our slow but steady advance while in Normandy the Allies had fought clear of the beach head, captured Caen and St Lô and were about to break out and take the whole of Normandy.

After a day of bridge bombing there was a visit from ENSA (Entertainments National Service Association) who laid on a performance called 'Fun Fare'. ENSA frequently provided the troops with excellent performances and sometimes far flung and isolated units would be able to enjoy the presence of famous stars of stage and wireless – Gracie Fields or Vera Lynn 'The Forces Sweetheart' – but frequently the shows featured actors, singers and comics of rather dubious quality[1]. Nevertheless, all were equally welcome and there was always the opportunity to invite the chorus girls to come to the Mess after the performance. The squadron diarist recorded that the evening's entertainment 'provided quite a change from the usual squadron evening.'

Operations resumed over the next few days with army targets such as field guns and bivouacs. A house that was straffed in a dive 'emitted a streak of white smoke' that passed over the guns that were the target and exploded on a hill opposite.' On 27 July the Wing was visited by HM King George VI who drove past the squadron dispersal in an open staff car to the cheers of all ranks.

The first operation on the 28th spotted two Re2000s, a small stubby, radial engined fighter which the Italian navy had procured as catapult-launched aircraft for use on their battleships of the Vittorio Veneto class. Curiously enough a British Air Ministry

[1] as the author remembers from his National Service days

delegation had visited the Reggiane factory in December 1939 and had ordered 300 of these machines, a deal which the Germans vetoed in April 1940. Very few of these aircraft were built and the bulk of the production was exported to the Hungarian and Swedish air forces. After the fall of Sicily and Sardinia the *Regia Marina* was unable to operate any seaborne aircraft but it would seem, if the aircraft were correctly identified by 112 Sqn, that at least two were still flying, possibly from the Reggiane factory at Reggio Emilia, about 65 miles north of the front line.

Operations on the 29 July were two armed recces and an attack on a railway bridge. MT workshops were bombed by the second mission and the area was reported to be a 'shambles'. A three-span metal bridge was attacked by the third formation and two spans were left hanging in the water by the time they left. That day Flt Lt Ray Hearn rejoined the squadron for the start of his second tour and took over 'B' Flight from Capt McLean.

On 30th there was an attack on a gun pit which resulted in a volume of black smoke. The last day of the month saw three operations that included a railway bridge as a target but which looked the same after the attack as it did before. On the second mission the aircraft attacked a cross roads and generally made a nuisance of themselves. At one place they found 'one small tank' which they attacked but it must have survived as they made no claim. That day 'Tex' Gray was persuaded that it was time his tour was over having completed it plus an extension of 50 operational flying hours. Thus one of the squadron's best remembered characters departed, whither we know not as a letter sent to his only known address in Chillicote, Ohio, USA, in 1957 went unanswered. This was hardly surprising as he has been described as something of a nomad.

August began with more of the same, a catalogue of attacks that would become boring were it not for the incidents that enlivened almost every day, some curious, some amusing, some tragic. To report that the 1 August saw the loss, after one month on the squadron, of Lieut A H Jones, whose engine cut on take off so that he crashed and was killed in FB317 'T', only provides the barest record of how this young man met his end. The squadron probably hardly knew him and within a few days he would have been forgotten – only back in South Africa would his death be mourned and his memory kept fresh for a few years. Those pilots who survived through most of a tour, became squadron stalwarts, remembered for their idiosyncrasies, their humour, their ability on the Mess piano or their skill in the air were different. If, at the last, they were 'plucked from the sky', their going left a gap that it seemed time would never heal; they are remembered to this day by their ageing comrades more vividly perhaps than by anyone in their immediate family. Occasionally, rarely, there was someone whose death seemed not all that untimely. One would hardly admit publically to disliking someone so much that you actually hoped he would be shot down sooner or later, but several ex-squadron members have hinted as much, and because human nature is what it is this is scarcely surprising. In this event a man's departure might be taken as being not such a bad thing for those remaining on the squadron.

Operations continued on 2 August and Sgt K R Mann (FB291 'F') also crashed on take off, but he lived to fight and fly once more. Lieut Jones was buried in Foiano military cemetery. In the evening torrential rain made the airstrip unfit for any flying so on the 3rd and personnel went out and explored the neighbourhood. On the 4th

Florence were captured; here the medieval bridges over the Arno was dynamited by the retreating Germans with the sole exception of the Ponte Vecchio which was left standing only because it was considered too narrow for military traffic.

On the 5th Sgt Kenneth Mann lost his life. Flying on his first operational mission in FR296 'R' he was hit in the dive by an 88mm flak shell. He went down steeply and hit the ground with a large explosion, fire and black and white smoke. Eighteen sorties were flown on the 6th, a busier day than usual. At the end of it hundreds of Italians enjoying one of their public holidays visited the landing ground and displayed great interest in the aircraft landing and taking off. 'There was no holiday on the squadron' the diarist commented on the 7th (August Bank Holiday in UK). Both operations were flown with 260 Sqn against lock gates and sluice gates in a canal. Results were good and one gate seemed to have been blown in.

In beautiful weather the next day operations continued against the canal system of Northern Italy resulting in two 100' barges being comprehensively hit. Guns were the targets on the 9th and the day was enlivened by Sgt D C Goodwin (FB340 'Z') who swung on take-off and crashed into a Kittyhawk III. Both machines were written off and Sgt Goodwin was lucky to escape with nothing more serious than a fractured skull. The next day was a stand-down for the squadron but little could be done because of torrential rain.

On the 12 August operations resumed on a limited scale attacking guns. In the meantime 'A' Party had been warned of an impending move to undertake 'a special duty', about which there was much speculation. On the following day the squadron continued operations from Crete LG while 'A' Party left for Rossignano, some 70 miles to the west, close to the coast. The aircraft meanwhile attacked two enemy landing grounds north of Ghedi and three Do217s, two Bf110s and an Me410 were successfully straffed. On the second mission Modena marshalling yards were bombed.

The squadron aircraft flew to Rossignano on the 14 August, leaving most of the squadron personnel at Crete LG trying to guess what was going on. The next day it was revealed that 112 were to support 'Operation Dragon' (part of 'Operation Anvil' or the invasion of southern France) which had begun that morning. The squadron flew 12 sorties that day, one of which was led by Gp Capt Eaton, CO 239 Wing. At 16.30 hrs the aircraft took off and flew with starboard wing drop tanks only, flying first to Bastia in Corsica, then to Lerins island where they patrolled from 17.45 to 18.40 hrs. At 17.50 hrs 40-plus DC3s towing Horsa gliders appeared from the east and the squadron split up into pairs and formed a top cover to the stream until the gliders were cast off. This 1st Airborne Task Force landed at Le Muy, inland from Fréjus, and was one of the best executed operations of the invasion. At 18.00 hrs four DC3s dropped supplies by parachute and between then and 18.40 hrs over a 150 DC3s, towing Waco gliders, flew to the dropping zone. No enemy aircraft were seen and the only observed disaster appeared to be when a supply ship struck a mine and blew up. Numerous landing craft and ships and fleet escort vessels could be seen lying off the coast. At 18.40 hrs the aerial cover was relinquished to 260 Sqn.

The squadron flew one more operation over the beach head the next day between 06.30 hrs and 09.30 hrs. At 07.55 hrs the aircraft jettisoned their drop tanks and five minutes later 50-plus Liberators were seen at 8000' going north-west. A lot of activity was seen on the ground, including a dive-bombing attack by 24 P47 Thunderbolts, and barges unloading on the shore. Otherwise the area seemed very quiet. Once established, Patch's 7th Army moved quickly inland and by the 28 August was past Grenoble and lying along the east bank of the Rhône north of Montélimar. Nevertheless luck and good fighting enabled the bulk of Wiese's 19th Army to escape north with the loss of 57,000 prisoners.

After this 112 was withdrawn from supporting the beach head and returned to Crete LG, followed shortly afterwards by 'A' Party. The next day, 17th, two E-boats[1] were attacked in the Venice area. On the 18th 12 aircraft flew to support ground troops and were vectored on to guns, infantry concentrations and mortars, also buildings believed to be strong-points were destroyed.

Armed recces, the most popular type of operation with the pilots, resumed on the 20th after a day of bad weather. The first target was an Italian cruiser lying behind submarine nets, but the formation leader called off the attack when it became apparent that the vessel was already a wreck. A motor vessel was inspected, but not attacked because of intense flak. Little else of interest was seen and there were no enemy aircraft on Reggio airfield, which also appeared to be unserviceable. Sqn Ldr Bluett straffed a staff car and left it smoking. On the second operation a railway line was bombed, undermining the track in two places, an airfield was straffed, then a railway junction where several locomotives were observed. Flt Lt Reg Wild led the last mission that day, flying his aircraft GA-? (HB900).

On 22 August 1944 'A' Party left for Iesi, returning once more to the Adriatic coast, to a landing ground some 12 miles south-west of Ancona. The squadron was to support the forthcoming attack on the Gothic Line and the move was made in the utmost secrecy, from the left to the Allied line to the right as the full weight of the new offensive was planned to cause the enemy the maximum surprise. WO Hooper and 'A' Party reached Iesi at 16.00 hrs on the 23rd while operations continued from Crete. This was an attack on the Modena marshalling yards. Lieut J C Hoyle (HB895 'N') was hit by flak in the dive and he struck the ground in a sheet of flame. The next day the squadron roamed around the Arno valley searching out MT.

On 25th a Dakota brought a reinforcement party consisting of 10 fitters, nine armourers and four pilots to Iesi so that operations could start immediately the aircraft arrived. Twelve aircraft, having completed their mission, flew to Iesi that afternoon and by 07.00 hrs the squadron was operational at the new LG. The 8th Army had opened its attack on the previous day and the initial surprise was enough to carry it through the Gothic Line. The invasion of southern France had convinced Hitler that the 5th and 8th Armies had been weakened to supply men for this invasion and consequently he had withdrawn five of Kesselring's best divisions, thus leaving the Germans thin on the ground. The 8th Army's attack in the east resulted in the enemy moving troops from the western portion of the line to try to shore up the crumbling defences of the Gothic Line.

On 26 August the squadron was flying close-support missions under Rover Jimmy's control. A farm house, mortars and infantry were attacked on the first operation and the aircraft attacked field guns in the late afternoon, the aircraft not landing until 20.10 hrs. The ground battle was now in full swing and all operations on the 27th were in

---

[1] 'E' (or 'Enemy') boat was an Allied name for the German *Schnellboot* or fast torpedo boat

support of the army. Guns were bombed and straffed and a strong-point at a cross roads. On the final operation Sgt L G Daniell (FB338 'C') crashed on take off, but he seems to have survived this incident.

By the third day it was apparent that the 8th Army's offensive had begun with some success. The loss of men from the Allied armies for 'Operation Anvil' was made up by reinforcements from Greek, Italian and Brazilian troops until no fewer than eleven nations were represented in the two armies. The fighting that followed was described by Lieut-General Sir Oliver Leese[1] 'as some of the bloodiest in the history of the British Army'. Nevertheless the Germans had been taken by surprise and, in some instances, the British infantry were able to capture their preliminary objectives with no losses.

Flying continued for the next couple of days with armed recces on the 28th and direct support operations on the 29th. In the third operation that day, an attack on a railway junction, Sgt Arthur Banks (HB936 'A') realised he had been hit by flak and that his engine temperature and oil pressure were 'off the clock'. He flew as far south as was possible and ended by force-landing behind enemy lines. The aircraft was last seen surrounded by peasants and with Sgt Banks getting out.

What subsequently happened to Sgt Banks, who had been on the squadron less than three weeks, is an amazing story of courage and fortitude, and is best told in the words of '*The London Gazette*' of 5 November 1946. 'The KING has been graciously pleased to approve the posthumous award of the GEORGE CROSS to: – 1607992 Sergeant Arthur BANKS, Royal Air Force Volunteer Reserve, No. 112 Squadron, Desert Air Force. On 29th August, 1944, this airman took part in an armed reconnaissance of the Ravenna and Ferrara areas. During the sortie his aircraft was damaged by anti-aircraft fire and he was compelled to make a forced landing. After the aircraft had been destroyed Sergeant Banks decided to try to reach Allied Lines. He made contact with a group of Italian partisans, amongst whom, in the following months, he became an outstanding figure, advising and encouraging them in action against the enemy. Early in December, 1944, an attempt at crossing into Allied territory by boat was planned. Sergeant Banks and a number of partisans assembled at the allotted place, but the whole party was surrounded and captured. Sergeant Banks was handed over to the German commander of the district, who presided at his interrogation. During the question-ing Sergeant Banks was cruelly tortured. At one stage he succeeded in getting hold of a light machine gun with which he might have killed most of his captors had not one of the partisans, fearing more severe torture, intervened and pinned his arms to his sides. Sergeant Banks was badly knocked about before he was taken to another prison. On 8th December, 1944, Sergeant Banks was taken, with a number of partisans, to a prison in Adria. He remained there until the 9th December, 1944, when he was handed over to the commander of a detachment of the 'Black Brigade'. He was then transferred to another prison at Ariano nel Polesine. Here, in the presence of Italian Fascists, he was stripped of his clothing and again tortured. Sergeant Banks was eventually bound and thrown into the River Po. Despite his wounds, even at this stage, he succeeded in reaching the river bank. The Fascists

---

[1] '*The Times*', 18 October 1944, quoted by Fuller, *op cit*

then took him back to the prison, where he was shot through the head[1]. At the time of his capture Sergeant Banks was endeavouring to return to the Allied lines so that he might arrange for further supplies to the partisans. He endured much suffering with stoicism, withholding information which would have been of vital interest to the enemy. His courage and endurance were such that they impressed even his captors. Sergeant Banks' conduct was, at all times, in keeping with the highest traditions of the Service, even in the face of most brutal and inhuman treatment.'

Further enquiries produced the following information from the files of the Directorate of Army Legal Services in 1960: 'Two Italians, Sergio Viegi and Olimpio Ferracini, were tried by a British Military Court at Naples, from 29th of August to the 25th of September, 1946 on charges of being concerned in the ill-treatment and killing of Sergeant Arthur Banks, and on being found guilty were sentenced to five years and twenty years imprisonment respectively. Findings and sentences were confirmed in each case. Two other Italians, Carlo Borrini and Dino Marsili were also tried by a British Military Court at Padua, from the 23rd of January to the 6th of February, 1947, on a similar charge and on being found guilty, by special finding, of being concerned with the ill-treatment of Sergeant Banks, were sentenced to four years six months and five years imprisonment respectively. Both sentences were subsequently confirmed.'

It would seem that Sergeant Banks was tortured under the direction of a certain *Tenente* Rinaldi, of the Fascist Militia, who was subsequently executed by the Italians. An Italian woman, Anna Paola Cattani, and two German nationals, Georg Joachim Geiger and Hugo Saggau, were also tried by a British Military Court in Naples for their part in the crime and sentenced to five and eight years imprisonment respectively[2].

The month of August finished with the squadron operating intensively against ground targets. Many of the targets cannot now be identified as they are referred to in the Ops Record Book solely by map references, although the village of Monte Calvo, 'a defended locality' is mentioned as having been attacked. In two cases the same target was also being attacked by Mustangs of 260 Sqn (although the Ops Diary either gets the squadron incorrect or wrongly identifies the aircraft as Marauders).

That month the squadron had 27 aircraft pass through its hands. Total operational flying time was 788 hours 25 minutes; non-operational flying 88 hours 40 minutes; operational sorties 516, an average of about 17 a day throughout the month. 390 tons of bombs were dropped and the claims amounted to four locomotives, 26 railway trucks, six barges and four motor transport vehicles destroyed, three MT probably destroyed and five damaged, one 2000-ton motor vessel damaged and two enemy aircraft damaged on the ground.

The fifth year of the European war opened 'in glorious weather' and the squadron diarist went on to record that 36 sorties were completed in support 'of our ground forces besieging Rimini'. In fact the total was 32 sorties not 36 as the first four missions were of four aircraft and the final one of 12. Two defended houses, two groups of guns and a road bridge were amongst the targets. Plt Off Jack Greenaway failed to return from the second mission the following day. During an attack on some enemy mortar positions a large explosion was seen which was later believed to have been FB297

---

[1] He died, it is believed, on 20 December 1944
[2] from information supplied by The Foreign Office, 10 May 1960.

Some Shark designs used by the Squadron

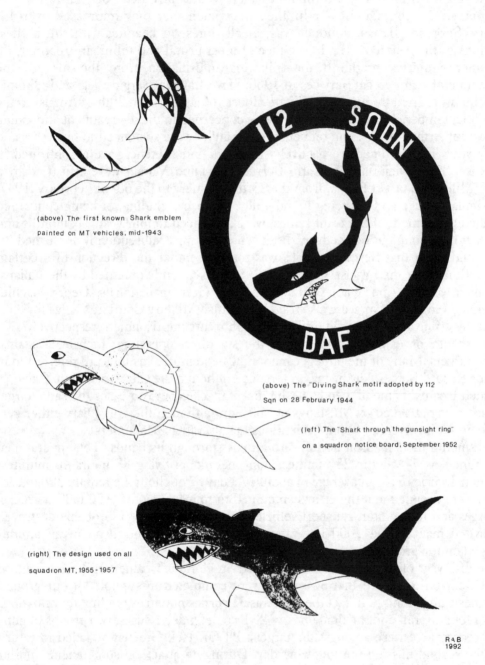

(above) The first known Shark emblem
painted on MT vehicles, mid-1943

(above) The "Diving Shark" motif adopted by 112
Sqn on 28 February 1944

(left) The "Shark through the gunsight ring"
on a squadron notice board, September 1952

(right) The design used on all
squadron MT, 1955 - 1957

R&B
1992

(GA-X), although no sign of wreckage was seen on the subsequent recce.

Poor weather kept most of the ground crew in their tents on the 3rd, although there was operational flying that day and MT concentrations were bombed. Some unease was expressed regarding the health of the airmen with winter coming. The runway was partly unserviceable the next day, due to the rain, but this doesn't seem to have interfered with flying as armed recces took off at 10.55 hrs. With better weather on the 5th a full day's flying was undertaken. Six operations were flown —

(1) Six aircraft took off at 06.35 hrs and started by flying south and west of San Marino to recce the Rimini road but without seeing any movement. Fifteen railway trucks were seen in Forli railway station, but they were not attacked. Two Tac-R Spitfires were contacted. A road bridge was then bombed and straffed and there were some near misses.

(2) Four aircraft took off at 06.50 hrs, flying west of Rimini, then north-west along Route 9 to Bologna. A lot of railway trucks were seen in Modena and Reggio. Thirty of these were attacked and straffed and the locomotive was left with steam pouring from it.

(3) Six aircraft took off at 10.30 hrs for a two hour trip. The formation flew to Rimini at 9000' and then along Route 9, but no movement was seen. They then bombed a railway bridge, but despite two near misses the line remained intact. Then, flying along Route 8, then went north of Bologna to Crevalcore. Open trucks and MT were straffed.

(4) Six aircraft, airborne from 11.15 hrs to 13.05 hrs flew on a course 300° to a road bridge target. There was one direct hit on the approach and other near misses. MT were then attacked but railway trucks, which were seen at various places, were apparently left in peace. The aircraft then straffed some barges, two vehicles and a staff car.

(5) The next operation, of five aircraft, led by Flt Lt Wild in GA-?, flew first to its primary target, a road bridge, but it was still intact after the bombing. The formation then flew east to the coast south of Rimini and observed two (Allied) destroyers shelling the port. Some vehicles then straffed and roads recced. The formation landed at 15.55 hrs after one hour forty minutes airborne.

(6) Six aircraft took off at 16.00 hrs and set course of 330° at 9000' to a point on the River Po. They then cruised along until they came upon some barges which they attacked. There was one direct hit and three barges were sunk. After straffing the aircraft re-formed north of the river, and then flew to Padua airfield but they found no enemy aircraft there. They then came upon a small convoy which included a *PzKw VI* Tiger tank, two smaller tanks, one armoured car and a few MT vehicles. The formation straffed and inflicted some damage on the Tiger tank, left one of the smaller tanks in flames and two armoured cars burning. A truck with quadruple 20mm guns mounted on a semi-turret was also silenced[1].

As a gauge of aircraft serviceability and turn-round that day fifteen aircraft were used, 'F', 'K', 'R', 'S', 'W' and '?' flew three times, 'B', 'C', 'E', 'J', 'Q' and 'V' flew twice and 'A', 'N' and 'Z' once. 'C' nearly flew three times but on the fifth mission it didn't manage to get airborne.

---

[1] Probably an *SdKfz 251* half-tracked armoured vehicle

There was no slackening of effort the next day, 6 September, and it was described as 'one of the best days for some time'. The first show was led by Gp Capt Eaton, DSO, and was the most successful. Twelve aircraft took off at 06.20 hrs and returned at 09.05 hrs. To start with the aircraft attacked a 5000-ton motor vessel along with three large and two smaller tugs which had been turned into flak boats. Bombs, however, fell short, and no damage was done. A 6000-ton vessel was then seen but 'Commander' could not be contacted so the Gp Capt detached two aircraft to return to base with the information. The rest made landfall near Grado and four airfields were then recced, but no aircraft were seen until they reached the easternmost one, where seven Ju87s and one FW190 were found and straffed. There were strikes on all the aircraft and the Focke-Wulf was left smoking. Six unidentified low-wing monoplanes were also attacked. Then 12 radial engined aircraft and one Bf109 were seen with the result that one Stuka was left smoking, a Ju52 and the 109 were also damaged. The aircraft then went further and found a train with seven carriages. This came to a halt when attacked and the driver and fireman were seen to 'bale out'. The aircraft continued along the line with similar targets of opportunity. Amongst these were twelve flat-bed trucks carrying ten unidentified 'conical tanks'. This story continues with variations until the aircraft had run out of ammunition and they were obliged to return to base. Claims included five locomotive destroyed, one MT flamer, two smokers, one ammo truck which blew up, one light tank left smoking and nine more damaged plus the aircraft that had been attacked.

In comparison the remaining missions that day were quite tame. The next day, the 7th, was a rest day and there was no operational flying. The squadron personnel amused themselves by going to the cinema shows and the theatre in Iesi. There was only limited flying the following day, a weather recce and two armed recces, fourteen sorties in all. During the second operation a train, which was about to be attacked, had the admirable presence of mind to take cover in some ground-level cloud.

The 9 September was another red letter day for the squadron, equal, it was considered, to the great days in Greece. The score at the end of the day was

> One Ju88 destroyed in aerial combat
> Thirteen locomotives destroyed
> One 2000-ton ship sunk
> One Heinkel He111 destroyed on the ground
> Three SM79s destroyed on the ground
> One Ju52 destroyed on the ground
> Thirteen other aircraft damaged on the ground
> Two oil trucks damaged
> One observation post dealt with

The first operation was an armed recce of north-eastern Italy led by the CO, Sqn Ldr Bluett, with 11 aircraft which were airborne for two and three-quarter hours. The first thing they spotted was the Italian luxury liner *'Rex'* lying on its side, with its stern on fire. A 2000-ton single funnel ship received two direct hits which caused a large explosion with clouds of smoke and steam. The ship made for shore and beached itself, listing heavily to port. The formation attacked some barges and inspected Trieste harbour, then flew to Grado where they found a train. The engine was straffed. The formation continued on to Rivolto where the airfield was straffed and two Reggiane Re2001s and two Bf109s were damaged. Aviano airfield was found to contain six SM79s, four of which were attacked. A visit to various marshalling yards accounted for eight of the locomotives claimed in the total. One pilot, Sgt Les North, reported engine trouble and was told to go back to base with his No 2, Sgt T R E Williams. On the way home the faulty engine picked up again so the pair went off on a lone strafe and found an airfield where a Heinkel 111 was set alight and two SM79s damaged.

There was a sequel to the attack on the 2000-ton ship. Sgt Williams, who was responsible for destroying it, was later interviewed by a newspaper correspondent. Sgt Williams' casual hyperbole about dropping his bomb 'straight down the funnel' was taken literally and the feat was headlined as such, much to everyone's amusement.

The squadron commander also led the second operation as the pickings seemed to be rich and a railway bridge was attacked near Forli, although it was still intact after the bombing. The third mission was led by Reg Wild against a reported observation post in a church steeple. The bombs were all near misses but the subsequent strafe left the structure burning. The army signalled 112 later with the message 'Just the job, many thanks.'

Another armed recce at 17.00 hrs was led by Flt Lt Ray Hearn and a railway station near Cesena was bombed. About 300 camouflaged waggons were seen there, including some flat-bed trucks with Italian armoured cars on board. The next target was an airfield where three aircraft were attacked and damaged, followed by another airfield where three SM79s were left burning and another damaged. One Ju52 was strafed on Vicenza airfield and left in flames. Just after that Hearn sighted a Ju88 flying very low. He gave chase and closed on it. With only one gun operating he obtained hits on the starboard engine which began to smoke. The enemy machine started to bank and then crashed on the airfield in a cloud of dust and was destroyed.

The day was not yet over as the fifth mission was airborne from 17.10 hrs to 19.00 hrs, led by Flt Lt P W Lovell. This was an escort of six aircraft to 12 Marauders, with four Spitfires as close cover. After the Marauders had finished bombing the Mustangs went their own way and bombed a bridge near Imola which they damaged with near misses.

Intensive operations continued the next day, 10 September, and the diarist commented that 'Northern Italy is proving a happy hunting ground for our pilots' and the score that day, as if to show just how happy these huntsmen were, was seven locomotives destroyed, seven damaged, eighteen railway trucks destroyed and more than twenty damaged – all at Padua and Vicenza marshalling yards. Three *PzKw IVs* were destroyed on the second mission and a 20mm gun silenced. The 11th day was a day of close-support missions for the army and six operations were flown. The AOC, Air Vice Marshal Dickson sent a congratulatory message to 112 on the 12th after a railway bridge at Poggio was demolished. The 13th saw the start of General Alexander's second phase of the offensive, with both the 5th and 8th Armies attacking along the whole German line. A week of bitter fighting began.

The strain of the ceaseless work was beginning to have its effect on the squadron, not least upon the 23 pilots. There was no rest on the 14 September which was the busiest day of the month with 48 sorties, several of the pilots flying more than twice.

The first two operations were against defended positions, then Cab Rank patrols, then attacks on field guns followed finally by another Cab Rank operation. One of the targets was 300 troops but all the pilots could see were civilians fleeing the battle zone, carrying their possessions.

Only 28 sorties were mounted on the 15th, which was observed as 'Battle of Britain Day'. Two SM79s and four Bf109s were straffed on the second mission resulting in one Messerschmitt on fire and all the rest damaged. Alternating attacks on communications and close support seems to have been the idea as the railway lines of Northern Italy were the targets on the following day, and Cab Rank patrols to start with on the 17th, followed by armed recces.

By the 18th the Americans and the British were through the Gothic Line at many places but improvised German defences kept the advance down to a slow pace. Major-General Fuller, that unwavering critic of so much of the strategy of the Allies in the Second World War wonders 'What for?'[1] Was General Alexander trying to keep Kesselring pinned down to prevent him sending reinforcements elsewhere? 'Then this could have been more effectively accomplished by keeping him closer to Rome, because then his lines of communication would have been longer, and the longer they were the bigger the target they would offer to air attack'.

There were some close-support missions on the 18th in the Bologna – Ferrara areas but there was not much to show for the effort. This part of the front was called 'Dead Loss Area'. Cab Rank patrols, which continued the next day, were not very popular with the pilots because of the poor returns they gave for the time spent in the air. The most popular activity undoubtedly was armed recce when they were allowed to swan off miles behind enemy lines, under no one's control, playing havoc with whatever caught their attention. The RAF Regiment personnel were withdrawn that day, much to the dismay of the groundcrew who would once again have to mount guard on the aircraft.

Close support continued on the 20th and the squadron earned a 'Good Show' from Control after the first operation which was bombing some guns located in a farm yard. A road bridge that was attacked on the third mission was cut successfully. Flt Lt Lovell, who had been on the squadron since the end of August, was posted as a Flight Commander to 260 Squadron. That day the 1st Canadian Division of the 8th Army entered Rimini.

Sqn Ldr Bluett led a long range armed recce across northern Italy on the first mission on the 22nd. Six aircraft began by bombing a ship, despite the heavy flak, although one aircraft had its canopy shot away. Then they went east to Lavariano LG where they saw some dummy Bf109s which they did not attack, then to Vill LG where they found some real aircraft. Strikes were observed on an SM79, a Henschel Hs129 and two MC200s. One unidentified aircraft was left smoking. Seven steam locomotives and a diesel engine were claimed destroyed. The Hs129, a rare bird as far as 112 were concerned, had been produced as a ground-attack aircraft and were mostly employed on the Russian front, although some had served rather ingloriously in Tunisia.

The 23rd saw the squadron doing Cab Rank duties again and on one mission three armoured cars were attacked but on the third attack they sent up a yellow smoke signal which indicated they were friendly. On the 25th there was a casualty, Lieut G McFie

[1] Fuller, *op cit*

(FB323 'E') was seen to be missing after an attack on some field guns. A search of the area failed to disclose any sign of a crashed aircraft. The second mission, also a Cab Rank, attacked some mortars located between two houses. This mission was uneventful until the aircraft returned to Iesi. Here one of the NCO pilots, flying FB304 'J', who had just completed his landing run, did not continue to the end of the psp strip, but turned his aircraft round and taxied back the other way. Another aircraft, HB925 'R', which had just landed swerved towards the edge of the runway and both collided and were destroyed, the pilots were unharmed.

Graham McFie was later reported killed, but, had he lived, he was due to face a court martial because of the over-informative letters he had sent to his mother from which great chunks had had to be cut by the censors. Generally speaking private letters from the airmen and NCOs were censored by the squadron officers, but officers' were supposed to know what should or should not be included in their own letters home.

There were close support missions all day on the 26 September and an attack on the marshalling yards at Suzara resulted in a direct hit on the engine sheds which caused a large explosion and the collapse of the centre of the building, with much steam and smoke. On 27th Sqn Ldr Bluett again led a long range recce of ten aircraft. Red Section started by attacking shipping in Parenzo harbour, though without much success as the bombs fell on land amongst the houses. Blue Section had more luck with a direct hit on a 2500-ton vessel which erupted in clouds of steam as the boilers exploded. Rolling stock was then attacked in the Portogruaro and Treviso areas and 11 locomotives were destroyed. Red Section, in the meantime, had also gone loco-busting in the Gorizia – Pordenone – Sacile areas and returned with claims for eight locomotives destroyed and two trucks. Raids led by the CO were somewhat unpopular with the pilots as he tended to lead them, unnecessarily it was thought, into too much danger.

Rain not only closed the airstrip the next day but began to bog down the advance on the ground. The Americans were within sight of Bologna, looking down into the valley of the river Po, and at the beginning of October General Mark Clark committed his reserves in a desperate attempt to take the city. The Germans stood firm and this attack was destined to peter out.

Reg Wild led a long range armed recce over northern Italy on the last day of September and again attacks were concentrated on shipping and rolling stock in the Treviso area. The second operation, flown only by Gp Capt Eaton and Flt Lt Hearn, disappeared for two and a half hours on what was described in the diary as a 'Secret Mission', but no further details were forthcoming.

The end of month summary by the squadron commander pointed out that September 1944 had been one of the most successful in the squadron's history. It was certainly one of the busiest: 712 sorties flown, making 1040 operational flying hours, 363 tons of bombs dropped and 179,540 rounds of .5" ammunition fired. Comparing 112's activities in another busy month, February, 1943, prior to the battle of Mareth when a mere 17,400 rounds of ammunition were fired and 16 tons of bombs dropped, Sqn Ldr Bluett's figures amply demonstrate the squadron's vastly increased capabilities.

Support for the army continued as October began with attacks north of Florence on suspected bivouac areas, but with autumn setting in and torrential rain, the rate of flying began to slow down. A conference was held at Wing HQ to determine the possibility of housing the personnel in billets rather than continuing under canvas. On the 4th Lieut C J Liebenberg had a narrow escape when a bomb dropped of his aircraft (HB917 'N') just as he was getting airborne. It presumably did not explode as the only damage was to his wing flaps, so he jettisoned the remainder of his bomb load over the sea but making a flapless landing he overshot the runway onto the soft earth and the aircraft turned onto its back. Chris Liebenberg was unhurt.

Flying days seemed to alternate with days when the weather kept aircraft on the ground, but when they did get airborne the targets continued to be listed as enemy ground positions, machine gun positions, guns and road bridges. On the 11th Flt Lt Wild led an eleven aircraft mission on a long range recce. They flew first to Parenzo harbour where Red Section bombed a 3000-ton ship. Then Red Section flew north where it straffed rolling stock between Basiliano and Treviso, claiming seven locomotives destroyed, and one more on the way back. Blue Section, under Fg Off Newton, had flown to Cervignano and started on another stretch of line. From there they flew to Palazzolo, Latisana and Portogruaro straffing everything that moved and returned claiming seven locomotives and one vehicle destroyed.

Lieut Chris Liebenberg was reported missing on the 12 October. He was the last one to attack a railway bridge which was defended by flak positioned in San Felice. He called up to say that his aircraft (FB263 'M') was on fire and that he was baling out, but nothing more was heard or seen of him. In fact he was taken prisoner and later escaped. Also that day Sqn Ldr Bluett led another successful long range recce. Taking off at 14.30 hrs they flew back to Parenzo harbour, where they again attacked shipping. Then, as before, the formation split into its two sections, Red and Blue, and went their different ways. Red Section flew to Gorizia and straffed a train so that the engine exploded in a satisfactory cloud of smoke and steam. They then made their way to Udine where they saw some aircraft which were judged to be dummies. From there they flew to Codroipo, Pordenone and Padua, shooting at rolling stock all the way. Blue Section flew along the railway line to Treviso and Castelfranco and Vicenza. Here they had a look at the airfield, then to Padua where they rejoined Red Section and returned to base, score: fifteen locomotives destroyed and one damaged.

Italian locomotive drivers, people who must have once considered themselves in a relatively safe occupation, found themselves in the front line again on Friday 13 October. The CO led five machines on another loco-busting mission to the Chioggia – Treviso – Sandona – Venice and Padua areas, but found nothing but low cloud and mist. However at Carsarsa marshalling yards it was clear enough for them to attack 30-plus trucks. Now they could fly below cloud to Villorra, Conelgliano and back home. Blue Section, which took off independently of Red, flew to Codroipo by way of Parenzo and Grado and there found 50 trucks and some locomotives with steam up. This collection was bombed and then straffed. The claims for that day were three engines destroyed and two damaged. The third mission attempted to bomb a Bailey-type bridge near Cesena, which was not damaged in the attack. There was heavy flak there which seemed to indicate the Germans were determined to defend their lines of communication and were, by now, well aware of what the Mustangs would be targetting.

The 14 October was another busy day, but the first two operations were cancelled due to poor weather. The third mission was under Cab Rank control and the aircraft were vectored on to a house that was reported to be a strong point and one direct hit was recorded. Mortars and some troops were attacked by the next Cab Rank mission. Flt Lt Reg Wild, flying GA-?, led his last operational sortie on 112 in the afternoon, a rhubarb, which accounted for one small vehicle that exploded.

On the 16th aircraft attacked what was supposed to be a German battalion headquarters and they succeeded in silencing a nearby 20mm gun. At Accuarola the squadron was specifically requested not to undershoot the target as our own troops were in the area – an indication of how close 'close support' could be on occasions. Ray Hearn received a bar to his DFC.

Thirty-six sorties were flown on the 20 October, the busiest day of the month. This was also the day that General Mark Clark reluctantly abandoned his efforts to force through the German defences to Bologna. Nevertheless Kesselring's shortage of troops had obliged him to bolster his line opposite Keyes' II Corps and this allowed the 8th Army to push forward, but 'both (Allied) armies were now exhausted. Casualties had been heavy and replacements few. Ammunition stocks were dangerously low; the weather worsened steadily.'[1]

112 Sqn continued relentlessly in its efforts to cut lines of communication and that day they had the pleasure of seeing the centre span of one bridge they bombed collapsing into the river beneath. Other bridges were also attacked that day with varying success. Red Section, having had some near misses on one bridge, saw people coming out to inspect the damage even before they had left the target area. They reported that although the northern span appeared to be missing it seemed possible that it had been lowered out of sight into the water on cables, ready to be hauled back into position when required.

Twenty-eight locomotives were 'clobbered' before breakfast on 21 October by Red and Blue Sections who had taken off at 06.30 hrs. Their bombs had been used up on 20 barges on the Adige river, destroying two and badly damaging two more. Red Section claimed 11 locomotives in the Padua – Vicenza and Istrana – Treviso areas. Flt Lt Hearn leading Blue Section went to Udine and they returned with claims of 17 locomotives destroyed. Sgt O G Jones, who had joined the squadron on the 19th of the month, was hit by flak in HB925 GA-Z, and called that he was baling out. His parachute was seen to open and he descended into the sea and was last seen swimming for the shore with his Mae West inflated. The aircraft stayed with him as long as they could. Later Sgt Daniell and Lieut J R Lund returned to cover Jones's rescue and at 10.25 they saw a Walrus touch down and fish him out of the water. The Walrus now came under shell fire and was unable to take off again so a Catalina was called up. The Walrus, in the meanwhile, was taxying around on the sea but apparently couldn't get airborne and the Catalina, which was behind it, couldn't get it to stop. A Vickers Warwick, a Wellington derivative used for air-sea rescue work, was also in the area and so the Warwick pilot asked Daniell and Lund to do a beat up of the Walrus to get it to stop. This was successful and the Walrus hove-to and eventually Jones was transferred to the Catalina. Lund and Daniell were relieved by two other squadron aircraft at which point a Spitfire pilot radioed that he was in difficulties and was baling out. The

---

[1] Esposito, *op cit*

Warwick dropped a dinghy and the Catalina picked him up also and then took off. The Walrus was last seen setting a course of 180°, taxying off homewards across the water. Lund was a casualty on the 22nd, which was a day of rhubarbs. Bad weather hampered operations and there were only 12 sorties, all in pairs. Lieut Lund, who was No 2 to Fg Off J J Roney, flying HB893 'K', failed to return. Roney didn't see what happened to him but he was probably shot down when they were straffing two tanks through intense 20mm flak. Later it was learned that he had been killed. Thus, as in all good theatre, comedy and tragedy take the stage alternately.

There were continuing close-support operations the next day and enemy troops and some houses were all attacked. A monastery was bombed on the third mission, the building supposedly being full of soldiers, and there was one direct hit in the courtyard. That day the elementary school in Iesi was commandeered for the airmen and adjacent flats were allocated to the NCOs. The drawback was that they all had to go back to the LG for their food.

The weather cleared on the 25th and the squadron was allowed off on one of its most popular entertainments, long-range recces of northern Italy. The CO, as always, led the first operation, which started off with a railway bridge as its primary target. Red and Blue Sections both bombed and then split up with Red going to Vicenza railway station. Here they were disappointed as some other aircraft had been there before them and the only two locomotives had already been dealt with. They found two engines at Castelfranco and one was destroyed and the other described as being a 'dribbler'. After flying to Sacile they returned with claims of five locos destroyed and one damaged. Blue Section under Ray Hearn straffed rolling stock in that happy hunting ground which was Treviso marshalling yards. Their score was six engines destroyed and some barges damaged near Muzzana.

Weather intervened over the next couple of days and no significant operations were flown until the 29 October when two operations were mounted at midday and 13.30 hrs. Both attacks were on an SS Headquarters in a town near Lake Commacchio. The second attacks seems to have been more successful and all the bombs fell in a close group.

On the 30th there was only one operation, a 12 aircraft formation led by Peter Bluett which took off at 11.15 and returned at 13.35 hrs. Crossing the coast at Fano the aircraft flew north at 8000' making landfall again and reducing height to 6000' below 10/10ths cloud cover. A storage dump, two large camouflaged sheds, were seen and both sections attacked with bombs. There were two large explosions and a lot of black and yellow smoke and a 'general pyrotechnic display'. The sections then went their different ways with Red going towards Padua and Treviso where five locomotives were claimed, plus one dribbler. Blue Section flew north to Vicenza, Treviso and Sacile and then to San Vito. It was here that Lieut D F Prentice, who was flying No 6, 'Tail end Charlie', was hit and glycol started streaming from his engine. Don Prentice set course for the coast and when he was over the sea he baled out. He was seen to alight safely in the water and then get into his dinghy, about 300 yards from the shore. People started to gather on the beach, which was in hostile territory, so it was supposed that he was made a PoW. The score that day was eight locomotives destroyed.

The final operation that month was an attack on a road bridge. A railway bridge had been their assigned target but it was found to have been destroyed already so the

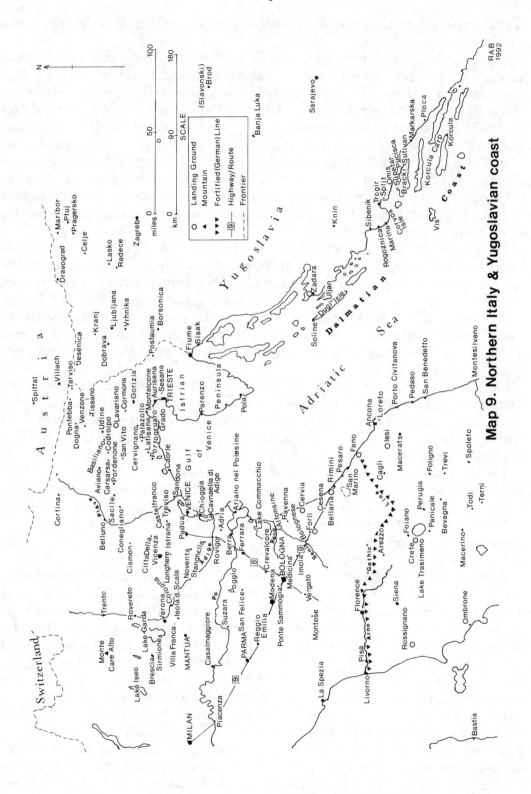

Map 9. Northern Italy & Yugoslavian coast

SCALE

Landing Ground
Mountain
Fortified (German) Line
Highway/Route
Frontier

aircraft turned their attention to the first undamaged bridge they could find and blew a hole in it.

November began with poor weather and there was no flying until midday when aircraft departed on an armed recce to Yugoslavia, the first time they had been there since April. Six locomotives were destroyed and one damaged in the Sarajevo – Slavonski Brod area. The second mission flew to Maribor and Zagreb and brought the total to 13 railway engines destroyed in one day. Rain prevented any flying on the 2nd and the Pilots' Mess was marooned when a Bailey bridge over the river was washed away during the night making it difficult to reach the landing ground, some 4½ miles distant. It was decided that the Mess would have to be moved into Iesi.

Flying was resumed on the 3 November on a limited scale and the CO went looking for some billets for the pilots. Eventually one was obtained in the main street, near the mayor's office.

There were two long distance recces on the 4th, the first, led by the CO, flew to Fiume harbour where they attacked installations by bombing and straffing. They then roamed around looking for MT and shipping. They spotted a destroyer which took evasive action when it saw them and a motor vessel going in the direction of Trieste. Laurie Usher led the second operation which was also briefed to go to Yugoslavia but about halfway the plan was changed due to the long-range fuel tanks not feeding and, on the advice of 'Commander' they returned to bomb bridges over the Reno river south of Lake Commacchio.

Lieut D W Featherstone had arrived on the squadron on the 2nd and, as his own letter recounts, he was almost immediately 'on the carpet' before Gp Capt Brian Eaton 'for beating hell out of Iesi LG. He accepted my "excuse" that it was through sheer jubilation at being at long last "operational" that I had acted so recklessly, and with a twinkle in his eyes, he awarded me a week's Orderly Officer duties!'

The shortening days now meant that fewer operations could be mounted in daylight and long range missions had to get airborne before 13.30 hrs if they were to return before dark. Rolling stock between Slavonski Brod (usually just referred to as Brod) and Sarajevo were the first target on the 5th and four locomotives were destroyed. Seven more were taken out by the second operation which took off at 13.35 and landed at 17.05 hrs–3½ hours airborne.

Plt Off R J Deeble (FB320 'N') was missing after the first operation on the following day, it being only his second operational trip on the squadron. The aircraft were engaged in an armed recce between Zagreb and Maribor. It was unfortunate that one of the aircraft was having R/T trouble which cut out all the other aircrafts' transmissions, so it was not known if he had made a distress call. It later transpired that he had been killed. Six railway engines were destroyed and one more in the afternoon mission. On these trips the Mustangs jettisoned their long-range tanks once they were empty and these allowed for the 3-hour flights which they were now undertaking.

Total cloud cover over Yugoslavia on the 8th made the leader decide to go back so the formation jettisoned their long-range tanks over the Adriatic and 'Commander' gave them an alternative target. Plt Off Clark took over the lead as he happened to be carrying maps of northern Italy. They were instructed to bomb the sluice gates at Cavnaella di Adige. This was successful but shortly afterwards Paul Forster, the original leader, saw a mushroom of white smoke rising from a flooded area near the target. He called Plt Off Clark but nothing more was seen or heard of him and later it was confirmed that he had been killed.

The squadron had a new adjutant posted in that day, a Flt Lt W H E Marriott, to replace the long-suffering 'Taffy' Evans, now promoted to Sqn Ldr. 'Taffy' (or 'Yanto') Evans was the longest serving officer in the squadron, having joined in June 1942. There was a party on the following night to see him safely on his way. The SIB[1] were called in to investigate the death of LAC Wadsworth who had been found at the foot of the billet stairs that morning. It was presumed that he had accidentally fallen over the bannisters.

Despite very bad weather operations were resumed on the 10 November when the CO led a formation to bomb a railway line between Celje and Maribor. One near miss covered the track with debris but that was all. The aircraft were obliged to fly round a very heavy snowstorm. Wintry conditions then descended on the whole area.

The following day the squadron flew into Austria for the first time. The aircraft left at 10.10 hrs and flew by way of Venice and Villach where a railway bridge was bombed, scoring one direct hit. Locomotives were then attacked and on Ljubljana airfield a Heinkel 111 and a small biplane were attacked. The score that trip was nine railway engined destroyed, one truck left smoking, one bridge and two aircraft damaged. The pilots remarked on how beautiful the scenery was in the brilliant sunshine. That evening the pilots attended the opening of the new Officers' Club in Iesi but they complained that five girls were not enough for the hundred officers of the Wing!

On the 12th there was supposed to be an escort for Halifax bombers but they didn't make the rendez-vous and 'Commander' instructed them to do a railway recce in the Udine – Treviso area. This was done and four locomotives were destroyed and a dribbler. It was back to close support of the army the next day and nine aircraft attacked a road bridge and scored one direct hit on the eastern approaches and some near misses. Bad weather stopped flying then for a couple of days and there was a rumour that the Wing was about to go forward again, this time to Fano about 20 miles further up the coast, a story that was confirmed on the 15th but the move was postponed due to a shortage of accommodation and the fact that civilians would have to be moved out.

Yugoslav rolling stock was the target on the next fine day, the 16th, when 12 aircraft attacked the Ljubljana – Celje railway line, destroying two locomotives. Fg Off Roney crashed after take off. A nut left in the feed pipe to the carburettor choked the flow of fuel. From 350' he tried to regain the runway but his engine cut and his aircraft collided with two Marauders and a petrol bowser, all of which caught fire. He was extricated from the wreckage but died a few hours later in No 1 Canadian General Hospital.

Flt Lt Hearn and Flt Lt Forster went on an air-sea rescue search for a Catalina which was found six miles off shore with a dinghy afloat alongside. The aircraft was seen to be smoking and then ammunition started exploding and it began to go down by the bows. They left it at 16.35 hrs when another aircraft took over from them. The next day the adjutant went to Fano to organise the billets and 'A' Party was briefed to be ready to move on the 18th.

The squadron again took over the task of giving top-cover to the Catalina. Another

---

[1] The RAF Police's Special Investigation Branch.

had touched down nearby and two dinghies were being taken on board. At that moment the Mustangs saw two aircraft, believed to be Re2001s, approaching from the north and they were chased away. When the Catalina's survivors had been safely rescued the Mustangs sank the dinghies with machine gun fire. This precaution was necessary to avoid the empty drifting dinghies causing another search and rescue alarm.

With 'A' Party travelling north a formation of 11 aircraft went to the Zagreb area and attacked a railway bridge at Sisak. One bomb appeared to fall right through the bridge's girders without touching them, to explode below. No apparent damage was done but four locomotives were disabled in the subsequent beat-up. Lieut J H Weeber (KH627 'B') failed to return and was later reported killed. There was a similar operation in the same area that afternoon and three more locomotives were claimed. The aircraft returned to the new landing ground at Fano. Sgt B T Routledge, in KH531 'E', had unserviceable brakes and the aircraft went off the end of the runway and ended up on its nose; he was unhurt. There was little flying the next day and the only mission was escorting a Westland Lysander 'on special duty', which was apparently abortive due to lack of ground co-operation. The airmen spent the day settling into their new homes.

On the 21 November there was an operation carrying what was called 'fire bombs'. In fact these were long range drop tanks filled with napalm which were dropped in a dive at about 150′–100′ above ground level and 300 knots. Nine aircraft flew to Yugoslavia on the 22nd to attack railway rolling stock. Four railway engines were destroyed and one probably damaged. The CO's aircraft developed engine trouble on the second mission, an attack on some German mortars, and he landed at Bellaria LG.

Denis Featherstone, whose week's Orderly Officer duties were completed, remembers his first operational sortie. At that stage, although 112 was his first squadron, he had already logged no fewer than 1570 flying hours on fifteen different aircraft types, which was about a thousand more hours than most of the seasoned fliers on the squadron. He decided to keep quiet about this fact and 'thought that I'd just quietly show these bods what an "ace" I was! Flying No 2 to Bluett I followed him down to bomb a road bridge at San Pancrazio, saw a lot of puffs around which I knew must be flak, trembled so violently that my Mustang must have seemed as though it was suffering from St Vitus's Dance, pressed the bomb release button, closed my eyes, pulled up so violently from the dive, blacked out, promptly lost myself. After blatantly breaking R/T silence for 10 minutes I was found by my leader and was led back to base where I was considerately treated at de-briefing and was called nothing worse than a stupid bloody sprog!' The story doesn't end there though as later Bluett was contacted by Wing HQ and congratulated by the Commander of the Indian Division. Apparently a German headquarters building, half a mile from the target bridge, had been demolished by Denis Featherstone's wayward bomb and all inside killed.

Featherstone's flying experience stood him in good stead on the 23rd when he had engine trouble on take off. He had sufficient speed to gain some height, retract the undercarriage and belly-land unharmed in the grass overshoot. Luckily this was an acceptance check and he was not carrying bombs. The trouble was traced to water in the carburettor. The next few days were too bad for any flying and the pilots amused themselves at 'The Desert Air Force Cinema' in Ancona, and by collecting firewood for the Mess fire.

Operations continued on the 26 November when Ray ('Steely Grey') Hearn led an attack on Pola harbour. The target was seen through a gap in the clouds and attacked. Despite the heavy flak the bombs were dropped well and Denis Featherstone was able to position his 1000-lb bomb near the target this time. There was no flying the next day but in the evening there was a dance in the Pilots' Mess and nurses were roped in from five different military hospitals and everyone had a good time. The music was provided by No 18 Sqn's dance band, so it would seem plain that conditions had altered out of all recognition from the dusty days in the western desert. Venereal disease, so long a subject that was totally taboo, had increased dramatically during the war years and it was not until the autumn of 1942 that the Ministry of Health had launched a campaign to make the facts about syphilis and gonorrhea more widely known. From then on there was intensive advertising on all military camps to alert personnel to the dangers, the institution of FFI[1] parades and the provision of ET or early treatment rooms so that men could take some emergency precautions themselves after sexual intercourse.

There was a first-light mission the following day by Flt Lt Forster and Lieut 'Feathers' Featherstone, coming straight from the party, took off on a weather recce. There was another weather recce a little while later and at 14.35 hrs, by which time no doubt the remainder of the pilots had sobered up, there was an attack on the railway line between Carsarsa and Merserva but the line was shielded by embankments and this prevented any damage being done. The last day of the month was unfit for flying and the pilots went to inspect the new Officers' Club in Fano but they decided it was more like a railway waiting room than a club.

Denis Featherstone tells of a 56-hour drinking session around this time that he had with Peter Crews and Laurie Usher 'we drank, smoked, ate a bit, talked, sang, and didn't sleep and at the end of it all Doc Crews did about 30 innoculations and had his patients petrified, but they felt no physical pain – he was terrific!'

Peter Bluett's end of the month summary set out the balance sheet with 66 locomotives disabled, one probable and five damaged, nine trucks destroyed and two damaged, two barges destroyed and two damaged on the credit side against three pilots missing and one killed.

December 1944 began with 11 aircraft attacking a railway bridge north-east of Treviso. Once again no direct hits were claimed but the line was hit south of the bridge and since the bridge was only about 20' long it was considered that a direct hit would have been extremely lucky.

The airmen now had a place for themselves in Fano, 'The Shark Club'. It consisted of three rooms, one for reading and writing, one a games room and the third a bar. The airmen, by virtue of their lowly unexciting tasks, get less than due mention in any war story. One of their many mournful dirges ran —

> 'It's the rich wot gets the pleasure,
> It's the poor wot gets the blame,
> It's the same the whole world over,
> *cres* Isn't it a f****** shame!'

Featherstone remembers his fitter, AC 'Benny' de Hond. 'Born within the sound of

---

[1] FFI – Free From Infection, also known as a 'short arm inspection'

Bow Bells, Benny was the life and soul of the ground staff, chief organiser, chief scrounger, and always with a smile. It was my good fortune to have him and "Yippie" as my erks right through my tour, and I will never forget the time I returned from a nocturnal session at a neighbouring squadron's pub at midnight to find these two wonderful fellows *polishing* my aircraft with wax to make it the fastest kite on the Wing!' Benny was knifed to death after the war when he was working as a bouncer in a London night club.

On 2nd the squadron held its first ever dance. An Italian seven-piece band was obtained after a lot of bickering with AMGOT[1] to obtain the necessary late passes which permitted some 75 Italian girls to be out after curfew. On the 3rd, following an unsuccessful attack due to bad weather, Ray Hearn crash-landed his aircraft (KH701 'Q') and although it was completely written off Ray emerged without any injury.

The 4 December was a slightly better day but even then there were only two missions, one of five aircraft and one of four. The first was an abortive escort to a Westland Lysander which was trying to get into Yugoslavia but cloud cover prevented it landing. The second operation carried napalm drop tanks and flew, with USAAF Thunderbolts of the 79th Fighter Group, to attack defended houses and a HQ. Flt Lt Paul Forster got a direct hit but the two napalm bombs failed to explode and the rest of the formation only claimed near misses. That evening the CO opened a squadron discussion group which, it was hoped, would have meetings once a week. It is possible that this innovation was related to the ABCA[2] scheme which was designed to provide compulsory adult education for the troops, and eventually was extended to all theatres of the war and provided newspapers, educational films, information rooms and reference libraries. After the 1945 general election the defeated Conservatives concluded that ABCA had been a 'monstrous left wing plot'[3] on the basis that it permitted the troops to discuss social and political issues that would require attention after the war of which they would otherwise have remained in ignorance.

Nine aircraft were just taxying out for an operation over Yugoslavia on the 5th when they were recalled due to a bad forecast over the area. No 5SAAF Sqn had unfortunately already gone and they ran into dreadful weather and out of ten aircraft that took off only four returned. There was a hurried conference with the CO of 5SAAF Sqn and it was decided that the next day aircraft would fly to Vis and see if any of the lost machines had landed there while Flt Lt Hearn would lead a sea search. However the bad weather continued until the 9th and nothing more could be done.

On that day two aircraft did a weather recce over Yugoslavia, which was still cloud covered, so the squadron bombed the village of Traversara near the front line instead. Napalm bombs were used and various houses were left smoking. It was said that the napalm blazed for about 30–60 seconds.

There was an armed recce of the Udine area on the 10th by aircraft carrying 500-lb bombs. The target was about ³/₄-mile of railway track just north of a tunnel and they were successful and cut the line in five places. The squadron returned to Yugoslavia

---

[1] AMGOT – Allied Military Government of Occupied Territories, an acronym that unfortunately meant something rather indecent to our Turkish allies.

[2] ABCA – Army Bureau of Current Affairs

[3] '*The People's War*' by Angus Calder

the next day also for an armed recce in the Zagreb area. They bombed a railway bridge but failed to hit it and afterwards they went train hunting at which they had more luck. The claims by both sections on their return amounted to 13 locomotives destroyed, one truck which exploded, one set alight, one truck and one vehicle left smoking.

Nothing much happened except weather recces and training flying for new pilots until the 15th when Rover Paddy kept them loitering for an hour before they were allowed to go to their secondary target, some supposed gun pits. No pits were seen but the bombs were dropped anyway. The second mission had more luck with Rover Paddy who directed them to attack some farm buildings and here there was a big explosion and dense black smoke. On the subsequent recce the farmyard was seen to have vanished into a dark smoking crater.

Six Mustangs were detailed to RV with a Catalina over Rimini for an air-sea rescue mission. The dinghy was seen and the Catalina alighted and rescued the pilot so promptly that 'Commander' sent a message to the squadron saying that it was the most perfect ASR mission he had ever handled. 10/10ths cloud at 800′ the next day and the 19th made flying impossible and the pilots were sent off to gather logs for the Mess fire and holly for the Christmas decorations. Conversation naturally tended to veer towards the possibility that the bad weather might last over the Christmas period.

However the skies cleared the next day, 20 December, and four Mustangs escorted some B-26 Marauders to Treviso marshalling yards. Their bombs overshot. One Marauder, with its engines smoking, was escorted back by two Mustangs until they lost it in cloud. The operation was repeated the next day with two B-26 formations, ten minutes apart, and this time the squadron reported that they had seen excellent bombing.

The 20 December was also the day that Sgt Arthur Banks died at the hands of the Fascists in prison 100 miles further north, at Ariano nel Polesine. He died in ignorance that his captors would be suitably punished and that his unflinching heroism would not only be acknowledged by HM The King but also remembered long after his death.

Two bad days followed with no operational flying and it seemed to the squadron that it was time to settle down for a good Christmas. On the 23rd the pilots were taken to see their MORU to talk to their controllers and here they were given such a very good welcome that most of them were asleep on the return journey. On Christmas Eve night there was a squadron concert, 'The Sharks Christmas Cocktail' subtitled 'A ridiculous revue'. The proceeds of the sale of programmes were sent to the mother of the late LAC Bill Wadsworth.

However Christmas Day was fit for flying and this being war, the squadron flew. There was an early morning recce of the Yugoslavian coast but their report was not favourable so instead the Mustangs again escorted Marauders to Treviso marshalling yards and found the flak gunners off duty. A large fire was seen in Rovigo with smoke rising to 10,000′. The leader of the bombers exchanged Christmas greetings with 112 as they returned from the target. As a result the airmen's Christmas dinner was not held until 17.00 hrs and the diarist concluded with a tribute to the cooks for their excellent meal.

There was another escort mission on Boxing Day, uneventful as far as the Mustangs were concerned. That night the pilots had their Christmas dinner. On the 27th Treviso marshalling yards were again hammered and again there was no opposition. Some of the bombers got separated which necessitated the escort splitting up to shepherd them home and all aircraft were back on the ground by 14.10 hrs. That evening 112 Pilots' Mess was 'Open House' to the pilots of the other squadrons on the Wing.

On 28 December the target for the Marauders was Celje in Yugoslavia. The bombers were flying in boxes of six but 10/10ths cloud cover over the target decided the leader to alter course for Udine instead and the marshalling yards there were bombed again. Intense and accurate flak was thrown at them and two B-26s were hit.

Eleven aircraft were dispatched on the 29th to attack a railway bridge near Cismon. They found the northernmost span already lying on its side, a mess of tangled wreckage and, after 112's attack, the embankment seemed to be undermined also. Railway lines west of Rovigo and Noventa were attacked by the other two missions. After a day without any flying the year ended with an attack on a railway bridge on a diversion line west of Citta Della, again only near misses could be claimed.

It seems probable that everyone must have known on New Year's Day 1945 that this would really be the last year of the war. In Italy the Germans had been pushed back so that the front line lay just south of Imola and Veragato. Here it was to stay until the start of Alexander's spring offensive, but in the west the final German thrust in the Ardennes was being held and by the 16 January Montgomery and Eisenhower would have their troops facing the old Siegfried Line. In the Ardennes offensive the Germans had squandered the bulk of their mobile reserves which otherwise might have stood up to the Russian spring campaign. The *Luftwaffe*, too, had its final fling on New Year's Day with a *blitz* of airfields – in which 156 Allied aircraft were destroyed – but in doing so lost many of its own best men and aircraft.

On the Italian front, stalemate. This lasted from January to April, the longest period of inaction on the ground since the invasion of Italy. Vietinghoff, now in command of Army Group Southwest, had under him two armies, the 14th (Lemelsen) and 10th (Herr). Facing him were Truscott with the American 5th Army and McCreery with the British 8th Army. The Germans had spent the intervening time methodically strengthening their defences but the Allied air forces' constant attacks on their lines of communication had resulted in slowly dwindling stocks of motor fuel and ammunition so that even oxen had to be pressed into service. Vietinghoff, realising it was only a matter of time before Alexander and Clark would be ready to strike, requested permission to be allowed to withdraw behind the river Po as he would no longer have the mobility to disengage once the Allied offensive began but, predictably, Hitler refused.

On 1 January the squadron flew again to the bridge on the loop line near Citta Della but again they were unable to make a direct hit. The next day the Borsonica viaduct was bombed, again without any result although the squadrons that bombed later claimed that the western span had been dislodged. The 3rd again saw attacks on the Yugoslavian railway network, this time near Vrhnika. This was more successful and two direct hits were claimed and the bridge was left hanging in the water. This was followed by an armed recce which accounted for seven railway locomotives destroyed. On the next day a railway bridge at Ptuj was attacked, but without result, but five more engines were destroyed with others damaged and trucks destroyed.

The Yugoslavian partisans under Tito were becoming somewhat less co-operative now that the defeat of the Germans was getting nearer, and were becoming more

Sharksteeth! *Matt Matthias*

No 260 and 112 Squadrons lined up on Pachino LG in Sicily. In the background two machines are about to take off. *Matt Matthias*

The interior of the Pilots' Mess at Pachino LG. The Adjutant, 'Taffy' Evans is seated at the end of the nearest table, with 'Doc' MacKenzie to the left. Behind the camera, on the right, is another photographer, possibly Matt Matthias. *James Longmore*

Fg Off Ray 'Goose' Guess strapping in to his machine. With two enemy aircraft to his credit, Guess went missing on 4th August near Randazzo but survived as a prisoner of war. *Matt Matthias*

Kittyhawk MkIII, GA-R, FR509, bombed up and ready for take off at Pachino LG. This machine was on 112 Squadron from April to July 1943. *Matt Matthias*

A comparison. A complete fin and rudder unit of a Kittyhawk, held by AC 'Slim' Potter, compared with all that remained of Flt Lt Bluett's rudder, held by Sgt Lillyman. 5th August, 1943. *Matt Matthias*

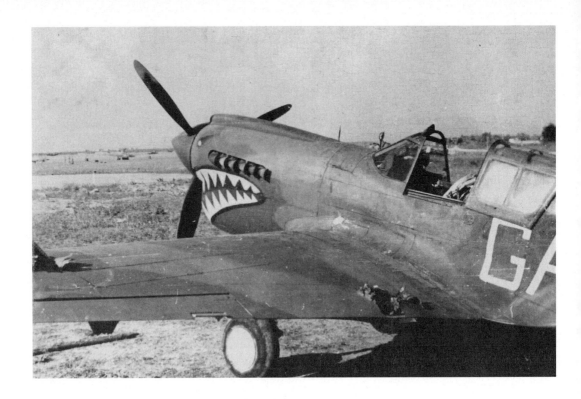

Flak effect. Reg Drown in GA-F must have been pleased to get back to base. *Matt Matthias*

An underside view of the damage to Reg Drown's wing, showing daylight all the way through.
Bert Horden

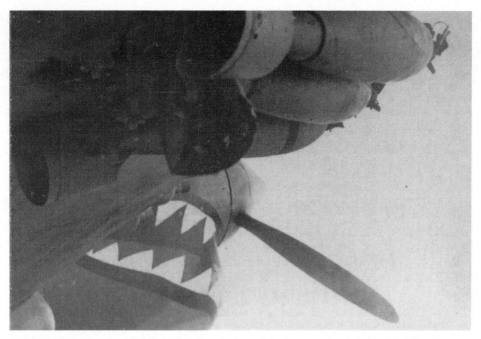

Another view showing the underside of the starboard wing and the damage to the stick of 40 lb bombs.
Bert Horden

One of the American 9th Air Force B-24D Liberators that had to land on the airstrip at Pachino on 1st August 1943 after raiding the oil refineries at Ploesti. The crew of the "Dogpatch Raiders" pose after their hazardous operation and equally hazardous landing. Wally Rutherford grins from the cockpit.   *Bert Horden*

Sgt Nordstrand's bivvy at Pachino. These small tents might be shared by two pilots, using a dugout covered by a tarpaulin tent. *Matt Matthias*

The Pilots' Mess tent, once the denizens had departed. An example of Matt Matthias's determination to record all aspects of squadron life, even down to the jar of pickles and the notice board where the "Dear John" letters were pinned up. *Matt Matthias*

On Catania airfield Matt Matthias discovered a wrecked Re2001, MC202 and a Fieseler *Storch*. *Matt Matthias*

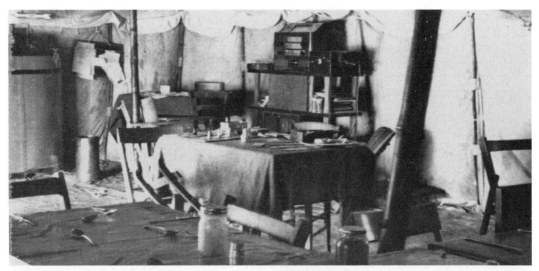

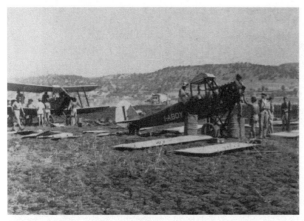

Assembling the three Caproni Ca100s found on Catania airfield. *James Longmore*

"The Shark Light Aeroplane Club" is airborne. *James Longmore*

A souvenir from Messina. GA-D (FR860) with flak damage to the fin. *Matt Matthias*

Martin Barnes and the 112 Sqn Field Battery, consisting of two 75mm *Cannoni da 75/27 modello 11.*
Bert Horden

The bomb cradle devised by WO Smith to allow the carrying of two American 250 lb bombs. The rotating air driven arming fuses can be clearly seen. The ground clearance was critical on take off, especially on the soft lava soil surface of the Sicilian LGs. *Matt Matthias*

The 112 Shark motif as applied to squadron transport. *Matt Matthias*

A close up of the Kittyhawk's 1,325 h.p. Allison V.1710.73 (F4R) engine. *Matt Matthias*

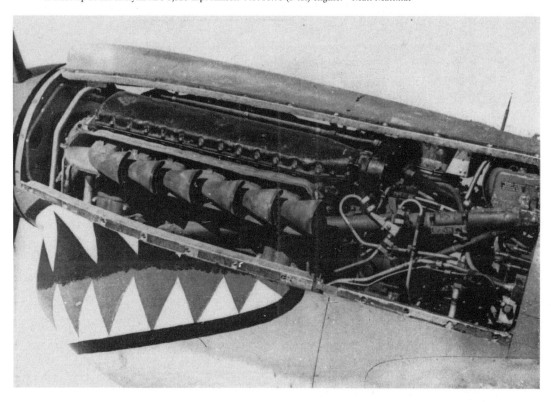

The squadron ops room, fitted out in the rear of a 3-ton truck. The large scale maps pinned to the side of the truck appear to show south-central Italy and the Yugoslavian coast. Bert Horden (left), Ray Hearn (right) and an Australian sergeant in the background. *Bert Horden*

At Agnone, Sicily, about August 1943. Lunch *al fresco* (left to right): Doug Holmes, Reg Wild, Stan Worbey and Nordy Nordstrand. *Matt Matthias*

Flak damage to Kittyhawk GA–B, FR455, September 1943. *Matt Matthias*

Doc MacKenzie and Johnnie Burcham at Grottaglie, September 1943. In the background are the airship sheds that were built by the British between the two World Wars. *Bert Horden*

Friendly Italian "co-belligerents" at Foggia Main Airfield. In the background is Kittyhawk MkIII, GA-K FR439. The turn-over rate of aircraft was lessening by this time and FR439 is recorded as having lasted six months on the squadron. *IWM (CNA1655)*

A Kittyhawk carrying a 60 gallon ventral drop tank. *Bert Horden*

An engine run in progress at Foggia Main. In the distance, to the left of the goalposts GA-N, FR796, is visible, with bombs and tail fins scattered around the middle distance. *IWM (CNA1652)*

Sqn Ldr Pete Illingworth, strapped in to his machine. The airmen with his back to the camera is Tom Walls, ex-Army, now a Fitter IIE. The date for the photograph is given as 19th October, 1943, when the CO led an attack on a railway line north of Termoli - the first rail interdiction operation flown by 112 Sqn. The aircraft is probably GA-M, FR864, shot down 20th December 1943. This occasion is also featured on a news-reel film. *IWM (NA7931)*

A group of pilots at Cutella LG, early 1944, gathered round a collection of 1000 lb bombs. Reg Drown is in the foreground with the cigarette.   *G. Hirons via Chaz Bowyer*

GA-K showing the huge bomb load carried by the Kittyhawk in 1944. One 1000 lb bomb mounted ventrally and two 500 lb bombs under the wings. The pilot is probably Tex Gray and the aircraft possibly FL886 which force-landed on 29th February in the Anzio beachhead.   *G Hirons via Chaz Bowyer*

Above Sqn Ldr Pete Illingworth, CO of 112 from July 1943 to March 1944. *Bert Horden*

Right 'Tex' Gray. *G. Hirons via Chaz Bowyers*

A Warhawk belonging to 3RAAF Sqn damaged by American Thunderbolts at Cutella, April, 1944. *Jack Barber*

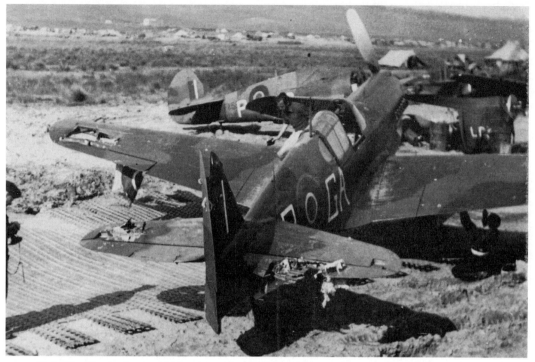

Flt Lt Nev Ahern's aircraft exhibiting signs of damage inflicted by an FW190 during the last aerial combat of the war, 7th April 1944. The aircraft in the background is probably not a 112 Sqn machine. Note psp tracking. *Matt Matthias*

More examples of the effect of an MG151 cannon. A close up of the damage to GA-Jinx, FR474, after the same dog-fight. *Matt Matthias*

112's Kittyhawks at Cutella LG where the squadron remained for nearly four months, their longest stay anywhere during the war. The airstrip was built on the beach, as can be seen by the foreground. The presence of GA-X, a MkIV carrying a rarely used aircraft letter, suggests that this photograph was probably taken in May 1944.
Matt Matthias

Re-arming the Kittyhawk's .5" wing-mounted machine guns, showing the trays that fed the breech mechanism.
Matt Matthias

interested in the setting up of a post-war Communist state under their leader Marshal Tito. Consequently it seemed necessary to issue all 112's pilots with a typed and duplicated identity pass, should they be forced to land or bale out over Yugoslavia.

> Sopstvenik ove isprave............(Pilot's name) vazduhoplovac savezničke avijacije. Molimo sve vlasti narodnooslobodilačke vojske i partizanske odrede Jugoslavije, da mu u slučaju potrebe pruze svu mogucu pomoc i da ga dovedu do više komande.

> Smrt fašizmu — Sloboda narodu.

> Za vojnu Delegaciju NOV kod Saveznička vojske (signature)

An example of a Yugoslavian partisan pass issued to 112 Sqn pilots

Further attacks on bridges followed on the 10th but on 11th there was a particularly busy day. Seven aircraft were targetted on a ship reported south-east of Livorno. The instructions were passed by 'Commander' over the R/T but were misunderstood by the formation leader so instead the aircraft went to attack a rail bridge south-east of Treviso. 'Commander' enquired about the ship so the formation went to have a look but they were unable to find it, although they searched as far as Trieste. The aircraft ended up bombing a railway line which was successfully cut for a distance of about 15 yards. The next operation was in support of the army and consisted of an attack on a rail bridge at Alfonsine. The north-east span was destroyed. WO J S Duncan, who had been on the squadron since September, was hit by flak in the dive, but he managed to get his aircraft (FB255 'M') over our side of the lines before it burst into flames and crashed one mile from Ravenna. Duncan was rescued by an elderly peasant who dragged him from the cockpit and he was rushed to hospital with burns.

Poor weather the next day allowed some pilots to visit WO Duncan in hospital and the following day Fg Off R Page, the squadron Engineering Officer, went to the scene of the crash to discover the name of the Italian who had rescued Duncan. On the 15th there were eighteen sorties and two missions. The first, from 10.45 hrs to 12.55 hrs, was sent to attack the railway station at Gorizia, followed by the standard strafe of rolling stock, barges and roads. The second operation was again near Gorizia, where it was reported that the railway line was apparently completely unserviceable. An airfield near Udine was then straffed by Denis Featherstone and 'Koos' Whelehan, and one twin-engined and five single-engined unidentified aircraft were seen. One was left burning along with a petrol bowser and a 20mm flak gun silenced. There were strikes on seven other aircraft. The apparent inability of the pilots to identify the aircraft they straffed was due to camouflage.

On the 17th the aircraft returned again to northern Italy when eight aircraft swanned off to cut the railway line near Cervignano and Monfalcone.

Capt G W Schwikkard led the only operation on the 18 January which was an armed recce with the rest of the Wing over the Celje – Zagreb area. Fourteen locomotives were put out of commission that day and one flak truck was silenced. Blue Section straffed an airfield and an unidentified aircraft was observed. Denis Featherstone remembers his 'first taste of Trieste' when he was part of a formation of 12 led by Ray Hearn on the 20th. Ten aircraft bombed an E-boat, resulting only in one near miss astern. Understandably the E-boat hurriedly returned to port. Another ship was bombed by the rest of the formation. The formation then flew round the coast to Parenzo where they obliged the sole occupant of a small boat to seek the safety of the water and a tug to take refuge against the boom. Featherstone went on to write 'Ray Hearn's cool, calm and collected leadership on this particular sortie did me a world of good, as I tried from that day to follow his example. I later led dozens of Flight, and a few Squadron sorties, and was always mindful of his wonderful example. I could never hope to pay sufficient tribute to his truly indomitable spirit and fine character.'

On the 21st there was an attack on a railway bridge in northern Italy which was left cut in the centre and on the 23rd, after a day of poor weather, the railway bridge at Ptuj, last attacked on the 4th, was revisited and this time successfully bombed. Seven locomotives were straffed and destroyed and another flak truck silenced. Sgt P L Greaves, who had been on the squadron since the 11 December, was hit by flak when attacking a train. He was seen to bale out and his aircraft (FB280 'X') crashed. The rest of the formation could not hang around to see how he fared as they were getting short of fuel.

Snow fell on the 24th, followed by ice and biting winds. The airfield was snow covered to the depth of 3″ and all the squadron was mobilised to clear the runway and taxy tracks but flying was not resumed until the 30th. The target that day was a railway bridge near Latisana and one span was destroyed. The last day of the month they bombed a bridge over the Piave, but the damage was difficult to assess because of the number of craters in the area. Over the month the squadron had claimed 36 locomotives destroyed – a remarkable comment on the way the armed recces must have been slowly throttling all rail traffic in northern Italy and Yugoslavia.

The squadron had eighteen aircraft that month, two of which appear to have been Mustang Mk IVs (P-51-Ks) with aircraft letters including the now traditional '?' and also Denis Featherstone's 'π', the Greek letter 'pie' which apparently was a tender allusion to his wife's nickname.

February began with several days of bad weather, with low cloud and heavy rain. Featherstone's memories of squadron life would include days like these spent on the ground with the squadron's gramophone playing Bruce Routledge's favourite tune 'Embraceable You', or the squadron's dog, 'Sharky', a cross between a Great Dane and 'something else', the binges, singing the squadron's favourite song 'The Codfish', although as Featherstone explains 'since the words are impossible to publish, I merely mention it in passing . . .' The characters: 'Robbie' Robinson ('who married a really lovely WREN') Fred Brett the Intelligence Officer, and that 'true-life character from Don Iddon's "Two Types" cartoons, Flt Lt Peter Crews, the MO. "China" Gauntlett, that excellent pilot who gave Jerry such a lot to think about[1], and who will forget Bob Strever's miraculous escape from death at Fano when he landed with two 1000-lb bombs which had hung up, and they both exploded as he touched down! And who can

---

[1] Killed circa 1957 flying a Spitfire in Hong Kong

ever forget the clear, encouraging voices of "Commander" and of Rovers "Paddy", "David", "Jack", "Tom", "Timothy" and others who spoke to us over the R/T and guided us so accurately and expertly to our targets and sometimes out of tricky situations?' He concludes with what must be the almost stereotyped remark of a man with so many memories 'I just love reminiscing about the old 112 days . . . and always regard them as some of the happiest days of my life.'

Operations began on the 4th with a weather recce followed by seven aircraft being sent to attack Dobrava marshalling yards. As the weather over the target was bad the alternative, Pontebba, was bombed. Two hundred trucks were seen and all the bombs fell in or around them. One aircraft (possibly KY586 'J') was hit by flak over Lake Commacchio on the return trip and was damaged. The bad weather then clamped down and again there was no flying until the 8th when they went to Dobrava once more. On the way home they watched Gorizia marshalling yards being bombed by Marauders. There then followed eight days without any operations – certainly the longest the squadron had been grounded by weather. The squadron occupied itself with various amusements which included an airmen's dance on the 11 January and some Wing rugger trials which resulted in Ray Hearn, Lieut D G Paul and the adjutant being chosen to play for the DAF team against the 8th Army.

The squadron got airborne again on the 17th to attack a railway diversion at Venzone in Northern Italy, resulting in a couple of near misses. These railway diversions that are mentioned were usually newly built loop lines which by-passed a badly damaged bridge or viaduct by taking a new route.

The DAF lost to the 8th Army by 8 points to 0. In this match Ray Hearn played 'a brilliant game' according to the squadron diarist. The next day he was missing, believed killed when, after leading an attack on the Dogna viaduct he took the formation to strafe Aviano airfield. He was hit by flak and his aircraft (KH820 'Q') was seen to be on fire. He climbed to 2000' by which time the machine was a mass of flame, with pieces dropping off. It then spiralled in and exploded and there had been no sign of a parachute. Hearn had originally joined 112 in May 1943 and had returned for his 3rd tour in July 1944 as 'B' Flt commander and, cruelly, this was the last sortie he was to have flown on ops. He had been due to marry a Canadian nursing sister within a few weeks.

The next day the squadron flew to Yugoslavia and attacked a railway bridge and then went on to look for rolling stock, destroying two locomotives. Northern Italy was all that was clear on the 20th and a railway bridge at Carsarsa was broken. Lieut G A P Reynolds swung on take off and struck a parked Dakota and finished up on top of the ambulance parked outside the watch office. Miraculously neither he nor anyone else was hurt.

Bob Strever's equally miraculous escape from death which Denis Featherstone describes took place on the following day. He had returned early from an operation with engine trouble and had been unable to jettison his two bombs. As he touched down they fell off. His aircraft was destroyed but he survived, although suffering from severe burns. On their way to Yugoslavia on the 22nd the squadron saw what they described as 'gaggles' of Liberators returning. They were unable to land at Fano due to a Lockheed P-38 Lightning having crashed and blocked the runway so they diverted to Bellaria, some 30 miles to the north.

Coming several days after the rumours began, the squadron was told it would be moving on the 25th from Fano to Cervia. In the meantime Plt Off W D Musther led nine aircraft to attack a rail bridge at Rovereto on the 23rd, resulting in one direct hit on the eastern span. In the afternoon another similar operation against the railway bridge at Stanghella. Although bombs fell in the area the bridge was still intact when the formation left. 'A' Party left for Cervia the following morning, about 38 miles as the crow flies but nearer 50 by road. On the 25 February the aircraft attacked a rail bridge at Portis and then, after a road recce when only one staff car was seen, they flew to the new airstrip. The pilots were pleased to find that their billets, which were houses, were better than had been expected with the only complaint that the bar was too small. The airmen, however, were unhappy to find that they were back to living in tents although these, at least, were sheltered by buildings and fir trees. Some pioneers were prevailed upon to put up a couple of Nissen huts, one for the cookhouse and one for the thriving 'Sharks Club'.

The month ended with the Wing leader, Gp Capt Eaton taking a four squadron show, 112, 5SAAF, 250 and 260 Sqns, to attack some sheds containing stores just north of the bomb line. Eleven of 112's aircraft, carrying a total of 18 1000-lb and two 500-lb bombs between them left the sheds burning. 'F/Lt to G/Capt in 18 Months' was the headline in a newspaper cutting that described Brian Eaton's career. Coming from Victoria, Australia, he reached the rank of Gp Capt at the age of 26 after having been CO of one of the RAAF squadrons.

One new arrival on 112 about this time was the ex-squadron member, Flt Lt 'Matt' Matthias who had left in July 1944, in place of Ray Hearn as 'B' Flight Commander. A supernumary member of the squadron was Sqn Ldr J S Hart, a Canadian, who had flown on ops in the Far East and who had 500 operational hours in his log book.

The squadron was now re-equipping with Mustang IVs. The P-51-K, a variant on the P-51-D and without rocket stubs and with a slightly inferior performance. For recognition purposes the main difference between the K and the C was the bubble canopy and the addition of a dorsal fairing leading to the fin, but it also had a useful tail-warning radar, which was probably more use to the Mustangs flying bomber escorts than to 112's machines. Of the twenty aircraft listed in February 1945 six were Mk IVs by the end of the month. Gp Capt Eaton ('BAE') still had a Mk III. The aircraft letter 'Q', which had been Ray Hearn's was not used again until the days of the de Havilland Vampires, by which time his sad fate had been forgotten on the re-formed 112. March began with thick sea fog covering everything at Cervia and there was no flying all day. On the 2nd it cleared enough for two aircraft to be air tested before the fog rolled in again off the Adriatic. On the 3rd the whole Wing got airborne to attack one target, the Carsarsa railway bridge. Sqn Ldr Hart, still supernumary on the squadron, led the first attack, with 112 acting as middle cover. Five aircraft acted in the anti-flak role and they bombed the gun positions while the remainder attacked the bridge. The railway line on the approach was cut and there was a concentration of near misses. The second operation was similar except that this time a direct hit landed plumb centre of the bridge. The significance of the Carsarsa rail bridge was that it carried one of the principal railway lines into Italy from Yugoslavia.

Apparently this last strike was still not good enough as the next day ten of the squadron's aircraft were sent there again, carrying, in all, twelve 1000-lb and eight

500-lb bombs. As before four aircraft concentrated on the gun positions. Again one direct hit was claimed on the bridge and the rest were near misses. The Venzone diversion bridge on the line from southern Austria was the target for the second mission. The aircraft flew near the Carsarsa bridge and reported that it appeared to be buckled and on the way back it was being attacked by Marauders.

Lasko rail bridge in Yugoslavia was the target on the 5th. This was a strongly constructed bridge of steel deck with a seven span masonry support. It lies on the main rail line from Zagreb to Ljubljana and thence to Villach and Salzburg. Capt Schwikkard led the first operation and they managed to buckle one of the spans. Two locos were also attacked. Flt Lt P M Forster, 'A' Flt Commander since the departure of Flt Lt Wild, led another dozen aircraft to Lasko in the afternoon and it was confirmed the damage, without, however, adding to it. One locomotive was left with clouds of steam escaping from the boiler.

The 6 March was a lovely spring day with clear blue skies and brilliant sunshine. The railway bridge at Longhere, on the line between Vicenza and Padua, was the day's target and it was attacked in the morning and afternoon. Bombing accuracy was not too good on the morning's raid, but the second mission had more success and the bridge was left with the second span completely destroyed and the railway line thrown out of alignment.

Another rail bridge, this time south of Gorizia, was the target for 112 and 5SAAF Sqns on the 7 March, and this was led by the Gp Capt. 112 attacked first and they were highly successful and, after 5 Sqn's attack, the bridge was seen to be cratered and the supports damaged. The second operation, which took off at 15.40 hrs, attacked a road bridge in Yugoslavia which was described as consisting of nine spans of strong masonry. There were two direct hits and a couple of near misses but the roadway surface was only cratered. The engine of one of the aircraft cut out in the dive and the pilot had to jettison his bombs along a railway line. There was some slight but accurate flak from the area and one aircraft was damaged near the oil cooler and port petrol tank, but it returned to base safely.

The Lasko rail bridge was again the target on the 8th, but the forecast bad weather was correct and this obliged them to jettison their bombs and return to base. The next day there was an attack on a rail bridge west of Carsarsa and there was one direct hit and the rail line was cut in five places. The target on the 10th was a bridge near Crisolera but the post-strike recce was unable to see the result due to cloud. Laurie Usher led an attack on a petrol dump in the afternoon and this resulted in an explosion and smoke and a fire that was still burning when the aircraft left.

Two operations concentrated on a rail bridge near Padua on the 11 March and by the end of the day it was badly damaged but not severed. Flt Sgt O G Jones, almost tour expired, was shot down in the first attack (KH635 'E'). He was the last in Blue Section to bomb and was seen to go over onto his back streaming glycol. Later the wing of an aircraft was seen by the river bank south of the target.

Two sections of six aircraft took off at 10 minute intervals on the 12th to join with No 3RAAF, 5SAAF and 260 Sqns to bomb a rail diversion. 112 attacked the gun pits while the others bombed and a pilot on 3 Sqn was seen to score a direct hit on the southern bridge. There was no flying the next day due to poor weather. Things improved again on the 14th and three operations were flown. After a weather recce Flt Lt Usher led an attack on a rail bridge at Calceranica, near Vicenza. The bridge was already cratered and the line was not continuous even before the bombing. A rail recce revealed no movement at all between Belluno and Treviso. The next operation split up into Red and Blue Sections and some large yellow boxes on trucks in a marshalling yard attracted the attention of Red Section. When attacked these burnt with a slow burning explosion which resembled cordite on fire. The aircraft then flew north towards Cortina where they saw some trucks carrying the Red Cross. They attacked a small lorry but the driver saw them coming and baled out. The driverless vehicle hit a parapet and came to a halt.

After a day of bad weather Capt Graham Schwikkard led the first operation on the 16 March. This formation was briefed to land at Zadara in Yugoslavia, behind the enemy's lines, to refuel. The target was the railway bridge at Brod but an error in navigation took them along the wrong railway line which they followed to Banja-Luka where they settled for an attack on a road bridge instead. The aircraft landed at Zadara after 2 hours 50 minutes flying. They were on the ground for 1 hour 25 minutes refuelling and then returned to Cervia, landing finally at 18.10 hrs. Flt Lt Matthias had to stay behind though as his aircraft's undercarriage leg was twisted. There was no flying for the next two days except for new pilots. 'Robbie' Robinson ferried an aircraft to Naples where he was able to see his wife, the WREN, who was stationed there.

The new squadron commander, Sqn Ldr Usher, led a formation of 12 aircraft to Yugoslavia again on the 19th and Red Section went to attack the bridge at Brod and managed to make it unserviceable. One bomb was seen to pass right through the platform of the bridge without exploding. Blue Section attacked a road bridge successfully. Two aircraft were obliged to land at Zadara short of fuel but the rest reached Cervia after a flight of 2 hours 45 minutes. The final operation that day had been an armed recce of northern Italy but there was very little movement and few worthwhile targets and the score amounted to only three trucks destroyed and one damaged.

The CO led an attack the next day, 20th, on the Ljubljana marshalling yards. They began by doing a recce of the railway line from Trieste to Ljubljana and when they got to their target they found some activity which they stifled by bombing and straffing it. A fire was started and this was still burning 30 minutes later. Near Kranj they straffed a train and it was here that Laurie Usher's machine (KH793 'L') was seen to be streaming glycol. He pulled away from the formation and baled out and was left hanging in his harness from a tree with locals hurrying towards him, so it was hoped that he might be safe and in the hands of the partisans.

The second operation that day was an armed recce from Cervia to Aurisina, then to Sesana, Postaumia, Ljubljana and Jesenica. The aircraft came upon a train emerging from a tunnel and about to cross a bridge so they bombed and straffed it with the result that the locomotive was destroyed. The recce then continued to Villach and Udine. The third mission, also in the same area, returned with claims for one truck destroyed and three damaged. The fourth operation returned to Yugoslavia, to the Ljubljana – Radece – Dravograd areas. The total number of sorties that day was 24.

The next day, 21 March, the squadron took part in the well-remembered 'Operation Bowler', so called because any failure by the attacking aircraft to drop their bombs with precision would result in the AOC, Air Vice-Marshal Foster, and his staff being given their bowler hats and retired. It had been obvious for some time that the Germans had been using the port of Venice to supply their troops and that shipping and barge traffic was gradually increasing as the rail network was destroyed. In February the notion of attacking the port had been agreed provided that no building of historical or artistic value was hit. War had already done irretrievable harm to Italy's cultural heritage and Venice was a unique monument which, at this late stage in the war, it would have been inexcusable to damage. However, the shipping basin, which would be the target, was only 950 by 650 yards in size.

All the squadrons in the Wing were detailed to take part, as well as other squadrons of American Thunderbolts from the 79th Fighter Group, six squadrons in all. Photo reconnaissance had shown that the *SS Otto Leonhardt* was there, taking on stores and nearby there was a coaster and a number of barges. Poor visibility delayed the attack

Some Daily Mirror *cartoon characters used as mascots*

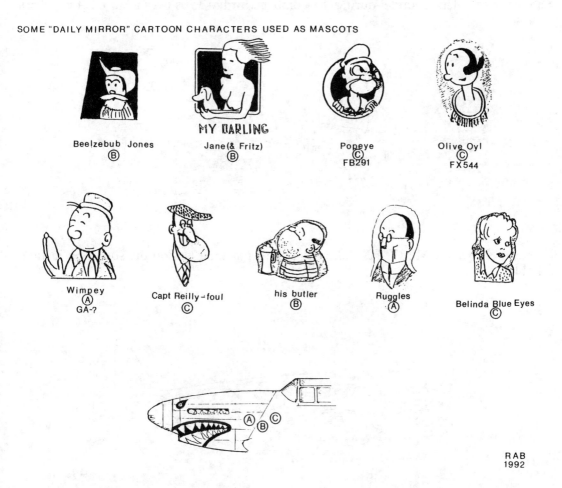

Diagram to show the position of the mascots

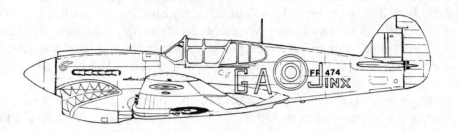

(above) Flt Lt Mattias's Kittyhawk Mk III, FR472, GA-J, "Jinx" was badly holed just above the fuselage roundel during the combat with FW190s over Rieti LG on 7 April 1944.

(above) Kittyhawk Mk IV, FX760, GA-T This machine was on the squadron in June 1944.

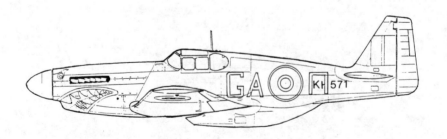

(above) Denis Featherstone's Mustang Mk III, KH571, GA-Π (Greek letter "pie"). This machine was on the squadron as GA-V from November to December 1944 and as GA-Π from January to May 1945.

until the 21st, by which time the coaster had come alongside the *Leonhardt* and one small vessel had disappeared. Two of the Thunderbolt squadrons and 3RAAF Sqn were to deal with the flak and then forty-eight Mustangs and Kittyhawks were to deliver their bombs. All this while a Spitfire PR aircraft flying at 20,000′ would be taking photographs so that there could be no argument as to what happened.

The raid was led by Wg Cdr Westlake, DFC, and began with 250 Sqn, commanded by Major Feilix Weingartz, attacking the *Leonhardt*. Weingartz scored a direct hit 'down the smoke stack' and Capt Peter Cheadle also scored a hit. The result from the first wave was that the *Leonhardt* was badly damaged and caught fire and there was a near miss on a torpedo boat. Then followed 450 Sqn, 112 (led by Paul Forster the acting CO), and 5SAAF. The second wave inflicted damage on two warehouses, set fire to three more warehouses along with the coaster and a supply barge; the third wave hit the escort vessel, two barges and warehouses. Soon flame and smoke rose upwards obscuring the whole target for the fourth and final wave. The only casualty was Lieut Senior of 250 Sqn who had to bale out over the sea and was rescued by a Catalina. One bomb, a hang-up, fell outside the target area and this destroyed a private garage. It is said that the Italians, who soon realised that they were in no danger, treated the whole thing as a *spettacolo* and climbed up onto the rooftops and crowded into their windows to enjoy this aerial entertainment, perhaps little realising what skill was being demonstrated. A total of 86,000 lb of bombs were dropped along with the expenditure of some rockets and .5″ ammunition.

The next day, the 22nd, the squadron was sent up in three sections each of four aircraft to give cover to Marauders bombing Carsarsa marshalling yards. The 88mm flak, the pilots reported, was directed only at the bombers. In the afternoon there were railway recces into Yugoslavia and seven trucks were left smoking. It was considered now that rail traffic was only moving at night. Escorts continued the next day when Marauders flew to marshalling yards near San Vito. There was no flak and most of the bombs were seen to fall in the target area.

Armed recces continued the next day but little was seen, although an unidentified aircraft on Udine airfield was straffed and damaged. By the 25th the squadron diarist was beginning to complain that it was getting very difficult to find anything to attack. Four sections each of four aircraft covered the best part of northern Italy and returned with a score of no more than two locomotives, five trucks and one MT vehicle destroyed and some trucks damaged. The railway line at Caorle was the target on the 25th and the first section of six aircraft cratered the track and then divided up into pairs to see what they could find. One staff car was seen and attacked three times and left riddled although they couldn't get it to catch fire. The second section also cratered the same piece of railway line but had nothing else to report.

The next couple of days were unfit for flying and it wasn't until the 29th that operations recommenced after a weather recce. A bridge was attacked and a good concentration of bombs was reported and even though it was not squarely hit it was believed that the supports had been damaged, making it unsafe for traffic. Red and Blue Sections then split up and came home after destroying four locos and one vehicle damaged. The second mission attacked lock gates near the mouth of the river Po. Damage was done but observation was difficult due to smoke from a burning building which was drifting across the target.

On the 30th the weather recce aircraft stayed up for three hours thirty minutes and, during their flight, managed to cover most of Yugoslavia and northern Italy. Their report, however, was that the weather was not good enough and so there were no operations. On the last day of the month the lock gates near the mouth of the Po were again attacked and more damage was done.

At the end of the month it was learned that Laurie Usher, last seen hanging by his parachute harness from a tree, had been awarded the DFC. Five 'old hands' had left or were due to leave the squadron, tour expired, Graham Schwikkard, Plt Off (ex Sgt) Dave Musther, the MO Flt Lt Peter Crews, the Engineering Officer Fg Off Bob Page and the CO, Sqn Ldr Bluett.

By April 1945 the whole of Germany itself was being over-run by the British, Americans and Russians. In the west armoured thrusts were advancing on average 30 miles a day and by the 1st the Ruhr, the industrial heartland, had been surrounded, cutting off Model and his Army Group B; Army Group H under Blaskowitz in Holland had been forced back by Montgomery's offensive and by the 4th elements of the Allied armies were lying along the Ems and the Weser. In the east the Russians were approaching the river Oder and by the middle of the month Vienna had been captured. German forces in Italy consisted of the 10th Army (Herr) and the 14th Army (Lemelsen) under the command of Army Group Southwest (Vietinghoff), in all 74,500 infantry and about 200 tanks in 25 divisions. Against these the Allies had 17 divisions and ten brigades, about 82,100 infantry and 3000 tanks. In the air the *Luftwaffe* could muster barely 130 aircraft against the Allies' 4000. The enemy's flak defences, however, as has been shown in this narrative, was of the highest order, the Germans having about 1000 heavy and 2,200 light flak guns.

April, for the squadron, opened with a recce of the Latisana bridge to see whether it was serviceable. They found it was not, with the western span down and the approach to the bridge cratered. On their way back 'Commander' asked them to look for a dinghy but although they searched for 45 minutes south of Caorle they found nothing but some floating wreckage. The next operation was an attack on a well-defended bridge near Slavonski Brod. Two direct hits were claimed but accurate observation was difficult due to dust and flak. The generally expressed wish was that life would be simpler if the Russians were to capture Brod soon. In the afternoon Sqn Ldr Hart, who had now taken over as CO, led an armed recce. The first weather recce on the next day was followed by three armed recces.

On the second the squadron had the misfortune to lose 'Matt' Matthias. He was leading a four which flew via Ljubljana – Radece – Celje – Pragersko – Maribor and Ptuj. Some captive balloons were seen over one marshalling yard, presumably as a defence. Two aircraft returned to base with engine trouble leaving a pair to continue alone. Somewhere near Graz Flt Lt Matthias's aircraft (KM135 'K') was hit in the glycol tank when at only 200'. He climbed to 1500' and then went into a glide and stalled. The parachute appeared briefly but the aircraft fell amongst some trees. His end was typical of the man – it seems as if he spent so much time giving his No 2 details of how to get home that he didn't leave himself enough to bale out. Flt Lt Maurice Neville Matthias, from Thika in Kenya, had joined the squadron in April 1943, when the squadron was at Kairouan in Tunisia and had served for over a year at that time, returning for his second tour in February 1945. He was a keen photographer and many of his photos appear in this and other books about the DAF. His own album is now in the possession of the Imperial War Museum, London.

On the second operation that day, again an armed recce, Sgt C Walker who had joined the squadron barely nine days before, flying FB288 'Z', called up near Graz to say that his engine was packing up. He was ordered to bale out but his aircraft was seen to go into a spin from 2000', too low an altitude to recover. No parachute was seen and he was presumed killed. His body has never been found. After a second weather recce there was another operation in the Celje – Dravograd – Zeltweg areas. The next day, 4 April, there were two operations, both against the railways. The 5th was a busy day mostly concerned with the rescue of a Lieut Veitch of 260 Sqn who had ditched not far from Trieste. The squadron had already done two armed recces, both in the Udine – Villach area and when they returned they were ordered to do a quick turn-round, not to bother about bombing up, and to fly to cover the air-sea rescue. When the aircraft reached the scene they found a Catalina already orbiting but the pilot was unhappy about alighting because of sea mines. Blue Section covered the dinghy while Red guarded the flying boat. A torpedo boat appeared out of Trieste so Blue Section 'made a pass at it' and received some pom-pom fire in return, but the enemy vessel took the hint and returned whence it had come. A relief patrol now appeared and the 112 aircraft went off on a recce, although their bombs were not fused owing to the hurried turn-round. After lunch another 112 section took over but just as they were departing a Warwick appeared with a dinghy. At 15.40 hrs when the third squadron top cover arrived they found that Lieut Veitch had boarded the dinghy and was under way. At this point some German coastal batteries opened up causing Ray Veitch to make haste to get out of range. He was last seen seven miles north of Salnore Point where he was finally picked up by the Catalina.

That evening a pair of aircraft were scrambled to try to intercept a German jet aircraft that was rumoured to fly over each evening at 23,000'. The Mustangs went up to 30,000' again the next evening but although they spotted an aircraft even higher than this they were told it was friendly. The squadron undertook some rail and bridge attacks but nothing was seen except an armoured car which was beaten up.

In an attempt to catch rolling stock before it was hidden for the day, nine aircraft took off before dawn on the 7 April. In this they were successful and they caught several trains before they could run for cover. Some were seen making for Udine and it was considered that this may be where they were hidden, a notion that was supported by the amount of flak that was always thrown up from the place. Nine locomotives and six trucks were destroyed and three damaged. Another wild goose chase for the German jetplane had no success that day either.

On the 9 April a massive artillery bombardment opened up on the German front line along the front of V Corps and the Polish Corps. The infantry attack went in at 19.00 hrs but the Germans fought stubbornly. That day the squadron was on close-support missions all day. It was a beautiful morning but the aircraft did not take off until the afternoon. Even so five missions (21 sorties) were flown that day with guns, gun pits and troops along the Senio River as targets under control of Rover David and Rover Frank. The sky was full of aircraft of all descriptions – Flying Fortresses, Liberators,

Mitchells and Marauders included. The CO, Sqn Ldr Hart, a Canadian, nearly 'had his chips' that day, when, according to Denis Featherstone, he and Bruce Routledge were straffing gun positions near Bolognese and Hart had to fly home with a 'man-sized hole through his port tailplane and a smack in the ammo bay'. After dark there was no respite from the aircraft going overhead and the windows of the Pilots' Mess rattled with the detonations.

The effectiveness of the aircrafts' ground support was such that, once again, the German troops were obliged to keep their heads down while the Allied troops moved forward onto their positions. The New Zealand Div was able to cross the Senio, a major tactical obstacle, without a single casualty.

Excellent weather aided the DAF the next day and all targets were attacked without incident. The only untoward occurrence was that a pilot of 450 Sqn nearly had his pants blown off when he landed with an unsafe bomb still attached. This exploded, cratering the runway, but as the aircraft was about 300 yards further along the psp by that time he was all right. The remaining aircraft had to divert to Forli, a few miles to the west.

Eight missions were flown on the 11th, an uneventful day, but busy. The next day it was all Cab Rank patrols but on the second mission Flt Sgt T P Roberts (KM127, 'X') eighteen days on the squadron, failed to return. He was observed to pull out after the attack but was not seen again and was listed as missing, believed killed. On the sixth operation a road bridge at Bastia was attacked. Lieut E N Roberts (HB913 'S') was seen in a dive with flames coming from the port mainplane, near the fuselage. Another fire began on the starboard side and the aircraft turned onto its back and flew into the ground just north of the bridge at 18.15 hrs.

The next day the mission was abortive due to low cloud and the bombs had to be jettisoned. The second mission was another attack on the bridge at Bastia that resulted in a direct hit on the steel centre section which damaged it. On the 14th the 5th Army joined the offensive sending its IV Corps forward behind the heaviest air support yet seen in Italy. Truscott massed his forces on a 20 mile front opposite Bologna, employing specially trained mountain troops who snaked their way rapidly through the German defences.

That day the squadron straffed a staff car, bombed a railway line, attacked a heavy duty vehicle but merely 'observed' two flak-cars! There were then two close support missions, the second of which made a successful attack on four heavy calibre guns. The bombs fell close enough to chuck earth and debris into the gun pits. By the end of the day the first of the three 'River Lines' had been breached by the army and the advance was gathering momentum.

The DAF's efforts in support of the army for this final offensive was to be the culmination of everything that had been learned, AVM Foster's 'swan song' embodying all the DAF's experience. There were to be very fine limits on the bombing ahead of the troops, a mere 500 yards separating the aircrafts' bombs and the Allied front line. 'Rovers', sometimes now working from tanks since they were so close to the fighting, had to sustain the rolling continuity of the close support. Afterwards Vietinghoff was to say that the period between the 9th and 20th was the time of the most effective employment of the Allied Air Forces. The Germans suffered badly at the crossing of the Senio from the DAF dropping numerous small-calibre fragmentation bombs and, with the severing of all the lines of communication, supplies of all sorts were impossible to bring forward, while, to the rear, rail traffic was continually harassed, particularly by the destruction of bridges. *Blitzkreig*, the German conception, had finally come home to roost. The *Luftwaffe* had never recovered from its defeat in North Africa so that whereas in the desert the DAF had had to chose between gaining air superiority, interdiction or close support operations, in Italy the choice was reduced to the latter two.

The next day, 15 April, there were three armed recces and two close-support operations. The first roamed along the roads from Imola – Bologna – Verona – Vicenza – Padua and to Ferrara. They saw nothing the whole way except an ambulance and a motor cyclist. It turned out to be the motor cyclist's unlucky day. He appeared on the road ahead just after the section had decided it should be bombed. The squadron diarist supposed that he must have been a bit 'shaken' while the ops log suggests that he may have been 'upset' at having six 1000-lb bombs falling around him.

The second armed recce went along Route 9 to Parma, then north to Casalmaggiore (given as Castel Maggiore in the diary), Lake Garda and west to Brescia where two pill boxes were bombed, then to Villa Franca and Isola della Scala where a bonanza of 50-plus trucks was seen and dealt with.

At 17.30 hrs there was a Cab Rank patrol which was detailed to attack a defended house near Castel Guelfo, resulting in some near misses. Castel Guelfo appeared to be burning and in the church ammunition was exploding. The 5th Army that day captured Montese and Veragato. From then until the 19th there was some very heavy fighting in the mountains but the Polish Division made progress along the road towards Bologna. By the 20th the Americans had debouched from the mountains and cut the main road at Ponte Sammogia.

In threes and fours the squadron continued with Cab Rank patrols. Slit trenches, heavy duty vehicles loaded with troops, horse-drawn transport, vehicles and a DR (whose body was picked up by an ambulance), HDVs towing guns, scout cars and staff cars were all attacked that day. On the second mission four aircraft were directed on to two tanks hidden in a courtyard. The building was thoroughly hit resulting in the tanks beetling off in the direction of Medicina. Two more tanks were attacked and bombed on a road and one was covered in debris by a near miss. On the fourth mission 'B' Flt Commander, Flt Lt Hirons, leading the section, had a narrow escape when his engine cut on take-off. He jettisoned his bombs 'safe' (which just missed a farm house) and crash landed in a field two miles north of the airstrip, causing little damage to his aircraft and none to himself. His formation carried on without him to attack a tank concealed in a garage.

On the 17th 24 sorties were flown, all Cab-Rank patrols. The third mission pinned a tank down in a garage and bombed it. It received a direct hit and there were two explosions and the tank was seen to have been destroyed. Several other tanks were attacked, but short of a direct hit or a near miss by a bomb, the straffing did not appear to worry them too much. Some of the bombing that day was only about 200 yards away from our own forward troops. The next day the CO led a first light mission to catch the locomotives before they ran for cover. In this way eleven engines were claimed as damaged. The rest of the day's operations were in close support of the troops. Capt Featherstone led the fifth operation when one tank was bombed and a near miss left the gun barrel bent. The tank was still moving until a further bomb landed within 15' of it, after which it caught fire.

Close support work continued all the 19 April, including an attack on the village of Ferrarese where troops were reported to be forming up in a house. The building was attacked and demolished and Rover Paddy called up to congratulate them. That day the German front line started to crumble, opposition in front of the American IV Corps practically collapsing although the troops in the centre of the line began withdrawing in good order.

Flt Sgt Bruce Routledge led a successful armed recce over Yugoslavia for the first operation on the 20th. One locomotive and 20 trucks were seen near Trieste, about 50 yards from a tunnel. Two aircraft bombed and managed to derail the engine. At this point Lieut J H Nixon (KH467 'Z') must have been hit by flak as his aircraft exploded in mid-air and the wreckage flew into the ground above the tunnel. The formation continued and eventually made its way into Austria, returning to land at Ravenna as Cervia LG was shrouded in mist. The claim was for two locomotives destroyed, three damaged, six trucks destroyed, five MT and four HDVs destroyed or damaged.

The rest of the day's operations were close support and on the fifth mission a house was attacked when Rover Paddy was able to confirm that the troops in it were not our own, they being barely 100 yards distant from the target.

On the 21st the squadron sent off a dozen aircraft together for the first time since the start of the offensive, along with 250 Sqn, on an anti-flak mission near a bridge on the River Reno. They pressed home their attack through an intense barrage of 20mm fire but they succeeded in silencing five of the guns. 'Bodies' were observed scattering during the attack. The second operation was against a pontoon wharf at Berra where a direct hit destroyed the target. Vietinghoff's defences were now ruptured and the Germans began to flee towards the Po, an enormously strong defensive line had they been able to defend it. With all bridges destroyed, the Po unfordable and lacking bridging equipment the enemy was, in effect, trapped. No attempt was made to hold Bologna and, as the Americans and British debouched onto the flat plain, which was served by excellent roads, the extent of the German defeat was visible on every side. Thousands of prisoners, bewildered by the speed and suddenness of the Allied advance, were rounded up. The enemy planned to hold Ferrara but now the Italian partisans rose *en masse* to do their utmost to hinder the Germans' efforts.

The determination of the Allied commanders to shatter Army Group Southwest, even at this late stage in the war, may have been connected with the fear of the much vaunted 'Alpine Redoubt', a largely imaginary defensive position in the depths of the south German and Austrian mountains. The fact that there was no such redoubt was incidental, but, as the war began to enter its final phase, it was important that no troops were allowed to make their way there. By the 22nd it was plain to the squadron that the enemy were in full retreat across the Po and a ferry terminal was the squadron's first target that day. After the attack the boat had vanished although the staging still remained.

On 23 April there were attacks on pontoons and wharfs and on the second mission four aircraft did a recce of the Adige River and some close support near Cologna. This final mission returned with their bombs, which had to be jettisoned, as it had become too dark to drop them on any target. That day Modena fell to the Allies. On the 24th

Ferrara and Mantua were taken and the squadron was given a variety of targets to attack to hinder the Germans' retreat. The next day Verona, Spezia and Parma were captured.

Armed recces ranged far and wide on the 26th but there was little to be found and the day's total was three vehicles destroyed and four damaged. There was great excitement in the evening when an American aircraft reported that it was shadowing a huge convoy of 300 vehicles moving north out of Verona, but the attack was cancelled when it was found to be our own troops. Piacenza and Genoa fell on the 27th and on the next day there was only one operation of 12 aircraft led by Flt Lt Hirons which caught some MT in the open and came back with a claim for six destroyed, seven left burning and eleven smoking. That day Mussolini and his mistress Clara Petacci, two Fascist leaders Carlo Scorza and Allessandro Pavolini, were shot by Communist partisans and strung up by their ankles in Milan's Piazza Loretto.

On the 29 April there were three operational missions, armed recces and attacks on MT in the Conegliano areas and towards Sacile and Carsarsa. Seventeen vehicles were destroyed. Venice and Padua were captured; the next day Turin fell and it was reported that what was left of the enemy formations were completely disorganised. It was said that a whole Wing of Spitfires had to be engaged in nothing more than keeping track of where our own forward troops had got to. Targets were now non-existant and there was no operational flying.

May opened with Gp Capt Eaton leading a formation, which included 3RAAF and 5SAAF Sqns to attack some shipping. Bombs were dropped on a collection of three small vessels and six barges towed by tugs, all full of troops, coming out of Trieste. The vessels were straffed. It was later learned that these may have been Germans on their way to surrender but nevertheless they had 20mm and 40mm flak guns to protect themselves with. Then 'Commander' ordered the attacks to cease as it was learned they were prisoners of war being escorted by Yugoslavs on their way to Monfalcone.

The next day, 2 May, there was an armed recce led by the CO into southern Austria where five railway engines and three vehicles were damaged. The remaining sorties that day were patrols over shipping, all of which were flying the white flag. In the evening came the announcement that all enemy troops in northern Italy had surrendered unconditionally that afternoon. Surprisingly the Pilots' Mess was quiet that night. Sgt Greaves, who had been shot down on 23 January, returned from Yugoslavia.

The war in the Balkans did not end until 8 May and so, in the afternoon of the 3rd, eleven aircraft patrolled the Istrian peninsula. They were fired on by flak and from Fiume came one 4-star red Verey signal, but otherwise there was no incident. There was another day's patrolling over the Istrian peninsula after which the squadron was stood down on the 5th. This was the first free day they had had for many months and liberty runs were organised for the airmen to go into Bologna and Ferrara.

On 6 May the four last operational sorties of the war were flown. Lieut E F Blatchford and Lieut W O Davenport went on a recce from 06.10 hrs to 08.35 hrs to Belluno – Peravola – Dubbiaco – Lienz – Spittal – San Michael, then back via Spittal and Villach to Tarviso and Vergone. There was some movement noted on roads and railways but nothing was attacked. The second mission, which was airborne from 16.50 hrs to 19.35 hrs, again led by Lieut Blatchford (KH774) and with Flt Sgt R B

Robinson (KM107), flew a similar route, Dubbiaco – Lienz – Spittal – Villach – Tarviso – Pontebba and back to Cervia.

Tuesday, 8 May 1945 was proclaimed Victory in Europe (VE) Day, and the squadron was stood down. All ranks listened to Churchill's speech at 15.00 hrs and the evening dissolved into celebrations. Luckily precautions had been taken to collect all arms and ammunition three days previously and so no serious damage was done to property or persons.

Thus, for 112 Sqn, the war ended. It was credited, by official reckoning, with 164 confirmed destroyed, 48 probably destroyed and 81 enemy aircraft damaged. It had lost, by a curious coincidence, 163 aircraft destroyed or badly damaged. 106 squadron pilots had been killed, taken prisoner or been killed in flying accidents since the start of hostilities. From the squadron records it would appear that about 308 pilots passed through the squadron between June 1940 and May 1945 which would indicate that the chances of being killed or captured were under 1 in 3, a reminder, if one is needed, that wartime flying was a high risk activity. Twelve pilots lost their lives in flying accidents, 41 pilots remain missing, even to this day (including one on an air test), 33 are known to have been killed, including 2 who were PoWs, 17 pilots were captured by the Germans and two temporarily incarcerated by the Yugoslavians and one pilot died of wounds. 21 NCOs and airmen had been made PoWs in Crete, possibly some more had been captured in the retreat in January 1942 but the squadron records have left us no details and only one airman appears to have lost his life as a result of enemy action.

The squadron was ordered to move once more, this time to Lavariano, eight miles north of Udine and the CO and Flt Lt Hirons flew to inspect it and returned to say that it was quite a pleasant spot. The rest of the day, 9 May, was spent packing up for the move and 'A' Party set off on the 10th for a journey of some 230 miles.

On the 13th, Sgt Greaves, who had only recently returned to the squadron, became the first post-war casualty. After an engine failure at 3000' he was advised to select somewhere to force land; he attempted to put his Mustang down in a field but the aircraft overshot, hit a ditch, overturned and burst into flames. He was buried at Forli British Military Cemetery the next day.

By the 19th the squadron was at Lavariano. Here one of their duties was to prepare for a Victory fly-past on 25th May, Empire Air Day. The formation to be adopted was a 12 aircraft line abreast, a very difficult formation to fly successfully. Nevertheless the preparations occupied everyone for the time being. On the 28th, the display having been postponed due to weather, all went very well. Gp Capt Eaton led 250 Sqn which was first in the fly-past, with 112 the fourth. The American 79th Fighter Group was adjudged the best, flying over in a formation that spelled '79' and then again spelling 'DAF'.

The diary starts the month of June 1945 with the remark that the CO was beginning to find it difficult to keep up the interest of the pilots and groundcrew who supposed that now the war was won there was no more work left to do. As a result all sorts of schemes and ideas were put into operation. On the 14th the CO flew to Villa Franca, the nearest airfield to Lake Garda, where a requisitioned hotel, the *'Albergo Catullo'* at Sirmione, was being turned into an airmen's leave hostel.

One of the highlights of the month was the return of Laurie Usher who had been missing since 20 March. He had been rescued from his tree and hidden in a farmhouse by local Yugoslavians and well cared for at first. After a while, though, they began to suspect, for some unspecified reason, that he was a Gestapo agent and he was placed in solitary confinement. It was only after strenuous efforts had been made on his behalf that he was released. His return was celebrated with a party and he related that, while in captivity, he had befriended a spider who had told him all sorts of stories! In honour of his release the pilots rang the local church bells in the middle of the night, which was at first considered to have been a frightful black until it was learned that this was indeed a local custom on the return of prisoners of war!

Training flying continued and on 20 July Capt G H Edwards found that he could not get his flaps or undercarriage to come down. After all else had failed Edwards was faced with the choice of crash landing or baling out. Possibly influenced by the fate of Sgt Greaves, he chose the latter option. He landed safely within a few yards of his wrecked machine, into the flames of which he thought he was going to fall.

'Black Thursday', 26 July 1945, was one of the saddest days in the squadron's history. Nine aircraft took off at 09.55 hrs, led by Capt Edwards, on a practice recce. Of these, two returned shortly afterwards with engine trouble. Later on that morning it appeared that something must have happened to the formation and eventually two more returned, Lieut A van Aardt and Sgt M Klibanksi who had been flying Nos 6 and 7 respectively. Their story was as follows – they had started by doing some practice straffing in a valley somewhere between Trento and Lake Iseo. The formation then re-formed in line astern and set course up a valley under cloud. After only a few seconds van Aardt and Klibanski realised that this was not an open-ended valley but that cloud covered mountains lay directly ahead. Van Aardt immediately stall-turned his machine and miraculously escaped hitting the mountain side while Klibanski[1], a pilot who came from Palestine, opened up full throttle and climbed as hard as he could, missing the mountain top, in his estimation, by only a few feet. Behind him he felt or saw a series of explosions in the cloud. Both pilots called the others but there was no reply. Those who failed to return were Capt Edwards (KM216), Lieut R D Park (FB259), Lieut W D Blom (KH235), Lieut R H Templer (KM107) and a new pilot Sgt G P Eyears (KH720).

That afternoon Van Aardt and Ted Oosthuizen took off again in an attempt to locate the scene of the disaster but were unable to find it and as the mountains were still cloud covered it was considered advisable not to venture in too far. Ground search parties were immediately organised by the Aircraft Safety Branch but it wasn't until 2 August that information was received that all five bodies had been found on Monte Care Alto (height 3463 metres) and were awaiting identification in the mortuary at Trento. They were buried that evening with the assistance of an American honour guard.

The South African pilots were now starting to return home and in a short time the whole character of the squadron had changed. South Africans, who had made up such a large proportion of the pilots towards the latter part of the war had, in fact, been associated with 112 Sqn since June 1940, but particularly from December 1943 and from the latter months of 1944 after which 25 SAAF pilots had been posted in but, although these 'Yarpies' formed the largest contingent from the Empire, they were not unique since 112 had had its share of Australians, New Zealanders and Canadians. In

---

[1] One authority refers to this man as Klabinski, not Klibanski

March 11 of the pilots had been SAAF but by August there was only one and even he was awaiting posting.

The Wing too was now changing and there were rumours that the squadron would soon disband. Nos 450 and 3RAAF had already departed and 260 was in the process of disbanding, its place being taken by No 318 Polish Squadron and 225 Sqn, both equipped with Spitfire IXs. Nevertheless instructions were received to find winter billets near Tissano airstrip, a small concrete LG, but this proved difficult as there were very few houses locally and what ones could be found were already crammed with Italian civilians bombed out of Udine. For the time being the squadron remained at Lavariano.

Cpl J Kerslake, writing in 1957, remembers that when the Australian squadron was disbanded 112 and 260 Sqns shared out the aircraft, tentage and the MT. Shortly afterwards some local Italians turned up, clutching spurious 'bills of sale' and asking where they could find the vehicles and equipment they had bought from the departing Aussies. The airmen moved in to winter quarters in a village called Santa Maria de Longa, which lay either side of the highway from Trieste to Udine, referred to as 'Long Mary' in their parlance.

By October the squadron diarist, that anonymous observer of all aspects of the squadron's existence, reported that spares for the Mustangs were now becoming increasingly hard to procure. On the 23rd a new CO arrived, Sqn Ldr P S Blomfield, DSO, DFC, who had had 260 Sqn until its disbandment in August. Geoff Hirons left in November bearing home his new Italian bride Gelsa from Udine, with whom he lived happily until his death in 1991, and a DFC. After the war Geoff remarked that his fitter had commented that the award of the DFC must have been for 'regular attendance'[1]

On 27 November there was a fatal accident. Three aircraft had been detailed to climb to 30,000' for an oxygen test. The leader, Plt Off Bruce Routledge, heard his No 2 say that he was not feeling too good. Routledge then looked round for his No 3, a Sgt A E Headland, one of the post-war postings in, and found that he was not there. Calling him on the R/T he received only an intermittant reply. Calling 'Control' and any other aircraft produced no further information but later that day the Americans reported that an aircraft had crashed near Cormons, south-east of Udine. This was found to be Sgt Headland's machine and his body was found nearby. Anoxia, resulting from lack of oxygen at height, is now known to have the insidious effect of slowly causing mental paralysis and death but with the victim being quite unaware – even light-heartedly accepting – that he is losing consciousness.

Sqn Ldr Blomfield left the squadron in December on posting and 112 was taken over by Flt Lt P M Forster. The following day the Wing Dental Officer was found dead in his mobile surgery, gassed by exhaust fumes. It was believed that he had committed suicide rather than return to England, although it was also understood that he was under investigation as a result of his partiality for under-age Italian girls.

On the 14 December the squadron was ordered to patrol the Istrian peninsula and the Italo-Yugoslav border as the 'Jugs' were beginning to menace Trieste. By the end of the year 112 was down to 50% establishment and on 22 January 1946 the long-delayed move to Tissano, a few miles to the east, was finally put into effect. Poor

[1] in a letter from Hirons to J E ('Ali') Barber, 23 September 1985

weather reduced flying and the few remaining airmen were obliged to act as aircraft guards every other night.

On 4 March ten aircraft took off on a Wing Balbo[1] led by the OC Flying Wing, Wg Cdr Storrar. The CO, Sqn Ldr Forster, somehow managed to break the undercarriage selector lever and was just preparing to land wheels up when he thought of undoing his safety harness and standing on the remaining portion of the undercarriage lever. This had the desired effect and he made a normal landing. In early May the squadron moved back to Lavariano under canvas. Sqn Ldr Forster, who had been on the squadron since June 1944, was replaced by Sqn Ldr M J Wright.

That summer flying continued and 112 was engaged in patrolling the 'Morgan Line', the provisional frontier between Italy and Yugoslavia and in August there was a bombing demonstration at Gorizia, close to the frontier, probably designed as a show of strength at this disputed piece of territory. That month the Yugoslavs shot down a DC3 Dakota and kidnapped some British soldiers and the Mustangs continued to patrol the Morgan Line. In September 112 moved to Treviso airfield.

An extract from the diary: 'Friday. No flying. However it was made up for by a big party in the Sergeants' Mess. Chiefly celebrating the Wing Commander's last night as a celibate. It was very nearly the Wing Commander's last night, period.' In November there was a detachment to Lavariano for a week where conditions were pretty grim. By the end of the month the squadron was down to nine pilots and Sqn Ldr Maurice Wright had been replaced by Sqn Ldr R T Llewellyn. Now there were none of the old specialist officers – adjutant, engineer, medical, intelligence – all had long since left and the Administrative Echelon as it had been called was a thing of the past. By December everyone knew that the end was not far off.

On 31st, as a grand gesture, the squadron flew on a long cross-country trip that lasted four hours and which took them to Paris and back.

That day the squadron diary ends. The last piece of paper, dated 16 January 1947, was a letter from the CO to Air Headquarters, RAF Italy, returning the squadron's badge for safe keeping. 'Double one twice' was no more.

Along with the disbandment of the squadron, the Desert Air Force was now slowly being wound down. Under men like Collishaw, Coningham, Broadhurst, Dickson, Foster and Tedder it had developed into a magnificent fighting machine which was personified, at squadron level, by such fighters as 'Imshi' Mason, 'Pat' Pattle, Neville Duke, Clive Caldwell, Billy Drake, and Jackie Darwen – a list which could be extended to fill the page. The extraordinary mixture of Allied nationalities – Canadians, South Africans, British, Poles, New Zealanders, Free French and Americans had coalesced to form a highly effective team. The privations of the desert bonded men into a unique brotherhood from the humblest erk to the Air Officer Commanding and it was this comradeship that led inexorably to the success of the DAF, whether they flew or serviced the bombers, the day and night fighters, the air-sea-rescue, the recce, the ground attack, the coastal or the transport machines.

---

[1] A 'Balbo' was a name given to any particularly large formation of aircraft and it perpetuates the memory of the pre-war exploits of the Italian Marshal Balbo who led a number of aircraft on long distance flights.

As the war progressed and essential lessons were learned, the DAF and their brothers in arms, the men of the Eighth Army also grew together. It was Montgomery who recognised this when he said 'I don't suppose that any army has ever been supported by such a magnificent air striking force. I have always maintained that the 8th Army and the RAF in the Western Desert together constitute one fighting machine, and therein lies our great strength.'[1]

112 (Shark) Squadron formed only a small part of this great team but because somehow the squadron's wartime records survived virtually intact, it has been possible to compile their story in some detail. 112 is merely representative of all the other squadrons that fought in the Mediterranean theatre but perhaps, in Lord Howard of Effingham's words of several hundred years before, 'God send me to see such a company together again when need is' would be particularly appropriate for 112 (Shark) Squadron. Great men say one thing, humbler men put it differently. If I were to summarise all that 112 Sqn had achieved I can produce no sincerer words than those written by one of 112 (Home Defence) Squadron's airmen in the Great War, Mr A W James – '*What a job all members of the squadron did in Greece, Crete, amongst the dust, sand, flies and heat of the desert and the changing fortunes of war. It makes me thank God we had such pilots and men to stick it out and win through.*'

---

[1] '*El Alamein to the River Sangro*', Field Marshal Sir B L Montgomery

CHAPTER SEVEN

Germany and the Bloodhounds

Four years and five months later, on 12 May 1951, 112 Squadron was re-formed. In the intervening time the wartime alliance with the Soviet Union had crumbled in the face of Stalin's uncompromising view of the destiny of Communism world wide. In 1948 the Russians had attempted to force the western allies out of Berlin and the British and American 'air bridge' had been the only way the beleaguered city could be supplied. The next year Mao Tse Tung completed his rout of the Kuomintang armies and China fell to the Communists. The so-called Free World braced itself for what appeared to be the inevitable conflict of the democracies against the perceived menace of the Russian empire which loomed, massively armed, behind its outworks of the satellite states in eastern Europe.

In October 1949 the Russians tested their first atom bomb, to the alarm of the west. It seemed inevitable that, sooner or later, the world would surely descend into a nuclear holocaust. The RAF, which had been whittled down at the end of the war, had now begun to expand once more. In 1950 North Korea invaded the south and the Americans found themselves embroiled in war.

NATO, the North Atlantic Treaty Organisation, had been set up in 1949 with the aim of co-ordinating the defence of western Europe and so when 112 Sqn was re-formed as part of the 2nd Allied Tactical Air Force in Germany, it was also part of a multi-national air force which included squadrons from Belgium and the Netherlands.

No doubt when a decision was made to increase the number of ground-attack squadrons, a search was made of the histories of units which had distinguished themselves in this role, and 112 Sqn must have been almost an automatic choice. 112, based at RAF Fassberg, as part of No 2 Group, was located well forward, barely 20 miles from the inter-zonal border with Soviet occupied East Germany. Fighter ground-attack squadrons were to be found at Celle, Wunstorf and Fassberg while the day fighters were slightly further to the rear, at Oldenburg, Jever and Wahn. The Recce Wing was based at Gütersloh and the night-fighters at Ahlhorn and Wahn. HQ 2nd TAF was to be found in the pleasant, wooded purlieus of Bad Eilsen, near Bückeburg.

The airfield at Fassberg had, like all the other 2nd TAF airfields, been a pre-war *Luftwaffe* station and, as such, was a well-built facility, served by road and rail, with attractive brick buildings for the Messes and barrack blocks. Commanded by a Group Captain, the airfield would have contained three Wings, Flying, Technical and

Administrative, and, at Fassberg, three flying squadrons beside 112, Nos 14, 98 and 118 all equipped with de Havilland Vampire FB5s.

The most fundamental change that had occurred in the 4½ years since 112 Sqn was disbanded, was the universal advent into squadron service of the jet fighter. Although the RAF had employed Meteor Mk 1s in 1944 to combat the V.1 Flying Bombs, Vampires had not been supplied to squadrons until 1946. By 1951 the jet fighter was commonplace both in U.K. and 2nd TAF, and by 1949 the Canberra jet bomber was also in production. In 2nd TAF virtually no piston-engined aircraft now remained except at the Air-to-air firing camp at RAF Sylt and on the Group and HQ Communications Flights. Flying training still began with tuition on propellor-driven aircraft, the Prentice and Harvard, but within a few years this too would be altered to *ab initio* jet training. From the Mustang's top speed of 439 mph at 26,000', the Vampire could touch 540 mph, while the Mustang's initial rate of climb of 3475'/min had been boosted to the jet aircraft's 4200'/min.

Apart from this, though, there was little difference. Fighters were still fitted with forward firing cannon or machine guns which the pilot aimed by means of his gyro gunsight or, if preferred, fixed ring and bead. Ground attack aircraft were now fitted with rockets as well as bombs but in air-ground firing and in fighter interception the rules were still much as they had been in the 1940s. The principles of air combat taught at the Day Fighter School at RAF Stradishall were still those propounded by Wg Cdr 'Sailor' Malan for the simple reason that air fighting had, in its essentials, not altered greatly from the Battle of Britain days or, to extend the theory even further, from the Western Front in 1916.

The pilots on the squadron were mainly officers, although there was a sprinkling of NCOs with wings. The first PC (permanent commission) officers were now beginning to come out to the squadrons from Cranwell although, for a while, Short Service and National Service commissions predominated. Flight commanders and those of higher rank had almost all served in the war and had a chest of medal ribbons to show it. To some extent, the old wartime ethos of heavy drinking, smashing up of Mess furniture, brawling at Dining-In nights still persisted, although, gradually over the next few years, flying discipline would begin to tighten up as pilots lost their lives needlessly and foolishly through taking risks or because of inadequate supervision.

The Korean war had accelerated the requirement for new squadrons and men who perhaps did not necessarily have the skills or capacity to cope with the stresses of high speed, high altitude flight, were selected to pass through the RAF's training machine in order to fill the new squadrons. At the same time the RAF was endeavouring to revert to many aspects of pre-war life. Dining-In nights soon began to have a sprinkling of officers wearing Mess kit instead of battle-dress with white shirt and bow tie, visiting cards were reintroduced with the practice of 'calling' on senior officers encouraged, also promotion exams were begun again for those who intended to rise in the service. However some concessions had to be made and obligatory church parades on Sundays were abolished, work usually ending at midday on Saturday. Officers was still obliged to obtain their CO's approval before getting engaged or married and this was rarely granted to junior officers. Married quarters on RAF stations were few and virtually all the squadron pilots, save perhaps the squadron and flight commanders, lived in the Mess. Lack of private cars also meant that life on a 2nd TAF station revolved round the

Mess with the bar as its epicentre and, with alcoholic drinks selling at very low prices, life was uproarious, hectic and unforgettable.

The first officer to arrive on the squadron was Fg Off W G Holmes, on 12 May 1951 and within a short time several more pilots were posted in. On the 24th the new squadron commander, Sqn Ldr I D Bolton, DFC, arrived. By the end of the month 112 had six Vampires and a Meteor Mk 7 two-seat trainer. These all carried two letter identification on the tail booms, the aircraft letter forward of the roundel and the letter 'T', for 112 Sqn, aft of it. Ground-attack training began and, a change from wartime training, night flying was instituted. In July the ground crew strength was 54, about half the establishment, while the pilot strength of five was increased by two when Plt Off G D Dawkins and Plt Off K A Williamson arrived. Keith Williamson, a Cranwell graduate, was to end his service career as Chief of the Air Staff with the rank of Marshal of the Royal Air Force. Flt Lt R B Robinson was posted in during August as Flight Commander having served on 112 as an NCO and Plt Off in 1944 and 1945. No doubt it was from this man that the notion of carrying the sharksteeth markings was to be revived. In the meantime Battle Flights began. This required the squadron to be at 'Readiness' for the daylight hours with relays of pilots strapped into their aircraft positioned near the end of the runway prepared for take off in the minimum amount of time to intercept any hostile incursions across the zonal border. During September the squadron was detached to the Armament Practice Camp at RAF Sylt for a month's air-to-air gunnery training. This involved live shoots on a banner target towed behind Mosquito aircraft of the Target Towing Squadron.

When at Sylt they were visited by the C-in-C 2nd TAF, Air Marshal Sir Robert Foster, KCB, CBE, DFC, who perhaps remembered that it was 112 Sqn, amongst several others, who had saved him from a premature bowler hat over Venice in March 1945. Another visitor that month was Air Vice Marshal Sir Harry Broadhurst who also may have recalled 112 in the days of the attack on the Mareth Line. So, from the C-in-C and SASO down to the Flight Commander, the experience of the old DAF was well represented in Germany.

By November the squadron was actively considering reintroducing the sharksteeth markings and the pilots were discussing how best they might be positioned on the nose. The Fassberg Wing was identified by having a lightning flash painted below the cockpit canopy and wing tips and fin fillets in different colours for the different squadrons – green being the colour for 112. Central upon the lighting flash was a white disc carrying the 'Helwan cat' motif. Later the whole of the fin of the CO's aircraft (WA331 'A') was painted green, even over the fin tricolour and a large white disc and the Helwan cat superimposed. The finalised sharksteeth design departed from tradition insofar as the new scheme had red lips, white teeth and the interior of the mouth black. At some date the squadron code letter was changed from 'T' to 'A'.

On 11 February 1952 Flt Lt Robbie Robinson drove to RAF Jever to have a look round as a squadron move was imminent. On the whole this was not a popular decision as Jever was rather remote, situated in the rather dreary plains of Ostfriesland, not far from the North Sea coast. After a farewell party 112 Sqn left Fassberg on the 7 March. The squadron diarist remarked that the new station 'didn't look so bad . . . after an alkaseltzer'.

The de Havilland Vampire FB5 could trace its inception back to a design on the drawing board in 1942 based on an Air Ministry specification E.6/41. The first prototype machines led to a production order in 1944 and the Vampire Mk 1 entered squadron service in 1946 as an interceptor fighter. The Mk5 first flew on 23 June 1948 and was soon replacing the standard Mk 3s in Fighter Command but it was in Germany that the greatest number were eventually to be seen. It was probably the last relatively unsophisticated front-line aircraft to see service in the RAF having manually-operated controls, no radar, gyro gunsight, and a simple jet engine – the de Havilland Goblin producing 2700-lb of thrust. The jet engine allowed for a three extremely short undercarriage legs so that, when taxying, the pilot was very close to the ground. This and the comic little solid rubber nosewheel made the machine trundle along the runways and taxy-tracks and gave rise to the rather unkind nickname of the 'kiddy car'. Nevertheless it was a very easy and simple aircraft to fly, very sensitive on the controls but pilots trained on piston-engined aircraft had to learn that the jet engine was sluggish to respond to demands for power which meant that power-on approaches were always necessary to anticipate the need to overshoot.

On 16 April 1951 the squadron was again detached to Sylt for one of its biannual air-to-air firing practices. Sylt was enjoyed most during the summer months when the pleasures of the long sandy beaches could be best appreciated – especially the so-called Abyssinia beach where bathing and sunbathing was reserved for the '*Freikörperkültur*' nudists. In the winter, autumn and spring months the resort was virtually deserted and bad weather and North Sea fog frequently kept all the aircraft grounded for days on end.

In June that year Fg Off W G Holmes was posted to No 77 RAAF Sqn on active service in Korea, a duty that fell on a number of RAF pilots who were thus able to obtain valuable jet combat experience. The squadron's first fatal accident occurred during a detachment to RAF Odiham on 27 July 1951 when Plt Off C R Donaldson (WA283) flying No 2 to Fg Off Keith Williamson was involved in a dog-fight with the Odiham Meteors. He appears to have lost control and dived away vertically, startling a passing Anson pilot who thought he was being bounced, but the Vampire never pulled out.

By the end of the year the squadron had taken part in a number of exercises and been on several detachments. The squadron strength in November was fourteen pilots, eight SNCOs, 11 corporals and 66 airmen.

On 29 January 1953 the squadron was sent to RAF Butzweilerhof, near Cologne, to take part in some taxying trials on psp runways. Fg Off A J A Sagar (WA114 'D'), a new arrival on the squadron, ran out of fuel and he was obliged to bale out. He came down safely by parachute and his aircraft crashed near a pumping station. The rest of the formation landed rather low on fuel due to the bad weather and lack of radio contact. Sagar's particular shortage was due to having left his flaps down. The trials on the psp resulted in a number of nose wheel and main wheel tyres having to be changed.

On 17 March during a practice for an impending visit by HRH The Duke of Edinburgh, Fg Off R A Hancock had engine failure in VZ115 'C' when in the circuit. He misjudged his approach and passed the runway caravan, going the wrong way, at about 200 knots. The aircraft disintegrated and Fg Off Hancock was lucky to escape with little more than a broken arm.

On 6 July 1953 the squadron moved from Jever to RAF Brüggen, one of the group of brand new NATO 'clutch' airfields sited between the Rhine and the Maas. The pilots were pleased to be returning to something approaching civilization and the fact that Brüggen 'seems to be within striking distance of four major cities in four different countries' – presumably Mönchen-Gladbach (Germany), Eindhoven (Holland), Liége (Belgium) and Luxembourg. 112 Sqn was the first squadron to arrive at the new airfield, with its 2700 yards of runway and brand new facilities. In August some of the pilots were posted out to form the nucleus of NO 130 (Punjab) Sqn, also based at Brüggen.

Sqn Ldr Ian Bolton handed over command of the squadron in November to Sqn Ldr F M Hegarty and a short while later, on 2 November, Plt Off E J Kitwood was killed. He was air-testing a Vampire and bounced another aircraft, then flick rolled and spun in from about 8000'. The aircraft, WZ261, was not one belonging to 112. That year the squadron Christmas card carried the plea 'All we want for Christmas is our wings swept back!'

This was in the hope – shortly to be realised – of being re-equipped with the new F86 Canadair Sabre Mk4s. In January the first batch of pilots from 'A' Flight started their Sabre conversion at RAF Wildenrath. Sqn Ldr Frank Hegarty is recorded in the squadron's authorisation book as having flown the first Sabre (XB893) on 23 January. By 29th all the squadron pilots were back at Brüggen, fully equipped with the fashionable 'bone domes', anti-G suits, and copies of the voluminous and copiously illustrated Canadair Pilots' Notes.

If the Vampire had been the last of the RAF's unsophisticated aircraft, then the Sabre 4 was the first of the sophisticated ones. For much of its history 112 had been equipped with out-dated machines but now it had (in a term unknown in those days) a 'state of the art' aircraft. The Sabre still ranks today with some of the greatest aircraft of all time and it immediately placed all the day-fighter squadrons in 2nd TAF on a par, or superior to, the current Soviet Air Force machines.

The North American Aviation Company had begun work on the Sabre in the late autumn of 1944. Initially it was conceived with straight wings but during the planning stage the design team learned of German wartime wind-tunnel reports that detailed the advantages of swept-back wings for transonic flight. Low speed stability was, however, a problem but this was overcome by adding leading edge slats. The aircraft was powered by a General Electric J-35-C-3 engine which produced 4000-lb static thrust and the first prototype was delivered to the USAF in November 1948 and the first production machines reached squadrons in February 1949. The development of the Sabre had been keenly watched by other nations and the Royal Canadian Air Force obtained a licence to manufacture and in August 1949 100 aircraft were ordered. It was fortunate that by the time the Russian MiG 15 appeared in the skies over Korea, in November 1950, the Americans were able to deploy the Sabre to counter it and prevent the North Koreans and Chinese from acquiring air superiority. The RAF had decided to obtain the Sabre as a stop-gap aircraft until the first Hawker Hunters could be produced and, as a result, about 400 Sabres were supplied.

Despite the complications involved in flying the Sabre for the first time – the unfamiliar instrument panel, the fuel gauges reading in pounds instead of gallons, the huge oxygen mask, the heavy helmet with its visor – you were committed on your first flight to tackling a machine unlike any aircraft you had ever flown before. There was no

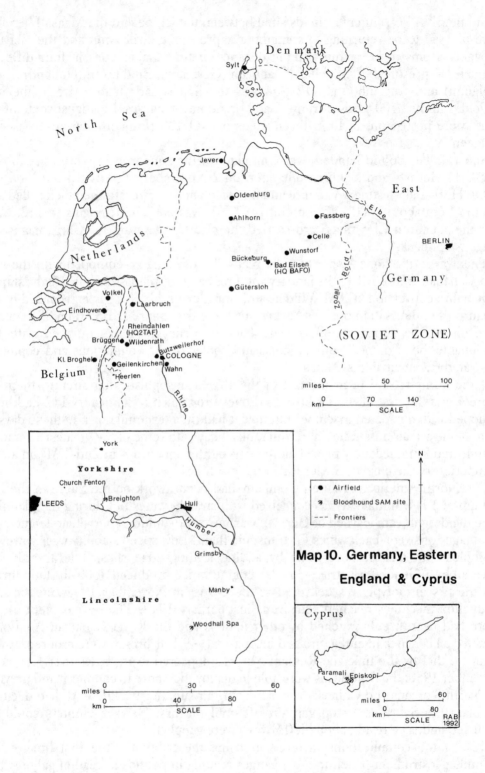

Map 10. Germany, Eastern England & Cyprus

two-seat Sabre for a dual familiarisation trip, you spent some time at Ground School, mugged up on Pilots' Notes and sat in the cockpit trying to remember what the plethora of dolls' eyes, knobs, levers, switches and displays were supposed to do and then, with a cheerful parting word of encouragement from your instructor, the hood closed on you and you were alone.

To 112 Sqn the problem with the Sabre was how to adapt the sharksteeth markings to the enormous gaping air intake. To be rational it might be supposed that this mouth ought to be incorporated into the design but just above the intake was the radar gunsight panel which could not be painted, so, in the end, the sharksmouth was (somewhat incongruously) painted on below and passing underneath the fuselage. By the end of January 112 had 13 Sabres, of which two were serviceable. On 3 March came the first accident when Fg Off L R Francis had a loss of power when overshooting and crash-landed a short distance from the airfield. XB912 was written off.

By May the squadron had grown considerably and had 31 pilots on strength and 22 aircraft, a large increase from the Vampire days. The Sabres though were found to be temperamental and required a lot of servicing. Frequently the radar gunsight failed to operate correctly and there was a limitation on flying above 400 knots due to a fault in the undercarriage. The squadron began receiving a later version of the Mk4 with 'hard' leading edges instead of the slatted ones. On 16 June Fg Off Roger Mansfield (XB884) was obliged to eject after a series of malfunctions ended with the power-controls freezing up on finals. He managed to gain enough height to eject at 1000' and, apart from being struck on the head by the seat that he had just parted company from, he landed unharmed. The aircraft came down in the bomb dump but luckily without a major disaster happening apart from .5" calibre bullets starting to explode. One of these further injured Fg Off Mansfield in the hand as he was helping to extinguish the heath fire that his aircraft had started. After that he retired from any further activity.

In June the squadron received official sanction to carry the sharksteeth markings instead of having to conform to an edict from Air Ministry which stated that all squadron markings had to be confined within rectangles on either side of the fuselage roundel. The officially suggested design had been a dreadful set of dentures on a red background which, if adopted, would have looked quite ridiculous.

There was, inevitably, immense kudos attached to being a pilot on a Sabre squadron, and amongst your peers you were the envy of those still flying Meteors, Venoms or

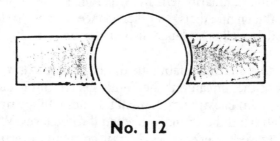

No. 112

No. 112 *From 'Fighter Squadron Markings', issued by Air Ministry*

NF11s. Those flying Sabres were issued with extremely comfortable calf-length black boots which were designed to stay on during an ejection, unlike the standard lace-up shoes worn up until that time. The trousers could be, unofficially, tucked into the tops of these boots, a sartorial detail which instantly identified a Sabre pilot, much in the same way as the undone top tunic button had been the mark of those in the Desert Air Force. In addition the Canadair Sabre representatives handed out little lapel badges which could be worn with civilian clothes, either a small brass Sabre or the circular 'Mach Busters Club' badge which was awarded once you had been through the sound barrier. *In hoc signo . . .* by these signs they were recognised.

On 26 September Fg Off J E A Jenkins and a Fg Off Weir (not from 112) were killed in the Meteor 7 trainer. On 5 July 1955 Fg Off M J Smith flying XB950 'S' crashed near Heerlen in Holland and was killed. On the 15th of that month the CO of 71 Sqn, Sqn Ldr L C Cherry, stalled on finals and was also killed – an ex-member of 112 Sqn during the Tunisian, Sicilian and Italian days of 1943 and 1944.

About August that year there was a showing in the Astra Cinema at RAF Brüggen of the film 'Desert Victory'[1]. The squadron pilots attended *en masse* and sat silently until, for one brief instant there was a shot of a Sharksteeth Kittyhawk, at which the pilots leaped to their feet and cheered madly and then, in complete silence, solemnly filed out of the cinema!

Flying the Sabre was an experience shared by only a small number of pilots.

'There you are, all alone – that is one immensely satisfying condition. You are your own master, away from all restraint, able to do what you want, to play all alone amongst the huge billowing deserts that are the cloud tops while, above you, the sky is absolutely blue and clear, a deep deep blue except near the horizon where it grows delicately lighter. I bank and dive under the cloud and there is the earth, with roads and towns and the river Rhine flowing seawards, broad and sinuous. Smoke pours from the chimneys of the Ruhr and where the cloud shadows lie it is darker and more sinister. But all I have to do to escape this sombre scene, this abode of earthbound mortals, is to pull back on the control column and effortlessly the aircraft emerges like a flying fish from the depths, out again into the brilliant sunshine. Further north, near Wesel, the cloud begins to break up into scattered woolly fragments floating like a fleet of galleons. Here I can play hide and seek amongst them, turning, weaving, darting, diving, climbing, avoiding them, passing through them, going down into the gloom for a bit or up into the dome of blue. Within the cockpit all is quiet. Every now and again I stop looking out at the passing scenery and let my mind dwell for a few moments on the instruments. Increasing familiarity tells me which need the closest attention – the fuel gauge for instance, the engine dials – a quick glance because so long as the needles lie within two limits, all is well – a glance also at the fire warning lights and my engine settings.

Outside the engine is making a fabulous din but down below, 7 or 8000 feet below perhaps, the shriek of the jet can only be faintly heard. In my cockpit all is quiet, and the only sound is the faint background hum of the radio. In my right hand is the control column and in my left hand the strangely shaped throttle lever. With these I control the aircraft – small though it is, perhaps, as aircraft go – but nevertheless weighing about

[1] last seen by squadron personnel on 9 April 1943, see above page 98

14000-lb, so that it sweeps across the sky like a swallow. We are all one, the aircraft and I. Without me it cannot fly, without it nor can I. If part of it were to break away we would tumble to earth, if I was destroyed, it would fall also. I am bound to it by four thick straps and two heavy tubes, so tightly as to be secured as firmly as the radio or the oxygen bottles.

So there I am, my Sabre and I, playing in the clouds and enjoying ourselves. I hope you would not say 'Well, why not get on with it and do some work?' because everything one does in an aircraft is work, the same way that everything one does when training a horse to be obedient can be said to be work, even if you appear to be just passing the time. Up in the clouds where I am enjoying doing things that millions of people will never be able to do, I am learning about my aircraft so that between us two, we make a fighting machine'[1]

On 26 April, 1956, after a detachment to the French Air Force base at Luxeuil, the squadron received its first Hawker Hunter Mk4, XF306, later to become 'E'. The pilots sat brooding over Pilots Notes and trying out the Hunter cockpit for size. It was smaller and more cramped than the Sabre cockpit but the pilots were pleased to have the Martin Baker ejection seat with the face blind, an improvement, it was considered, on the American 'bang seat' which was operated from the arm rests. By the 10th the aircraft were being painted with the sharksteeth, and the general opinion was that the Hunter looked better than the Sabre with the markings.

The painting was a difficult and quite laborious task and was specifically the business of the pilots – the ground crews had more important work to do. The area to be painted had first to be thoroughly cleaned of oil and grease and then a cardboard template had to be fixed on by means of sticky tape so that the outline of the teeth could be drawn on in pencil. The first colour was the white of the teeth, which was sprayed onto the mouth and centre of the eyes. This was left to dry for about 24 hours and then the template was stuck back on again and the outlines of the teeth covered so that the black of the mouth interior could be applied. Finally, after another delay to allow this paint to dry, the red of the lips was sprayed on. The whole operation could take about 48 hours although, if it was a weekend, about six or eight aircraft could be done at the same time with four or five pilots working on one aircraft as the masking alone took several hours. A large amount of the fuselage, wings and cockpit had to be covered to prevent the spray paint drifting and settling on the rest of the aircraft. A problem arose when the Aden gun packs were dropped and replaced with packs from another aircraft as, if there had been any variation in the positioning of the paintwork, the design would not fit together exactly.

Towards the end of August 1956 the squadron was detached to Sylt. Sqn Ldr Hegarty accompanied the squadron although he was due to leave[2], his place being taken by Sqn Ldr A R Wilson. The squadron's air-to-air scores on this detachment were extremely good, with Fg Off Pete Frame achieving 46% on one shoot and Sqn Ldr Hegarty 54%. On the 13th Flt Lt Keith Wiliamson, recently back from Korea, was obliged to eject from WV412 'A', when his engine failed on the downwind leg. He parachuted into the shallow water off Keitum village, inflated his dinghy and was soon

---

[1] Author's diary.
[2] Sqn Ldr Hegarty was later killed flying a Meteor 7

rescued by the Sylt helicopter none the worse for his experience.

The squadron was starting an aerobatic team at this time, led by Flt Lt Lee Jones and with Keith Williamson as No 2, Pete Frame as No 3 and Pat Reeve as No 4. Frame stood down shortly afterwards on the arrival of Plt Off Norman Lamb who had been No 3 in 43 Sqn ('The Fighting Cocks') aerobatic team.

The Hawker Hunter, which, from mid-1954, began to take the place of the Meteor 8 was the development of Hawkers P.1067 prototype that had first flown in 1951, which itself was the product of earlier designs, the P.1040, P.1052 and P.1081. These elegant machines, which had originally had Nene engines and straight wings, were evolved into a longer and slimmer aircraft with swept wings powered by a Rolls Royce Avon turbojet. The Hunter F1 first entered RAF service in July 1954 but by October that year the improved Mk 4 had appeared with increased fuel tankage and was supplied to 94 Sqn in Germany in April 1955. It was armed with a gun pack containing four 30mm Aden guns, the whole assembly being quickly and easily removed and replaced on a fast turn-round. It was an attractive-looking aircraft and was a pleasure to fly even if, as it seemed at the time, its performance was no great improvement on the Sabre 4s.

Two aircraft came to grief in a minor fashion on the 23 October, the first when Fg Off 'Bonx' Baker aborted his take off and rolled into the overshoot, then, on taxying back to the hangar, his brakes caught fire. The second incident involved Fg Off 'Taffy' Heath who had brake failure on landing and also ended up in the overshoot. Neither aircraft was damaged.

Two major crises came to a head in October and November with the Suez invasion and the Russian repression of the Hungarian uprising. Both of these resulted in the Wing (112, 71, 67 and 130 Sqns) being warned to be ready for war. The wives on the 'married patch' were strongly advised to learn to drive, if they didn't know already, and be prepared to make their own way to the Channel ports. However, by Christmas, the panic had subsided.

Sqn Ldr Wilson was promoted early the following year, 1957, and the squadron was taken over by Sqn Ldr C J. Homes. Homes, who had come straight from Air Ministry, gave the pilots a talk on the development of the fighter aircraft after which, as the squadron diarist put it, 'there was a deathly silence'. The reason for this silence was that current forward thinking concerning the interception of enemy aircraft in the future could only be done by guided missiles and that manned fighters would soon be obsolete. It seemed as though the writing was on the wall. 'All sorts of rumours wandering around, engendered by the official political talk of economies in the forces and withdrawing troops from NATO. People say that squadrons will be disbanded, there shortly won't be jobs for anyone . . . one can't help feeling that fighter squadrons as we know them today will soon be a thing of the past . . .'[1] At Robin Brown's suggestion, he being deep in the squadron's historical records, the old custom of having an aircraft painted with the query symbol was revived. XF319, the squadron commander's machine, was so painted, much to the amusement of the other squadrons on the Wing.

On 1 March 1957 a few telephone calls produced a 'Balbo' of 16 aircraft, eight from

[1] Author's diary

112, 5 from 67 and three from 3 Sqn at Geilenkirchen, which flew south over the American Zone. Led by 'A' Flt commander, the formation flew at contrail height in order to scramble the F86 Dogs for a huge aerial combat. In the past this had brought up every kind of jet fighter from the USAF airfields near the Mosel but on this occasion they seemed unwilling to mix it, much to everyone's disappointment. Group were interested to hear how we got on when we returned and the Wg Cdr Flying was happy. Had the Brüggen Wing continued in existence there were plans to repeat the performance.

April 1957 saw Sqn Ldr Homes' dire prediction come true inasmuch as the Gp Capt announced to the whole station the implications of Duncan Sandys' Government White Paper on Defence which was to result in all four squadrons at Brüggen being disbanded. The news was followed very swiftly by its implementation and by mid-April several squadrons on the Wing were being wound down. Thursday, 16 May, the anniversary of 112's re-forming in 1939, was the last day the squadron was operational. That day, after taking part in an exercise, Robin Brown (XF295) led a squadron farewell flypast, 'Eclipse' Red and Black Sections, comprising eight aircraft (none of them 112's as it happened) with Fg Off Pat Reeve (WV382), Plt Off Norman Lamb (XF298), Fg Off Len Amor (XF715), Flt Lt Pete Frame (XF291), Fg Off Jim Edwards (XF292), Plt Off 'Jock' Carnegie (XF275) and 'The Fluid Druid', Fg Off 'Taffy' Heath in XF294. The formation took a route so as to overfly as many of the local airfields as was possible, namely Laarbruch, Volkel, Eindhoven, Kleine Broghel, Geilenkirchen, HQ 2TAF and finally Brüggen itself. The aircraft landed at 1730 hrs.

After this, once the aircraft had been ferried away, all that remained was to pack up the squadron silver and other possessions to send into storage in UK. By 31 May, the date on which 112 officially ceased to exist, only three pilots remained at RAF Brüggen. One of the final decisions was to form 'The 112 Lonely Sharks Club' which was to meet at some venue in England from time to time to enjoy a meal, good wine and good company. For several years this venue was 'The White Hart' inn at Brasted in Kent but gradually pilots became scattered across the globe and the idea lapsed.

112 nevertheless received a certain amount of post-mortem publicity from 'Flight' magazine which published a digest of the squadron's history on 16 January 1959, and Chris Wren the cartoonist of 'The Aeroplane' wrote up one of the reunion dinners at 'The White Hart'. With his flair for prediction Chris Wren commented that '112 with its appropriate "motif" was perfectly in line for re-forming as the first Guided Weapons squadron and to get its fourth life' – 'as a glorified artillery regiment' in Wg Cdr James Longmore's rather more pointed phrase.

Early in 1960 there were rumours that 112 was indeed about to be re-born as an Air Defence Missile Squadron and this event took place on 1 August 1960. Squadron Leader Peter Shaw, having completed the Long Guided Weapons Course at the RAF Flying College at Manby, found himself in command of a large area of drying concrete and wet mud at RAF Breighton, near Church Fenton. Thus it was that, after a lapse of 41 years, 112 Sqn was once again concerned with the home defence of the British Isles.

The squadron's beginnings were really at Church Fenton which, even after Breighton, an old wartime dispersal airfield, was open, remained the parent station. 112 was equipped with 32 Bloodhound Mk 1 missiles and manned by eight officers, 21

SNCOs, 92 airmen supported by five police dogs, and became operational on 7 November that year. To begin with, however, the daily travel for personnel who were billeted at Church Fenton, a round trip of 54 miles, was raising considerable difficulties with the MT section, apart from the strain imposed on the personnel themselves. The precise design criteria of the Bloodhound missiles however prevented the squadron reintroducing the sharksteeth markings.

In 1961 the term Air Defence Missile Squadron was changed to Surface-to-Air Missile (SAM) Squadron and 112 was transferred from 12 Group to 11 Group Fighter Command. Sqn Ldr Shaw handed over to Sqn Ldr M Kaye in August 1962, who, in turn, handed over to Sqn Ldr M A MacKenzie in January 1964. On 8 November that year HQ Fighter Command announced plans to disband the squadron once more and at the end of the year operations ceased. On 31 March 1964, RAF Breighton was closed.

This disbandment was only temporary as on 8 November that year 112 re-emerged as a SAM Sqn equipped with Bloodhound Mk 2 missiles based at RAF Woodhall Spa. The squadron became operational on the 4 January 1966 under the control of the Supreme Allied Commander in Europe (SACEUR), with Sqn Ldr G Middlebrook in command. His tour expired in October that year and his place was taken by Sqn Ldr J R Davies. In 1967 112 was informed that it was to be transferred to RAF Episkopi, in Cyprus, as part of the Air Defence System there and in September the equipment sailed in the *SS African Prince*, with an Advance Party flying from RAF Lyneham. The squadron became operational once more on 1 January 1968. In March, however, there was a move to Paramali West.

On 5 July 1969 command of the squadron was transferred to Sqn Ldr L J Wright and that month the squadron completed 25 years qualifying service and became eligible for a squadron standard. The submission was made to Her Majesty on 1 April 1971. In November the previous year an Australian Air Force detachment, commanded by Sqn Ldr J L Hulbert, RAAF, was formed alongside 112 to become familiar with the operation of the Bloodhound. On 29 September 1972 the squadron standard, proudly bearing eight battle honours, was presented to 112 by Air Marshal Sir Derek Hodgkinson, KCB, CBE, DFC, AFC., AOC-in-C Middle East, with Flt Lt N M Pedley as standard bearer. On that occasion, as can be seen from photographs, the Bloodhound missile that was also on parade, bore sharksteeth markings.

On 4 October 1972 Sqn Ldt Wright handed over command to Sqn Ldr B Leefarr but on 1 July 1975 112 Squadron was finally disbanded without, one might add with some satisfaction, ever having fired a missile in anger.

The squadron colours are laid up in Ely Cathedral in Cambridgeshire.

POSTSCRIPT

When this history was first undertaken, about 30 years ago, it was found that many of the officers and airmen who had taken part in the events of 1917 to 1919 and 1939 to 1945 were still around. Today, in the natural order of things, hardly any of the men from the Great War are still alive and those from the Second World War are getting elderly. Without the evidence supplied by people such as Nan Ricketts, C J Chabot, A C S 'Earwig' Irwin, J I Blackburn, A B Yuille, A W James and J Tucker there would have been very little to say about the squadron in the time it was at Throwley.

Throwley, after all, was where this story began and the author has visited it several times. It was one of the group of airfields that were strung along the North Downs and almost all these have reverted to agriculture – Biggin Hill and Detling being exceptions, at least until recently. In 1957 when Throwley was visited for the first time, the author was astonished at what still remained of this First World War airfield. Bells Forstal Farm, the Officers' Mess, was very much the same while, on the airfield, there were many surprises. The guardroom was, by then, a pebble-dashed private bungalow and the old recreation hall and chapel was used as the Throwley Forstal village clubhouse. A triple line of concrete blocks in the grass showed where No 188 (NT) Squadron's wooden hangar once stood, while, in the fringes of Dodds Willows, a semi-underground ammunition and pyrotechnic store was found (lacking only its roof). The concrete foundations of rows of wooden huts within the woods were still to be seen and, out on the old airfield, the circular concrete compass-swinging base was almost as good as the day it had been built. Further away, in the next field, the firing butts were recognisable and .303 bullets and rounds from .45 revolvers could be prised out of the brickwork. Along the road between Bells Forstal Farm and the guardroom the hedges were still not replanted – they had been grubbed out to permit the aircraft to make a safer approach. An examination of some aerial photographs also showed with astonishing clarity that even after so many years it was still possible to make out depressions in the turf caused by the canvas Bessoneau hangars and the foundations of the new brick hangar that was in the course of construction when the war ended in 1918.

By 1992 though much had changed. The airfield, under grass for so many years, is now cultivated and, in consequence, the compass-swinging base had gone and the foundations for the hangars had been rooted out like rotten teeth and dumped in the fringes of Dodds Willows. The concrete bases for the wooden huts had also vanished, overgrown by grass and bluebells so that they are virtually impossible to trace any longer. Nevertheless there are some strange, enigmatic foundations still remaining and these are said to be dangerous so that local children are warned not to go into the woods for fear of falling into old cellars.

The old guardroom has been rebuilt and enlarged although the present day occupant (who told me that Throwley is pronounced with the middle letters sounding like 'owl') said that the old wooden structure is enclosed within the new brick shell. The Camp Hut has all but disappeared with only the stumps of the chimney stacks remaining. The pyrotechnic store still stands, slowly filling with rubbish but otherwise unchanged. The gun-firing range is falling victim to old age and is slowly collapsing under the stress of tree roots, rabbit burrows and brambles. In the ploughsoil, where the hangars and offices once stood, there is much evidence in the form of half bricks, fragments of old drains and roof tiles and, perhaps on the site of the old squadron workshop, a lump of iron slag.

Nevertheless it takes only a little imagination to stand there and look across to the gap between the old Guardroom and Bells Forstal and see in your mind's eye, the Sopwith Camels coming in over the road, banking round to land.

Appendix A

SQUADRON COMMANDERS & WARTIME FLIGHT COMMANDERS
(decorations listed are contemporary, not subsequent)

Squadron Commanders 1917–1919	**in command from**
1. Captain G Allen	30 7 17
2. Captain B F Moore[1]	21 11 17
3. Major C A Ridley, DSO, MC	3 12 17
4. Major C J Q Brand, DSO, MC	13 2 18
5. Major G W Murlis Green, DSO & bar, MC & 2 bars	9 7 18
6. Major C O Usborne	5 10 18

Flight Commanders 1917–1919
(Note: little information survives for this period)

'A' Flight	**'B' Flight**	**'C' Flight**
Lieut D F Lawson	Lieut Baker	Capt T M B Newton
		Lieut A S C Irwin

Squadron Commanders 1939–1946	**in command from**
1. Sqn Ldr D M Somerville	16 5 39
2. Sqn Ldr A R C Bax (temporary)	1 8 40
3. Sqn Ldr H L I Brown	29 9 40
4. Sqn Ldr L G Schwab	4 4 41
5. Sqn Ldr D W Balden	27 6 41
6. Sqn Ldr H P Cochrane	13 10 41
7. Sqn Ldr F V Morello	28 10 41
8. Sqn Ldr C R Caldwell, DSO, DFC & bar	13 1 42
9. Sqn Ldr P D M Down	27 4 42
10. Sqn Ldr B Drake, DSO, DFC	25 5 42
11. Sqn Ldr G W Garton, DFC	15 1 43
12. Sqn Ldr G H Norton	17 5 43 (Killed)
13. Sqn Ldr P F Illingworth	15 7 43
14. Sqn Ldr W K Watts	29 3 44 (PoW)
15. Sqn Ldr L N Ahern, DSO, DFC	5 5 44
16. Sqn Ldr A P Q Bluett, DFC+bar, C-de-G	20 7 44
17. Sqn Ldr C L Usher	19 3 45

[1] This officer was never in post, selecting to go to the Western Front

18.	Sqn Ldr J S Hart	4 4 45
19.	Sqn Ldr P S Blomfield, DSO, DFC	23 10 45
20.	Sqn Ldr P M Forster, DFC	4 12 45
21.	Sqn Ldr M J Wright, DFC	29 4 46
22.	Sqn Ldr R T Llewellyn, DFM	29 11 46

Flight Commanders 1939–1946 showing dates in command

'**A' Ftl**	'**B' Flt**	'**C' Flt**
1 Flt Lt W C Williams (16 5 39–18 7 40)	Flt Lt K H Savage (16 5 39–31 8 40) [*became 'K' Flt Sept 1940*]	Flt Lt C H Fry (16 5 39–18 5 41) [*became 'B' Flt Sep 1940*]
2 Flt L G Schwab (23 7 40–3 4 41)	Flt Lt J F Fraser (18 5 41–13 6 41)	
3 Flt Lt A R Costello (3 4 41–9 6 41)	Flt Lt H P Cochrane (19 6 41–13 10 41)	
4 Flt Lt H W Harrison (9 6 41–31 10 41)	Flt Lt C F Ambrose (24 11 41–12 12 41)	
5 Flt Lt D F Westenra (3 11 41–7 4 42)	Flt Lt P H Humphreys (? 1 42–12 4 42)	
6 Flt Lt P D M Down (7 4 42–27 4 42)	Flt Lt J P Bartle (12 4 42–27 5 42)	
7 Flt Lt E Dickinson (KIA) (28 4 42–28 5 42)	Flt Lt R M Leu (PoW) (31 5 42–21 6 42)	
8 Flt Lt J A Walker (6 6 42–22 7 42)	Flt Lt G W Garton (24 6 42–16 11 42)	
9 Capt E C Saville (15 8 42–17 5 43)	Flt Lt R R Smith (PoW) (17 11 42–10 3 43)	
10 Flt Lt A P Q Bluett (22 5 43–29 3 44)	Flt Lt C L Usher (14 3 43–18 7 43)	
11 Flt Lt L H Ahern (29 3 44–5 4 44)	Flt Lt W J M Longmore (18 7 44–14 4 44)	
12 Flt Lt E Ross (6 4 44–29 5 44)	Capt A E McLean (22 4 44–28 7 44)	
13 Flt Lt M N Matthias (29 5 44–15 7 44)	Flt Lt R V Hearn (KIA) (29 7 44–18 2 45)	
14 Flt Lt R A Wild (15 7 44–11 11 44)	Flt Lt C L Usher (18 2 45–19 3 45)	
15 Flt Lt P M Forster (11 11 44–20 11 45)	Flt Lt M N Matthias (KIA) (20 3 45–2 4 45)	
16 Flt Lt J Dickerson (20 11 45–2 9 46)	Flt Lt G L Hirons (2 4 45–16 11 45)	
17 Flt Lt S Walker (12 9 46–31 12 46)	Flt Lt E S Hughes (23 11 46–31 12 46)	

Notes:

KIA = Killed in action; PoW = Prisoner of War

Flt Lt Matthias was the only officer to serve both as 'A' and &'B' Flight commander.

Squadron Commanders 1951–1957   **in command from**

1.	Sqn Ldr I D Bolton, DFC	29 5 51
2.	Sqn Ldr F M Hegarty, AFC	24 11 53
3.	Sqn Ldr A R Wilson	1 9 56
4.	Sqn Ldr C J Homes	17 2 57

Squadron Commanders 1960–1975

		in command from
1.	Sqn Ldr P Shaw	1 8 60
2.	Sqn Ldr M Kaye	16 8 62
3.	Sqn Ldr K A MacKenzie	? 1 64
4.	Sqn Ldr G Middlebrook	2 11 64
5.	Sqn Ldr L J Wright	5 7 69
6.	Sqn Ldr B Leefarr	4 10 72

Appendix B

SQUADRON MOVES & LOCATIONS

1917–1919

1.	Formed at Detling, Kent	25 Jul 1917
2.	To Throwley, near Faversham, Kent	30 Jul 1917
3.	Disbanded at Throwley	13 Jun 1919

1939–1946

1.	Formed aboard HMS *Argus*, Portsmouth, Hampshire	16 May 1939
2.	Disembarked at Alexandria, Egypt	25 May 1939
3.	Helwan	
	'B' Flt detached to Sudan 2 Jun 40, sub-flts at Port Sudan, Khartoum, Gedaref, (finally detached from 112 Sqn 31 Aug 1940)	26 May 1939
4.	Maaten Gerawla	19 Jul 1940
	'A' Flt sub-flt detached to Sidi Barrani	3 Aug 1940
	'A' Flt at 'Z' LG	17 Aug 1940
	'C' Flt at 'Y' LG	17 Aug 1940
	'C' Flt at Sidi Barrani (E & W satellites)	30 Aug 1940
5.	Sidi Barrani LG30	3 Sep 1940
6.	Sidi Haneish	7 Sep 1940
	'C' Flt at 'Z' LG	14 Sep 1940
7.	Amiriya	1 Jan 1941
8.	Eleusis (Greece)	23 Jan 1941
9.	Yannina	1 Feb 1941
	'A' Flt to Paramythia	7 Mar 1941
10.	retreat, arrived Agrinion	16 Apr 1941
11.	Hassani (Athens)	17 Apr 1941
12.	aircraft left for Heraklion (Crete)	22 Apr 1941
	ground personnel left for Argos	22 Apr 1941
13.	ground personnel moved to Naphlion	24 Apr 1941
	ground personnel arrived Suda Bay, Crete	25 Apr 1941
14.	'A' Flt to Aboukir, then Lydda, Palestine	29 Apr 1941
15.	Fayid	31 May 1941
	sub-Flt to Haifa	
	detachment from 'A' Flt to Mariyut	11 Aug 1941
16.	Sidi Haneish, LG 102 (via LG92)	12 Sep 1941

17.	Sidi Barrani, LG 110	14 Nov 1941
18.	Fort Maddelena, LG 122	19 Nov 1941
19.	El Adem	19 Dec 1941
20.	Msus	21 Dec 1941
21.	Antelat Satellite	13 Jan 1942
22.	Msus	21 Jan 1942
23.	Mechili	24 Jan 1942
24.	Gazala	28 Jan 1942
25.	El Adem	2 Feb 1942
26.	Gambut Main	5 Feb 1942
27.	El Adem	16 Feb 1942
28.	Gambut Main	17 Feb 1942
	Gambut Satellite No 2	22 Feb 1942–9 Mar 1943
29.	Sidi Azeiz	17 Jun 1942
30.	Sidi Barrani, LG 75	18 Jun 1942
31.	Sidi Haneish, LG 102	24 Jun 1942
32.	El Daba, LG 106	27 Jun 1942
33.	Amiriya, LG 91	28 Jun 1942
34.	Amiriya, LG 175	25 Aug 1942
35.	El Daba, LG 106	6 Nov 1942
36.	Sidi Haneish, LG 115	8 Nov 1942
37.	LG 76 (south-west of Maaten Bagush)	9 Nov 1942
38.	Gazala No 2	15 Nov 1942
39.	Martuba	19 Nov 1942
40.	Belandah No 2 (Alam-el-Gzina)	6 Dec 1942
41.	Hammraiet	9 Jan 1943
42.	Bir Dufan	19 Jan 1943
43.	Castel Benito	25 Jan 1943
44.	El Assa	15 Feb 1943
45.	Neffatia (Tunisia)	8 Mar 1943
46.	Medenine	21 Mar 1943
47.	El Hamma	3 Apr 1943
48.	El Djem	14 Apr 1943
49.	Kairouan	18 Apr 1943
50.	Zuara	21 May 1943
51.	advance detachment to Safi (Malta)	9 Jul 1943
52.	Pachino (Sicily)	18 Jul 1943
53.	Agnone	2 Aug 1943
54.	Grottaglie (Italy)	15 Sep 1943
55.	Brindisi	20 Sep 1943
56.	Bari	23 Sep 1943
57.	Foggia	3 Oct 1943
58.	Mileni	26 Oct 1943
59.	Cutella	30 Jan 1944
60.	San Angelo	23 May 1944
61.	Guidonia	13 Jun 1944
62.	Falerium	24 Jun 1944
63.	Creti	10 Jul 1944
	detachment to Rossignano	15 Aug–16 Aug 1944
64.	Iesi	25 Aug 1944
65.	Fano	18 Nov 1944
66.	Cervia	25 Feb 1945
67.	Lavariano	19 May 1945
68.	Tissano	1 Mar 1946

69.	Lavariano	4 May 1946
70.	Treviso	23 Sep 1946
	detachment to Lavariano	11 Nov–18 Nov 1946
71.	Disbanded at Treviso	31 Dec 1946

1951–1957

1.	Formed at Fassberg, West Germany	12 May 1951
2.	Jever	7 Mar 1952
3.	Brüggen	6 Jul 1953
4.	Disbanded at Brüggen	31 May 1957

1960–1975

1.	Formed at Church Fenton, Lincolnshire	1 Aug 1960
2.	Breighton	7 Nov 1960
3.	Disbanded at Breighton	31 Mar 1964
4.	Re-formed at Woodhall Spa	2 Nov 1964
5.	Episkopi, Cyprus	1 Oct 1967
6.	Paramali	20 Jun 1969
7.	Disbanded at Paramali	1 Jul 1975

Appendix C

NOMINAL ROLL OF SQUADRON OFFICERS & NCO AIRCREW

Abbreviations used:

Adjt	Squadron adjutant
AFC	Air Force Cross
(Aus), (Can), (NZ) (SAAF)	Dominion Pilots
BNF	Body never found
CO	Squadron Commander
DFC	Distinguished Flying Cross
DSO	Distinguished Service Order
DFM	Distinguished Flying Medal
Engr Off	Engineering Officer
Eqpt Off	Equipment Officer
F/Cadet	Flight Cadet
Flt Cdr	Flight Commander
Gnd Def Off	Ground Defence Officer
IO	Intelligence Officer
MBE	Member of the Order of the British Empire
MC	Military Cross
MO	Medical Officer
(Notts & Derby)	parent regiment
5×V (example)	5 victories in aerial combat*
PoW	prisoner of war
Tech Off	Technical Office
WO	Warrant Officer
† accid	accidentally killed

* only victories gained on 112 noted

Part 1 1917–1919

Rank	Name	Service No	Posted In	Posted Out	Remarks
Lieut	Aitken	?	?	?	
Capt	G Allen	?	30 7 17	21 11 17	CO, (Connaught Rangers)
Capt	Baker	?	?	?	'B' Flt Cdr
Lieut	F B Baragar	?	?	20 5 19	(Can)

Rank	Name	Service No	Posted In	Out	Remarks
Lieut	L A A Bernard	?	?	?	
F/Cadet	J I Blackburn	?	?	?	
Lieut	J G Blane	?	?	18 5 19	
Lieut	G N Blennerhassett	?	?	?	MC,
Major	C J Q Brand	?	13 2 18	9 7 18	CO, DSO, MC, DFC, 1×V
Lieut	T Broome	?	?	?	DFC, AFC
Lieut	G Cameron	?	?	6 5 19	
Lieut	E W Carmichael	?	?	30 4 19	
Capt	C J Chabot	?	?	17 4 19	
Lieut	R N Chandler	?	?	?	(NZ)
Lieut	C Cockerall	?	?	?	AFC,
Lieut	J Collier	?	?	?	DFC
Lieut	W J Corney	?	?	?	attach from 143 Sqn
2/Lieut	G J Cross	?	?	?	
Lieut	Davies	?	?	?	
2/Lieut	C Edwards	?	?	20 5 19	Aviation Instructor
Lieut	Frampton	?	?	?	
Lieut	A E Gates	?	?	6 5 19	
Lieut	Gilbertson	?	?	?	
Lieut	E A Halford	?	?	20 5 19	Observer
Lieut	G S L Hayward	?	?	18 5 19	
2/Lieut	E Hazell	?	?	20 5 19	
2/Lieut	E G Hill	?	?	20 5 19	
Lieut	F J Horrell	?	?	20 5 19	Aviation Instructor
Lieut	R E Horsfield	?	?	1 5 19	(Notts & Derby Regt)
Lieut	E W F Hopgood	?	?	14 10 18	(Can Gren Gds) † accid
Lieut	A C S Irwin	?	? 10 17	20 5 19	'C' Flt Cdr
2/Lieut	E J Jordan	?	?	19 3 19	Administrative
Lieut	B J Kirchner	?	?	22 3 19	
Lieut	D F Lawson	?	?	?	'A' Flt Cdr
F/Cadet	T R Mace	?	?	3 9 19	
Capt	T J C Martyn	?	30 5 19	?	MC, AFC, Act. Adjt.
2/Lieut	J T Mitchell	?	?	24 1 19	(Can) † accid
Capt	B F Moore	?	21 11 17	3 12 17	CO designate
Lieut	H A Morley	?	?	6 5 19	
Major	G W Murlis Green	?	9 7 18	5 10 18	CO, DSO+bar, MC+2 bars, *Karageorge*,
2/Lieut	A F Nethey	?	?	?	Eqpt Off
Capt	T M B Newton	?	?	?	'C' Flt Cdr
Lieut	C Olliver	?	?	?	Wireless Off
Lieut	W Partridge	?	?	20 5 19	(Can)
Capt	H S Preston	?	6 5 19	?	
Major	C A Ridley	?	3 12 17	13 2 18	CO, DSO, MC
Lieut	R T Robbins	?	?	?	Administrative
F/Cadet	A B Robertson	?	?	?	
Lieut	E T Rogers	?	?	20 5 19	
Lieut	Scotcher	?	?	?	
Lieut	O M Sutton	?	?	?	
2/Lieut	Turton	?	?	?	
Major	C O Usborne	?	5 10 18	13 6 18	(Can) CO
Lieut	G J Wilde	?	?	20 5 19	

Rank	Name	Service No	Posted In	Posted Out	Remarks
Lieut	D Wills	?	?	?	
Lieut	C F Wolley Dod	?	25 6 18	? 10 18	(1 Sherwood Foresters)
Lieut	Wykes	?	?	?	
Lieut	A B Yuille	?	30 3 18	14 6 18	DFC,

Part 2 1939–1946

Rank	Name	Service No	Posted In	Posted Out	Remarks
Lieut	A van Aardt	580774V	14 4 45	1 8 45	(SAAF)
Flt Lt	R J Abrahams	37663	29 8 40	4 3 41	V×2½, 1 damaged
Plt Off	R A Acworth	40496	16 5 39 / 25 10 41	28 10 40 / 11 11 41	Fg Off; V×7½, 1 prob
Sgt	E Adye	776184	14 4 42	11 6 42	V×1½; Missing, returned
Flt Sgt	J B Agnew	?	5 6 42	31 3 43	WO, Plt Off, V×1, 2 prob, 1 damaged
Fg Off	L N Ahern	X402781	17 9 43	31 7 44	Flt Lt, 'A' Flt Cdr, Sqn Ldr, CO, DSO, DFC (Aus) V×½, 2 damaged
Plt Off	G F Allison	402782	3 5 42	27 2 43	(Aus), V×1 prob
Sgt	J Alves	1001427	31 10 41	12 12 41	PoW, released 1944
Fg Off	C F Ambrose	42583	21 11 41	12 12 41	V×2 prob
Sgt	P W Amis	1804379	27 3 45	17 4 45	
Plt Off	E Atkinson	J8414	25 5 42	4 6 42	Missing, BNF
Sgt	W Bain	518517	7 6 41	15 10 41	
Plt Off	A C Baker	64892	? 2 42	22 8 42	V×1, 1 damaged; DFC
Sqn Ldr	D W Balden	33154	27 6 41	13 10 41	CO
Sgt	A Banks	1607992	9 8 44	29 8 44	PoW, murdered 20 Dec 44 George Cross
Plt Off	E T Banks	40978	16 5 39	13 3 41	Fg Off, 2×V, 6 damaged, 1 prob, † accid
Fg Off	G P Barclay	78223	4 1 41	5 6 41	MO
Sgt	Barlow	RCA83050	? 8 42	28 9 42	PoW, safe Aug 1944
Plt Off	H J M Barnes	122407	19 1 43	15 2 44	Flt Lt
Plt Off	J S Barrow	118054	? 6 42	22 7 42	V×2 damaged; Killed
Plt Off	J P Bartle	406171	31 8 41	27 5 42	(Aus) Flt Lt, 'B' Flt Cdr 4½×V*, 2 damaged, 1 prob
Fg Off	S P Bartlett	40875	17 11 40	12 2 41	
Plt Off	L L Bartley	42182	30 7 40	31 5 41	PoW Crete, escaped 1943 2×V
Sgt	P O Bates	779038	2 4 41	5 9 41	
Sqn Ldr	A R C Bax	33018	1 8 40	24 6 40	Temporary CO
Plt Off	R J Bennett	40982	16 5 39	31 5 41	PoW Crete, 3×V, 1 prob
Sgt	R J K Bird	180115	22 7 45	22 11 45	Flt Sgt
Lieut	W A Blackburn	206143V	26 4 45	28 7 45	(SAAF)
Sgt	P M Blair	1583246	5 6 44	5 1 45	Plt Off
Sgt	W R Blake	R97463	14 1 43	? 6 43	(Can)
2/Lieut	E F Blatchford	580779V	5 10 44	22 5 45	(SAAF), Lieut
Lieut	W D Blom	581737V	16 4 45	26 7 45	(SAAF) † accid
Sqn Ldr	P S Blomfield	47767	23 10 45	4 12 45	CO, DSO, DFC

* Bartle claims 2 additional confirmed, but there is no record of these.

Rank	Name	Service No	Posted In	Out	Remarks
Flt Lt	A P Q Bluett	43539	22 5 43	29 3 44	'A' Flt Cdr
			20 7 44	19 3 45	Sqn Ldr, CO, 2nd tour; DFC + bar, Croix de Guerre
Flt Sgt	V E R Booth	1806930	20 5 46	28 11 46	
Fg Off	W A Booth	33358	16 5 39	13 2 40	
Lieut	A C J Bosch	32874V	17 1 45	28 7 45	(SAAF)
Plt Off	N Bowker	5R89773	15 2 41	27 12 41	(Can), Flt Lt, DFC, PoW 10×V, 1 damaged
Fg Off	I D D Brett	115330	1 7 45	5 10 45	IO
Sgt	L W Brierly	1581057	19 6 44	24 8 44	(later killed)
Sgt	D B Brown	1381428	2 9 42	9 12 43	Flt Sgt, WO, V×1 prob
Plt Off	E H Brown	41777	30 10 40	14 4 41	Fg Off, V×1, 1 damaged
Flt Lt	H L I Brown	37060	4 9 40	3 4 41	Sqn Ldr, CO, V×3, 1 damaged
Flt Sgt	W D Brown	R86267	? 10 42	19 9 43	(Can), WO, Missing, BNF, V×2, 1 probable, 2 damaged
Flt Sgt	C T O Bruce	528156	1 5 44	10 5 44	
Plt Off	D A Bruce	80213	27 5 42	10 3 43	Fg Off, Missing, BNF V×1, 1 probable, 1 damaged
Plt Off	P C L Brunton	89774	14 1 41	3 2 42	Fg Off, killed, V×1, 2 damaged
Plt Off	J A Burcham	119713	24 2 43	7 3 44	Fg Off, PoW
Sgt	H G Burney	402343	8 8 41	30 5 42	Plt Off, Missing, BNF, V×4½
Plt Off	J H Bullock	293135	15 10 41	18 8 42	(Aus) Cypher Officer
Plt Off	A R Butcher	70104	16 5 39	30 10 40	
Flt Sgt	W H Butterworth	1474220	26 9 45	20 6 46	
Sqn Ldr	C R Caldwell	402107	13 1 42	27 4 42	(Aus), CO, DFC+bar, V×2½
Flt Lt	A C Camm	100468	28 5 45	10 11 45	MO
Sgt	J R Carr	1620942	24 5 44	2 6 44	Killed
Fg Off	G Carroll	101105	5 6 41	14 3 43	IO
Sgt	K F Carson	404233	? 10 41	16 6 42	(Aus) Plt Off, V×1½, ½ prob, 1 damaged, PoW
Sgt	W E Carson	404168	? 10 41	? 1 42	(Aus)
Sgt	Cassell	402307	18 2 42	12 6 42	(Aus) Flt Sgt.
Plt Off	R H Chapman	36161	16 5 39	10 9 40	
Fg Off	L C Cherry	114723	14 2 43	6 3 44	Flt Lt (killed 1955)
Sgt	R H Christie	?	? 11 41	14 4 42	V×3, 1 probable, 1 damaged
Lieut	H F Churchill	207324V	3 1 44	5 6 44	(SAAF) PoW
Sgt	G G Clark	1624052	6 5 44	9 11 44	Plt Off, killed
2/Lieut	D A H Clarke	328908V	28 5 44	30 9 44	(SAAF)
Fg Off	E J Clarke	56853	28 8 46	31 12 46	
Sgt	N A Clarke	1169208	22 2 42	13 1 43	Plt Off
Plt Off	R H Clarke	40513	16 5 39	31 10 40	Fg Off, V×1 dam; Missing BNF
Sgt	K M Cockram	1425541	3 6 43	24 6 44	
Plt Off	H P Cochrane	40991	16 5 39	13 10 41	Flt Lt, 'B' Flt Cdr, Sqn Ldr CO; V×5, 1 prob, 2 damaged
Sgt	W E Cocks	1393866	17 9 43	7 4 44	V×1, F/Sgt; killed.
Sgt	W E C Cordwell	1260984	20 1 42	1 5 42	V×1
Lieut	A Colenbrander	102267	10 6 40	? 7 40	(SAAF) attached
Plt Off	A R Costello	41781	30 10 40	6 10 41	V×1
			? 2 42	1 5 42	Flt Lt
Flt Lt	E W Crews	120425	14 2 44	17 3 45	MO

Rank	Name	Service No	Posted In	Posted Out	Remarks
Plt Off	J M S Crichton	J5032	25 5 42	11 1 43	(Can) V×2, 2 damaged; Fg Off, PoW
Sgt	A T Crocker	1259818	? 1 42	4 1 42	† accid
Sgt	W J Crowther	1670847	5 6 44	30 12 44	Plt Off
Plt Off	B A F Cuddon	115619	1 5 42	11 12 42	V×1 prob; Missing, BNF
Plt Off	L H Curphey	J7769	5 7 42	13 1 43	(American), Fg Off, V×3, 1 prob, 1 damaged; Missing BNF
Sgt	L G Daniell	1602798	5 6 44	14 1 45	Plt Off
Flt Lt	C W W Darwin	42050	21 2 42	21 4 42	
Lieut	W O Davenport	542975V	30 4 45	28 7 45	(SAAF)
Sgt	J V Davey	R74906	22 2 42	18 5 42	(Can) Missing, BNF
Sgt	R D Davies	1422019	19 6 44	28 6 44	Injured, posted
Sgt	G F Davis	1614505	1 5 44	31 5 44	Killed
Plt Off	T H Davison	39863	16 9 39	12 3 40	
Lieut	J K N Dawes	543152V	18 4 45	28 7 45	(SAAF)
Lieut	G N Dawson	580784V	16 4 45	28 7 45	(SAAF)
Sgt	R DeBourke	R79049	10 7 42	10 3 43	(Can) WOII, Missing BNF V× 3, 1 prob
Plt Off	R J Deeble	181078	? 10 44	6 11 44	Killed
Sgt	J Derma	784742	9 2 42	5 5 42	(Pole)
Sgt	J M Dick	1672409	5 6 44	1 7 44	(later killed)
Flt Lt	J Dickerson	150325	1 1 46	2 9 46	'A' Flt Cdr
Plt Off	E Dickinson	64920	? 12 41	28 5 42	Flt Lt, 'A' Flt Cdr; V×1, 1 damaged, missing, BNF
Sgt	G M Donaldson	580315	16 3 40	30 5 41	V×5, 2 prob
Sgt	A T Donkin	1055285	23 11 41	8 2 42	Killed
Flt Lt	Dorrington	?	? 4 42	27 5 42	
2/Lieut	E W Dottridge	328288V	21 12 43	23 7 44	(SAAF)
Sgt	A Dowling	1803433	21 5 44	24 8 44	(later killed)
Flt Lt	P D M Down	39934	22 3 42	21 5 42	'A' Flt Cdr, Sqn Ldr, CO
Sqn Ldr	B Drake	39095	25 5 42	15 1 43	CO, DSO, DFC+bar; V×13, 2 probables, 2 damaged
Sgt	R A Drew	407415	30 10 41	17 6 42	F/Sgt, V×2; Missing, BNF
Flt Sgt	R W Drown	1190809	24 4 43	19 5 44	WO, V×1 damaged
2/Lieut	S de K Dudley	?	10 6 40	? 7 40	(SAAF) attached
Plt Off	B B E Duff	40684	16 5 39	12 11 40	
Plt Off	N F Duke	61054	12 11 41	22 4 42	V×5½. 1½ prob, 2 damaged
WO	J S Duncan	R131740	19 9 44	11 1 45	(Can) Injured
Flt Lt	E J F Eberle	110805	2 5 42	2 6 43	MO, MBE
Plt Off	F F J Edwards	80140	14 4 42	13 6 42	V×1; Killed
Capt	G H Edwards	11208V	22 4 45	26 7 45	(SAAF) † accid
Sgt	P T Elliott	404618	30 10 41	9 3 42	(Aus), wounded 21.2.42, killed
Sgt	G W Elwell	1160921	20 1 42	8 2 42	V×1; Killed, BNF
Plt Off	D V S Evans	40047	16 5 39	31 8 40	
Plt Off	E Evans	61615	27 6 42	9 11 44	Adjt., Fg Off, Flt Lt, Sqn Ldr
Sgt	R B Evans	?	20 1 42	1 5 42	V×1 prob, wounded 14.3.42
Sgt	G P Eyears	575856	7 7 45	26 7 45	† accid
Plt Off	I G A Faulk	83803	30 7 40	2 5 41	Cypher Officer
Lieut	D W Featherstone	103902V	2 11 44	24 7 45	(SAAF), Capt
Sgt	A H Ferguson	404542	30 10 42	20 12 41	Killed, BNF
Plt Off	J R Fisher	118192	3 5 42	18 5 42	Killed, BNF

Rank	Name	Service No	Posted In	Posted Out	Remarks
Plt Off	V D Fletcher	88518	24 11 40	8 5 42	IO
Flt Lt	P M Forster	106650	19 6 44	29 4 46	'A' Flt Cdr, Sqn Ldr, CO, DFC
2/Lieut	W E Foster	207365V	21 12 43	23 4 44	(SAAF), Lieut., killed
Plt Off	J F Fraser	70229	16 5 39	13 6 41	Flt Lt, 'B' Flt Cdr, DFC, V×8, 2 damaged
Flt Lt	C H Fry	40047	16 5 39	18 5 41	(Aus), 'C', later 'B' Flt Cdr PoW Crete, DFC, V×5 2 prob, 1 damaged
Plt Off	Gale	?	8 5 42	25 5 42	IO
Plt Off	K R Gardener	103554	12 6 42	26 10 42	Fg Off, killed
Flt Lt	G W Garton	67034	24 6 42	16 11 42	'B' Flt Cdr, DFC; V×1½, 2 prob, 1 damaged
			15 1 43	13 5 43	Sqn Ldr, CO, 2nd tour.
Lieut	E J G Gauntlett	542882V	8 3 45	28 7 45	(SAAF) (killed post-war)
Flt Lt	F Gazda	PO414	10 2 42	5 5 42	(Pole)
Fg Off	R Geddes	162242	23 7 45	20 6 46	Flt Lt
2/Lieut	H H Geraty	?	27 9 40	19 11 41	(SAAF)
Sgt	R J A Gibson	1569002	5 8 45	15 11 46	F/Sgt
Sgt	F D Glasgow	402469	? 11 41	25 11 41	(NZ), Killed, BNF
Plt Off	A J Goar	75723	7 4 40	30 8 40	IO
Sgt	D C Goodwin	1601215	5 6 44	? 11 44	Injured 9.8.44
Plt Off	E D Gosschalk	75940	2 3 40	3 11 41	Eqpt Off
Sgt	G W Graham	1522182	10 7 44	23 2 45	Plt Off
Plt Off	J O Gray	J16543	18 9 43	31 7 44	(American) Fg Off; V×1 dam
Fg Off	A Gray-Worcester	33338	16 5 39	18 7 40	† accid
Sgt	D F Greaves	?	21 2 42	20 10 42	V×1 prob, 1 dam.; PoW
Sgt	P L Greaves	1808528	11 12 44	23 1 45	V×1 prob, 1 dam., Missing
			2 5 45	13 5 45	(returned) † accid
Plt Off	P O V Green	41015	16 5 39	31 8 40	V×1
Sgt	J H Greenaway	184791	6 5 44	2 9 44	Plt Off, killed
Sgt	R Gregory	1807193	7 7 45	28 11 46	F/Sgt
Sgt	S Grondowski	782063	15 2 42	5 5 42	(Pole), (killed later)
Plt Off	J L Groves	42305	30 7 40	6 12 41	DFC, V×6, 5 damaged
Sgt	D W Grubb	1323923	26 4 44	22 5 44	PoW
Plt Off	R D Guess	J10277	18 1 43	4 8 43	(Can) V×2; Flt Lt, PoW.
Fg Off	K C Gundry	81371	? 4 42	22 5 42	Killed, BNF
Plt Off	J Hamlyn	40109	16 5 39	31 8 40	V×1
2/Lieut	H J Hanreck	207359V	6 12 43	29 7 44	(SAAF); V×1 damaged;
Plt Off	C J Harman	170726	28 8 45	20 9 45	
Fg Off	L A Harris	184819	19 8 45	17 11 45	
Plt Off	H W Harrison	40910	3 2 40	31 10 41	Flt Lt, 'A' Flt Cdr
Sqn Ldr	J S Hart	41696	4 4 45	19 8 45	(Can) CO, DFC
Plt Off	J M Hayward	40111	16 5 39	31 8 40	(killed later)
Sgt	A E Headland	1584911	7 7 45	27 11 45	† accid
Fg Off	R V Hearn	102547	22 5 43	17 11 43	
			29 7 44	18 2 45	2nd tour, Flt Lt; 'B' Flt Cdr; V×1, DFC+bar, killed
Plt Off	P R M v.d. Heijden	40190	16 5 39	28 7 40	injured
Plt Off	J E Helfield	75717	22 8 40	?	IO

Rank	Name	Service No	Posted In	Out	Remarks
Flt Sgt	G L Hirons	1190809	26 9 43	21 5 44	
			31 12 44	16 11 45	2nd tour; Fg Off; Flt Lt, 'B' Flt Cdr; DFC
Sgt	B P Hoare	404365	26 11 41	8 2 42	Killed, BNF
Sgt	D Hogg	748555	14 4 42	21 10 42	V×1, damaged, PoW
Plt Off	R P Hogg	176313	12 2 42	?	Gnd Def Off
Fg Off	A P Hollis	163285	19 8 45	27 6 46	
Sgt	N Holman	932152	15 11 41	11 2 42	Killed
Fg Off	T Hooper	264704	5 12 43	15 7 45	(Aus), IO, Flt Lt
Sgt	E D Holmes	403927	31 5 43	12 2 44	† accid., BNF
Fg Off	H A Horden	120778	14 3 43	14 5 44	
Sgt	J T Hounsell	1268030	6 2 43	22 4 43	F/Sgt, killed, BNF
Sgt	W E Houston	402473	? 11 41	12 12 41	(NZ), killed, BNF
Flt Sgt	D J Howe	RCA74045	? 10 42	?	(Can)
Plt Off	D E de la Hoyde	40517	16 5 39	3 11 40	
2/Lieut	J C Hoyle	282449V	3 8 44	23 8 44	(SAAF), Lieut, killed
Flt Lt	E S Hughes	144000	23 11 46	31 12 46	'B' Flt Cdr
Fg Off	P H Humphreys	84961	12 11 41	22 4 42	Flt Lt, 'B' Flt Cdr; V×1½, 1 prob, 1 damaged
Plt Off	E C Huntley	173645	14 6 44	11 11 44	Eqpt Off
Sgt	D Ibbotson	1107760	16 6 42	12 10 42	Plt Off; V×1, 2 prob, 1 dam.
2/Lieut	W J Illidge	328963V	16 5 44	11 12 44	(SAAF), Lieut
Sqn Ldr	P F Illingworth	35929	15 7 43	30 5 44	CO, (Missing 22.3.44–5.4.44)
Flt Sgt	G A Ivatt	1876657	28 3 46	31 12 46	
Sgt	Jackson	RCA75046	22 1 42	27 2 42	(Can) Killed
Fg Off	W Jander	76746	8 2 42	21 2 42	(Pole), wounded (killed later)
Plt Off	R J D Jeffries	406179	31 8 41	13 12 41	V×1, 1 prob, killed, BNF
Sgt	J L Jellett	1318164	26 9 43	31 7 44	F/Sgt
Sgt	S C Johnson	404504	30 10 41	5 1 42	(Aus), † accid
Plt Off	Johnson	?	? 7 42	24 7 42	V×2 damaged, Missing[1]
Sgt	F K Johnstone	711002	8 8 41	20 8 41	† accid
Lieut	A H Jones	524665V	29 6 44	1 8 44	(SAAF) Killed
Sgt	A W Jones	1621438	9 8 44	30 8 44	F/Sgt
Sgt	J K Jones	170728	28 8 45	20 9 45	
Sgt	O G Jones	570249	19 11 44	11 3 45	F/Sgt, killed
Fg Off	C Joseph	78653	20 8 41	1 5 42	MO
Plt Off	H B Kirk	70808	16 5 39	31 8 40	
Sgt	M Klibanksi	7765616	21 7 45	? 8 45	
Plt Off	K H Knapik	P1302	10 2 42	26 5 42	(Pole), Fg Off
Fg Off	F Knoll	P0768	8 2 42	10 7 42	(Pole) Killed
Sgt	M H Lamont	776196	? 9 42	22 4 43	V×1 probable, 1 damaged; Killed, BNF
Plt Off	J T Lean	74163	25 4 40	23 8 40	Armament Officer
Sgt	J G R Lecours	R79289	? 10 42	5 2 43	(Can) V×1, 1 damaged, Missing, BNF
Flt Lt	K N T Lee	72998	30 5 42	7 7 42	
Sgt	F C Lees	1577276	11 5 45	7 3 46	F/Sgt
Plt Off	H T Legg	?	?	5 6 43	Engr Off, Flt Lt
2/Lieut	W D Lemkus	581884V	18 4 45	28 7 45	(SAAF)

[1] No more is known about this pilot, he is mentioned a couple of times before being shot down.

Rank	Name	Service No	Posted In	Posted Out	Remarks
Flt Sgt	G Lenton	1529520	21 2 46	5 5 46	WO
Sgt	R M Leu	404178	? 9 41	21 6 42	(Aus) DFM, Flt Lt, 'B' Flt Cdr, V×6, 1 prob, PoW
Plt Off	E D Lewis	?	15 3 40	?	IO
Lieut	C J Liebenberg	542464V	29 6 44	12 10 44	PoW, escaped
Plt Off	R T Littlewood	199527	13 8 45	30 1 46	DFM
Plt Off	T Livingstone	61167	27 8 42	20 6 43	V×1, 1 prob, 2 damaged
Sqn Ldr	R T Llewellyn	47380	29 11 46	31 12 46	CO, DFM
Flt Lt	W J M Longmore	40723	18 7 43	14 4 44	'B' Flt Cdr
Plt Off	J E Loree	J7471	5 7 42	28 8 42	(Can) V×1; PoW
Flt Lt	P W Lovell	42351	30 6 44	21 9 44	
Lieut	J R Lund	329087V	29 6 44	22 10 44	(SAAF) Killed
Flt Lt	L G Lunn	157825	7 12 46	31 12 46	
Sgt	J M MacAuley	RCA77152	1 8 42	2 7 43	(Can) V×1, 2 damaged
Plt Off	D G H MacDonald	76160	20 9 40	7 11 41	Fg Off, V×1 prob, 1 dam.
Plt Off	R H MacDonald	42316	30 7 40	9 3 41	Injured, died
Fg Off	R H Madgett	48202	16 3 45	22 1 45	Engr Off, MBE
Plt Off	T Magner	83097	25 7 40	4 7 42	Adjt
Sgt	K R Mann	1332895	5 6 44	5 8 44	Killed
Fg Off	W H E Marriott	100167	7 11 44	? 1 46	Adjt., Flt Lt
Sgt	A Martin	RCA97115	28 8 42	30 10 42	(Can)
Sgt	T A Marsden	993301	3 10 42	27 2 43	V×1 prob: killed, BNF
Lieut	A Q Masson	P1026561	10 6 40	? 7 40	(SAAF) attached
Fg Off	M N Matthias	119867	23 4 43	15 7 44	Flt Lt, 'A' Flt Cdr
			22 2 45	2 4 45	2nd tour, 'B' Flt Cdr, killed
Fg Off	C Matusiak	P0304	8 2 42	12 2 42	(Pole) † accid
Flt Lt	L McBryde	407005	7 5 43	3 12 43	(Aus)
Sgt	E McCormack	404181	? 9 41	16 9 41	(Aus) † accid (attached from 274 Sqn)
Sgt	J H McDermott	776098	24 2 43	23 7 43	
Lieut	G McFie	524252V	29 6 44	25 9 44	Killed
Fg Off	D McGregor	75359	22 4 40	5 7 40	MO
Plt Off	M McIntyre	46140	23 6 41	22 4 42	Engr Off
Flt Lt	R H McKenzie	79346	29 5 43	18 2 44	MO
Capt	A E McLean	47852V	22 4 44	28 7 44	'B' Flt Cdr, DFC,
Sgt	D N McQueen	402530	30 10 41	15 2 42	(Aus) V×1 damaged
Sgt	C F McWilliams	404185	20 5 41	28 10 41	(Aus)
Sgt	K F Middlemist	1376378	13 11 42	15 9 43	WO, killed
Sgt	E H Mills	404180	? 7 41	31 8 41	(Aus) † accid
Fg Off	J A Milne	42758	12 6 42	26 6 42	Injured, posted
Plt Off	F E Mitchell	199414	4 1 46	3 4 46	Fg Off
Flt Sgt	P A Mitchell	1621361	5 8 45	25 6 46	
Plt Off	S S Mitchell	41348	25 5 42	31 5 42	Killed, BNF
Fg Off	P F Mollan	201330	28 6 46	31 12 46	
Sgt	W Money	1378132	24 8 42	24 6? 42	V×1, 1 damaged
Plt Off	W N Monteith	70471	17 8 40	28 6 41	PoW
Sqn Ldr	F V Morello	39256	28 10 41	4 1 42	CO
Sgt	J H Morrison	41144	18 8 42	30 9 42	(NZ) injured, posted
Sgt	W E Mould	1623064	3 8 44	5 10 44	
Sgt	W D Musther	1399599	19 6 44	29 3 45	Plt Off

Rank	Name	Service No	Posted In	Out	Remarks
Sgt	R H Newton	411437	25 5 42	? 4 43	(NZ) F/Sgt; V×1 prob,
			1 7 44	25 12 44	2nd tour, Flt Lt, DFC
WO	N R N Nichol	1027201	28 9 45	2 2 46	
Lieut	J H Nixon	542313V	15 3 45	20 4 45	(SAAF) Killed
Sgt	G S Nordstrand	41220	3 6 43	16 5 44	(NZ)
Sgt	L W North	1682639	6 5 44	14 10 44	
Fg Off	L W North	187358	8 1 46	19 3 46	
Sqn Ldr	G H Norton	89308	17 5 43	13 7 43	CO, killed, BNF
2/Lieut	P Nuyten	207347V	21 12 43	16 9 44	(SAAF)
Sgt	J H Oliver	R84086	? 2 43	10 3 43	(Can) WO, killed, BNF
Lieut	E D Oosthuizen	205796V	2 11 44	28 7 45	(SAAF) Capt
Plt Off	L M Page	78155	20 5 40	18 8 40	Cypher Officer
Fg Off	R Page	49511	22 4 44	16 3 45	Engr Off
Lieut	R D Park	53052V	2 4 45	26 7 45	(SAAF) † accid
Plt Off	F E Parker	A406260	31 8 41	15 10 41	(Aus) injured, posted
Plt Off	T E Parker	190332	17 7 45	10 9 45	
Sgt	C J Parkinson	1800971	24 5 44	29 5 44	Killed
2/Lieut	D G Paul	543129V	16 11 44	28 7 45	(SAAF) Lieut
Fg Off	J H Pepper	103294	6 8 42	14 12 43	Tech Off, Flt Lt
Sgt	B H Peters	A409439	26 9 43	31 7 44	(Aus) F/Sgt; V×½
Plt Off	H Phillips	J8653	24 7 42	11 11 42	(Can) V×1, 2 prob, 1 dam. injured, posted
Fg Off	N L H Piper	181506	28 8 45	20 9 45	
Fg Off	W E S Pittuck	141721	13 12 43	27 3 44	Eqpt Off
Sgt	W E Pollock	RCA63166	21 8 42	21 11 42	V×1, 1 damaged; returned after forced-landing, prob posted
Sgt	A E Prain	1366355	14 3 43	22 4 43	Killed, BNF
Lieut	D F Prentice	329061V	3 8 44	30 10 44	PoW, escaped 8.5.45
Fg Off	W B Price-Owen	39829	1 1 40	18 8 40	
Flt Sgt	D M Preston	1787395	22 7 45	? 8 46	WO
Plt Off	I G Probert	163311	7 7 45	22 11 46	Adjt, Fg Off
Sgt	G Rae	1179958	30 9 42	2 10 42	† accid
Sgt	P L Rees	930745	6 5 44	30 5 44	PoW
Fg Off	M H Reid	57535	28 6 46	31 12 46	
2/Lieut	G A P Reynolds	580826V	26 10 44	28 2 45	(SAAF) Lieut
Plt Off	S J Rhodes	108850	4 9 42	1 6 43	Gnd Def Off
Lieut	E N Roberts	32870V	26 10 44	12 4 45	(SAAF) killed
Flt Sgt	T P Roberts	1623387	25 3 45	12 4 45	Killed, BNF
Sgt	R B Robinson	576014	19 11 44	10 11 45	F/Sgt, Plt Off
Fg Off	J J Roney	156137	2 7 44	16 11 44	† accid
Fg Off	A M Ross	40142	16 5 39	9 12 40	
Fg Off	E Ross	115030	24 2 43	29 5 44	Flt Lt, 'A' Flt Cdr
Sgt	B T Routledge	1324827	26 10 44	14 8 46	F/Sgt, Plt Off, Fg Off
Sgt	A G Rowe	1336895	3 6 43	31 7 44	F/Sgt
Plt Off	G W Rutherford	J16545	29 4 43	17 11 43	(Can) Fg Off
Sgt	J W Rozanski	P1818	9 2 42	18 5 42	(Pole) (killed later)
Plt Off	J P Sabourin	J3519	12 11 41	27 12 41	V×3, 3 damaged; crashed, posted (killed later)
Plt Off	J H Sanderson	39189	16 5 39	31 8 40	
Plt Off	K R Sands	406265	31 8 41	23 12 41	V×1; shot down, returned, posted

Rank	Name	Service No	Posted In	Out	Remarks
Flt Sgt	A Salkin	1623665	22 7 45	28 8 45	
Flt Lt	K H Savage	37483	16 5 39	31 8 40	'B' Flt Cdr; (killed later)
Capt	E C Saville	10325	15 8 42	17 5 43	'A' Flt Cdr; DSO, DFC+bar, V×3, 2 probable, 3 damaged
Plt Off	R G Sayle	115773	15 9 42	13 1 43	PoW;
Sgt	H V Schofield	RCA83903	1 8 42	15 8 42	(Can), F/Sgt,; † accid
Flt Lt	L G Schwab	37831	23 7 40	25 6 41	'A' Flt Cdr, Sqn Ldr, CO, v×5, 2 prob, (died post-war)
Lieut	G W Schwikkard	205771V	27 8 44	29 3 45	(SAAF), Capt, DFC
Fg Off	M O Searle	57746	8 10 46	31 12 46	
2/Lieut	N G Sharp	328278V	21 12 43	13 9 44	(SAAF)
Sgt	L C Shaver	J17058	17 12 42	26 9 43	(Can) F/Sgt, WO, Plt, Off, V×1
Sgt	A Shaw	RCA83102	1 8 42	19 2 44	(Can) V×½
Sgt	R E Simonsen	RCA69710	? 1 42	14 3 42	(Can) V×1, 1 damaged; Killed
Sgt	Simpson	402987	18 2 42	13 3 42	(Aus)
Plt Off	P H Skey	78588	10 8 40	18 1 41	Cypher Officer
Plt Off	D H V Smith	70631	18 8 40	22 10 41	Fg Off, V×1 prob, 3 damaged
2/Lieut	E R Smith	?	27 9 40	29 10 41	(SAAF)
Sgt	R C C Smith	J16175	10 7 42	10 3 43	V×1; 2 probable, 1 damaged, Plt Off, killed, BNF
Plt Of	R H Smith	36161	16 5 39	10 9 40	V×1
Flt Lt	R R Smith	40952	? 10 42	10 3 43	'B' Flt Cdr., DFC, V×4, PoW
Plt Off	G B Smither	41484	6 12 39	2 1 40	
Sgt	H S Snelgrove	?	? 10 42	9 12 43	F/Sgt, WO,
Fg Off	J F Soden	42903	? 11 41	27 12 41	V×1, 2 damaged
Sqn Ldr	D M Somerville	32113	16 5 39	29 9 40	CO,
Flt Sgt	R W Stapley	1629859	23 11 46	31 12 46	
Sgt	R W Staveley	1231263	14 3 43	18 9 43	F/Sgt, killed
Sgt	I H Stirrat	404186	? 8 41	3 10 41	
Sgt	J L Stinson	?	30 10 41	?	(not mentioned)
Flt Sgt	K S Stokes	656779	26 9 43	21 5 44	WO
Fg Off	P E Stone	162101	7 12 45	20 6 46	Flt Lt
Plt Off	P E C Strahan	36154	16 5 40	24 9 40	V×1
WO	P Strange	656370	21 7 45	10 9 45	
2/Lieut	R W Strever	543007V	14 11 44	21 2 45	(SAAF) injured
Flt Sgt	N E Swinton	401547	31 5 43	27 5 44	(NZ) Plt Off
Sgt	T Tackaberry	R261069	22 1 42	9 2 42	(Can)
Sgt	C J W Tait	565362	3 1 40	18 6 40	† accid
Fg Off	K Taussig	163112	28 8 45	20 9 45	
Sgt	Taylor	404188	? 11 41	?	(Aus)
Lieut	A K Taylor	328249V	3 1 44	4 4 44	(SAAF), wounded, posted
Lieut	R H Templer	581465V	15 3 45	26 7 45	(SAAF), † accid
Sgt	H G E Thomas	405000	3 5 42	5 9 42	(NZ) missing, perhaps OK
Fg Off?	S Thompson	?	? 4 41	? 5 41	Cypher Officer[1]
Lieut	P du Toit	207341V	26 4 45	28 7 45	(SAAF)

[1] Nothing more is known about this officer. He published an article *'Escape from Greece'*, in 'Air Pictorial', November 1954 describing events similar to Plt Off Magner's account.

Rank	Name	Service No	Posted In	Posted Out	Remarks
Flt Sgt	W J Thorne	1605514	21 7 45	30 9 45	
Sgt	E Tickner	1800763	6 5 44	5 6 44	Killed
Plt Off	E Trees	181077	17 8 44	6 11 44	
Flt Sgt	I Treloar	401551	31 5 43	7 8 43	WO, killed
Flt Sgt	T R A Underdown	1609583	30 11 46	31 12 46	
Sgt	Z Urbanczyk	781038	9 2 42	5 5 42	(Pole) V×½
Flt Lt	G L Usher	88251	14 3 43	18 7 43	'B' Flt Cdr, DFC
			26 9 44	20 3 45	CO, Missing. returned
Flt Sgt	F R Vance	R80721	24 4 43	13 7 43	(Can) WO. killed
2/Lieut	L R Viljoen	?	10 6 40	? 7 40	(SAAF) attached
Sgt	C Walker	553859	25 3 45	3 4 45	Killed, BNF
Flt Lt	J A Walker	40768	6 6 42	22 7 42	'A' Flt Cdr, DFC
Flt Lt	S Walker	181180	12 9 46	31 12 46	'A' Flt Cdr
Sgt	D S Watson	1596995?	? 10 42	13 1 43	V×1, 1 damaged, PoW
Sgt	J J Walton	576995	22 7 45	? 11 45	
Sgt	K C Warburton	1435351	31 12 43	7 4 44	F/Sgt, PoW
Sqn Ldr	W K Watts	400827	29 3 44	6 4 44	(Aus) CO, PoW
Sgt	R Webb	1313162	23 10 42	7 11 42	Killed, BNF
2/Lieut	J H Weeber	280286V	5 10 44	18 11 44	(SAAF), killed
Sgt	Weir	?	5 41	5 41	(possibly attached only)
2/Lieut	D E Whelehan	543191V	26 10 44	6 5 45	(SAAF)
Plt Off	D F Westenra	89782	4 3 41	21 4 42	(NZ) V×4½, 1 prob, Flt Lt 'A' Flt Cdr, DFC
Plt Off	J Weston	49706	3 6 43	27 4 44	Engr Off, dep Adjt
Fg Off	W M Whitamore	102107	13 5 42	20 8 43	DFC, V×2, 3 dam,
Sgt	D J B White	1016777	30 4 42	15 12 42	
Lieut	M C White	75645	6 12 43	3 5 44	(SAAF), killed
Plt Off	R B Whittington	40159	16 5 39	31 8 40	
Plt Off	P R W Wickham	33403	16 5 39	30 10 40	V×3
Sgt	R A Wild	X407884	28 8 42	4 9 43	(Aus), Plt Off, Fg. Off,
			1 6 44	11 11 44	2nd tour, DFC, 'A' Flt Cdr V×2, 2 dam
Flt Sgt	G W Wiley	J7234	1 8 42	10 3 43	(Aus) Fg Off, Flt Lt, PoW (murdered 30.3.44)
Plt Off	R M Wilkinson	?	25 5 43	20 12 43	PoW
Flt Lt	J E A Williams	40652	11 4 42	21 4 42	
Sgt	T R E Williams	1673051	10 7 44	? 4 45	F/Sgt, Plt Off
Flt Lt	W C Williams	39010	16 5 39	18 7 40	'A' Flt Cdr,
Plt Off	R K Wilson	115949	3 5 42	1 6 42	PoW
2/Lieut	H O Winter	76848V	31 3 43	11 10 43	(SAAF) IO
Plt Off	G A Wolsey	41811	30 1 40	31 8 40	
Sgt	E N Woodward	566289	3 1 40	31 8 40	
Sgt	S T Worbey	1380985	6 2 43	13 3 44	Plt Off, PoW, escaped
Plt Off	A G Worcester – see Gray Worcester –				
Fg Off	H C Worcester	?	16 5 39	? 8 40	V×4
Plt Off	J G Wright	J7233	5 7 42	24 5 43	(Can) Flt Lt, injured, DFC, posted; V×2, 1 prob., 1 dam.
Sqn Ldr	M J Wright	117704	2 5 46	29 11 46	CO, DFC
Sgt	R A Wright	1024883	26 10 44	16 12 45	F/Sgt, WO
Sgt	Young	411490	10 7 42	15 9 42	(NZ) V×1 damaged, wounded, posted

Appendix D

SQUADRON VICTORIES

1. Victories in the air

The official squadron score for the 1939–1945 war was given by the (then) Air Ministry Historical Branch as 164 enemy aircraft destroyed, 48 probably destroyed and 81 damaged in aerial combat. The information in this Appendix is drawn straight from the contemporary, day-by-day, squadron records and results in a score considerably greater than the totals quoted above.

Attempts have been made to reconcile the figures and now and again the illusion of being able to make the totals correspond tempts one to start altering the figures. No doubt, were the Italian Air Force historical records office to be as forthcoming as the German air force, some sort of correlation could be arrived at overall. As early as February, 1941 there is a difference of four confirmed victories which may point to four probables being confirmed– but which four? There are measures of agreement in the totals until about March 1942 when discrepancies again emerge. By December 1942 the total claimed by the squadron is 198 enemy aircraft destroyed, which is 7¹/₂ more than the total arrived at by reading the squadron diary and combat reports but more than 30 above the figure given by the Air Historical Branch for the squadron's total in the whole war.

One can always imagine that, either deliberately or by mistake, individual pilots inflated their personal score or that a falling enemy aircraft was honestly supposed by two or more pilots to be the result of their effort alone. No doubt later intelligence may have altered claims but the squadron diarist probably did not bother to amend his figures. From the narrative it is also plain that on more than one occasion 112 Squadron aircraft must have seemed to the enemy pilots to be doomed and was notched up as destroyed in *Luftwaffe* or *Regia Aeronautica* when in fact the aircraft successfully returned to base, and no doubt the same happened on the enemy side. Where correlation is made possible by post-war research, as in Chris Shores and Hans Ring's books on the Desert and Tunisian campaigns, many instances are revealed to show that both sides claimed victories where none existed (see 21st February 1942, Sgt Carson's claim).

To this end, believing that it is probably now impossible to arrive at the whole truth, the contemporary claims are given in this Appendix exactly as they appear in the squadron records, and no attempt has been made to modify or alter them.

Date	Pilot	Claim
1917–1919		
19/20th May 1918	Major C J Q Brand	1 Gotha G5 destroyed
1939–1945		
29th June 1940	Plt Off J Hamlyn	1 SM81 destroyed
29th June 1940	Plt Off P R W Wickham	1 Ro37 *bis* destroyed
		1 CR32 destroyed
4th July 1940	Fg Off H C Worcester	4 CR42s destroyed
	Fg Off R H Smith	1 CR42 destroyed
	Fg Off R J Bennett	1 CR42 destroyed
25th July 1940	Fg Off P E C Strahan	1 CR42 destroyed
1st August 1940	Plt Off P O V Green	1 Ca133 destroyed
17th August 1940	Flt Lt L G Schwab	1 SM79 destroyed
	Plt Off P R W Wickham	1 SM79 destroyed
31st August 1940	Fg Off J F Fraser	1 SM79 damaged
15th September 1940	Plt Off E T Banks	1 SM79 damaged
	Plt Off R H Clarke	1 SM79 damaged
31st October 1940	Flt Lt L G Schwab	2 CR42s destroyed
	Plt Off R A Acworth	1 CR42 destroyed
18th November 1940	Flt Lt L G Schwab	1 SM79 destroyed
20th November 1940	Flt Lt R J Abrahams	1 ½ CR42s destroyed
	Fg Off R J Bennett	1 CR42 destroyed
	Plt Off R A Acworth	1 ½ CR42s destroyed
	Plt Off A R Costello	1 CR42 destroyed
	Plt Off L L Bartley	2 CR42s destroyed
	Sgt G M Donaldson	1 CR42 destroyed
20th February 1941	Flt Lt L G Schwab	1 G50 destroyed
	Flt Lt R J Abrahams	1 G50 damaged
	Fg Off E T Banks	1 G50 damaged
	Plt Off J L Groves	1 G50 damaged
27th February 1941	Fg Off R A Acworth	1 CR42 destroyed
28th February 1941	Sqn Ldr H L I Brown	1 G50 destroyed
	Flt Lt Fraser	1 G50 destroyed
		1 CR42 destroyed
	Flt Lt C H Fry	1 G50 destroyed
		1 CR42 destroyed
	Flt Lt R J Abrahams	1 G50 destroyed
	Fg Off D H V Smith	1 CR42 damaged
	Fg Off H P Cochrane	1 CR42 destroyed
	Fg Off E T Banks	1 CR42 destroyed
		1 CR42 damaged
		1 BR20 damaged
	Fg Off J L Groves	1 CR42 destroyed
	Sgt G M Donaldson	2 G50s destroyed
28th February 1941	Fg Off R A Acworth	1 CR42 destroyed
3rd March 1941	Fg Off R A Acworth	1 Cant Z 1007 destroyed
4th March 1941	Flt Lt J F Fraser	1 G50 destroyed

	Sqn Ldr H L I Brown	
	Plt Off D G H MacDonald	shared 1 G50 destroyed
	Plt Off J L Groves	
4th March 1941	Sqn Ldr H L I Brown	1 G50 damaged
	Flt Lt C H Fry	1 G50 probable
	Fg Off R A Acworth	1 G50 probable
	Fg Off E T Banks	1 G50 probable
	Fg Off H P Cochrane	1 G50 damaged
	Plt Off J L Groves	1 G50 damaged
	Plt Off D G H MacDonald	1 G50 damaged
	Sgt G M Donaldson	1 G50 probable
9th March 1941	Sqn Ldr H L I Brown	1 G50 destroyed
	Flt Lt C H Fry	1 G50 destroyed
	Flt Lt J F Fraser	1 BR20 destroyed
	Fg Off R A Acworth	1 G50 destroyed
	Fg Off H P Cochrane	1 G50 damaged
	Fg Off R J Bennett	1 G50 probable
	Plt Off J L Groves	1 G50 destroyed
	..	1 BR20 damaged
	Sgt G M Donaldson	2 G50s destroyed
11th March 1941	Sqn Ldr H L I Brown	1 G50 damaged
	Flt Lt C H Fry	1 G50 probable
	..	1 G50 damaged
	Flt Lt J F Fraser	1 G50 damaged
	Fg Off N Bowker	1 G50 destroyed
	Fg Off D F Westenra	1 G50 destroyed
	Fg Off H P Cochrane	1 G50 destroyed
	Fg Off E T Banks	1 G50 destroyed
		2 G50s damaged
	Fg Off R A Acworth	1 G50 destroyed
	Fg Off E H Brown	1 G50 damaged
	Fg Off D H V Smith	1 G50 damaged
13th March 1941	Sqn Ldr H L I Brown	1 G50 destroyed
	..	1 G50 damaged
	Flt Lt J F Fraser	3 CR42s destroyed
	Fg Off H P Cochrane	3 CR42s destroyed
	Fg Off E H Brown	1 CR42 destroyed
	Plt Off J L Groves	2 CR42s destroyed
	..	1 CR42 damaged
	Plt Off D G H MacDonald	1 CR42 probable
	Plt Off P C L Brunton	1 CR42 destroyed
14th March 1941	Flt Lt C H Fry	1 BR20 destroyed
	Flt Lt J F Fraser	1 G50 destroyed
	Fg Off R J Bennett	1 G50 destroyed
	Fg Off H P Cochrane	1 G50 probable
	Fg Off D H V Smith	1 G50 probable
	..	1 BR20 damaged
	Plt Off P C L Brunton	1 G50 damaged
	Sgt G M Donaldson	1 G50 probable
26th March 1941	Flt Lt L G Schwab	1 G50 probable
	Plt Off P C L Brunton	1 G50 damaged
13th April 1941	Sqn Ldr L G Schwab	1 G50 probable
12th May 1941	Sgt Weir	1 prob Ju52 destroyed
14th May 1941	Plt Off N Bowker	1 Bf110 destroyed

15th May 1941	Flt Lt C H Fry	1 Bf110 destroyed
	Plt Off D F Westenra	1 Bf110 destroyed
14th September 1941	Plt Off N Bowker	1 SM79 destroyed
3rd October 1941	Fg Off J L Groves	1 Bf109 damaged
12th October 1941	Fg Off J L Groves	1 Bf109 destroyed
	..	1 G50 destroyed
	Plt Off R J O Jeffries	1 Bf109 destroyed
20th November 1941	Fg Off J F Soden	1 Bf110 damaged
	Plt Off R J O Jeffries	1 Bf110 probable
	Plt Off N Bowker	
	Sgt R M Leu	shared 1 Bf110 destroyed
	Sgt R H Christie	
	Sgt K F Carson	1 Bf110 destroyed
21st November 1941	Plt Lt R J O Jeffries	
	Plt Off N Duke	shared 1 CR42 destroyed
	Sgt K F Carson	
	Sgt R M Leu	1 CR42 destroyed
22nd November 1941	Plt Off N Duke	1 Bf109 destroyed
	Plt Off J P Bartle	1 Bf109 destroyed
	unknown pilot	1 Bf110 damaged
25th November 1941	Flt Lt D F Westenra	1 CR42 probable
	Fg Off P H Humphreys	1 CR42 destroyed
	..	1 Bf109 probable
	Plt Off N Bowker	1 Bf110 destroyed
30th November 1941	Plt Off N Bowker	1 MC200 destroyed
	Plt Off N Duke	1 G50 destroyed
	..	1 Bf109 damaged
	Sgt R M Leu	1 G50 destroyed
	unknown pilot	1 G50 damaged
4th December 1941	Flt Lt D F Westenra	2 G50s destroyed
	Fg Off P H Humphreys	1 Bf109 damaged
	Plt Off N Bowker	1 G50 destroyed
	..	1 Ju87 destroyed
	Plt Off N Duke	1 MC200 destroyed
	..	1 Ju87 destroyed
	..	1 Ju87 damaged
	Sgt R H Christie	1 Bf109 destroyed
	..	1 Bf109 probable
5th December 1941	Flt Lt C F Ambrose	1 MC200 probable
	..	1 G50 probable
	Fg Off J F Soden	1 Ju87 destroyed
	..	1 Bf109 damaged
	Plt Off N Bowker	3 Ju87s destroyed
	..	1 G50 damaged
	Plt Off J P Sabourin	1 Bf109 destroyed
	..	1 G50 destroyed
	..	1 Ju87 destroyed
	..	1 G50 damaged
	..	2 Bf109s damaged
	Plt Off J P Bartle	1 G50 destroyed
	..	1 Ju87 destroyed
	Sgt R M Leu	1 MC200 destroyed
	..	1 Bf109 probable
12th December 1941	Plt Off J P Bartle	1 Bf109 destroyed

	..	1 MC202 damaged
	Plt Off E Dickinson	1 MC202 damaged
	Sgt D N McQueen	1 Bf109 damaged
14th December 1941	Sgt S C Johnson	1 Bf109 damaged
20th December 1941	Plt Off K R Sands	1Bf109 destroyed
	Sgt H G Burney	1 Ju88 destroyed
22nd December 1941	Flt Lt D F Westenra	shared
	Plt Off J P Bartle	1 Ju87 destroyed
	Plt Off N Duke	1 Ju52 probable
	..	shared
	Sgt K F Carson	1 Bf109 probable
25th January 1942	Sgt R M Leu	1 Bf109 destroyed
8th February 1942	Flt Lt P H Humphreys	shared
	Sgt H G Burney	1 Bf109 destroyed
	..	1 Bf109 destroyed
	Sgt G W Elwell	1 Bf109 destroyed
14th February 1942	Plt Off E Dickinson	1 MC200 destroyed
	Plt Off N Duke	1 MC200 destroyed
	..	½ MC200 (shared with Sgt Reid, 3RAAF Sqn)
	Plt Off J P Bartle	1 Bf109 probable
	..	1 Bf109 damaged
	Sgt R M Leu	2 MC200 destroyed
	Sgt H G Burney	1 prob MC200 destroyed
	Sgt R A Drew	2 MC200s destroyed
	Sgt R E Simonsen	1 MC200 destroyed
	..	1 MC200 damaged
	Sgt R H Christie	2 MC200s destroyed
	..	1 MC200 damaged
	Sgt W E C Cordwell	1 Bf109 destroyed
	Sgt R B Evans	1 MC200 probable
21st February 1942	Sqn Ldr C R Caldwell	1 Bf109 destroyed
	Sgt K F Carson	1 Bf109 destroyed (probably only damaged)
13th March 1942	Sgt H G Burney	1 MC202 destroyed
14th March 1942	Sqn Ldr C R Caldwell	1 MC202 destroyed
	..	shared
	Sgt Z Urbanczyk	1 Bf109 destroyed
7th May 1942	Plt Off F F J Edwards	1 Bf109 destroyed
6th June 1942	Plt Off A C Baker	1 Bf109 destroyed
	Plt Off K F Carson	shared
	Sgt E Adye	1 Bf109 destroyed
	..	1 Bf109 destroyed
26th June 1942	Fg Off W M Whitamore	1 Bf109 destroyed
2nd July 1942	Sqn Ldr B Drake	1 Bf109 probable
4th July 1942	Fg Off W M Whitamore	1 Ju87 destroyed
	..	1 Bf109 damaged
	Sgt D Ibbotson	1 Ju87 destroyed
8th July 1942	Sqn Ldr B Drake	1 Bf109 destroyed
	Plt Off Johnson	1 Bf109 damaged
19th July 1942	Sqn Ldr B Drake	1 Ju88 damaged
	Plt Off A C Baker	1 Ju88 damaged
	Plt Off Johnson	1 Ju88 damaged
	Sgt Young	1 Ju88 damaged

Date	Pilot	Claim
20th July 1942	Flt Lt G W Garton	1 MC202 damaged
	Fg Off J M S Crichton	1 Ju88 damaged
	Fg Off W M Whitamore	1 Bf109 damaged
	Plt Off D A Bruce	1 Ju88 damaged
	Plt Off J S Barrow	2 Ju88s damaged
	Sgt D Ibbotson	1 Ju88 damaged
22nd July 1942	Fg Off W M Whitamore	1 Bf109 damaged
	Sgt D Ibbotson	1 Bf109 probable
24th July 1942	Sqn Ldr B Drake	1 Bf109 destroyed
	Plt Off J E Loree	1 Ju88 destroyed
	Plt Off J G Wright	1 Bf109 destroyed
1st September 1942	Sqn Ldr B Drake	2 Ju87s destroyed
	Capt E C Saville	2 Ju87s destroyed
	..	1 Bf109 probable
	Plt Off H Phillips	1 Ju87 destroyed
	Plt Off T Livingstone	1 Ju87 damaged
12th September 1942	Capt E C Saville	1 Ju87 probable
	..	1 Ju87 damaged
	..	1 Bf109 damaged
	Sgt W E Pollock	1 Ju87 destroyed
	..	1 Ju87 damaged
	Sgt D F Greaves	1 Ju87 probable
	..	1 Ju87 damaged
	Sgt W Money	1 Ju87 damaged
	Sgt D Hogg	1 Ju87 damaged
13th September 1942	Sqn Ldr B Drake	1 Bf109 destroyed
	Sgt D Ibbotson	1 Bf109 probable
	unknown pilot	1 Bf109 damaged
	unknown pilot	1 Bf109 damaged
16th September 1942	Flt Lt G W Garton	1 MC202 probable
1st October 1942	Sqn Ldr B Drake	1 Ju87 probable
	..	shared
	Flt Lt G W Garton	1 Ju87 destroyed
	..	1 Ju87 probable
	Fg Off T Livingstone	1 Ju87 probable
	Plt Off L H Curphey	1 Ju87 destroyed
	Plt Off J G Wright	1 Bf109 damaged
	Flt Sgt R C C Smith	1 Bf109 probable
	Sgt M H Lamont	1 Ju87 damaged
2nd October 1942	Capt E C Saville	2 Bf109s destroyed
	Fg Off J M S Crichton	1 Bf109 damaged
	Fg Off T Livingstone	1 Bf109 damaged
	Plt Off H Phillips	1 Bf109 damaged
	Sgt J M MacAuley	1 Bf109 destroyed
20th October 1942	Flt Sgt R C C Smith	1 Bf109 probable
	Sgt J M MacAuley	1 MC202 damaged
22nd October 1942	Flt Lt R R Smith	1 Bf109 destroyed
22nd October 1942	Sqn Ldr B Drake	1 Bf109 probable
	Capt E C Saville	1 Bf109 damaged
	Plt Off L H Curphey	1 Bf109 damaged
26th October 1942	Sqn Ldr B Drake	1 Bf109 destroyed
	Plt Off J G Wright	1 Bf109 destroyed
27th October 1942	Sqn Ldr B Drake	1 MC202 destroyed
	Plt Off L H Curphey	1 MC202 destroyed

	Plt Off D A Bruce	1 MC202 destroyed
31st October 1942	Sqn Ldr B Drake	1 Ju87 destroyed
	Flt Lt R R Smith	1 Ju87 destroyed
	Fg Off J M S Crichton	1 Bf109 destroyed
	Plt Off L H Curphey	1 Bf109 probable
	Plt Off B A F Cuddon	1 Bf109 probable
	Plt Off H Phillips	2 MC202s probable
	Flt Sgt W D Brown	2 Ju87s destroyed
	Flt Sgt R H Newton	1 Ju87 probable
	Sgt R A Wild	1 Ju87 destroyed
	..	1 Bf109 damaged
	Sgt W Money	1 Bf109 destroyed
	Sgt M H Lamont	1 Bf109 probable
	Sgt D B Brown	1 Bf109 probable
	Sgt D S Watson	1 Bf109 damaged
1st November 1942	Flt Lt G W Garton	1 Ju87 destroyed
	Plt OffG F Allison	1 Ju87 probable
	WO J B Agnew	1 Ju87 destroyed
	..	2 Ju87 probables
	..	1 Ju87 damaged
	Flt Sgt R C C Smith	1 Ju87 destroyed
	..	1 Ju87 damaged
	Sgt R A Wild	1 Ju87 destroyed
	..	1 Ju87 damaged
	Sgt R DeBourke	2 Ju87s destroyed
	..	1 Ju87 probable
	Sgt T A Marsden	1 Ju87 probable
	Sgt D S Watson	1 Ju87 destroyed
4th November 1942	Flt Sgt W D Brown	1 Bf109 damaged
15th November 1942	Sqn Ldr B Drake	1 He111 destroyed
19th November 1942	Sqn Ldr B Drake	1 Bf110 destroyed
	..	1 Bf110 damaged
	Plt Off J G Wright	1 Me210 probable
10th December 1942	Flt Lt R R Smith	1 Bf109 destroyed
	..	1 MC202 destroyed
	Flt Sgt L C Shaver	1 Bf109 destroyed
11th December 1942	Sqn Ldr B Drake	1 Bf109 destroyed
	..	1 MC202 destroyed
	Fg Off J M S Crichton	1 Bf109 destroyed
	..	1 Bf109 damaged
	Plt Off D A Bruce	1 Bf109 probable
	Flt Sgt W D Brown	1 Bf109 probable
	..	1 Bf109 damaged
13th December 1942	Sqn Ldr B Drake	shared
	Sgt A Shaw	1 Bf109 destroyed
	Fg Off L H Curphey	1 Bf109 destroyed
	Sgt J G R Lecours	1 Bf109 destroyed
	..	1 Bf109 damaged
	Sgt R DeBourke	1 Bf109 destroyed
	Sgt J M MacAuley	1 Bf109 damaged
13th January 1943	unknown pilot	1 Bf109 destroyed
27th January 1943	unknown pilot	1 unidentified seaplane destroyed
5th February 1943	unknown pilot	1 Bf109 probable

		1 Bf109 damaged
27th February 1943	unknown pilot	1 Bf109 probable
10th March 1943	Fg Off T Livingstone	1 Ju87 destroyed
	Plt Off R D Guess	2 Bf109s destroyed
20th April 1943	unknown pilot	1 Ju88 destroyed
25th April 1943	unknown pilot	8/9ths Bf110 destroyed (shared with 3RAAF Sqn)
7th April 1944	Flt Lt L N Ahern	2 FW190s damaged
	..	shared
	Flt Sgt B H Peters	1 FW190 destroyed
	Lieut H J Hanreck	1 FW190 damaged
	Fg Off J O Gray	1 FW190 damaged
	WO R W Drown	1 FW190 damaged
	Flt Sgt W E Cocks	1 FW190 destroyed
	unknown pilot	1 FW190 destroyed
9th September 1944	Flt Lt R V Hearn	1 Ju88 destroyed

Totals of Aircraft destroyed, probably destroyed and damaged in air-to-air combat 1940–1945

Aircraft type		Destroyed	Probably destroyed	Damaged
1.	Bf109	44	20	30
2.	Bf110	8	1	3
3.	FW190	3	0	5
4.	Hel11	1	0	0
5.	Me210	0	1	0
6.	Ju87	32	11	11
7.	Ju88	4	0	8
8.	Ju52	1	1	0
9.	CR32	1	0	0
10.	CR42	38	2	3
11.	G50	31	12	21
12.	MC200	13½	2	2
13.	MC202	7	3	4
14.	Ro37 *bis*	1	0	0
15.	Cant Z1007	1	0	0
16.	BR20	2	0	3
17.	SM79	4	0	3
18.	SM81	1	0	0
19.	Ca133	1	0	0
20.	seaplane	1	0	0
Totals		194½	53	93

2. Victories against aircraft on the ground

Date	Pilots	Claim
22nd December 1941	Plt Off N Duke	1 Ju87 straffed, damaged
	Sgt K F Carson	1 Ju52 straffed, damaged
24th December 1941	Sgt D N McQueen	1 Ju52 straffed, left burning
17th June 1942	unknown pilots	1 Bf109 straffed, damaged
		1 Fi *Storch*. straffed, damaged
		7 other aircraft straffed, damaged

11th November 1942	Sqn Ldr B Drake	1 Bf109 straffed, damaged
	Flt Lt G W Garton	1 Ju52 straffed, probable
	Sgt D S Watson	1 Ju52 straffed, probable
	..	1 Fi *Storch* straffed, probable
	Sgt R A Wild	1 Bf109 straffed, damaged
21st January 1943	unknown pilots	2 MC202s straffed, destroyed
		1 MC202 straffed, damaged
7th May 1943	Flt Sgt F R Vance	1 Cant Z-506-B straffed, damaged
17th September 1943	unknown pilots	2 Ju88s straffed, burning
		2 Ju88s probably damaged
27th March 1944	unknown pilots	1 Fi *Storch* straffed, probable
29th March 1944	unknown pilots	1 MC202 straffed, smoking
25th April 1944	unknown pilots	3 Ju88s straffed, damaged
		1 unidentified Caproni damaged
		1 Fi *Storch* straffed, damaged
		1 Do215 straffed, damaged
		1 Ju52 straffed, damaged
13th August 1944	unknown pilots	2 Bf110 straffed, damaged
		3 Do217 straffed, damaged
		1 Mc410 straffed, damaged
6th September 1944	unknown pilots	8 Ju87s straffed, damaged
		1 FW190 straffed, damaged
		1 Bf109 straffed, damaged
		1 Ju52 straffed, damaged
		18 u/i aircraft straffed, damaged
9th September 1944	Sgt L W North	shared 1 He111 straffed
	Sgt T R E Williams	probably destroyed
	unknown pilots	1 Ju52 straffed, destroyed
		3 SM79s straffed, destroyed
		4 SM79s straffed, damaged
		2 Re2001s straffed, damaged
		2 Bf109s straffed, damaged
		1 u/i aircraft straffed, damaged
15th September 1944	unknown pilots	2 SM79s straffed, damaged
		2 Bf109s straffed, damaged
15th January 1945	unknown pilots	1 u/i aircraft straffed, probably destroyed
		2 u/i aircraft straffed, damaged
24th March 1945	unknown pilot	1 u/i aircraft straffed, damaged

Totals: 6 destroyed, 8 probably destroyed, 75 damaged

Note:

At the end of the Tunisian campaign in May 1943 the squadron considered that it had achieved a total of 200 confirmed enemy aircraft destroyed. If victories in aerial combat are considered alone, then this figure (from the extant squadron records) appears to be about 193. However it seems clear that 112 Squadron believed that aircraft destroyed on the ground in straffing attacks also contributed to their total, but this would only add 2 more unless it was believed that some of the enemy machines listed above as badly damaged were destroyed. As has been pointed out it seems unlikely, at this distance in time, that any definitive total can be arrived at.

Another point that requires emphasising to some degree is the fact that claims by individual pilots were subjected to considerable scrutiny by the squadron commander and the squadron intelligence officer before being accepted. Any doubt whatsoever and the claim was either modified or rejected. To claim a confirmed kill there had to be at least one independent witness or the evidence on the ground of a crashed aircraft. It is also possible that individual 112 Sqn pilots who were shot down and did not return would have filed claims had they been able to. It is more than likely that the totals shown in these tables are under – rather than overstatements.

"On lonely airfields of the war where hooded and tethered like hawks against the weather, the aircraft waited for their next release..." A 112 Sqn Kittyhawk under wraps. Aircraft would be refuelled and re-armed after every sortie so as to be ready to go again with the minimum of delay. *G. Hirons via Chaz Bowyer*

Eddy Ross taking off from Cutella LG in GA-?, FX561, with a full load of bombs in a characteristic nose down attitude with 20º of flap and a boot full of rudder. The Kittyhawks were carrying a bomb load equal to that of Baltimores and Marylands. May 1944. *Matt Matthias*

Above The squadron's anniversary, 17th May, 1944. Seated astride the propeller spinner; Sgt Rowe. On port wing: Flt Lt Crews. Standing (left to right): Fg Off Page; Fg Off Tex Gray; Fg Off Matt Matthias; Sgt Cockram; Flt Sgt Stokes; Sgt Jellett; Sgt Grubb; Sgt Nordstrand; Flt Lt Evans; Sgt North; 2/Lt Dottridge. Kneeling behind: 2/Lt Illidge; 2/Lt Clarke; Lt Churchill; (seated) Sgt Rees: 2/Lt Sharp. Kneeling (front) Sgt Tickner; 2/Lt Nuyten; Sgt Greenaway (slightly behind); Capt McLean; Sgt Davies; 2/Lt Hanreck; Sqdn Ldr Ahern; WO Drown; WO Hirons; Sgt Peters; Plt Off Swinton. *Robin Brown*

A 15-cwt truck taking the squadron pilots into Rome, 17th July, 1944. Johnny Burcham (left) and Tex Gray (standing left). *Matt Matthias*

The same day the pilots come upon a German "Tiger" tank and scramble all over it. Someone has slapped an 8th Army crest on its front and written "Water Closet" on its flank. *Matt Matthias*

Above At Creti LG in July 1944 (left to right): Capt McLean, OC 'B' Flt, Sqn Ldr Ahern, CO, and Flt Lt Reg Wild, OC 'A' Flt. *Jack Barber*

Left Flt Lt Ray Hearn, DFC & bar, OC 'B' Flt, killed in action 18th February, 1945. Seen here in the commandeered billet in Foggia. *Bert Horden*

Below 112 Sqn's headquarters staff with the CO, Sqn Ldr Ahern, the Adjutant, Fg Off 'Taffy' Evans and others. *Jack Barber*

Top Mustang MkIII GA-Q FB247, loaded with two 500 lb MC bombs, July/August 1944. *Robin Brown*

Centre Mustang MkIII GA-P FB327, taking off from Creti LG in July 1944. *Flt Lt Matthias*

Left Sergeant Arthur Banks, George Cross, from a painting commissioned after his death by his old school, St Edwards, Oxford. *With permission of the Warden, photo from Mrs Margaret Castle*

Above Mustang MkIII GA-?, either HB900 or KH589, carrying the mascot Wimpey from the Popeye cartoons. Summer/Autumn 1944. *Jack Barber*

Centre Two 500 lb bombs slung under a Mustang MkIII. *Matt Matthias*

Left A photograph taken late in 1944 with (left to right): Flt Lt Ray Hearn; Plt Off Bruce Routledge and (probably) Flt Lt Ray Newton. Fano LG. *Robin Brown*

Sqn Ldr Bluett and Lieut Dennis Paul in about January 1945. *Robin Brown*

Mustang MkIII GA-J KH586 at Zadara, a partisan held LG behind the enemy lines in Yugoslavia. The aircraft's name, partially obscured by the folded down perspex panel, is illegible. KH586 remained on the squadron from August 1944 to March 1945. This occasion was probably the operation on 16th March 1945.

Mustang MkIV GA-S KH774, April or May 1945.   *IWM (MH7980)*

Wg Cdr Brian Eaton's MkIV, BA-E carrying a DAF crest.   *G. Hirons via Chaz Bowyer*

At the war's end. A line up of aircraft, the nearest being GA-K KH832 at Lavariano in late May 1945. The occasion for the smart turn-out could be the Victory Fly-Past on 28th May. *G. Hirons via Chaz Bowyer*

Two airmen standing by a MkIII, Harry Futcher on the left and an un-named bowser driver, probably at Lavariano LG, about June 1949. *IWM (HU6980)*

An evocative photograph taken somewhere in northern Italy showing a Mustang MkIII leading a MkIV, possibly Wg Cdr Eaton's aircraft, along the psp taxi track. *IWM (CNA3494)*

Flt Lt Geoff Hirons, DFC, 'B' Flt Cdr (left) and Sqn Ldr Paul Forster. *G. Hirons via Chaz Bowyer*

Top At RAF Fassburg in the winter of 1951, the first attempt at the newly readopted sharksteeth markings, seen here is T-A, WA331, the CO's aircraft. Just below the open cockpit is a green lightning flash, the signature of squadrons on the Fassburg Wing. The tail fin and rudder were painted green with a superimposed white disc and the Helwan cat in black. The squadron's role as Ground-Attack is indicated by the pair of rockets under the port wing.   *Robin A. Brown*

Centre An air-to-air shot of Vampire Mk5 A-D, WA235, flying from Jever. The silver colour of the 2nd TAF air-craft has now been changed to drab camouflage.

Bottom One of the typical formal squadron photographs taken during the 1950s and frequently published in "Flight" or "Aeroplane". Here 112 Squadron pilots are arranged in front of a Vampire at RAF Sylt prior to the start of an air-to-air firing detachment in November 1953. Standing (left to right): Dicky Brown; Colin Buttars; Vic Little; Chan Biss; Chris Bryce; John O'Neill; Pat Reeve; Maurice Lackman; Reg Crumpton. Seated: Tommy Thompson; Bernard Lydiate; Ray Hancock; Barney Concannon; Bil Holmes; Mac Maconnel; Jonx Jonklaas; Dicky Duke; Jenks Jenkins; Pete Frame and Terry Hillman. On the hangar in the background can be seen a repre-sentation of the towed target banner used at Sylt.

Canadair Sabre IVs, XB960, G, and XB774, D, with underwing drop tanks, early 1956. *MoD (Air)*

An impressive formation in echelon starboard of eleven aircraft, led by Dennis Heywood. *MoD (Air)*

At RAF Brüggen the full complement of aircraft on one day fighter squadron, 22 aircraft, nearly exhausted the alphabet. K (nearest) XB920, and R (2nd) XB946, H (3rd) XB771.

The first sharksteeth Hunter 4 flies in formation with Sabre XB920, summer of 1956. *Roger Mansfield*

112 Squadron pilots, August 1956, RAF Brüggen. Standing (left to right); Brian 'Bonx' Baker; Ted Roberts; Jim Edwards; Roger Mansfield; Howard David; Paddy Glover. Seated: 'Taffy' Heath: Roy Davey; Reg Crumpton; Sqn Ldr Frank Hegarty, AFC; Robin Brown; Pete Frame and Dicky Brown. *MoD*

All that remained of WV412, A, after Flt Lt Keith Williamson had ejected over the island of Sylt, 13th September 1956. *MoD*

The author when 'A' Flt Cdr, seated in one of the squadron aircraft. Note how the unpainted replacement gun pack has disrupted the line of the sharksteeth. RAF Brüggen, 1956.
Robin Brown

The extremely complicated and laborious business of spraying on the sharksteeth markings on XF319, ?. Quantities of paper and masking tape were required. *Robin Brown*

The end result, XF319 with the revived query symbol. *Robin Brown*

One of 112 Squadron's Bloodhound missiles deployed at Episkopi in Cyprus. *MoD*

The presentation of the squadron standard on 29th September 1972. Flt Lt N. M. Pedley was the standard bearer. Note the addition of sharksteeth to the Bloodhound missile in the background. This was non-standard and specially for the occasion since the paint could have interfered with the flight of an operational missile. *MoD*

A vertical air photograph taken in 1957 by 80 (PR) Sqn, of the First World War airfield at Throwley, Kent. Forty years had obliterated much but a comparison with the Sketch Plan on page 9 shows that much remained. Top right the cluster of houses marks Bells Forstal. At the junction of the track with the road stands the old site guardroom. Between this building and the dark mass of Dodds Willows, which conceals the foundations of many huts, stands the Camp Hall. On the airfield itself traces of the foundations to the wooden hangar are visible and, by the white circle which was the compass-swinging base, the location of Bessoneau hangars are faintly visible. At the bottom right corner of the print, where the hedgerow curves, stand the firing butts. *MoD*

In November 1982 an air enthusiast, Mr A. J. Moor, took this photograph of the Throwley Camp Hall. At that time it was still in use as the local village hall but it has since been demolished. Dodds Willows is in the background and the flying field, where 112 HD Sqn's hangars were sited, in the foreground.   *A. J. Moor*

The Bf109G-2 Trop that once belonged to Lt Heinz Lüdemann of III/JG27 is seen here about to touch down at the Imperial War Museum's airfield at Duxford, near Cambridge. This machine was damaged by "Canada" Brown on 3rd November 1942. "Black Six" is believed to be the only airworthy Bf109G in the world.
Imperial War Museum, Duxford

Appendix E

SQUADRON AIRCREW LOSSES IN THE AIR

In brackets is the location of the grave, where known; those with no known grave (indicated by BNF) are commemorated on war memorials – at El Alamein and on Malta.

1. 1917–1919

14th October 1918	Lieut E W F Hopgood	Killed in flying accident (Throwley churchyard)
24th January 1919	2/Lieut J T Mitchell	Killed in flying accident (Throwley churchyard)

2. 1939–1946

18th June 1940	Sgt C J W Tait	Killed in flying accident (Khartoum New Christian cemetery)
4th July 1940	Fg Off A Gray-Worcester	Killed in flying accident (Cairo War Memorial Cemetery)
31st October 1940	Fg Off R H Clarke	Missing near Mersa Matruh, BNF (Alamein War Memorial)
9th March 1941	Plt Off R H MacDonald	Injured in combat. Died of wounds 7.5.41 (Cairo War Memorial Cemetery)
13th March 1941	Fg Off E T Banks	Killed in flying accident (Phaleron War Cemetery, Athens)
20th August 1941	Sgt F K Johnstone	Killed in flying accident (Hadra War Memorial Cemetery, Alexandria)
31st August 1941	Sgt E H Mills	Killed in flying accident (Fayid War Cemetery)
16th September 1941	Sgt E McCormack	Killed in flying accident (Cairo War Memorial Cemetery)
3rd October 1941	Sgt I H Stirrat	Killed in action, west of Sofafi (Halfaya-Sollum War Cemetery)
25th November 1941	Sgt F D Glasgow	Missing over Sidi Resegh, BNF (Alamein War Memorial)
10th December 1941	Sgt A H Ferguson	Missing near Marana, BNF (Alamein War Memorial)

12th December 1941	Fg Off R J D Jeffries	Missing over Tmimi, BNF (Alamein War Memorial)
12th December 1941	Sgt W E Houston	Missing over Tmimi, BNF (Alamein War Memorial)
12th December 1941	Sgt J Alves	Missing over Tmimi, PoW.
27th December 1941	Plt Off N Bowker	Missing Agheila-Agedabia road, PoW
1st January 1942	Sgt S C Johnson	Killed in flying accident (Halfaya-Sollum War Cemetery)
4th January 1942	Sgt A T Crocker	Killed in flying accident (Benghazi War Cemetery)
3rd February 1942	Plt Off P C L Brunton	Killed in action, Derna road (Beghazi War Cemetery)
8th February 1942	Sgt G W Elwell	Missing near Bomba, BNF (Alamein War Memorial)
8th February 1942	Sgt E P Hoare	Missing near Bomba, BNF (Alamein War Memorial)
8th February 1942	Sgt A T Donkin	Killed in action, Bomba (Knightsbridge War Memorial Cemetery, Acroma)
11th February 1942	Sgt N Holman	Killed in action near Gazala (Knightsbridge War Memorial Cemetery, Acroma)
12th February 1942	Plt Off C Matusiak	Killed in flying accident (Tobruk War Cemetery)
27th February 1942	Sgt Jackson	Killed in flying accident, Gambut Main (Knightsbridge War Memorial Cemetry, Acroma)
9th March 1942	Sgt P T Elliott	Killed in action over Gambut (Halfaya-Sollum War Cemetery)
14th March 1942	Sgt R E Simonsen	Killed in action, Bir Hackeim (Knightsbridge War Memorial Cemetery, Acroma)
18th May 1942	Plt Off J R Fisher	Missing over Temrad area, BNF (Alamein War Memorial)
18th May 1942	Sgt J V Davey	Missing over Temrad area, BNF (Alamein War Memorial)
22nd May 1942	Fg Off K C Gundry	Missing over Martuba, BNF (Alamein War Memorial)
28th May 1942	Flt Lt E Dickinson	Missing over Point 365395, BNF (Alamein War Memorial)
30th May 1942	Plt Off H G Burney	Missing over Point 359412, BNF (Alamein War Memorial)
31st May 1942	Plt Off S S Mitchell	Missing over Point 372483, BNF (Alamein War Memorial)
1st June 1942	Plt Off R K Wilson	Missing near Gambut, PoW
4th June 1942	Plt Off E Atkinson	Missing over Point 378372, BNF (Alamein War Memorial)
13th June 1942	Plt Off F F J Edwards	Killed in action (Knightsbridge War Cemetery, Acroma)
16th June 1942	Plt Off K Carson	Missing, PoW
17th June 1942	Flt Sgt R A Drew	Killed in action, Sidi Rezegh, BNF (Alamein War Memorial)

21st June 1942	Flt Lt R M Leu	PoW
10th July 1942	Fg Off F Knoll	Killed in action over LG 102. (Alamein War Cemetery)
24th July 1942	Plt Off Johnson	Missing near LG 20 (Alamein War Memorial)
22nd July 1942	Plt Off J S Barrow	Killed in action, Alamein area (Alamein War Cemetery)
15th August 1942	Sgt H V Schofield	Killed in flying accident (Alamein War Cemetery)
28th August 1942	Plt Off J E Loree	Missing near Deir-el-Abyad, PoW
28th August 1942	Sgt Barlow	Missing near Deir-el-Abyad, PoW
5th September 1942	Sgt H G E Thomas	Missing, but probably survived (did not return to 112 Sqn)
2nd October 1942	Sgt G Rae	Killed in flying accident, LG 91 (Alamein War Cemetery)
20th October 1942	Sgt D F Greaves	Missing near LG 21, PoW
21st October 1942	Sgt D Hogg	Missing near Gazal, PoW
26th October 1942	Fg Off K R Gardener	Died of wounds (Alamein War Cemetery)
7th November 1942	Sgt R Webb	Missing near Fuka, BNF (Alamein War Memorial)
11th December 1942	Plt Off B A F Cuddon	Missing near Marble Arch, BNF (Alamein War Memorial)
11th January 1943	Fg Off J M S Crichton	Missing near Buerat, PoW
13th January 1943	Fg Off L Curphey	Missing near Geddabia, BNF (Alamein War Memorial)
13th January 1943	Fg Off R C Sayle	Missing near Point R9070, PoW
13th January 1943	Sgt D S Watson	Missing near Point R9070, PoW
5th February 1943	Sgt R Lecours	Missing over Ras Agedir, BNF (Alamein War Memorial)
27th February 1943	Sgt T A Marsden	Missing over El Hamma, BNF (Alamein War Memorial)
10th March 1943	Flt Lt R R Smith	Missing over Foum Tatahouin, PoW
10th March 1943	Fg Off D A Bruce	Missing over Foum Tatahouin, BNF, (Alamein War Memorial)
10th March 1943	Fg Off G W Wiley	Missing over Foum Tatahouin, PoW, murdered after break out from *Stalag Luft III*, 30.3.44 (Posen/Poznan Old Garrison Cemetery, Poland)
10th March 1943	Plt Off R C C Smith	Missing over Foum Tatahouin, BNF (Alamein War Memorial)
10th March 1943	WOII R DeBourke	Missing over Foum Tatahouin, BNF (Alamein War Memorial)
10th March 1943	WOII J H Oliver	Missing over Foum Tatahouin, BNF (Alamein War Memorial)
22nd April 1943	Flt Sgt M H Lamont	Missing over Cape Bon, BNF (Alamein War Memorial)
22nd April 1943	Sgt A E Prain	Missing over Cape Bon, BNF (Alamein War Memorial)
22nd April 1943	Sgt J T Hounsell	Missing over Cape Bon, BNF (Alamein War Memorial)

13th July 1943	Sqn Ldr G H Norton	Missing near Lentini, Sicily, BNF (Malta War Memorial)
13th July 1943	Flt Sgt F R Vance	Killed in action near Lentini (Catania War Cemetery)
4th August 1943	Fg Off D Guess	Killed in action near Randazzo (Catania War Cemetery)
7th August 1943	WO I Treloar	Killed in action near Randazzo (Catania War Cemetery)
15th September 1943	WO K Middlemist	Killed in action near Pertosa, Italy (Salerno War Cemetery)
18th September 1943	Flt Sgt R W Staveley	Killed in action near Vallata (Salerno War Cemetery)
19th September 1943	WO W D Brown	Missing near Avigliano, BNF (Malta War Memorial)
20th December 1943	Fg Off R M Wilkinson	Missing near Ripa, PoW
12th February 1944	Flt Sgt D Holmes	Missing on an Air Test, BNF (Malta War Memorial)
7th March 1944	Fg Off J A Burcham	Missing near Rome, PoW
13th March 1944	Flt Sgt S T Worbey	Missing near Rome, PoW escaped June 1944
22nd March 1944	Sqn Ldr P F Illingworth	Missing near Trogir, returned
6th April 1944	Sqn Ldr W K Watts	Missing near Todi, PoW
7th April 1944	Flt Sgt K C Warburton	Missing over Rieti LG, PoW
7th April 1944	Flt Sgt W E Cocks	Killed in action, Rieti LG (Assisi War Cemetery)
23rd April 1944	Lieut W E Foster	Killed in action, Lake Trasimeno (Assisi War Cemetery)
3rd May 1944	Lieut M G White	Killed in action near Rieti (Beachhead War Cemetery, Anzio)
22nd May 1944	Sgt D W Grubb	Missing near Avezzano, PoW
29th May 1944	Sgt C J Parkinson	Killed in action near Frosinone (Beachhead War Cemetery, Anzio)
30th May 1944	Sgt P L Rees	Missing near front line, PoW
31st May 1944	Sgt G F Davis	Killed in action near front line (Cassino War Cemetery)
2nd June 1944	Sgt J R Carr	Killed in action near Subiaco (Beachhead War Cemetery, Anzio)
5th June 1944	Lieut H F Churchill	Missing near Highway 6, PoW
5th June 1944	Sgt E Tickner	Killed in action, Highway 6 (Bolsena War Cemetery)
1st August 1944	Lieut A H Jones	Killed in flying accident (Foiano Della Chiana War Cemetery)
5th August 1944	Sgt K R Mann	Killed in action north of Florence (Florence War Cemetery)
23rd August 1944	2/Lieut J C Hoyle	Killed in action at Modena (Milan War Cemetery)
29th August 1944	Sgt A Banks	Missing, PoW, later murdered (Argenta Gap War Cemetery)
2nd September 1944	Plt Off J R Greenaway	Killed in action near front line (Copiano Ridge War Cemetery)
25th September 1944	Lieut G McFie	Killed in action near front line (Forli War Cemetery)

12th October 1944	Lieut C J Liebenberg	Missing near San Felice, PoW, escaped
22nd October 1944	Lieut J R Lund	Killed in action near Ravenna (Forli War Cemetery)
30th October 1944	Lieut D F Prentice	Baled out near San Vito, PoW
6th November 1944	Plt Off R J Deeble	Killed between Zagreb and Maribor (Belgrade War Cemetery)
8th November 1944	Plt Off G G Clark	Killed in action, Cavnaella di Adige (Padua War Cemetery)
16th November 1944	Fg Off J J Roney	Died after flying accident (Ancona War Cemetery)
18th November 1944	Lieut J H Weeber	Killed in action near Sisak (Belgrade War Cemetery)
23rd January 1945	Sgt P L Greaves	Missing near Pragersko, returned
18th February 1945	Flt Lt R V Hearn	Killed in action at Aviano (Udine War Cemetery)
11th March 1945	Flt Sgt O G Jones	Killed in action near Padua (Padua War Cemetery)
20th March 1945	Sqn Ldr G L Usher	Missing near Ljubljana, returned
2nd April 1945	Flt Lt M N Matthias	Killed in action near Graz (Klagenfurt War Cemetery)
3rd April 1945	Sgt C Walker	Killed in action near Graz (Klagenfurt War Cemetery)
12th April 1945	Flt Sgt T P Roberts	Killed near front line, BNF (Malta War Memorial)
12th April 1945	Lieut E N Roberts	Killed in action near Bastia bridge (Coriano Ridge War Cemetery)
20th April 1945	Lieut J H Nixon	Killed in action near Trieste (Belgrade War Cemetery)

Post-War Casualties:

13th May 1945	Sgt P L Greaves	Killed in flying accident near Forli (Forli War Cemetery)
26th July 1945	Capt G H Edwards	Killed in flying accident near Trento (Padua War Cemetery)
26th July 1945	Lieut R D Park	Killed in flying accident near Trento (Padua War Cemetery)
26th July 1945	Lieut W D Blom	Killed in flying accident near Trento (Padua War Cemetery)
26th July 1945	Lieut R H Templer	Killed in flying accident near Trento (Padua War Cemetery)
26th July 1945	Sgt G P Eyears	Killed in flying accident near Trento (Padua War Cemetery)
27th November 1945	Sgt A E Headland	Killed in flying accident near Gorizia (Udine War Cemetery)

3. 1951–1957

27th July 1952	Plt Off C R Donaldson	Killed in flying accident near Odiham
2nd December 1953	Plt Off E J Kitwood	Killed in flying accident at Sylt (Hanover Military Cemetery)
26th September 1954	Fg Off J E A Jenkins	Killed in flying accident near Brüggen (Cologne Southern Cemetery)
5th July 1955	Fg Off M J Smith	Killed in flying accident near Heerlen, Netherlands (Cologne Southern Cemetery)

Appendix F

SQUADRON AIRCRAFT SERIAL NUMBERS

1917–1919

1.	Sopwith Pup:	B1772; B5910;
2.	Sopwith Camel:	C6748; C8349; D6403; D6405; D6415; D6473; D6664; E5153; F1369; F2091; F4175;
3.	Sopwith Snipe:	E6643; E6839; E6842; E6844; E6848; E7429;
4.	Avro 504:	C4378

1939–1946

5. Gloster Gladiator: (Mk 1)

K6130; K6134; K6135*; K6136; K6138; K6140; K6142; K6143; K6150; K7893; K7895; K7896; K7897; K7916; K7922; K7932; K7941; K7948; K7954; K7962; K7963; K7969; K7970; K7974; K7977; K7978; K7984; K7986; K7993; K7997; K7998; K8008; K8024; K8025; K8031*; L7612; L7619; L7622; L8007; L8011;

(Mk 2)

N5774; N5823; N5895; N5913; N5916; N5918;
* ferried to Greek Air Force, 2 December 1940

6. Gloster Gauntlet: (Mk 2)   K5292; K7792; K7870; K7881;
7. Hawker Audax: K7514
8. Curtiss Tomahawk IIB

The asterisk indicates the months that each particular aircraft was on squadron strength. This is only a rough guide as an aircraft flying operationally only on the last day of one month and the first day of the next would still qualify for two asterisks. The aircraft are listed as they appear in squadron records and therefore not strictly in alphabetical/numerical order. (↓ = shot down, damaged in combat or crash-landed)

1941/42	Sep	Oct	Nov	Dec	Jan
AK367	*	*			
AK413	*	*			
AK457	*	*	*	*	↓ 12.12.41
AK461 'A'	*	*	*	↓ 25.11.41	
AK495	*	↓ 25.9.41			
AK502	*	*			
AK503	*	*	*		
AK538	*	*	*		

1941/42	Sep	Oct	Nov	Dec	Jan
AK541	*	*	*	*	
AK382	*				
AM390	*	*	*	↓ 23.11.41	
AM396	*	*	↓ 12.10.41		
AM410	*	*			
AM438	*				
AM444	*	*	↓ 12.10.41		
AM474	*	*			
AM481	*	*	↓ 12.10.41		
AM495	*	*			
AN218	*	*			
AN220	*	*	↓ 12.10.41		
AN231	*				
AN331	*	*			
AN414	*				
AN442	*				
AM442		*			
AK531		*	*	*	
AN309		*	*	*	
AN330		*	*	↓ 22.11.41	
AN413 'K'	*	*	*	↓ 12.12.41	
AN415		*	*	*	
AN442		*			
AK327			*	*	
AK354 'L'			*	*	
AK377 'V'			*	*	
AK402 'F'			*	↓ 30.11.41	
AK405			*		
AK475 'J'			*		
AK509			*	*	↓ 9.12.41
AK533			*	*	
AK534			*		
AK565			*	*	
AM459			*		
AN242			*		
AN283			*	*	↓ 27.12.41
AN303			*	*	
AN327			*	*	
AN338			*	↓ 30.11.41	
AN340 'B'			*	*	↓ 20.12.41
AN372			*	*	↓ 20.12.41
AN381			*	*	
AN417			*		
AN436			*		
AN439			*		
AN446			*		
AK418				*	↓ 20.12.41
AK426				*	
AK476				*	↓ 12.12.41
AM406				*	
AM446 'P'				*	
AM459				*	

1941/42	Sep	Oct	Nov	Dec	Jan
AN265				*	
AN274				*	
AN289				*	
AN336				*	
AN337 'F'				*	↓ 5.12.41
AK330					*
AK561					*

       Total: 67 Tomahawk IIBs

9. Curtiss Kittyhawk Mk 1A

1942/43	Jan	Feb	Mar	Apr	May	Jun	July	Aug	Sept	Oct	Nov	Dec	Jan
AK578 'V'	*	*	*	*									
AK583 'X'	*												
AK595 'Y'	*												
AK602	*	*	↓ 3.2.42										
AK637	*	*											
AK651	*												
AK652 'D'	*	*	↓ 8.2.42										
AK653 'G'	*	*											
AK658	*	*											
AK667	*	*	*	*	*	*							
AK672	*	↓ 9.1.42 (a/c recovered)											
AK673 'F'	*	*	↓ 11.2.42										
AK675	*												
AK678	*												
AK682 'U'	*	*	*	*	*								
AK685	*	*											
AK700 'B'	*	*	*	↓ 9.3.42									
AK702	*	*											
AK728	*												
AK584		*											
AK585		*	↓ 8.2.42										
AK707 'Y'		*	(damaged in strafe)										
AK593		*	↓ 8.2.42										
AK630		*											
AK761		*											
AK762		*	*	*	*								
AK777		*	*	*	*								
AK781		*	↓ 21.2.42										
AK782		*	*										
AK784		*											
AK802		*	*										
AK804		*											
AK808		*	*										
AK814		*											
AK894		*											
AK910		*											
AK957 'D'		*	*	*									
AK959		*	*										
AK632			*	*	*								
AK766			*	*	*								

1942/43	Jan	Feb	Mar	Apr	May	Jun	July	Aug	Sept	Oct	Nov	Dec	Jan
AK772 'Y'			*	*	*	↓ 30.5.42							
AK787			*	*	*	↓ 22.5.42							
AK834			*	↓ 13.3.42									
AK878			*	↓ 14.3.42									
AK900 'A'			*	↓ 14.3.42									
AK906			*	*	*	↓ 18.5.42							
AK913			*										
AK936			*										
AK994			*	*	*	↓ 18.5.42							
AK680				*	*								
AK707 'Y' (returned)				*	*								
AK802				*									
AK859				*	*								
AK868				*	*								
AK924				*	*	*							
AK938				*	*	*							
AK990				*	*	*							
AK587					*								
AK763					*	↓ 18.5.42							
AK770					*	*							
AK805					*								
AK829					*								
AK907					*	*							
AK908					*								
AK909					*	*							
AK928					*								
AK929					*								
AK985					*	*							
AK999					*								
AL107					*	*							
AL121					*								
AL122					*	↓ 27.5.42							
AL158					*								
AL161					*	*							
AL185					*	*							
AL196					*	*	↓ 1.6.42						
AL211					*	*	↓ 8.6.42						
AL219					*	*							
AK571						*	↓ 21.6.42						
AK586						*	↓ 17.6.42						
AK614						*							
AK655						*							
AK677						*	*						
AK705						*	*						
AK778						*	*						
AK825						*							
AK852						*	*	↓ 27.6.42					
AK892						*	*						
AK918						*							
AK922						*							
AK925						*							
AK937						*	↓ 11.6.42						

1942/43	Jan	Feb	Mar	Apr	May	Jun	July	Aug	Sept	Oct	Nov	Dec	Jan
AK949						*	↓ 13.6.42						
AK977						*							
AK988						*	↓ 11.6.42						
AK992						*							
AK995						*	*						
AL105						*	↓ 16.6.42						
AL112						*							
AL127						*							
AL149						*	↓ 12.6.42						
AL156						*							
AL175						*	↓ 16.6.42						
AL192						*							
AL225						*	↓ 21.6.42						
ET510						*	*						
ET511						*	*						
ET526						*	↓ 26.6.42						
ET527						*	*						
ET910						*	*						
AL108							*						
AL204							*						
AL209							*						
AK583 (returned)							*						
AK590							*						
AK603							*	↓ 24.7.42					
AK634							*						
AK658 (returned)							*						
AK675 (returned)							*						
AK852							*	↓ 4.7.42					
AK677							*	↓ 20.7.42					
AK892							*	↓ 10.7.42					
AK685 (returned)							*						
AK788							*						
AK832							*	*					
AK853							*						
AK866							*	↓ 23.7.42					
AK890							*	↓ 5.7.42					
AK920							*	↓ 3.7.42					
ET510							*	↓ 23.7.42					
ET513							*						
ET515							*						
ET524							*						
ET529							*						
ET611							*						
ET685							*						
ET724							*						
ET783							*						
ET790							*	↓ 22.7.42					
ET794							*	↓ 10.7.42					
ET795							*	*	*	↓ 30.9.42			
ET853							*	*	*				
ET861							*						
ET865							*						

1942/43	Jan	Feb	Mar	Apr	May	Jun	July	Aug	Sept	Oct	Nov	Dec	Jan
ET902							*	*	*				
ET915							*						
ET919 'C'							*	*	*	*			
ET1017+							*	*	↓ 28.8.42				
ET1024+							*						
AK701								*	*	↓ 5.9.42			
AK703								*					
AK743								*	*				
AK744								*					
AK746								*	↓ 28.8.42				
AK882								*					
AK960								*	*				
ET909								*					
EV136								*	*	*			
EV162								*	*				
EV340								*					
EV368								*	*	↓ 9.9.42			
ET719 'C'								*					
ET265 'K'								*					
AL128 'D'									*	*			
AL178 'C'									*	*			
AL228									*	*			
AK694									*	↓ 15.9.42			
AK716									*				
AK792									*	*			
AK849									*				
ET195									*				
ET318									*				
ET789 'C'									*	*			
ET973									*				
ET1022+									*				
EV166									*	*			
EV168									*	*			
EV315									*	*			
EV318									*	*			
EV319									*	*			
EV339									*	*			
EV344									*				
EV360									*	*			
EV368									*	↓ 9.9.42			
EV365									*				
AL792 'B'									*				
AK685 (returned)									*				
AK847										*			
AL223										*			
ET787										*			
ET799 'W'										*			
EV139										*			
EV359										*			

+ These unusual four digit serials are genuine, but probably a mistake made by the American manufacturers

10. Curtiss Kittyhawk Mk III

1942–44	Oct	Nov	Dec	Jan	Feb	Mar	Apr	May	Jun	Jul	Aug	Sept	Oct	Nov	Dec	Jan	Feb	Mar	Apr	May	Jun
FR195+ 'F'	*	*	*	*	↓ 13.1.43																
FR211 'E'	*	*	*	*																	
FR212	*	*	*	*																	
FR213 'Q'	*	*	*	*	↓ 13.1.43																
FR214 'A'	*	*	↓ 7.11.42																		
FR215 'V'	*	*	*	*	↓ 11.1.43																
FR216	*	*	*	*																	
FR217 'C'	*	*	↓ 11.12.42																		
FR219	*	*																			
FR224 'B'	↓ 21.10.42																				
FR236	*	↓ 17.11.42																			
FR245 'B'	*	↓ 20.10.42																			
FR248	*	↓ 27.10.42																			
FR262	*	*	↓ 26.10.42																		
FR263 'X'	*	*		*																	
FR264	*	*																			
FR266 'H'	*	*	↓ 26.10.42																		
FR279 'J'	*	*	↓ 31.10.42																		
FR281 'D'	*	*																			
FR283	*	*	*																		
FR293	*																				
FR302 'T'																					
FR115 'B'		*	*	*																	
FR255	*	*	*																		
FR261																					
FR271	*	*	*																		
FR287 'X'	*	*	↓ 1.11.42																		
FR289 'Z'	*	*	*	*	*	*															
FR324 'E'	*	*	*	*	*	*															
FR326	*	*																			
FR789	*	*																			
FR879+	*	*																			
FR880+	*	*	*																		

1942-43	Oct	Nov	Dec	Jan	Feb	Mar	Apr	May	Jun	Jul	Aug	Sept	Oct	Nov	Dec	Jan	Feb	Mar	Apr	May	Jun
FR885+	*																				
FR919	*																				
FL880	*	*																			
FL890 'D'		*	*	↓ 13.1.43																	
FR320 'J'			*	*	*																
FR325			*	*	*	*															
FR338				*	*	*	*														
FR127			*	*	↓ 27.2.43																
FR130 'Z'			*	*																	
FR362+				*	*	*	*	↓ 22.4.43													
FR276				*	*	*	*														
FR292				*	*																
FR317 'H'				*	*																
FR357				*	*																
FR358				*	*	↓ 10.3.43		*													
FR361				*	*	↓ 10.3.43															
FR412 'D'				*	*	*															
FR413				*	*	*	*														
FR710+'C'				*	*																
FL321 'F'					*																
FL876					*																
FL882					*	*		*	*	*											
FL886'B'				*	*	*	*	*	*	*	*										
FL730				*	↓ 5.2.43																
245790++'B'				*	*																
FL901					*																
FR131					*	↓ 10.3.43															
FR325					*	↓ 10.3.43															
FL714					*	*	*	↓ 11.5.43													
FL891					*	*															

+ These serial numbers are listed in the squadron records as shown but they are recorded elsewhere as Mitchell serial numbers. This may be a squadron error and FR should perhaps read FL or it may be a case of duplicated serial numbers.

++ one of three unaltered American serial numbers

1943-44	Oct	Nov	Dec	Jan	Feb	Mar	Apr	May	Jun	Jul	Aug	Sept	Oct	Nov	Dec	Jan	Feb	Mar	Apr	May	Jun
FR118 'F'						*															
FR137						*															
FR140						*	*														
FR221						*	* ↓22.4.43														
FR691						*	* ↓10.3.43														
FR241						*	*														
FR275						*	* ↓10.3.43														
FR277 'E'						*	* ↓10.3.43	*													
FR295						*	* ↓10.3.43														
FR336						*															
FR345						*															
FR354						*	*	*													
FR385						*															
FR414						*	*														
FR422 'N'						*	*														
FR424						*	*														
FR440 'V'						*	*	*	*												
FR442						*															
FR443						*															
FR445						*															
FR453						*	* ↓22.4.43	*													
FR882						*	* ↓10.3.43														
245798 'D'						*	*														
FR115 'W' (returned)							*														
FR691							*	*	*												
FR472 'L'&'Z'							*	*	*	*											
FR474 'Jinx'							*	*													
FR478							*	*													
FR482							*	*													
FR483 'K'							*	*	*	*											
FR484							*	*													
FR489 'H'							*	*	*	*	*										
FR494 'W'							*	*	*	*	* ↓4.8.43	*									
FR502 'D'							*	*	*	* ↓13.7.43	*	*	*	*	*						
FR509 'R'							*	*	*	*											

1943-44	Oct	Nov	Dec	Jan	Feb	Mar	Apr	May	Jun	Jul	Aug	Sept	Oct	Nov	Dec	Jan	Feb	Mar	Apr	May	Jun	Notes
FR511							*	*	*	*												
FR516 'A'							*	*	*													
FR517							*	*														
FR520 'F'							*	*	*													
FR521							*	*														
245789							*															
FR315 'C'									*	*												↓ 30.7.43
FR860 'D'										*	*	*										↓ 19.9.43
FR392 'E'										*	*	*										
FR820 'E'										*	*	*										
FR793 'J'									*	*												↓ 13.7.43
FR864 'M'										*	*	*	*	*	*							↓ 20.12.43
FR796 'N'										*	*	*										
FR429 'P'										*	*	*										
FR806 'Q'										*	*											↓ 4.8.43
FR827 'V'										*	*	*										↓ 18.9.43
FR866 'T'											*	*										('K' in September)
FR790 'X'												*	*									
FR849 'Z'												*										
FR542 'C'												*	*	*	*							
FR511 'H'												*	*	*	*							
FR801 'H'												*	*	*	*							↓ 31.12.43
FR839 'J'												*	*	*	*							
FR823 'P'												*	*	*	*							
FR355 'R'												*										
FR282 'X'												*										
FR837 'Z'												*										
FL897 'A'												*										
FL882 'A'												*										
FR455 'B'												*	*	*	*							
FR825 'B'												*	*	*	*							
FR812 'B'												*	*	*	*	*						
FR521 'D'												*	*	*	*	*	*					
FR803 'F'												*	*	*	*	*	*		*			
FR439 'K'												*	*	*	*	*	*		*			

1943–44

Aircraft movement chart (Oct 1943 – Jun 1944). Asterisks indicate the months during which each aircraft was on strength.

Aircraft	Sept	Oct	Nov	Dec	Jan	Feb	Mar	Apr	May	Jun
FR389 'R'	*									
FR814 'T'	*	* ↓15.9.43								
FR132 'T'	*	*	*							
FR350 'V'	*	*	*	*						
FR835 'Z'	*	*	*	*						
FR388 'Z' (and J)	*	*	*	*	*	*	* ↓7.3.44			
FR824 'A'			*	*	*	*	*			
FR344 'R'			*	*	*	*				
FR838 'D'				*	*	*	*			
FR521 'N' (returned)			*	*	*					
FR491 'R'		*	*	*	*	*	*			
FR492 'V'		*	*	*	*	*	* ↓22.3.44			
FR257 'H'			*	*	*	*	*	*		
FR861 'M'				*	*	*	*			
FR872 'P'				*	*	*				
FR229 'Q'				*	*	*	*			
FR420 'R'				*	*	*	*			
FR236 'T' (later S')				*	*	*				
FR299 'V'				*	*	*				
FR429 'W'				*	*	*				
FR511 'D'				*	*	*	*			
FR823 'Q'				*	*	*	*	* ↓7.4.44		
FR288 'Z'				*	*	*	*	*		
FR795 'B'				*	*	*	*			
FR238 'F'					*	* ↓29.2.44	*			
FL886 'K'					*	*	* ↓7.3.44			
FR283 'P'					*	*	*			
FR902 'Q'					*	*	* ↓13.3.44			
FR812 'R'					*	*	*	*		
FR819 'V'					*	*	*	*		
FR299 'W'					*	*	*	*		
FL895 'A'					*	*	*	*		
FR222 'B' (later 'P')					*	*	*	* *		
FR871 'E'					*	*	*	*		
FR390 'F'						*	*			

1943-44	Oct	Nov	Dec	Jan	Feb	Mar	Apr	May	Jun	Jul	Aug	Sept	Oct	Nov	Dec	Jan	Feb	Mar	Apr	May	Jun
FR312 'J'																		*	*		
FR121 'K'																		*	*		
FT854 'P' (later 'B')+																		*	*		
FR309 'Q'																		*	*		
FR507 'R'																		*	*		
FR857 'V'																		*	*		
FR354 'W' (returned)																			↓7.4.44		
FR474 'Jinx' (returned)																			*	*	
FR862 'E'																			*		
FR811 'M'																			↓6.4.44		

+ This was a Mk IV

11.   Curtiss Kittyhawk Mk IV

1944	Apr	May	Jun	Jul	Aug
FX541 'A'	*	*	*		
FX731 'B'	*	*	*		
FT857 'E'	*	*			
FX563 'F'	*	*			
FT949 'H'	*	*			
FX552 'J'	*	*			
FX544 'K'	*	*	↓ 22.5.44		
FT947 'M'	*				
FX658 'N'	*	*			
FX516 'P'	*	↓ 23.4.44			
FX558 'Q'	*	*	*		
FX561 'R' (later'?')	*	*			
FX566 'S'	*				
FX710 'S'	*	*	↓ 29.5.44 (prob)		
FT945 'V'	*	*	*		
FX622 'W'	*	*	↓ 3.5.44		
FT921 'Z'	*	*			
FX781 'C'		*	*		
FX699 'R' (later 'E')		*			
FX776 'F'		*	*		
FX719 'H'		*	*		
FX687 'K'		*	*	↓ 2.6.44	
FT951 'M'+		*			
FX733 'N'		*	*		
FX800 'R'		*	*	↓ 4.6.44	
FX685 'T'		*	*		
FX670 'W'		*	↓ 30.5.44		
FX560 'X'		*			
FX641 'X'		*			
FX740 '?'		*	↓ 31.5.44		
FX831 'B'			*		
FX827 'C'			*		
FX762 'E'			*		
FX777 'E'			*		
FT948 'J'			*	↓ 4.6.44	
FX729 'J'			*		
FX749 'K'			*		
FX724 'K'			*		
FX804 'R'			*		
FX732 'S'			*		
FX799 'W'			*		
FX805 'X'			*		
FX792 'X'			*	↓ 3.6.44	
FX768 'X'			*		
FX788 'Z'			*		
FX760 '?'			*		

+ Squadron records give this as FX951, probably incorrectly
Total: 417 Kittyhawks (all Marks)

12. North American Mustang Mk III

1944–45	Jul	Aug	Sep	Oct	Nov	Dec	Jan	Feb	Mar	Apr	May	Jun
FB320 'A'+	*	*										
FB290 'B'	*	*	*	*	*							
FB338 'C'	*	*										
FB323 'E'	*	*	*	↓ 25.9.44								
FB291 'F'	*											
FB255 'F'	*	*	*									
FB326 'H'	*											
FB257 'H'	*											
HB830 'H'	*	*	*	*								
FB287 'Jinx'	*											
FB304 'J'	*	*	*									
FB262 'K'	*											
FB249 'N'	*	*										
FB327 'P'	*	*	*	*	*							
FB247 'Q'	*	*										
FB296 'R'	*	*	↓ 5.8.44									
HB827 'S'++	*											
FB328 'S'	*	*	*	*	*							
FB317 'T'	*	*										
FB244 'V'	*	*	*	*	*	*						
FB297 'X'	*	*	*	↓ 2.9.44								
FB340 'Z'	*	*										
HB900 '?'	*	*	*	*	*							
HB936 'A'		*	↓ 29.8.44									
HB940 'C'		*	*	*	*	*						
HB893 'K'		*	*	*	↓ 22.10.44							
HB895 'N'		*	↓ 23.8.44									
HB842 'N'		*	*									
FB309 'Q'		*	*	*	*							
HB925 'R' (later 'Z')		*	*	*								
HB908 'W'		*	*	*	↓ 30.10.44							
FB320 'Z'+		*										
FB339 'Z'		*	*	*								
FB257 'A'		*										
FB279 'F'+++		*	*	*	*	*						
KH586 'J'		*	*	*	*	*	*	*	*			
FB263 'M'			*	*	↓ 12.10.44							
HB917 'N'			*	*								
KH572 'R'			*	*	*	*						
HB897 'X'			*	*								
KH531 'E'				*	*							
KH597 'K'				*	*							
KH579 'L'				*	*	*	*					
FB280 'X'				*	*	*	*	↓ 23.1.45				
KH627 'B'					*	↓ 18.11.44						
FB320 'N'+ (returned)				*	*	↓ 6.11.44						

+ a Mk IIIb
++ Squadron records give this as FB827, probably incorrectly
+++ Squadron record give this as HB279, probably incorrectly

1944–45	Jul	Aug	Sep	Oct	Nov	Dec	Jan	Feb	Mar	Apr	May	Jun
KH635 'E'					*	*	*	*	*	↓11.3.45		
FB260 'K'					*	*	*	*	*			
KH636 'P'					*	*	*					
HB913 'S'					*	*	*	*	*	*		↓12.4.45
KH571 'W' (in January 'π')					*	*	*	*	*	*	*	
FB254 'Y'					*	*	*					
KH601 'Z'					*	↓8.11.44						
KH589 '?'					*	*	*					
KH512 'B'						*	*	*	*			
FB300 'C'						*	*	*	*	*	*	
FB255 'M' (returned)						*	*	↓11.1.45				
KH701 'Q' §						*						
KH628 'Z'						*						
KH793 'L' §								*	*	↓20.3.45		
KH820 'Q' §								*	↓18.2.45			
KH572 'R'								*	*			
KH579 'F'								*	*	*		

13. North American Mustang Mk IV (unless otherwise noted)

1945	Feb	Mar	Apr	May	Jun	Jul	Aug	Sep
KH852 'P'	*	*	*					
KH824 'V'	*	*	*					
KH589 'X'#	*	*	*					
KH628 'Y'# (later 'R')	*	*	*	*				
KH795 'Y' (later 'G')	*	*	*					
FB255 'Z'	*	*						
KM136 'B'		*	*					
KH586 'E'		*						
KM135 'K'		*	↓2.4.45					
KH832 'K'		*	*					
KM107 'M'		*	*	*	*	*	†26.7.45	
KH776 '?' (later 'K')		*	*					
KH734 'B'			*					
FB259 'E'			*					
KH763 'F'			*	*				
KH774 'S'			*	*				
FB272 'W'			*	*				
KM127 'X'			*	↓12.4.45				
KH862 'X'			*	*				
FB288 'Z'			*					
KH467 'Z'			*	↓20.4.45				
KM872 '?'			*	*				
KH832 'J'				*				

§ Mk IVs, although KH701 is probably a mistake
# Mk III; + Mk IIIB

Total: 86 Mustangs (all Marks)

The records stop at the end of the war in Europe and little information has come to light concerning Mustang serial numbers from May 1945 until the disbandment in December 1946. Noted from other sources are —

Those involved in the accident of 26 July 1945: KM216; KH235; FB259 & KH720; (also KM107, see above) and KM124 'S' (July 1946) and KH719 'B'

14. De Havilland Vampire FB 5

WA332 'A'; WF586 'B'; VV687 'C' (later to B Flt as 'O'); WA115 'C' (later to 'B' Flt as 'N'); WA218 'C'; WA235 'D' (later to B Flt as 'L'); WA114 'D'; WA279 'D'; WA233 'D'; WA343 'E'; VZ115 'E'; WA345 'F' (later to B Flt); WA283 'F'; WA244 'F'; WA337 'G' (later to B Flt as 'K'); VX462 'G'; WA372 'H'; WA393 'J'; WA337 'K'; WA235 'L'; WA389 'M'; WG844 'M' WA115 'N'; WA257 'N'; VZ268 'O'; VV687 'O'; VZ240 'P'; VZ343 'Q'; WA382 'R'; WA417 'S'; WA144 'T'; VV466 'T'; WG844 'V'; also WA295 and WG841 (aircraft letters not known)

15. Canadair Sabre Mk 4

XB576; XB591; XB593; XB629; XB675; XB804; XB746; XB808; XB812; XB818; XB822; XB829; XB865; XB884; XB893; XB912; XB913; XB914; XB915;

(The above group were the initial issue. They had leading edge slats and carried no aircraft letter or Sharksteeth markings)

XB917 'A'; XB995 'A'; XB979 'B'; XB649 'C'; XB774 'D'; XB793 'E'; XB976 'E'; XB939 'F'; XB960 'G'; XB771 'H'; XB958 'J'; XB920 'K'; XB944 'L'; XB978 'N'; XB802 'O'; XB926 'O'; XB772 'P'; XB947 'Q'; XB946 'R'; XB950 'S'; XB956 'T'; XB650 'U'; XB919 'V'; XB957 'W'; XB934 'X'

(The above group were 'hard edged' aircraft)

16. Hawker Hunter Mk 4

WV412 'A'; XF986 'A'; XF319 'A'(later '?'); XE672 'B'; XE673 'C'; XE674 'D'; XF306 'E'; XF307 'F'; XF293 'N'; XF358 'P'; XF366 'R'; XF362 'Q'; XF704 'S'; XF937 'T';

At the disbandment of the Brüggen Wing 112 Sqn inherited various aircraft from other squadrons: VW273; XF291; VW382; XE715; XF294; XF292; XF298; XF300; XF295; WV374; WV332. These did not carry Sharksteeth markings.

Appendix G

SQUADRON AIRCRAFT DESTROYED OR DAMAGED AS A RESULT OF ENEMY ACTION

No.	Serial No. & letter	Pilot	Date	Remarks
1.	?	Plt Off B B E Duff	31.10.40	A/C destroyed in combat, Mersa Matruh
2.	?	Plt Off R A Acworth	31.10.40	A/C destroyed in collision in combat, Mersa Matruh
3.	?	2/Lieut E R Smith	31.10.40	A/C destroyed in collision in combat, Mersa Matruh
4.	?	Flt Lt L G Schwab	31.10.40	A/C damaged in forced-landing after combat, Mersa Matruh
5.	?	Flt Lt R H Clarke	31.10.40	A/C destroyed in combat, Mersa Matruh
6.	?	Flt Lt R J Abrahams	28.2.41	A/C destroyed in combat over Sarande-Tepelene, Albania
7.	N5823	Plt Off R MacDonald	9.3.41	A/C destroyed in combat over Albania
8.	N5916	Sqn Ldr H L I Brown	14.3.41	A/C destroyed in combat over Kelcyre, Albania
9.	?	-	15.3.41	A/C damaged by bombing at Yannina, Greece
10.	?	-	26.3.41	A/C destroyed by bombing at Paramythia, Greece
11.	?	Plt Off P Brunton	13.4.41	A/C destroyed in combat over Koritsa
12.	?	-	16.4.41	Two a/c destroyed on the ground to prevent them falling into enemy hands
13.	?	-	1.6.41	Unknown number of a/c left in Crete and destroyed
14.	AK495	Plt Off D Westenra	24.9.41	A/C destroyed in combat over Sidi Barrani
15.	AK502	Sgt I H Stirrat	3.10.41	A/C destroyed in combat over Sidi Omar
16.	AN220	Plt Off F E Parker	12.10.41	A/C destroyed in combat over Sofafi
17.	AM396	Sgt R M Leu	12.10.41	A/C destroyed in combat over Sofafi
18.	AM444	Fg Off J L Groves	12.10.41	A/C badly damaged in combat
19.	AM481	Sgt C F McWilliams	12.10.41	A/C badly damaged in combat
20.	AN330	Plt Off J Sabourin	22.11.41	A/C destroyed by flak, Sidi Omar
21.	AM390	Sgt H G Burney	23.11.41	A/C crash-landed, El Adem
22.	AK461 'A'	Sgt F D Glasgow	25.11.41	A/C destroyed in combat over Sidi Resegh
23.	AN338	Plt Off N Bowker	30.11.41	A/C crash-landed at LG122
24.	AK402 'F'	Plt Off N Duke	30.11.41	A/C crash-landed near Tobruk
25.	AN337 'F'	Plt Off N Duke	5.12.41	A/C crash-landed at Tobruk
26.	AK509	Plt Off J Sabourin	9.12.41	A/C crash-landed amongst XXX Corps
27.	AK533	Sgt K F Carson	9.12.41	A/C badly damaged in action
28.	AN413 'K'	Plt Off R Jeffries	12.12.41	A/C missing in action near Tmimi

29.	AK457	Sgt W E Houston	12.12.41	A/C missing in action near Tmimi
30.	AK476	Sgt J Alves	12.12.41	A/C missing in action near Tmimi
31.	AN340 'N'	Sqn Ldr F V Morello	20.12.41	A/C damaged in action near Marana
32.	AN372	Plt Off K R Sands	20.12.41	A/C crash-landed after combat over Marana
33.	AK418	Sgt A H Ferguson	20.12.41	Missing in action near Marana
34.	AN283	Plt Off N Bowker	27.12.41	A/C crash-landed after combat in El Agheila-Agedabia area
35.	AK672	Sgt K Carson	9.1.42	A/C crash-landed after combat near El Agheila (aircraft was successfully recovered)
36.	?	-	28.1.42	Several aircraft abandoned in retreat from Msus
37.	AK602	Fg Off P C L Brunton	3.2.42	A/C missing in action near Derna
38.	AK593	Sgt G W Elwell	8.2.42	A/C missing in action near Derna
39.	AK652	Sgt A T Donkin	8.2.42	A/C missing in action near Derna
40.	AK585	Sgt B P Hoare	8.2.42	A/C missing in action near Derna
41.	AK673	Sgt N Holman	11.2.42	A/C shot down over El Adem
42.	AK781	Sgt P T Elliott	21.2.42	A/C badly damaged in combat over El Adem
43.	AK707 'Y'	-	27.2.42	A/C destroyed in enemy strafe of Gambut
44.	?	-	27.2.42	A/C destroyed in enemy strafe of Gambut
45.	?	-	27.2.42	A/C badly damaged in enemy strafe of Gambut
46.	?	-	27.2.42	A/C badly damaged in enemy strafe of Gambut
47.	AK700 'B'	Sgt P T Elliott	9.3.42	A/C shot down near Gambut Main
48.	AK834	Sgt J W Rozanski	13.3.42	A/C shot down near El Adem
49.	AK878	Sgt R B Evans	14.3.42	A/C shot down at Bir Hakeim
50.	AK900 'A'	Sgt R E Simonsen	14.3.42	A/C shot down at Bir Hakeim
51.	AK763	Plt Off J R Fisher	18.5.42	A/C shot down by flak
52.	AK906	Sgt R A Drew	18.5.42	A/C force-landed near Gambut
53.	AK994	Sgt J V Davey	18.5.42	A/C shot down over Temrad
54.	AK787	Plt Off K C Gundry	22.5.42	A/C missing north of Bomba
55.	AL122	Flt Lt E Dickinson	27.5.42	A/C missing near Point 385370
56.	?	Flt Lt E Dickinson	28.5.42	A/C missing near Point 365395
57.	AK772	Plt Off H G Burney	30.5.42	A/C ('London Pride') missing over Point 359412
58.	?	Plt Off S Mitchell	31.5.42	A/C missing near Point 372483
59.	AL196	Plt Off R K Wilson	1.6.42	A/C missing after combat
60.	AL219	Plt Off E Atkinson	4.6.42	A/C missing after strafe near Point 378372
61.	AL211	Sgt D J B White	8.6.42	A/C force-landed after strafe
62.	AK988	Sgt E Adye	11.6.42	A/C missing over Point 368414 pilot returned safely
63.	AK937	Sgt D F Greaves	11.6.42	A/C missing over Point 368414 pilot returned safely
64.	AL149	Flt Sgt Cassell	12.6.42	A/C missing over 'Rotunda', near El Adem, pilot safe
65.	AK949	Plt Off F Edwards	13.6.42	A/C missing after armed recce
66.	AL105	Plt Off K Carson	16.6.42	A/C shot down west of Sidi Resegh
67.	AL175	Sgt R H Newton	16.6.42	A/C missing, pilot safe
68.	AK586	Flt Sgt R A Drew	17.6.42	A/C shot down near Sidi Resegh
69.	AL225	Flt Lt R M Leu	21.6.42	A/C force-landed at Sidi Azeiz, behind enemy lines
70.	AK571	Fg Off J Crichton	21.6.42	A/C force-landed at Sollum
71.	ET526	Plt Off B Cuddon	26.6.42	A/C shot down in combat
72.	AK652	Flt Lt J Walker	27.6.42	A/C shot down
73.	AK920	Sgt D J B White	3.7.42	A/C shot down over Point 865269
74.	AK852	Flt Sgt J B Agnew	4.7.42	A/C badly damaged near Point 870290
75.	AK890	Sgt D Ibbotson	7.7.42	A/C force-landed
76.	AK892	Fg Off F Knoll	10.7.42	A/C shot down near LG106
77.	ET794	Sgt D J B White	10.7.42	A/C shot down into the sea near LG106
78.	AK677	Sgt R DeBourke	20.7.42	A/C damaged over El Alamein and force-landed
79.	ET790	Plt Off J S Barrow	22.7.42	A/C shot down by flak over battle area

80.	ET510	Flt Lt G W Garton	23.7.42	A/C force-landed at Point 877257
81.	AK866	Sgt Young	23.7.42	A/C force-landed
82.	AK603	Plt Off Johnson	24.7.42	A/C shot down over LG20 & LG104 (Qotafiyah)
83.	?	Sgt R C C Smith	1.8.42	A/C force-landed, possibly it was recovered
84.	AK703	Sgt Young	24.8.42	A/C force-landed at Point 895254
85.	ET1017	Plt Off J E Loree	28.8.42	A/C shot down at Deir-el-Abyad
86.	AK746	Sgt Barlow	28.8.42	A/C shot down at Deir-el-Abyad
87.	EV365	Sgt D Ibbotsen	3.9.42	A/C returned Cat 1 after dog-fight
88.	AK701	Sgt H G E Thomas	5.9.42	A/C shot down over Point 455275
89.	EV368	Plt Off H Phillips	9.9.42	A/C force-landed at 1 SAAF Bde Workshops
90.	ET789	Sgt D Hogg	19.9.42	A/C crash-landed, Cat. 2, in Alamein area; a/c returned to squadron in October
91.	?	Sgt J H Morrison	13.9.42	A/C shot down, crash-landed and was destroyed by fire
92.	AK694	Sgt Young	15.9.42	A/C shot down by own AA fire over Point 878282, destroyed
93.	ET795	Sgt J H Morrison	30.9.42	A/C caught fire and crash-landed, cause uncertain
94.	ET919 'C'	Plt Off G W Wiley	7.10.42	A/C force-landed at Point 452904
95.	FR248	Sgt D F Greaves	20.10.42	A/C shot down near LG21
96.	FR236	Sgt D Hogg	21.10.42	A/C shot down near Gazal
97.	FR279 'J'	Plt Off J G Wright	26.10.42	A/C crash-landed near front line
98.	FR263 'X'	Fg Off K Gardener	26.10.42	A/C shot down over front line
99.	FR262	Sgt A Martin	27.10.42	A/C crash-landed at Fuka
100.	FR281 'D'	Plt Off D A Bruce	31.10.42	A/C ditched near El Daba
101.	FR289 'Z'	WO J B Agnew	1.11.42	A/C force-landed in battle area
102.	FR215 'V'	Sgt R Webb	7.11.42	A/C shot down near Fuka
103.	?	Plt Off J Crichton	11.11.42	A/C destroyed on take-off
104.	?	Plt Off H Phillips	11.11.42	A/C destroyed on take-off
103.	FR245 'B'	Sgt W E Pollock	17.11.42	A/C force-landed 40 miles west of Msus
104.	FR217 'C'	Plt Off A B Cudden	11.12.42	A/C shot down in Marble Arch area
105.	FR255	Flt Sgt W D Brown	11.12.42	A/C force-landed in forward area, aircraft recovered
106.	FR216	Fg Off J M Crichton	11.1.43	A/C shot down in Buerat area
107.	FR195 'F' (FL195?)	Fg Off L H Curphey	13.1.43	A/C shot down over enemy lines
108.	FR214 'A'	Fg Off R G Sayle	13.1.43	A/C shot down near Point R9070
109.	FR320 'J'	Sgt D S Watson	13.1.43	A/C shot down near Point R7090
110.	FL730	Sgt J G R Lecours	5.2.43	A/C shot down near Ras Agedir
111.	FR130 'Z'	Sgt T A Marsden	27.2.43	A/C shot down near El Hamma
112.	FR325	Flt Lt R R Smith	10.3.43	A/C shot down near Foum Tatahouin
113.	FR295	Fg Off D A Bruce	10.3.43	A/C shot down near Foum Tatahouin
114.	245798	Fg Off G W Wiley	10.3.43	A/C shot down near Foum Tatahouin
115.	FR131	Plt Off R C C Smith	10.3.43	A/C shot down near Foum Tatahouin
116.	FR275	Flt Sgt R DeBourke	10.3.43	A/C shot down near Foum Tatahouin
117.	FR361	Sgt J H Oliver	10.3.43	A/C shot down near Foum Tatahouin
118.	FR691	?	10.3.43	'wrecked, enemy action in the air'
119.	FR453	Flt Sgt M H Lamont	22.4.43	A/C shot down near Cape Bon
120.	FR221	Sgt A E Prain	22.4.43	A/C shot down near Cape Bon
121.	FR276	Sgt J T Hounsell	22.4.43	A/C shot down near Cape Bon
122.	FL714	Sgt R W Staveley	30.5.43	A/C forced down, landed at Hammamet
123.	FR502 'D'	Flt Sgt F R Vance	13.7.43	A/C shot down by flak near Lentini, Sicily
124.	FR793 'J'	Sqn Ldr G H Norton	13.7.43	A/C shot down by flak near Lentini
125.	FR315 'C'	Sgt R W Staveley	30.7.43	A/C force-landed near front line
126.	FR429 'P'	Fg Off R D Guess	4.8.43	A/C shot down by flak near Randazzo

127.	FR489 'H'	Fg Off H J M Barnes	4.8.43	A/C crashed in the sea near Catania
128.	FR849 'Z'	Flt Sgt I Treloar	7.8.43	A/C shot down by flak near Randazzo
129.	FR814 'T'	WO K F Middlemist	15.9.43	A/C shot down by flak near Pertosa, Italy
130.	FR866 'K'	Flt Sgt R W Staveley	18.9.43	A/C shot down by flak near Vallata
131.	FR860 'D'	WO W D Brown	19.9.43	A/C shot down near Avigliano
132.	FR864 'M'	Fg Off R Wilkinson	20.12.43	A/C shot down near Ripa
133.	FR839 'J'	2/Lieut H Hanreck	31.12.43	A/C damaged and ditched off San Vito Chietino
134.	FL886 'K'	Fg Off J O Gray	29.2.44	A/C force-landed in Anzio beachhead
135.	FR824 'A'	Fg Off J Burcham	7.3.44	A/C shot down near Rome
136.	FR283 'P'	Lieut A K Taylor	7.3.44	A/C landed on beach near Cutella, damaged
137.	FR812 'R'	Flt Sgt S T Worbey	13.3.44	A/C shot down near Rome
138.	FR861 'M'	Sqn Ldr P Illingworth	22.3.44	A/C shot down near Trogir
139.	FR811 'M'	Sqn Ldr W K Watts	6.4.44	A/C shot down near Todi
140.	FR857 'V'	Flt Sgt K Warburton	7.4.44	A/C shot down near Rieti LG
141.	FR288 'Z'	Flt Sgt W E Cocks	7.4.44	A/C crashed near Rieti LG
142.	FR516 'P'	Lieut W E Foster	23.4.44	A/C shot down at Lake Trasimeno
143.	FX622 'W'	Lieut M C White	3.5.44	A/C shot down near Rieti
144.	FX544 'K'	Sgt D W Grubb	22.5.44	A/C shot down near Avezzano
145.	FX710 'S'	Sgt C J Parkinson	29.5.44	A/C shot down near Frosinone
146.	FX670 'W'	Sgt P L Rees	30.5.44	A/C shot down near front line
147.	FX740 '?'	Sgt G F Davis	31.5.44	A/C shot down near front line
148.	FX687 'K'	Sgt J F Carr	2.6.44	A/C shot down near Subiaco
149.	FX792 'X'	2/Lieut D A H Clarke	3.6.44	A/C shot down north of Ienne
150.	FT948 'J'	Sgt E Tickner	4.6.44	A/C shot down near Castel di Tora
151.	FX800 'R'	Lieut H F Churchill	4.6.44	A/C shot down near Castel di Tora
152.	FR296 'R'	Sgt K R Mann	5.8.44	A/C shot down near Florence
153.	HB895 'N'	2/Lieut J C Hoyle	23.8.44	A/C shot down at Modena
154.	HB936 'A'	Sgt A Banks	29.8.44	A/C shot down at Point G514123
155.	FB297 'X'	Plt Off J H Greenaway	2.9.44	A/C shot down over front line
156.	FB323 'E'	Lieut G McFie	25.9.44	A/C shot down near Rimini
157.	FB263 'M'	Lieut C J Liebenberg	12.10.44	A/C shot down near San Felice
158.	HB893 'K'	Lieut J R Lund	22.10.44	A/C shot down near Ravenna
159.	HB908 'W'	Lieut D F Prentice	30.10.44	A/C crashed in the Gulf of Venice
160.	FB320 'N'	Plt Off R J Deeble	6.11.44	A/C crashed between Zagreb & Maribor, Yugoslavia
161.	KH601 'Z'	Plt Off G G Clark	8.11.44	A/C crashed at Cavnaella di Adige
162.	KH627 'B'	Lieut J H Weeber	18.11.44	A/C shot down at Sisak
163.	FB255 'M'	WO J S Duncan	11.1.45	A/C crash-landed near Ravenna
164.	FB280 'X'	Sgt P L Greaves	23.1.45	A/C shot down near Pragersko
165.	KH820 'Q'	Flt Lt R V Hearn	18.2.45	A/C shot down at Aviano
166.	KH635 'E'	Flt Sgt O G Jones	11.3.45	A/C shot down near Padua
167.	KH793 'L'	Flt Lt G L Usher	20.3.45	A/C shot down near Ljubljana
168.	KM135 'K'	Flt Lt M N Matthias	2.4.45	A/C shot down near Graz
169.	FB288 'Z'	Sgt C Walker	3.4.45	A/C shot down near Graz
170.	KM127 'X'	Flt Sgt T P Roberts	12.4.45	A/C shot down near front line
171.	HB913 'S'	Lieut E N Roberts	12.4.45	A/C shot down at Bastia
172.	KH467 'Z'	Lieut J H Nixon	20.4.45	A/C shot down near Trieste

Bibliography

BOWYER, Chaz & **SHORES**, Christopher, *'Desert Air Force at War'*, Ian Allen, 1981
BRICKHILL, Paul, *'The Great Escape'*, Faber & Faber, 1951
BROWN, David B *'The Desert Sharks'* in 'The Air Enthusiast', March 1978
BROWN, Air Vice-Marshal Sir Leslie O, *'Flights of Memory'* (unpublished typescript)
BRUCE, J M, *'The Sopwith Camel'*, Part 1, in 'Flight', 22 April 1955
BRUCE, J M, *'The Sopwith F. 1 Camel'* Part 1 in 'Aeromodeller', January 1964
CALDER, Angus, *'The People' War'*, Jonathan Cape, 1969, Panther, 1971
CATTANEO, Gianni, *'The Fiat CR42'* in Profile Publication (No 16)
EDWARDS, Wg Cdr James F & **LAVIGNE**, J P A M, *'Kittyhawk Pilot'*, Turner-
    Warwick Publications, Canada, 1983
EPOSITO, Brig-General V J, ed., *'West Point Atlas of American Wars'*, Vol II, Frederick
    A Praeger, New York & London, 1959
FULLER, Major-General J F C, *'The Second World War'*, Eyre & Spottiswood, 1948
GREEN, William, *'Famous Fighters of the Second World War'*, MacDonald, 1957
GUINGAND, Major-General Francis de, *'Operation Victory'*, Hodder & Stoughton,
    1947
HERINGTON, John, *'The Air War against Germany & Italy'*, Vol 3 of 'Australia in the
    War of 1939–45', Canberra, Australian War Memorial publication
HINSLEY, Sir Harry, *'British Intelligence in the Second World War'*, Vols. I-VI, HMSO,
    1988
HMSO publication *'R.A.F. Middle East'*, 1945
HMSO publication *'Tunisia'*, 1944
HURREN, B J, *'Eastern Med'*, Frederick Muller, 1943
JEFFORD, Wg Cdr C G. *'RAF Squadrons'*, Air Life Publications, 1988
LYALL, Gavin, ed., *'Freedom's Battle'*, Vol 2., Hutchinson, 1968
MONTGOMERY, Field Marshal Sir Bernard L, *'El Alamein to the River Sangro'*,
    BAOR Printing & Stationery Services, 1946
MOOREHEAD, Alan, *'Mediterranean Front'*, Hamish Hamilton, 1941
MOOREHEAD, Alan, *'The End in Africa'*, Hamish Hamilton, 1943
NORMAN, Aaron, *'The Great Air War'* MacMillan, New York/Collier-MacMillan,
    London, 1968
OWEN, Roderic, *'The Desert Air Force'*, Hutchinson, 1948
SHORES, Christopher, **CULL**, Brian & **MALIZIA**, Nicola, *'Air War for Yugoslavia,*

Greece and Crete, 1940–41', Grub Street, 1987

SHORES, Christopher & **RING**, Hans, *'Fighters over the Desert'*, Spearman, 1969

SHORES, Christopher, **RING**, Hans & **HESS**, William N., *'Fighters over Tunisia'*, Spearman, 1975

RICHARDS, Denis & **SAUNDERS**, Hilary, *'The Royal Air Force, 1939–1945'*, HMSO, 1953

RING, Hans & **GIRBIG**, Werner. *'Jagdgeschwader 27'*, Motorbuchverlag, 1971

YATES, V M, *'Winged Victory'*, Jonathan Cape, 1934 & 1961

Index